THE DAMNED AND THE BEAUTIFUL

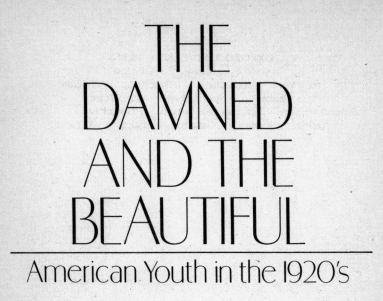

THE DAMNED AND THE BEAUTIFUL

American Youth in the 1920's

PAULA S. FASS

OXFORD UNIVERSITY PRESS
Oxford   New York   Toronto   Melbourne

OXFORD UNIVERSITY PRESS

Oxford   London   Glasgow
New York   Toronto   Melbourne   Wellington
Nairobi   Dar es Salaam   Cape Town
Kuala Lumpur   Singapore   Jakarta   Hong Kong   Tokyo
Delhi   Bombay   Calcutta   Madras   Karachi

Permission to reprint two stanzas of "Our Eunuch Dreams" from *The
Poems of Dylan Thomas*, copyright 1953 by Dylan Thomas, has been
granted by New Directions Publishing Corporation, J. M. Dent and
Sons, Ltd., and the Trustees for the Copyrights of the late Dylan Thomas.

Library of Congress Cataloging in Publication Data

Fass, Paula S
The damned and the beautiful.

Includes bibliographical references and index.
1. Youth—United States—History. 2. Conflict
of generations. 3. Subculture. 4. United States
—Social conditions—1918-1932. I. Title.
HQ799.7.F37   1979   301.43'15'0973   78-11904
ISBN 0-19-502492-3 pbk.

printing, last digit: 10 9 8 7 6 5 4

Printed in the United States of America

In memory of my gentle mother and dearest friend
Bluma Fass

After the fire and the stench of human flesh,
the sun gave us many mornings
and a night.
The covenant bound us once again.
And you—for whom the sacred stood
as in newborn Adam's eye—would not rest.
Nor forget
the promise and that love known
to only the chosen
and the good.

Contents

How they are provided for upon the earth (appearing at intervals),
How dear and dreadful they are to the earth,
How they inure to themselves as much as to any—what a
  paradox appears their age,
How people respond to them, yet know them not,
How there is something relentless in their fate all times,
And how the same inexorable price must still be paid for the
  same purchase.

Walt Whitman
"Beginners"

Acknowledgments

Many, many people helped to make this book. It would be impossible to thank them all or to thank them enough. My teachers and colleagues in the history departments of Columbia University and the University of California at Berkeley, respectively, have been unstinting in their kindness and generous assistance. I would like to thank especially Walter Metzger, Annette Kar Baxter, Lawrence Cremin, Leon Litwack, Winthrop Jordan, Kenneth Stampp, Richard Abrams, Reginald Zelnick, Natalie Zemon Davis, Sheldon Rothblatt, Ira Lapidus, and Robert Brentano, who have each read and commented on this manuscript at various stages of its evolution from the original dissertation. Robert Middlekauff read the manuscript with infinite care and I benefitted greatly from his excellent advice. My many delightful discussions with Lawrence Levine and his scrupulous attention to all aspects of the study were invaluable. My good friend Ruth Bloch helped me to improve the form and the content and, above all, helped me through the labors.

There are two men without whose advice, encouragement, and example this study would never have been begun or completed. Richard Hofstadter provided the first inspiration for this book and he carefully nurtured its earliest roots. He died before it was completed, but his example, his wisdom, his gentle humanity made it easier for me to labor through it even after he was gone. David Rothman provided extraordinary and continual assistance. His sharp and stimulating criticism and unfailing interest were essential from beginning to end. He has been a true friend and an outstanding teacher.

The generous assistance of a number of institutions facilitated my studies. I would like to thank the State of New York for a Herbert H. Lehman Fellowship, Columbia University for a Faculty Fellowship, the Woodrow Wilson Foundation for a Dissertation Fellowship, the University of California for a Regents Fellowship in the Humanities Summer Grant and the Committee on Research of the University of California, Berkeley for funds for typing and manuscript preparation. Sheldon Meyer of Oxford University Press gave me his kind support and active encouragement and helped to improve the manuscript. Leona Capeless at Oxford generously and meticulously supervised the final preparation. My research assistant, Mark Dimunation, and typist, Norma Montgomery, provided excellent services.

New York   P. F.
December 1976

My mother, to whom this edition is dedicated, can no longer be thanked. I only hope she knew how much of what is best in my work, and in myself, I owe to her.

Berkeley
August 1978

INTRODUCTION:
YOUTH IN THE 1920'S

They were sitting with disarming quiet upon the still unhatched eggs of the mid-twentieth century.

F. Scott Fitzgerald

Historians have long recognized that, for better or worse, American culture was remade in the 1920's. Robust with business styles, technologies, educational policies, manners, and leisure habits which are identifiably our own, the decade sits solidly at the base of our culture. We recognize, of course, that the difference between the twenties and an older America was not simply corporate power, or the automobile, or sexual liberation. It was more than the fierce energy, tone, and sensibility that came with conscious innovation; more than the sharp social tensions and frequent head-on collisions between new forces and traditional but still obstinate forms. All of this had occurred before. What made the twenties new was the finely textured tapestry where the many changes were knotted to form a wholly new design. Still, we too often find it easier to bypass the long-term changes that were firmly secured in the twenties when we remember either the surface excitements of the new or the remnants of the old. Perhaps by remembering the twenties merely as an enchanting series of novelties or the crude afterthought of a simpler past, we preserve the illusion of our own simple innocence. The result may be comforting, but it is scarcely enlightening. The structuring power of that primal modern age is too often lost as the decade sinks into insignificance, serving as a kind of comic relief between two crises—the Great War and the Great Crash—full of interesting signs but barren of deeper meanings.

The twenties seem to lend themselves to caricature. The complexities of politics, for example, are largely missing. In contrast to the decades which precede and succeed, both dense with political activity and reformist energy, the twenties are flat—a combination of simplistic business values, corrupt government practices, and stingy isolationism. And while none of this is pretty, all can be excused as a respite from the heavy issues of political and social reconstruction. It is not surprising that the twenties make most political historians, who are generally concerned with the dynamics of progressive change, uncomfortable.

They do not fit into a reform-oriented historiography. Better, therefore, to let the decade rest, indulging in its prosperity and luxuriant in its war-weary retreat from commitment.

Where politics in the twenties was dreary, the culture, at least, was lively. Few decades have been so often treated solely in cultural terms, as historians, in describing the period from 1901 to 1945, jump from decades of reform and war to a decade of culture and back again to reform and war. The image, once more, is that of relief and of much-needed rest. But when it is isolated in this way, even the richness of twenties culture is flattened and reduced to a less serious plane of social reality. Moreover, too often the culture of the 1920's is portrayed as a culture of negation, of war-weary cynics, despairing intellectuals, and decadent artists who simplified the society by renouncing it as phony and irrelevant. As the Babbitt businessmen, filling the void left by weary social reformers, took over the reins of government, the sensitive artist retreated into fantasy or to Paris, there to proclaim American life empty of vital sustenance, spiritually dead, driven to its grave by the WCTU, KKK, Comstockery, and a coven of fundamentalists. Recently, we have learned that even the ordinary man on Main Street, unable to afford Paris or to create rich fantasies, beat a retreat, refertilizing the roots of old American values to harvest them through a resuscitated Klan, old-time religion, and the personal heroics of Charles Lindbergh. Everyone was in flight. The reformer fled the government, the artist fled the country, and the ordinary man fled the reality of change through the fantasia of the past.

The portrait of an America in flight from reality permits the historian, too, to flee from the complex problem of the era—the knotty process by which Americans adjusted to change. The twenties has been so schematized, so crushed between a conservative business and politics, an avant-garde high culture, and an ostrich-like popular imagination that the solid substance of the society has disappeared. And instead of opening the door to ourselves, the twenties has become a meaningless passage, unstable, unwelcome, and unreal.

But what makes the twenties so meaningful is not the escape from change but the adjustment to change. Throughout the decade, personal adjustments, cultural accommodations, and social reconstruction were taking place everywhere in the society—certainly not without nostalgia, not without much frivolous nonsense, and not without frequent conflicts and painful anxieties, but remarkably swiftly and effectively nevertheless. That long-suspended ambivalence, the tension between modern and traditional modes of thought and behavior, was finally played out, and the social changes that had been remaking America for decades finally congealed into a pattern which would shape life in the twentieth century. This story of how Americans moved into the modern age, not away from it, has yet to be told.

This study attempts to tell part of that story by focusing on the youth of the twenties who were vigorously and visibly adjusting to the new society. The young are, of course, the most vulnerable to change. They are pliant, alert, and eager. And they exist at a splendid crossroad where the past meets the future in a jumble of personal anxieties and an urgent need for social self-definition. While this is true for all youths, it was particularly important for the youth of the twenties. For them, a personal crisis was absorbed into a social process. The youth of the twenties were at once the product of change and the agents of change, because they existed at a strategic point in history when their actions really did make a difference.

Youth has become so much a part of contemporary life that it is well to stop and ask ourselves how and why this should be. Youth is, after all, biologically, no more than a short and fleeting period of life, a transitional identity, the very boundaries of which are difficult to define. Yet, youth has become far more than this in our culture. At a time when the American population is aging, the young are ever more with us; their specialized habits, their music, dress, lingo, recreations, and sexual patterns loom large on the social scene. Youth has become a regular and normal feature of twentieth-century experience. The consumer market has been reshaped to youth's tastes, institutions like high schools, colleges, and multiversities created around youth's needs, politics reformed by youthful marches and demonstrations and most recently by the vote for eighteen-year-olds. The Constitution, the oldest and most venerable of American political institutions, has thus been recast by youth, which is now enshrined and legitimated as a national presence. Youth has become so real, so manifest, so omnipresent, that it is difficult to realize how recent all this really is. For youth is not simply a physical or biological fact. It is a cultural expression of social relationships and a product of a specific set of historical conditions. Those conditions which made modern youth possible, even necessary, are at the foundation of contemporary society, and it is precisely because this is so that youth is an important subject for historical analysis.

In the 1920's, youth appeared suddenly, dramatically, even menacingly on the social scene. Contemporaries quite rightly understood that their presence signaled a social transformation of major proportions and that they were a key to the many changes which had remade the society. Contemporary perceptions of youth were, as a result, heavy with the excitement and anxiety of that perception. Historians, too, have long been fascinated by the youth of the twenties, sensing their cogency in the context of the time. Too often, however, their approach to the subject has suffered from the caricatures and simplifications which have deflated the significance of the decade. For the youth of the twenties have been used as symbols and symptoms of that alienation which has become the catchword of the decade.

The image that teases the historical imagination is of a rebellious youth, iconoclastic, irreverent, frivolous, lost to social responsibility, and even more lost to traditional values and beliefs. While no longer tied to the past, they also rejected the present. They denied their elders the moral authority the artists denied their culture and the seriousness which historians still deny the politics of the day. They thus become part of that process of rejection which destroys the substance of the twenties by reducing its complexities. Historians are not wholly to blame for this picture. It was, in fact, a portrait carefully constructed by contemporaries in the twenties—in the creative literature, popular journals, and volumes of social analysis by educators, judges, and poets. Contemporaries caricatured youth in order to understand and finally come to terms with the many changes which youth represented and which had suddenly overwhelmed an older order. We must not, however, be misled by the culture's willful misrepresentation of its youth. It served a purpose and was, like youth itself, part of that process of cultural adjustment which was the governing spirit of the time.

Historians, unlike commentators in the twenties, have largely failed to appreciate just how meaningful the behavior of youth really was, and by dwelling on the symbolism of failure, they have missed the reality of success. The youth of the twenties did not reject the authority of their nurture, nor were they symptoms of the irrelevance of the society's norms. On the contrary, they were an indication of the success of both. The young translated the changes in nurture into new behavioral norms which continue to organize our lives. In this study I have tried to examine some of the changes of which youth was a product and youth's role in the process of social change. To do so I have narrowed the focus of investigation to one major segment of the youth population—native, white, middle-class, and almost exclusively college-going—and I have given particular attention to the role of the family and of school peer groups in determining the experience of youth. It was the changes in these two institutions which most directly influenced the behavior and attitudes of the young. These changes were, of course, only part of a much larger social process which affected youth in myriad ways: changes in work patterns and job training, social and economic legislation concerning school attendance and child labor, youth centers and agencies sponsored by the church, government, and private organizations, new cultural mediators like movies and advertising. All of these created the modern fact of youth. To understand youth fully would force us to examine the society in all its multidimensional complexity. This study does not pretend to do that. Rather, it limits itself to the crucial changes in the primary instruments of socialization, family and peers, and to those cultural patterns most immediately affected by the experiences of youth—sex, politics, work, and style.

White, urban, middle-class college youth were, of course, only one segment of the youth population. Rural and working youths, blacks and immigrants, exposed to different institutional influences, may well have behaved and believed differently than the young people portrayed here, and need to be studied as an integral part of the same process of social reorganization, no less than the native middle classes. My choice is meant neither to ascribe exclusive significance nor to describe a universal pattern. Rather, by limiting the investigation to a specific and highly visible subgroup among youth, it became possible to study a phenomenon broadly and deeply embedded in our social experience. My choice of this group was governed by a number of personal and practical considerations: the availability of sources, the concern of their contemporaries with what was happening to these youths, the implicit interest of the subject matter, and the strategic position of this group in the society. I was, moreover, interested in testing a number of sociological hypotheses about the role of youth in advanced industrial society, especially that of S. N. Eisenstadt, and this segment of the population appeared the most likely to serve as a model for such an investigation. My concern was, therefore, to limit and sharpen the investigation and to avoid as much as possible the interesting, but obfuscating, problems that would color any study of immigrant, black, or rural youth—problems of conflicting cultural orientation and of specific intergenerational tension, relating more to the group than to the time. Since I am interested in the relationship between youth and dynamics of social change, the white middle classes seemed least burdened by those separate issues of acculturation, out-group status, and conflicting identities with which other youths had to deal as they assumed their mature roles in the society.

At the same time, the sample studied here is both strategic and symptomatic. White college youths in the twenties were responding to a broad range of phenomena which increasingly touched everyone in the society—phenomena which were changing the culture dramatically and reducing local and particularistic differences. The fact and experience of youth was affecting the slum as well as the suburb, the workplace as well as the school, the ghetto as well as the country club. Youth was cutting across older patterns of identification and association, and the steamroller of change was making it harder and harder to confine the influences affecting one group from crossing the boundaries of space, class, and even race. Moreover, as the children of the native American middle classes, well cared for, well educated, socially and economically secure, this particular group of youth would go on to powerfully affect the substance and forms of American life down to our own day.

PART I

THE PLASTIC AGE

Nel mezzo del cammin di nostra vita
   mi ritrovai per una selva oscura,
   che la diritta via era smarrita.

Ahi quanto a dir qual era è cosa dura
   questa selva sevaggia ed aspra e forte,
   che nel pensier rinnova la paura!

Tanto è amara, che poca è più morte:
   ma per trattar del ben ch' I' vi trovai,
   dirò dell' altre cose, ch'io v'ho scorte.

Dante, Inferno

I

The Children of Our Discontent

By "our young people" is meant Americans of both sexes who are in the adolescent period, particularly those of secondary school and college age. That they are somehow different from the young people of "our generation" is a common remark of persons in middle age and beyond. As a rule, this difference makes us of the older generation uneasy. "Something ails" the youth of to-day. This opinion was in evidence for several years before the Great War, and since the War it has become an alarmed conviction.

George A. Coe, What Ails Our Youth? *(1924)*

Youth suddenly became a social problem in the 1920's. Part myth, part reality, the youth problem was for contemporaries a symbol for the strains of a culture running headlong into the twentieth century. As they concentrated the many facets of a complex social experience into their perceptions and descriptions of the young, contemporaries often used youth to condemn or to praise the network of change they came to represent. The problem of youth was connected to changes in family nurture, education, sex roles, leisure habits, as well as social values and behavioral norms. Above all, youth had become a challenge to an older social order. While it is often difficult to separate the youth problem from the many social issues to which it was linked in the public mind, contemporaries were quite right to understand that the problem of youth was not an isolated phenomenon. The public usually invested youth with too many hopes or fears, thus draining them of their specific reality, but the perception of youth's vital relevance was never misplaced.

Certainly the attention paid to youth in the twenties was not new. Anxiety about children has long been an American indulgence. During the late nineteenth century and the Progressive period, for example, adolescence was seen as a dangerous stage of life marked by stress and conflict.[1] But the problem, because it could be clearly defined, made effective solutions, however difficult, always manageable. The problem of youth was a problem of outsiders, of juvenile offenders, young prostitutes, children of the ghetto and the slum. The victims of exploitation and neglect, these youths needed to be assimilated or reformed and integrated into the wholesome norm of the society.

In the twenties, however, the youth were different, the problem ill-defined, and the public discussions both partisan and passionate. In the journals of middle-class opinion like the *Atlantic Monthly*, the *Literary Digest*, and the *Ladies' Home Journal*,[2] and in volumes of social analysis by judges, poets, and educators, the children not of the outsider but of the insider, of the native, urban middle classes, were pressed to the center of attention and debate. The issue was no longer assimilation to the mainstream, but changes within that very mainstream which now affected every facet of American life and the young in particular. And because the problem was so broad and the children were their own, the discussions of social commentators in the twenties were clouded with frustration—a frustration resulting from the sense that not only were old solutions inadequate, but the problem had been so radically altered that there might be no solutions.

The perception of the changed nature of the youth problem generally forced two kinds of responses: pessimism and despair by "traditionalists," who felt overwhelmed by the magnitude of the resulting social disorder and used the image of youth to denounce the society for failing to preserve old structures and values; or an urgent call for reconstruction and reorganization by "progressives," who saw the young as a positive force for needed change and as already charting the path toward the future. The youth question also forced contemporaries to an examination of American values and institutions. Traditionalists believed these had been unequal to the challenges posed by the changing society, while progressives saw them as outworn barriers to effective progress. The difference between the traditionalists and the progressives had less to do with the content of their observations than with the purpose to which these were enlisted and the intellectual frameworks within which they functioned. For the traditionalist, the young represented the fruit of social disorder, cultural disintegration, and a personal loss of coherence. They viewed the present from the perspective of what they believed was a formerly stable society which had been shattered, and they taunted themselves with the loss that came with change. The progressives were no less aware of these changes but set their sights on a new order and a new coherence which beckoned somewhere in the future toward which the young were already oriented.

The labels "traditionalist" and "progressive" are meant to define not a specific group or interest, but broadly two kinds of contemporary sensibilities, particularly as they related to attitudes toward the young. The traditionalists' position was best articulated in the popular journals of the period, especially those which registered the tastes and opinions of the respectable middle classes. The progressive voice emerged most clearly in books of social criticism which attempted a more thoroughgoing analysis. But examples of both can be found in either literary genre; Walter Lippmann's *A Preface to Morals* (1929), for example, sounded the traditionalist call, while the *New Republic* usually echoed that of the progressives. While these sensibilities are described here solely in terms of attitudes toward youth, they do highlight a more general reaction to the changes which youth represented. This does not mean, of course, that those who raged at the young were traditionalists on all the cultural and social issues of the period or that those who delighted in youth welcomed all change, but only that the attitudes toward youth divided along lines which were distinctly characteristic of the time.

Many of our impressions of the young of the twenties, as well as our understanding of the decade's tone, have been filtered through the traditionalist sensibility which was prominently featured in the journals. The progressive social critics who chose to look hopefully at the young and to incorporate them into their blueprints for the American future have received less attention from historians. But their much more optimistic social prognosis and their understanding of youth's behavior was very much part of the general dialogue of the decade. We need to examine both if we are to understand what youth meant to contemporaries, how the youth problem was related to other social issues, and the range of adult opinion that shaped the world of youth. Divided on this as on so many other cultural questions, the mind of the twenties was governed neither by black despair nor by blind enthusiasm, but by an anxious sense of change. For both progressives and traditionalists the youth problem described and symbolized a period of acute transformation. Neither believed that the behavior of youth was an indication of a new stability, for neither believed the period was anything more than a waystation, one that marked the further descent into chaos for the traditionalist and illuminated the forthcoming ascent to clarity and integration for the progressive. In the highly dramatic perceptions of a dramatic era, youth was either damned or beautiful.

I

Decrying the lamentable state to which the nation's youth had come, the journals of the 1920's repeatedly reminded their readers, often in frenzied prose, that the society was failing to produce a moral progeny. What is striking about these descriptions is how little they really had to do with the offenses of the young, except in a derivative way. The central issue was always the failure of modern society; rarely were specific solutions for the youth problem more than an afterthought. The repetition of the catalogue of youth's faults was, in fact, not intended to describe or reform. It was, instead, a form of ritual incantation which, by bringing the problem forward again and again, created a painful consciousness that became a substitute for action, and indeed, even a way of coming to terms with the situation. James Truslow Adams grasped this fact when he observed, "Here in these United States in this post-war period, realizing that all is not right with our world, we have found the scapegoat which permits us to go about our business with a free mind. The name on its collar is 'The Younger Generation.' " [3] As a dreadful reminder of social shortcomings, the theme of youth was used in the journals like a literary leitmotif, conjuring up visions of disastrous social consequences. It was just this technique of relief by exposure that F. Scott Fitzgerald used so successfully in his novels and stories. Employing the symbols of his time to tease his readers' curiosity while he exploited their alarm, Fitzgerald was able to best express the period's aching sense of frustration.

What was being paraded before the public was not the behavior of youth, but the psychological defenses of a society. The young rake or flapper, strutting defiantly in the pages of the *Atlantic* or the *Ladies' Home Journal,* or even the *New Republic,* had about as much to do with the average high school or college youth as Jay Gatsby did with the average bootlegger. They were not real but fictionalized, emotion-packed distortions of a type that was meant to evoke rather than to describe and finally to comfort through rebuke. Youth served the traditionalist sensibility as a device for social self-exposure, for uncovering the deeper wound of social disorder, and as an excuse for reflecting on the changes which had undermined social order. Launching his attack on the young, the traditionalist found the rubble of a once-stable society and the ruined structures of a former world: sexual morality, family authority, school and church control, ideological direction. And the bomb that shattered them all came appropriately from the war.

In the 1920's, the war provided traditionalists with the first and most persistent explanation for the post-war behavior of youth, as well as a starting point for an exploration of that behavior.[4] At the beginning of the decade especially, the problems of youth, like so many others, were attributed to the war's shattering effects, and the theme of war like the theme of youth carried an emotion-charged fuse. According to traditionalists, the war had awakened the young to the sad realities of life, and the imminence of death turned young men and women to pleasure-seeking. Having ripped the rosy veil from a self-confident civilization, the war permitted the young to see through the sham idealism of their elders. "Our youth have lost their illusions" became at once an explanation and a description as the war and the resulting peace made a mockery of the ideals for which so much youthful blood had been spilled. As the theme of war was linked with that of youth, the descriptions of youth became heavy with the effects of betrayal. John F. Carter, Jr., a self-proclaimed member of the "Wild Young People," taunted readers of the *Atlantic* (long an arbiter of middle-class respectability, literary tastes, and civilized morality) with the observation that "the older generation had certainly pretty well ruined this world before passing it on to us." "Now my generation is disillusionized, and, I think, to a certain extent, brutalized, by the cataclysm which *their* complacent folly engendered. . . .

We have been forced to live in an atmosphere of 'tomorrow we die,' and so, naturally, we drank and were merry." [5]

The war had proved to youth how unreliable, if not also culpable, their elders were, forcing them to live their lives on their own terms and by their own lights.[6] The young were described as hard-boiled, cynical, smug, and ravenous for experience. Devoted to truth and candor, they refused to accept the counsel of their elders; they had to experience life for themselves and to snatch its pleasures at a hurried pace. Mary Borden told readers of *Harper's* that youth "exalts sincerity, truth, naturalness." "Young America," she noted, "is enamored of life, real life, life in the raw, life lived at the highest pitch of excitement." And in an editorial entitled, "They Want To Know," the liberal *New Republic* explained that the young rejected "a religion of opinion or of conventional conduct." "They are not sure that they can learn by living, but they feel sure that they cannot learn without living." [7]

More than a shell-shocked and war-weary hedonism worried those in the older generation who saw the world they knew falling around them. In the process of discovering life for themselves, the young were consciously and knowingly rejecting the conventions in manners and morals, according to traditionalists. They now called hypocrisies those same behaviors and beliefs that had stabilized the prewar world. For the young, the past was worse than irrelevant, it was pretentious, and they proceeded to strip manners of their gentility, language of its pomposities, and morality of its righteous deceptions. Searching for truth in all its naked crudeness, they denied their elders any moral authority, denouncing their conventions as cant. "How do they [the young] see us?" Mary Agnes Hamilton asked in the pages of the *Atlantic.* "The answer can be put in a word: as frauds." The result, according to an *Atlantic* editorial, was that "The old and the young" were "as far apart in point of view, code, and standard, as if they belonged to different races." [8]

In fact, however, it was not the substitution of one set of standards for another that was most threatening to these observers, but the fact that for young people there were apparently no effective standards or controls at all. Once released from traditional restraints, their behavior appeared to be characterized only by licentiousness and self-gratification. Each individual, seeking his own raw truth, did just as he pleased: "This sense of overwhelming fact," Hamilton noted, "is at the root of modern 'license.' " In *Harper's Magazine*, Avis Carlson, a college professor of English, observed that morality was something from which the young were "rapidly emancipating themselves." Morality, Carlson noted, "the right-and-wrong standard is based on authority," but authority of any kind, whether of government, church, or family, was unacceptable to the young. According to Carlson, youth organized their behavior on the basis of personal expediency, with the veto of public opinion their one effective limitation. "They keep a shrewd weather-eye out for what they call 'stuff you can't get by with.' 'Getting by' is almost the twentieth century equivalent for morality." [9] Fearful that all standards were being destroyed, Carlson urged that aesthetic considerations be adopted as a substitute for morality. Far less significant than the specific proposal (which was, of course, deeply moral) was Carlson's urgent sense of the need for some universally acceptable standard. That a member of the college community and a patron of the moral establishment should recommend in a journal like *Harper's* a substitute for morality suggests just how far-reaching the repudiation of standards was believed to have gone among the young.

The young had come to represent the unhinging of the social order, and the journals of the twenties were filled with an image of youth out of control, of energy released from social restraints, and of raw forces unleashed. At the very beginning of the decade, in an editorial appropriately entitled "The Release of Youth," the *Nation* wondered whether the youthful energies tapped by the war could be harnessed in peacetime to a social purpose, especially in the context of the profound social changes that had taken place. Those energies, which had once been drawn into socially necessary channels through work and child-rearing, appeared now to threaten social order as adult enterprises were delayed and leisure time expanded.[10]

The dangers of unchanneled and potentially disruptive energies attendant upon an unprecedented new leisure and new social conditions were at the root of the denunciations of youth. Not surprisingly, traditionalists equated the unharnessed energies of youth with license, and sexual license above all became the most powerful bogeyman of the twenties. Youthful sexuality was at once the sign of social demoralization and a continuing threat to social order. Sexuality symbolized both disorder and rebellion: disorder because it meant energy unrestrained, and rebellion because it was the most obvious line of attack in the onslaught against the pretensions of prewar morality.[11]

Behind all the descriptions of youth's defiance, their attitudes, manners, fashions, amusements, and above all their morals, lurks this double-barreled threat of sexuality. As one young woman sharply put it in the solid, old-fashioned *Forum*, "This tremendous interest in the younger generation is nothing more nor less than a preoccupation with the nature of that generation's sex life." The traditionalist collapsed all the facets of the youth problem into this one issue of sexual license. Their frankness and devotion to reality and truth were equated with an uninhibited acceptance of sexuality. The rejection of genteel manners, which were for the young only "worn-out hypocrisies, unsuitable and worthless relics of an elaborate insincerity," suggested that the young were stripping social relations of all previous controls and conventions. As they challenged former affectations, the young grasped at a new sexual candor.[12]

The peeling away of genteel manners was only the first line of attack. Clothing styles, especially as they affected women, considered liberating by the young, were demoralizing in the eyes of their elders. Bobbed hair ("the badge of flapperhood"), short skirts, silk stockings for everyday wear, cosmetics (once "confined to a class representing the victims of the social order rather than its makers") were all outward signs of the escape from convention which made women appear cruder and purposefully solicitous of the rawer instincts in men. Smoking for women and drinking by both sexes were said to be prevalent among the young. Youth even had a language. It was slangy, coarse, often profane, and not infrequently lewd. Men and women openly talked and joked about sex to each other.[13] The behavior of youth was defiant, raunchy, implicitly sexual.

So too, traditionalists looked at youthful pastimes like jazz and dancing and saw rude passion, Negro lewdness, sensuous movement. In the early twenties, the *Ladies' Home Journal,* the housewife's companion and guide, seethed with rage against "Unspeakable Jazz" and launched an anti-jazz "crusade" which it believed to be "of as great importance to-day to the moral well-being of the United States as the prohibition crusade was in the worst days of the saloon." Jazz and modern dancing were the sign of American decadence heralding the collapse of civilized life. "Anyone who says that 'youths of both sexes can mingle in close embrace'—with limbs intertwined and torso in contact—without suffering harm lies. Add to this position the wriggling movement and sensuous stimulation of the abominable jazz orchestra with its voodoo-born minors and its direct appeal to the sensory center, and if you can believe that youth is the same after this experience as before, then God help your child." [14]

Stirring his readers with this almost visceral description, John McMahon then informed parents of the dangers implicit in the fashion: "In so far as jazz dancing relaxes morality and undermines the institution of the family, it is an element of tremendously evil potentiality." New York, the corrupt Gotham, laying waste to the virtues of the Republic, came in for the lion's share of denunciation, and there was the inevitable comparison to Rome in her final orgiastic plunge to destruction.[15] The *La-*

dies' Home Journal urged the "legal prohibition" of jazz dancing. The call for legal action was characteristic of the frenzied response of traditionalists in this as in so many other social areas in the twenties. Impotent to stop what they saw as social disintegration, the traditionalists saw the law as the final barrier to chaos and the ultimate instrument of control.

While the behavior of all youth was cause for concern, a special apprehension was reserved for the manners and attitudes of young women.[16] The American woman had been the special stabilizer of nineteenth-century society, and it was the change in female behavior which underlined the overall changes that had taken place. It was the new definition of equality that was most troubling, for it was apparently not the same thing that the old feminists had in mind. According to Dorothy Dunbar Bromley, " 'Feminism' has become a term of opprobrium to the modern young woman," who defined equality not as political rights or economic opportunities but as something more subtle and more threatening: freedom—the right to self-expression, self-determination, and personal satisfaction. To traditionalists this smacked of immorality, self-indulgence, and irresponsibility.[17]

This was alarming for it meant not merely a granting of rights but an upheaval in social relationships and the destruction of formerly effective controls. According to Bromley, the new woman of the twenties was not dissatisfied with the kitchen if it was freely chosen, but she refused to be consigned to a single role and she expected to be satisfied in each. Asking for more than merely to have a man choose her as a wife and the mother of his children, the new woman expected to be satisfied "as a lover and a companion," and she insisted on *"more freedom and honesty within the marriage."* Married or not, she was likely to have a "pagan attitude toward love itself." [18]

All this appeared to portend the collapse of noble womanhood as it had been understood. Once released from previous controls and well-defined roles, women risked the danger of succumbing

to impulse, of entering upon a path from which there was no return, of teetering on the edge of sexual promiscuity. "Mr.
Grundy" reminded readers of the *Atlantic* that "When lovely
woman stoops to folly, she can always find someone to stoop
with her but not always someone to lift her up again to the level
where she belongs." The right to freedom of choice, to broad
social participation, and to sexual satisfaction seemed to
threaten above all the stability of the home, once the keystone
of the social order, for it undermined the imperatives to marriage.[19]

The change in female behavior was especially apparent in the
nation's cities. "In the great cities," Alyse Gregory reported in
Current History, "in those circles where women twenty-five to
thirty-five can control their own purse strings many of them are
apt to drift into casual or steady relationships with certain men
friends which may or may not end in matrimony." Indeed, the
Literary Digest believed that it was necessary to warn country
girls of the dangers of migrating to the city for work. Twenty-
five thousand girls were reported to be adrift in New York,
"victims of the room shortage." That migration was "a national
menace. We must carry our campaign from the city into the
country. We must portray to the young women and men on the
farms the disadvantages of forsaking the farm for the city and
make them realize how fortunate they are on the farm." "A nationwide movement to keep girls away from the city is urged on
the Association to Provide Proper Housing for Girls in New
York." [20] Here again was the implied need for legal control,
for a means to hold back the impending chaos.

The manners, habits, and styles of youth all seemed to describe a new attitude which rejected traditional roles and norms.
Not everyone agreed that changes in manners and styles necessarily reflected immorality among the young,[21] but most admitted that the sexual attitudes of young women who considered
"free love" not so much immoral as "impractical" had been
profoundly altered. "A woman is no longer ashamed of pas-

sion," declared one young woman in the *Forum,* but "she does not gratify it unless there is justification for it." She implied, of course, that each woman would and should judge for herself when passion was justified, satisfaction taking precedence over social control. This was ominous, for it granted a latitude in personal behavior that undermined the very idea of morality. Moral strictures were never meant to correspond to desire or conduce to self-expression. The implicit faith in the rectitude of conventions kept society stable and uniform. But the manners, attitudes, and styles of the young all implied a rejection of traditional conventions.[22] Thus everything about the young, no matter how seemingly minor, threatened the traditionalist. Language, manners, clothes, pastimes, each undercut the uniform commitment to the traditional moral order. When he saw old conventions and styles questioned, the traditionalist assumed there was no morality and no order.

It was this frantic fear of sexual promiscuity, of the upheaval in social relationships and the destruction of definitions and limitations, that characterized the reaction of the traditionalists to the youth of the twenties. Gazing at the young women of the period, the traditionalist saw the end of American civilization as he had known it. Its firm and robust outlines, best symbolized by the stable mother secure in her morality and content in her home, were pushed aside and replaced by the giddy flapper, rouged and clipped, careening in a drunken stupor to the lewd strains of a jazz quartet.

II

From the instant he stepped onto its stage, F. Scott Fitzgerald became inseparable from the twenties, his art capturing the public's mind, his life a prisoner of its mood. Fitzgerald gave the twenties its symbols: flappers, jazz, gin. He still forces us to remember the decade through his fantasies: its fairy-tale quality;

its winter-dreams unreality; its diamonds-as-big-as-the-Ritz extravagance; its oceans of gin and champagne; its frantic gaiety. But Fitzgerald's art is important for more than its symbols or its fantasies. Fitzgerald transformed the urge to self-exposure and condemnation into a luminous art. With uncanny insight into the contemporary mood, he was able to play on the public sensibility and its alarm, to expose the way in which the culture had betrayed its past, all the while feeding the public's hungry curiosity about the present. It is this barometric sensibility and the bombshell effect that his art had on the contemporary American public that make the intimate world of Fitzgerald's art a worthy historical testament.

This Side of Paradise (1920), Glenway Wescott recalled, "haunted the decade like a song." The notoriety of Fitzgerald's first book has become legendary, but the modern reader would be hard-pressed to say why it stirred such passion or why it caught fire at all. Surely not a very good book, it is also young and terribly innocent. But *This Side of Paradise* struck a responsive chord in the twenties precisely because it strives to be naughty, sophisticated, and shocking. By portraying the young as he did and by posing as their spokesman, Fitzgerald was brilliantly telling his audience what it was eager to know but unable to condone. Fitzgerald was aware that the American public would be aroused and shocked by the behavior of college youth, as indeed it was when articles on the subject appeared in respectable journals. And like those articles, Fitzgerald's book exploded on the public scene. Fitzgerald, moreover, portrayed himself as one of the young—and the wildest and most raucous of all. He was not an outraged observer but a willing participant. That served to accentuate the public reaction. But Fitzgerald's own offended sensibilities are as obvious as those of any traditionalist. The sophistication of Amory Blaine is all too clearly an affectation; the petting, the drinking, the automobile-carousing that Blaine describes and takes part in were unnatural to him. They are a mode of expression, a proof of his nonchalant identification with the newest of the new. That sophistication betrays his discomfort. Fitzgerald rightly assumed the public's pained reaction.

Fitzgerald was considered "nervy" precisely because he threw the behavior of America's youth in the public's face, thinking that by so doing he was shamelessly rattling the surface calm and naive optimism of which he was himself victim. He touched a sensitive nerve. Almost immediately he was damned and maligned, accused of being a consciously naughty young man, and paid the highest compliment of all, that of being widely read and imitated. *This Side of Paradise* was a blow to the public calm, because by describing the behavior of college students as he did, Fitzgerald reminded readers of an older order and the values and standards that had been rendered conspicuously inoperative among the young. And the eagerness with which it was received (even then its literary merits were questioned) reveals an American public eager to have a smart young kid thumb his nose at it, just as it readily exposed its own shortcomings by bewailing its young.

Like *This Side of Paradise*, *The Great Gatsby* (1925) is an exposé. And like *Paradise*, it relies on the double technique of shocked sensibility and the implicit contrast between a formerly stable world and the loss of that world. *Gatsby* exposes the decadent rich much as *Paradise* exposes sophisticated youth. It is not necessary to examine the many subtle ways in which Fitzgerald juxtaposed the richness of old dreams and the emptiness of dreams realized in the new world to appreciate the powerful comparison Fitzgerald draws between a former stability and the flux of the present. It is sufficient to note that both in the narrator and in Gatsby himself, Fitzgerald provides his readers with ample opportunity to compare the old and the new. As narrator, Nick Carraway observes and exposes the dissipation, the luxurious self-indulgence, and the promiscuity of Gatsby's world. Carraway, the aloof observer, provides a point of stability and brings to bear the stern standard of the Midwestern minister's son. It is Carraway who finally leaves the enticing "distortion" of the East to return to the greater stability of the American heartland, to "my Midwest," as he calls it. But it is above all the past and the present of Gatsby himself that supply the power of the tale, the most poignant reminder of a lost world. Time and change, Fitzgerald reminded readers, had destroyed the idealism of Gatsby's dream and the purity of his vision, leaving him only the distortions of the present. It is the shattering loss of dreams and illusions, of young love and ideals that haunts the book and that finally makes the soft sentimentality of the past vastly preferable to the reckless reality of the present. Carraway put it perfectly when he called it a distortion.

Gatsby, like *Paradise* and the incantations in the journals, is predicated on a certain kind of American past and on the still powerful yearning for the stable values and virtues it represented. And it was Fitzgerald who most effectively played upon his audience's sense of the once-upon-a-time in America when things were stable and good and upon the acute consciousness of change which the youth of the period represented. The young of the twenties were less a threat to that former stability than an ongoing reminder that it had passed. Portrayed as responding to modern life with frivolous unconcern for the sterner ways of their predecessors, the young epitomized both what America had lost and what America had become. The ways of youth fascinated the twenties, much as Amory's campus affairs and Gatsby's social world fascinated their audience, because they teased and taunted, telling readers what they most feared but wanted to hear again and again in different and ever more alarming ways. The knowledge and the alarm were inextricably bound with the sense of change and the loss that came with it. Fitzgerald's heroes were gay but never light-hearted. Their gaiety was forced, even more uncomfortable than it was disquieting. It was gaiety based on the sense of loss, not gaiety secure in the possession of joy. The posing Amory Blaine had, after all, taken every kiss seriously and not promiscuously, and Jay

Gatsby could not throw himself lightly into the cotton-candy world with which he surrounded himself but which was the mere fallout of his dream. Both had carried over into the styles of the present the hopeless values of the past.

III

While Fitzgerald paraded as a gilded youth to remind his readers of the loss of a golden past, and traditionalists condemned the young for their careless part in the whirligig of the present, others found in youth the living inspiration of a spectacular future. The progressives also remembered the past—not, however, as a nostalgic embrace. For them, it was a deadly encumbrance, exercising an unmerciful grip over the possibility of social progress and renewal. And they called on Americans to give up finally and completely the last remains of an old order and consciously to complete the task of reconstruction. The progressives were as conscious of change and as concerned with the problem of disorder as the traditionalists, but they saw patterns where the traditionalists saw only chaos, and they saw those patterns most clearly in the behavior of youth.

Some of the progressive tracts, like George Coe's *What Ails Our Youth?* and Ben Lindsey's *The Revolt of Modern Youth,* were directly and centrally concerned with the youth problem. In others, like *The Bankruptcy of Marriage* by V. F. Calverton and Floyd Dell's *Love in the Machine Age,*[23] the young were seen as critical actors in a drama which focused on changes in family forms or sexual mores. These analyses, like those of the traditionalists, reflected the period's strong urge toward self-examination as well as the acute consciousness of change which characterized the social thought of the twenties. What unites these tracts and distinguishes them from most of the journal literature, however, is neither their special sense of the disorderliness of the present, nor even their specific description of the behavior of the young, but their attitude toward that behavior and its significance for the American future. Both defined a much more general social orientation and sensibility.

Perhaps to call these analysts "progressives" is to extend the term beyond its traditional historical limits. Yet in a real sense it is appropriate, for it conveys their sense of excitement and orientation toward a reformed and regenerated future. It is an orientation that alerts us to the fact that the progressive sensibility had found a very specific twenties voice. Some time between 1914 and 1919 the progressive temperament is believed to have retreated into a bomb shelter, to emerge after the war an eerie ghost of its former self, lifeless, anemic, and demoralized.[24] Certainly, progressivism as a reform package did not dominate national programs or foreign policies during the twenties. But progressivism as an angle of vision, as an optimistic approach to social problems, was very much alive. The twenties progressive was not anemic, though he was elusive. Usually dressed in a variety of intellectual wrappings borrowed and adapted from the latest scientific and socio-scientific schemas, his vision was studded with climactic turning points and etched with social stages rather than the gradual and consistent progress which had been his hallmark in the prewar years. He was now more generally interested in culture than in politics and economics, and he was armed with a view of human nature as hungry with drives and instincts.

The twenties progressive, like his predecessor, looked eagerly toward the future, but it was a future which often had millennial overtones, a future which embodied to the fullest what he called man's true nature and his real needs. The twenties progressive created a future order around what he believed were the basic drives of man's physical and psychological organism. Not only did he trust man's natural instincts, but he judged the present society by the degree to which it corresponded to them.[25] That was in large part why the progressives turned to youth as a guide: in youth, human nature was found in its purest, least inhibited form. The young represented what was best in man, what was least tainted by the distortions of an unregenerate society. George Coe, for example, described the young as naturally inclined toward the pure and simple ethics of primitive Christianity, to which he turned for inspiration and guidance and around which he constructed his vision of a new social order. Coe relied on John Dewey for his image of the natural potential of youth and their divine "variability" and malleability, but it was Coe's simple faith in the goodness of the natural man that made him expect that this "natural variability" would effect a new and better world. For the traditionalist, it was just that natural, unsocialized self and its potential variability that threatened the social order, for he equated it with personal license and self-seeking. For Coe, it was an inspiration, the "normal and proper order for the self-revelation of God," which would free man from his past and help to create God's "new earths." [26]

To the twenties progressive, human nature was good, but it was no longer "pure" as an earlier generation would have defined that term. Every progressive accepted man's sexuality. With a twist of the wrist, however, he transformed it from the basest of instincts to what can only be described as primal innocence. For the progressive, not only was human nature fully sexual, but sexuality became an almost spiritual force, making for moral rejuvenation. The progressive, like the traditionalist, often collapsed the youth problem onto this one plane, but while the sexual energies of youth effected a crisis in social order for the traditionalist, sexual vitality was the spring for social rebirth for the progressive.

In *The Revolt of Modern Youth*, Ben Lindsey brings this vision of the regenerative powers of youthful sexuality to its most fabulous limits. Contemporary sexual attitudes and behavior were for Lindsey the most critical, almost the only, significant social issue, and sexual repression was weighted with all the problems of American life. Lindsey transformed the conflict between the life-denying hypocrites of sex repression and the life-affirming liberators—the older and younger generations respectively—into a millennial drama. According to Lindsey, the young were seeking, above all, for sexual honesty, and they turned instinctively away from the sexual shams which had made American society repressive and no longer responsive to human needs. Ever sensitive to the moral requirements of life, youth emerge in Lindsey's tract from the dark mire of repression and falsehood like the veritable angels of life. Denizens of the world of light, they are all unconfounded innocence with "dreamy blue eyes," "golden hair," and faces of "delicate, ethereal beauty." It is as though "the angels literally took charge of them." "There is," Lindsey observed, "a delicacy, and fineness, a spirituality, an unearthly sweetness about these girls." The dragon of sex has been transformed into the lamb of God. With the primitive truth of their vital sexuality, Lindsey proclaimed, youth would "save the world." [27]

Not all the progressive tracts were quite so full of fanciful youth, but all were committed to the virtues of youthful sexuality. Indeed, for most progressives the sexual habits of youth were laying the basis for a new social order. To V. F. Calverton, youth's sexual attitudes held "forth hope as a rich incentive," a promise of that ideal classless society that would come with the impending socio-economic revolution. That society was man's destiny and would fulfill his social nature. Similarly, Floyd Dell ascribed to the sexual habits of youth the wisdom of just those mating patterns which would complete the bourgeois revolution of the Western world and bring about the final stage of man's psycho-sexual evolution.[28] To all the progressives, the next stage of man's ascent would be the last, corresponding finally to his most basic and primitive self. And they all seemed convinced that this stage was finally about to come because the youth of America had discovered sex.

The sexual consciousness of the twenties progressive was grounded in Freudian sensitivity, although it was very far removed from Freud's pessimism about human nature or his dark determinism about civilization. But Freud was only one of the many thinkers who provided the progressives with guidance. The progressives drew heavily on a variety of intellectual schemes to which the 1920's attached a furious relevance: Marx, Dewey, Freud; the new psychology, the new sociology, the new anthropology. Each had something to teach about human nature, and all reinvigorated the progressive's faith in man and his future. As intellectual tools these psychologies and philosophies provided guides to human behavior and social process which were broad-based and universal in their description, geared toward change, and, at least as interpreted by Americans, optimistic in their prognosis. The progressives usually drew on one or more of these intellectual constructs for their analysis of the present and relied heavily on them for their visions of the future. Thus, Coe permitted Dewey to lead him to Christ; Calverton used both Marx and Freud to understand the present and followed Marx into the future; Dell's analysis was influenced by cultural anthropology as well as by Marx, but its greatest debt was to Freud's sexual categories, which Dell transformed from psychological stages to historical periods. And Lindsey drew on both Freud and Dewey, while he placed his faith in a kind of *élan vital* that was both Bergsonian and heavily influenced by D. H. Lawrence. With these intellectual supports, the progressive was able to make sense of the present disorders in the interests of a perfected future.

Because they were directed toward the future, the analytic tools were often used to obscure, distort, or simplify the present. Dell, for example, disposed of contraception as irrelevant to sexual mores because it did not conform to his future-directed vision of a society in which sex was confined to a conception-oriented family. Calverton hastened to reduce the value-shattering effects of the war to a theoretical construct in which only economic processes made for social change. Lindsey overplayed the extent of sexual misbehavior among the young in order to impress his readers with the need for sexual reform and to illustrate that behind every angelic face there lay an erotic nymph. And Coe imitated Dewey in calling for a new ethic commensurate with modern industrialism, while inclining toward an ethic that was both pre-modern and anti-industrial. Nevertheless, the systematic intellectual tools provided the progressives with just that faith in the future which the traditionalists lacked. The traditionalist had only his remembrance of a stable American society as a measure and a method; the progressive had a system which illuminated his faith.

Finally, of course, it was that faith in a new social order which most clearly distinguished the progressive from the traditionalist. And it was the role they assigned to youth in those visions that made them delight in the behavior of the young while the traditionalist could only screech in despair. In a reformed future, the behavior of youth would be incorporated into an effective society. Each of the progressives had a different vision of that society: for Coe it was a Christian commonwealth, for Dell a middle-class utopia, for Calverton a classless community, and for Lindsey a sexual garden. For each the young were vital instruments in the creation of the new order. The young were instinctively sagacious. They naturally turned toward the direction of social evolution and devised means for their survival in the new society. They were for Coe closer to God, who evolved his ever-changing worlds through youth's Deweyan variability. They were closer to the springs of instinctive life-affirming sexuality, according to Lindsey, and their greater honesty and inner wisdom would cleanse the world of its corruptions and distortions. For Calverton, they picked up the pulse of the fateful evolution of society which would lead to the ultimate egalitarian order and were participating in the destruction of the old. For Dell, they were the instruments of the great second revolution of human sexuality which would lead to the perfect unfolding of man's sexual potential. Their natural instincts led them toward the conventions which would define the new world. Whatever the special quality of the future, for the progressive mind of the twenties youth provided the key.

It is easy now to rip apart their intellectual frameworks and their naive visions of youth as so many hopeful moral fantasies. But it is important to note that these provided more than an ongoing faith in the efficacy of change. For the progressives the conditions of change provided solutions to the problems of youth, and the progressive directed his readers' attention to how to align human institutions with the primitive values of human nature. The new world would come only when the needs for social order were one with the needs of human nature. He never questioned the congruence of the two, nor that a conscious recognition of one would affect the conscious creation of the other. Thus the progressive tracts were also a trumpet call to social action. And while the twenties progressives usually described the new order in terms of total transformation and the present as a climacteric between the past and the future,[29] they nevertheless offered specific proposals which would hasten the millennium. Committed to American institutions as they had once been, with all their authority intact, the traditionalists could offer few solutions and little hope. The progressive was not concerned with the maintenance of authority but with how institutions could best respond to human needs, and he thus directed readers' attention to how this could be effected. The dialogue between progressives and traditionalists about the nature of social institutions illuminates their respective concerns.

Ironically, both progressives and traditionalists were correct. The past, with its synchronized institutional structures, had been outstripped by a multitude of social changes and cultural innovations. The future was already hastening to effect new institutional bonds and behavioral norms. Both were wrong, however, to believe that the young were free either to reject institutional conventions or to create a wholly new social order.

IV

Progressives and traditionalists disagreed sharply about the significance of youth's behavior, but both insisted that contemporary youth were unlike previous generations, and neither would have challenged the truth of James Truslow Adams' observation that amidst all the hysteria about the younger generation no one was fool enough to believe "that the babies born between 1900 and 1910 all received a hypodermic injection of new original sin." [30] No, the source of youth's problems lay not in their nature but in their nurture, and whatever their orientation—to the traditional past or the reformed future—contemporaries directed their attention to American social institutions.

For the traditionalist, the war had dealt a final blow to the sustaining and stable values of American culture. But the war was, after all, only a limited instrument of destruction, effective because of the deterioration of that triad of institutions—family, church, school—entrusted with the discipline and direction of the young. Not surprisingly, the traditionalist found them lacking because none of them individually and not all of them together had sufficient authority to provide the young with social continuity and effective control. But rarely did the traditionalist believe that the necessary authority could be reinjected or the former controls resurrected. Instead, the traditionalist applied salt to the raw wound of self-exposure. One and only one order satisfied his sense of social felicity, and it had passed. The young were left adrift by the failures of the society to secure institutional structures and traditional values.

Less interested in a single event, effective or symbolic, the progressive searched for the source of youth's behavior in the multidimensional social transformation, which was yet to be completed. [31] Material changes had outdistanced institutional foundations, so he attacked these as ill-adapted to the needs of social progress. Thus, the progressive agreed to the inefficiency of older institutions, but he hoped to establish the basis for new authority by describing how social institutions could be made to respond to the twin imperatives of human nature and social order.

Of all institutions, the American family was the most critical and the most troublesome. The journals were unmerciful. Once the bulwark of social morality, the home was in the eyes of traditionalists a major source of the disorderliness of youth. The American parent, Avis Carlson noted in *Harper's,* was "famous for his subservience." Mothers, especially, who should have prepared their daughters to assume what the *Atlantic*'s Mr. Grundy called "the entire responsibility of the human race," had instead been indulgent and permissive, allowing their children to rule and dominate the household. The result according to the Dean of Women at Ohio State University, was that mothers trained their children to glorify "personal liberties and individual rights to the point that they are beginning to spell lack of self-control and total irresponsibility in the matters of moral obligation to society." Summarizing a survey on the younger generation, the *Literary Digest* concluded that "all through the mass of horrified onlookers runs the censuring of the American home. The great need, we are told, is a reassertion of parental authority," and the *Digest* reported that one group of parents in Brooklyn had already formed to draw up a specific code of conduct for the young.[32]

But the reassertion of parental authority, which seemed simple, was really not enough. Parents had failed not only to control but to instruct. "Beyond a constant solicitude for health, do the parents of today have the passion for the souls and minds of their children that used to be not uncommon?" William Phelps asked in *World's Week.* The question contained its own answer. The home failed to provide the young with fundamental moral training. But the problem of family competence was still more complex. "The tendency is," the *Digest* noted, "when once away from the restraining influence of the parents, to attempt to see and to learn as much of life as is possible." [33] Thus, not only had family discipline (where it still existed) failed to instill youth with lasting values and provided only the temporary fear of parental disfavor, but the young were now exposed to many social temptations over which the family had no control. Youth needed ongoing restraint and control during a period of continuing immaturity, a restraint the family could not provide, either through moral guidance or through explicit control. Complicated new conditions, aided and abetted by a deterioration of parental authority, had stripped the family of its former social role.

The application of old-fashioned family authority more often than not produced a problem in the view of the progressive. If the traditionalist lamented the fact that society had changed so fast that it left family control behind, the progressive accused the family of mortifying rigidity. Instead of catching up to the new social conditions, the family impeded the process of social adjustment. The young, caught between family authority and social reality, were led to revolt. According to Ben Lindsey, the repressive features of an older family culture inhibited the progress of youth toward a genuine morality and often led directly to social maladjustment and misbehavior. Unable to understand the young's search for sexual honesty, parents withheld essential sexual knowledge ("the conspiracy of silence," he called it) and later withheld compassion when youth strayed from the conventional paths of righteousness. [34] The family, according to Lindsey, often applied its controls with a vengeance, punishing sincere sexual experimentation and forcing the young to revolt.

In Lindsey's view, the whole structure of the family was ill-suited to modern needs. Rigidly tied to old forms and unresponsive to individual needs for affection and security, it was glued together by tradition and convention. Instead, Lindsey announced that the family must be revised, streamlined, and adjusted to those very changes which to the traditionalist under-

mined its authority. On that point, Lindsey fully agreed with
the traditionalists; both understood that the old family could no
longer serve the new society without resorting to repressive control.

Companionate marriage, Lindsey announced, would provide
the solution. A simple legal device which would offer young
men and women an alternative to the confining commitments of
ordinary marriage, companionate marriage would sanction explorations in mate compatibility. By facilitating divorce and
requiring the full application of contraceptive procedures, companionate marriage would restrict adolescent sexual experimentation to institutional channels, while obviating the irrepa-
rable damage of ill-suited mating choices. It would relieve the
young from sexual and economic anxieties, free wives to work,
and free both partners from childbirth. Companionate marriage
would also reconfirm family authority. Lindsey ascribed most of
the problems of youth to family sources: inadequate family instruction in sexual matters, inappropriate parental responses to
sexual deviance, unyielding marital commitments for sexually
ripe but socially and emotionally immature youthful partners.
Sex education and companionate marriage would replace parental authority as a control on youthful behavior. Once sex was removed as an issue between the generations, family authority
would return to normal channels, the young would not need to
revolt, and parents would have no need for repression. Lindsey
hoped to preserve the conventional family as an effective social
institution by supplementing it with a modern auxiliary form of
marriage to contain and channel adolescent sexuality. He was
thus quite candid when he claimed, "I am as much for what is
really meant by marriage, virtue, chastity, and so on, as any one
could be." "When I criticize many of our present standards and
conventions it is not because I do not favor them, because I do
favor them." [35] He asked for an effective system of supplemen-
tal social controls, not dependent on an unnatural and repressive
exercise of authority by the family, but effected through new in-

stitutional bonds which grew from adolescent sexual needs in new social conditions.

Lindsey was thus as interested in control as any traditionalist, but he was willing to adjust institutions to just those changes which the traditionalist most feared. Not tied to an unyielding vision of order, Lindsey sought to revitalize order with a pragmatic new proposal. The traditionalist, however, saw the family undercut from within and without, and feared that neither the family nor the society would survive the blow. Some traditionalists already feared that the family had, in fact, become largely irrelevant to the young. Mary Hamilton, for example, noted that, where once young people rebelled against the views of their parents, they now merely disregarded them. "Revolt," she observed, left "the parent in the center of the stage; now he is not so much as hovering in the wings." [36] Any change in family order would undermine it still further.

V. F. Calverton, a progressive and a Marxist, agreed. He too believed that the family was irrelevant to the young, who no longer subscribed to its values and norms. The bourgeois family which depended on a rigid adherence to monogamy and female purity had been undermined by the effects of war and contraception. The first dealt a final blow to all former ideals, including those of female virtue, the second to family practices. Together they forever did away with the twin myths of premarital chastity and female innocence, essential to the middle-class institution of marriage. [37] Calverton, like the traditionalists, believed that American society could not survive the social changes destroying older patterns of marriage and family. As a Marxist, Calverton of course gloried in the destruction, because the American family supported a middle-class social structure.

Both Calverton and the traditionalists were tied to a confining vision of social order. The traditionalists could conceive of order only as it had once been, with all the bricks in place, and Calverton, as a Marxist, insisted that all culture was of a piece, that each stage of social organization had one and only one strict set of institutional arrangements. Unlike the traditionalists, however, Calverton thought that the changes undermining family order would be reincorporated into a new family form in a new society. For the moment, because the values of youth were detached from older family norms, the young lived in a frenzied state of sexual excitement.[38] But this would pass, and sex would assume a proper and limited role in a more wholesome family life once the future social order was effected. In the Soviet Union, Calverton found just such a properly functioning, if also looser, family form, egalitarian and democratic, freely formed and freely dissolved. In the sexual misbehaviors of American youth, Calverton located not only the loss of an older family authority but the promise of a new family and its attendant social order.

In fact, Floyd Dell declared, American youth were already creating a freer, more natural family without fanfare and without revolt. Dell believed that the old-fashioned American family, whose authority was based on sexual repression, patriarchal authority, and hierarchical organization, had long been outdistanced by industrial and social realities, by middle-class forms of production, and by middle-class social organization. The older American family was not middle class at all, but a vestige of an aristocratic order, and it was fast being replaced by a truly middle-class family form based on love criteria in mating, implicit fidelity growing from vital sexual compatibility, and a deep commitment to child-bearing and democratic child-rearing. The "ideals of our time," Dell insisted, are "a courtship period in which one learns what one needs to know about oneself and love, in order to effect a genuine love-choice, and then the life-long marriage made possible by such emotional knowledge." [39] The new family, for which the young were preparing themselves through courtship patterns like petting, would be the perfected expression of human needs and social conditions.

Thus Dell, like the traditionalists, attributed adolescent behavior to family sources, but he gave that behavior form and direction. Dell tried to make sense of youth's behavior by describing it not merely as the result of family socialization but also as a preparation for family formation. Youth came from families, but they also created families. This took him far beyond the traditionalists and considerably beyond even Calverton and Lindsey. Lindsey and Calverton, like the traditionalists, still saw the young as escaped from the leash of older family controls, as rebellious or capricious, whereas Dell saw brilliantly that their behavior was already an indication of new controls, directed toward family order and effected by peers. Dell understood the behavior of youth not as a frantic response to disorder, but as purposive, arising from new conditions of socialization, and in turn anchoring those new conditions through norms and values. This the traditionalists would not see, for they looked to the family to cement an older order, not to direct change. The traditionalists understood that both the inner dynamics of family relations and the position of the family in the complex of the society had changed. But they could not believe, as Dell did, that this either reserved to the family an important social role or preserved its integrity. Partly by the accident of his personal inclination, and partly because he was a sharp observer, Dell understood that a differently organized family would exercise social control and authority in much more subtle but no less effective ways.[40]

If the family was in trouble, the church was in ruins, and the more the churches adjusted, the less they seemed to matter. In the stable world, the traditionalist remembered, the church had been the second pillar of social order and social morality. But the young had simply "thrown religion overboard." "We are not looking at this question from the religious viewpoint, from that of saving souls," the *Chicago Tribune* admitted, "but simply from the viewpoint of social behavior." And from that perspective, "skepticism in religion," as William Phelps observed, "is, in nine cases out of ten, followed by skepticism in morals."[41]

The progressives were generally less interested in the churches than the traditionalists, partly because they were less concerned with the maintenance of old-fashioned authority, partly because it was precisely the progessive-liberal reform of the churches which had apparently undermined religion.

Americans had spent the latter part of the nineteenth century wrestling with the consequences of Darwinian evolution and devising a makeshift alliance between religion and science. But, as S. K. Ratcliffe observed in *Century Magazine,* this "liberal" religion meant nothing to the young. "There is no more momentous social fact than the cool and decisive turning away of the young people from those forms of religious association which to the liberals of the last age seemed to be the natural and satisfying embodiment of an emancipated faith." Predicated on the inevitability of progress and the evolving perfection of the human race, the religious compromise had been wrecked by the war which betrayed what a flimsy patchwork of naive idealism it really was. "We have seen hideous peculation, greed, anger, hatred, malice and all uncharitableness, unmasked, rampant and unashamed," one of the "Wild Young People" informed the readers of the *Atlantic.* [42]

According to Katherine Gerould, a contributor to the *Atlantic,* Americans would have done well to heave to the orthodox line. Only firm dogmas and doctrines, not liberal idealism, could provide the young with the stable moral leadership which alone would make for socially responsible behavior. But her own generation had replaced authoritative control with humanitarianism and freely accepted ethical principles. They had done away with God and heaven and hell and thus deprived religion and the churches of the power of eternal sanction. They kept only the commandments, Gerould asserted, without the religious tenets upon which they were based. But these could not in turn be passed on to the young, who lacked the ingrained fear of transgression. Morals without religious absolutes could not keep youth in control. "This conduct is wrong," had been replaced by "this conduct is unsocial." But in the end, who was to say with authority that the standard morality was any more humane or beneficial than a deviant morality? "There is no reason why the young should not do anything they please, so long as it is not inexpedient. Society, escaped from its leash of authority, will soon see to it that anything it pleases to do shall be expedient." The churches, "afraid of being too narrow, afraid of offending their hearers," had erased the fundamental definitions and doctrines, which had been the basis of their authority, in the illusion of humanitarian ecumenicalism. And, in another effort to please communicants, Avis Carlson noted, churches now offered social service and entertainment instead of religious dogma, converting their buildings into "social centers with gymnasiums, club-rooms and billiard halls." [43]

By their liberal and misguided compromises, Americans had undermined the efficacy of the church as a moral guardian. The progressives had, of course, asked that religion be broad and humane, and writers in a liberal religious journal like the *Outlook* continued to believe that the young wanted "the windows of the Church . . . thrown wide open to reason," that they were seeking "for truth and will accept no compromises." A progressive like George Coe went further. Applying a Deweyite commitment to change and elasticity, Coe condemned the churches for remaining traditional, rigid, insufficiently given to questioning the ethical, social, and Christian foundations of the society which they served. Christianity, Coe insisted, must return to its humane and human roots of brotherhood and justice. For Coe, the churches were still narrow and bigoted, beholden to the interests of government and business whose practices they needed to examine and cleanse. Even when they could attract them, Coe asserted, the churches continued to tie the young to the leading strings of mindless authority, instead of liberating their creative Christian imaginations. But Coe's philosophy was lodged in just that open humanism which traditionalists attacked. Coe was intent on changing the world by changing religious institutions and was eager to have the churches serve human needs in a new social environment. The traditionalists looked to church authority to stop the world from changing, and to control, not express, human needs. Not even the religious aspirations of the young themselves could reassure the traditionalists. "I feel that the definition of religion has changed," "Last Year's Debutante" declared in the *Atlantic*. "The 'wild young people' don't believe that faith can be confined to a dogma or reduced to a creed. We think of religion as the spiritual stream in which we are floating or swimming, or struggling or sinking, and how can we deny the existence of the very element in which we live?" [44] In the end, however, it seemed highly unlikely that authority would ride the flux or that morality could be floated on a "spiritual stream."

While the traditionalists may well have overestimated the modernity of the churches, their perception of the erosion of church discipline in the lives of the young was certainly correct. Even the progressives agreed that the churches were not attracting the young. By the twenties the young had transferred their allegiance from the churches, broad or narrow, to a different sort of God, as they invested a kind of religious devotion to their leisure pursuits, to sports, dating, and song. And they engaged in these in the communion of peers. This means not that there was no religion among the young, but that even the most religiously inspired college youth, those who joined YMCA's and missionary societies, and even theology students, often found the churches ill-suited to their needs. These students often turned to social reform and politics just as their less spiritual brothers and sisters turned to football and jazz. Coe understood that the traditional religious institutions were not responding to the new social conditions. But even Coe was too much of a traditionalist to see how religious energies had been rechanneled. Some contemporaries, especially those connected with colleges and universities, sensed that religious energies had been redirected, and certainly Ben Lindsey and Floyd Dell understood how important peer conventions had become. But few realized how thoroughly the shift in allegiance and authority had been effected.

Few contemporaries could doubt the new significance of another traditional institution—the school. But while the schools were certainly attracting the young in ever greater numbers, they seemed to have lost effective control as the massive increase in high school and college enrollments threatened to undermine the traditional objectives and functions of education. "Youth goes toward youth," Princeton's Dean Christian Gauss observed, "and all youth goes to the colleges." [45] Huge and heterogeneous populations raised new and troubling issues in the traditionalist mind.

The schools were sorely plagued by the loss of specific direction. The hallowed halls had been only recently opened to "practical" courses, in partial recognition of the new professional orientation of an industrial society, and educators found themselves confronted by new student types—the "grind," the "poler," the distasteful social climber—attracted by the material or social advantages of higher education. There remained, of course, the gentleman loafer, who had no idea why he was there at all. Many began to question whether, on opening the schools to democratic populations, the gates had not been thrown so wide that the massed gatherings became inimical to all learning, practical or otherwise. "Young men and young women prefer the society of other young men and women to the society of their elders," Gauss noted. "With the general obscuring of the college's original purpose and function, it has unfortunately become a kind of glorified playground. It has become the paradise of the young." [46]

The schools had become centers of youth life and youth activities which had little to do with the basic aims of education as they had been heretofore understood. Educators were suddenly confronted by new social problems concerned with residence, recreations, youth organizations, and only casually related to academic concerns. These threatened to undermine the guided initiation of students into the intellectual and moral precepts the schools were meant to provide. Indeed, the schools appeared no longer even capable of providing that leadership, because on entering the colleges the young promptly scattered to a variety of fraternity houses, athletic fields, extra-curricular clubs, dances, and proms. Some withdrew altogether in that new menace to order, the automobile, to motion-picture houses and road-side dance halls. Others, because of a critical lack of housing facilities at schools unprepared for the sudden rush to the colleges, were forced to live in completely unsupervised boarding houses, usually located off-campus in downtown and unpatrolled districts.

Had the increased size and heterogeneity of school populations, together with the increased diversity of school activities, not in fact deflected the young from the course of a maturing experience under the influence of older minds and saner heads? "The student," Gauss observed, "lives too largely with his own classmates and life is too exclusively adolescent to stimulate the young or induct them into that social maturity which is, of course, one of the goals of education." The young seemed not to be gaining in social maturity. They showed instead a sense of independence from anything old or traditional.[47] Community morality and standards left when heterogeneous populations came in. In their place were undisciplined individualism, self-indulgence, self-expression.

Within the last two generations, Wilbur Abbott told readers of the *Atlantic,* "there has been evolved beside, or rather within, the framework of formal and official college and university another system of education, largely outside the authority of faculties, and largely independent of their intellectual impulses and disciplinary ordinances." Although this "student university" was not new (indeed, it had medieval roots), it had assumed an unprecedented intensity in twentieth-century America and was stirring passionate public debate and concern. Abbott asked the critical question: How could one "infuse into this mass of youthful energy something of judgment and direction more than is natural to youth; to connect this vigorous, undisciplined, loosely organized development with the saner standards and the worthier ends of maturer minds?" The problem must, above all, be recognized as an "integral part, not only of the situation as it exists, but of the education of our youth in its entirety." [48]

That was the crux of the matter: how to control the experiences of the young and to direct them toward responsible values and behavior? Even those most eager to defend students could not adequately answer. The *New Republic*'s education critic, W. H. Cowley, argued that the school curriculum was no longer adequate to the needs of the young, who were thus devising their own instruments to fill the gap. George Coe was more extreme. The schools were worse then irrelevant—they were dangerous. Education was "reproducing in youth, instead of correcting, the moral confusion which prevails in adult life." Tied to obsolete values and mechanical procedures, the schools deprived youth of the vital experience of active intelligence and repressed youthful creativity. Rather than guiding students to an unfolding of inner potential, they still adhered to a philosophy in which "school is something done by the teacher to the student." Still others, like the *Forum*'s Willard Thorpe, argued that all schooling was irrelevant to youth, who were eager for life and impatient with seemingly irrelevant learning: "The college boy is tremendously interested in life. He comes to four years of study when the romance of adventuring in the world, earning a living, raising a family and making a name are very near realities. Quiet poring over books seems an unessential pastime, pleasant enough perhaps, but pro-tem after all. Managing college organizations and forming lasting friendships are more nearly related to the life just outside." [49] The schools, progressives believed, must liberate youth's potential and serve their practical needs.

All these assurances about youth's eagerness for life, their creative potential, or their finer appreciation of the outside world could hardly allay the traditionalists' fears, for it was precisely the world outside that was most threatening. They turned to the schools both to halt the contagion and to repress youthful energies. This the schools seemed no longer capable of doing.

The traditionalist was concerned with the maintenance of standards and the exercise of controls, the progressive with adjustment to new social realities. One looked toward the past, the other to the future. Neither fully appreciated the degree to which the schools were directing youth to a balance between past and future, not in the classroom but in those very youth-controlled agencies that seemed most threatening to the traditionalists and represented the mere spillover of youthful vitality to progressives. The schools provided the setting and context for an effective set of institutional controls which utilized just those youthful energies suspected by traditionalists and over-glamorized by progressives. Those controls and the direction of youthful behavior had as little to do with the mythological society of the traditionalists' past as they did with the fanciful world of the progressives' future.

V

Tied as they each were to idealized conceptions of social order, past or future, the progressives and the traditionalists often found youth more useful as didactic examples of what had been or what would be rather than as guides to the contemporary scene. Youth was weighted with a baggage of social symbolism which more often concealed than revealed their experiences. Yet contemporary observations are critical to our understanding of what was happening to youth. First, contemporaries often vividly described the broader implications of youth's behavior as well as the institutional context making for that behavior, and some, like Floyd Dell, came very close to an inspired understanding of what was happening to the middle-class youth of the 1920's. So too, traditionalists were especially aware that not only specific institutions, but the whole network of socialization, had changed; the society had outgrown and overgrown older institutional structures. While they lamented those changes and despaired of effectively controlling them, this was often the better part of wisdom. It is well to remind ourselves that it was just this desperate nostalgia for an older order which underlay the kind of repressive social legislation that blackened the fair face of the decade. Americans looked to law in the twenties to provide the controls other institutions had been unable to maintain precisely because they believed that the older structures had failed and could not be reformed. The law could not correct socialization, but it could consciously punish misbehavior. Thus traditionalists hoped to deal with the effects, not the causes, of institutional misfunction. But the law was, after all, a precarious bulwark in a democratic society which extolled liberty and order based on shared ideals and individual virtue rather than on external constraint. The traditionalists were really concerned with the kind of lawlessness that came from a deterioration in a common morality and in shared values, not from law-breaking. When they turned to the law, they admitted defeat.

The progressives of the twenties rarely called on the law and, except for such proposals as companionate marriage, rarely needed it. Often they could not wholly understand the traditionalists' furor. Thus, a liberal journal like the *New Republic,* citing statistics from the Children's Bureau that "crime" among the young had not increased proportionately to their numbers, assured their readers that "whatever wildness of youth exists, if it be not serious enough to draw the attention of the law, cannot be worth as much excitement, as many millions of words of frenzied exhortation, as it has been receiving." [50] The *New Republic* missed the point. What concerned the traditionalists was not crime but the nature of American life, and the millions of words of frenzied exhortation, like the resort to law, was a frantic admission of failure.

The progressives generally trusted to the forward thrust of time and the specific actions of the young to effect the changes they yearned for, changes which went well beyond anything the behavior of youth really promised. What they hoped to do with their tracts was to change people's attitudes toward the young, to wean them from an obsession with the past, and thus to make the changes they described more smoothly realizable. Their trust in the young was not misplaced, extreme though it sometimes was, for material and institutional changes in conjunction with the behavior and attitudes of the young were pushing the culture forward to a different world.

Secondly, and perhaps more significant for the young, the attitudes of progressives and traditionalists described the sensibility of the world in which youth lived. Participant and observer were linked in a network of cultural attitudes which not only described but affected youth's behavior. Adult reaction to the young affected them directly through the actions of parents and teachers, churchmen and screenwriters. It also affected them indirectly, since it produced a degree of self-consciousness which exaggerated the real differences and discontinuities between the generations. The young could and did play on the alarm or the acclaim of a receptive audience. Fitzgerald understood this potential in his art, and the young understood it in their lives. "Do not flatter us," warned "Last Year's Debutante" in the *Atlantic,* "for it does flatter us even to be criticized." "Notoriety is the breath of life to the girls and young men who love to shock and scandalize their open-mouthed elders." The young were often consciously naughty in the twenties, and both the consciousness and the naughtiness reflected youth's perception of adult expectations.[51] Life, Oscar Wilde reminds us, imitates art, and the college youths of the twenties sometimes tried to make their lives into an art. This does not mean that youth's behavior was all play. On the contrary, as we shall see, much of that behavior was a necessary response to a new set of social and cultural conditions. It does mean, however, that a certain play-acting accentuated particular patterns which, in turn, interacted with and reinforced adult attitudes and sensibilities.

The young always live in a world that is maintained and restrained by adult institutions and values. The degree to which the young can manipulate or readapt these depends on various factors, not the least of which is the attention they get from their elders. In the 1920's, the young had that attention and used it. They also had the plastic conditions of new and changing institutions, an ever more quickly changing social stage, and an emerging self-consciousness grounded in those changes and in the almost reverent attention of an adult world.

2

The Family Redivivus: 1880-1930

The distinguishing feature of the modern family will be affection. The new family will be more difficult, maintaining higher standards that test character more severely, but it will offer richer fruit for the satisfying of human needs.

Ernest R. Groves and William F. Ogburn,
American Marriage and Family Relationships (*1928*)

It is the child's right to be wanted and to have a chance to grow up under conditions assuring the proper mental, spiritual and physical health.

J. F. Hayden, The Art of Marriage (*1926*)

"Daddy, what an ass you are." This was the final sentence in an argument which I had with my youngest daughter, aged five. I had not been able to convince her or to sway her opinion. . . . I ceased arguing and reflected. I tried to imagine what would have happened had I thus addressed my father some forty years ago. I shuddered and sighed. Fate was unkind in making me appear forty years too soon.

Bronislaw Malinowski,
"Parenthood, The Basis of Social Structure" (1930)

"The Child in Power Again," a simple subtitle in Bronislaw Malinowski's now classic essay on parenthood and social structure,[1] neatly summarized a half-century of changes in American middle-class homes. When the effects of these changes came to the fore in the 1920's, traditionalists denounced them, progressives welcomed them, and social scientists anxiously investigated their social ramifications. For the historian, the reorganization of the family as a child-rearing environment is the starting point for understanding youth then and since. The popular literature of the twenties recognized the fact implicitly, for while the young were symbols of vast social changes, they were first the products of specific families which had been critically, indeed drastically, changed as social environments and in relation to the complex body of social authority. This observation was not restricted to lay observers, On the contrary, the debate over the family among sociologists, psychologists, and social workers was at least as heated as the debate over youth. The two were, of course, related. From a welter of theories and conflicting views on the family, one central observation emerged almost unchallenged in the discussions. The child had assumed a new prominence in middle-class family affairs, and as a result in these families the care and rearing of children had superseded all other functions within the household.

To most social scientists, this primary reorientation was accompanied by other changes in family patterns—a democratization of family relations, increases in affection between husband and wife and parents and children, and more latitude for emotional expression for each member of the family. But while each of these changes was significant in its own right, their importance was above all to confirm and highlight the changes in the quality of the family as a child-rearing environment. This observation was by no means without its troublesome aspects, particularly as it related to the problem of family responsibility to the larger society, but on the whole, experts concurred in the fact. In time, the specific anxieties about the wholesomeness of the changes in family life gave way to confidence and finally to a radical rethinking of what the family was and how it related to other social patterns, and especially to social stability. But during the twenties, at least, most family experts were often more tremulous than confident about the changes which were suddenly so prominent. Discussions about the family in the twenties were full of the same anxious indeterminacy which characterized observations on youth; both defined a decade's response to changes which appeared to have suddenly overwhelmed society.

The family had, of course, been changing for some time. As one facet of the general repatterning of the society, the family reflected and reinforced changes which began after the Civil War with the rapid acceleration of the processes of urbanization, industrialization, and nationalization.[2] Over time, the slow process of family adaptation had produced a radical alteration which by the 1920's was both perceptible and effective. The change was two-pronged. Changes in internal order, in roles, relationships, and child-rearing patterns were paralleled by strategic revisions in the integration of the family into the complex web of social institutions and especially into the overall process of child socialization.

The internal changes can be briefly summarized: the democratization of family relations and the reorientation of family function toward child nurture broke down former rigidities in roles and opened the way for less structured, more emotional interaction between husband and wife and between them and their children. The term "affectionate," while laden with ambiguities and controversy, is nevertheless appropriate to describe this family pattern. It was a term used constantly and with little reservation by contemporary sociologists and psychologists to describe their sense of the new qualities of family life, especially among the urban middle classes.

At the same time, this emotional family unit became more and more separated from other social institutions and freed of direct responsibility to them. These institutions were also changing, but in the opposite direction from the family. More and more dependent on direct role performance, the school, the community, the workplace, and the market became impersonal social environments, registering the general rationalization and regimentation of urban industrial society. An elaborate system of differential roles and emotionally neutral relationships was being articulated as the effects of national markets, urban consolidation, and machine and clerical technology re-created the meaning of social identity. Nowhere was the process complete, and nowhere did it completely obliterate older patterns of community integration, but it was already widespread and prominent.

These two processes were mutually dependent and mutually reinforcing. The society was increasingly forced to rely on the emotional and expressive services of the family, while the family relied on the productive services of the society. They were, moreover, both dependent on a newly important mediatory institution, the school. As the family looked to its children's welfare and needs, education was an ever more significant extension of the services the family willingly assumed in relation to its children. For the society, education became more necessary as the skills required in the workplace came to be predominantly those of a highly literate, skilled, and educationally sophisticated population. The school thus became an expression of family solicitude at the same time that it became the primary requisite of a rationalized economy.

The divergence between the family and social spheres had other consequences as well. It called for an emotional readjustment from a personal to a social identity. And the extended school experience provided the young with a new and ever longer period of transitional dependence—a period of potential freedom and incipient responsibility. This juncture between the two worlds, between the family and the marketplace, created the modern span of youth.

It was this complex social transformation which both created the fact of modern youth and underlay its experience. For in the interstices between older institutions, peer groups firmly grasped a critical role in socialization.[3] Mediating between family nurture and social performance, they controlled and directed habits, attitudes, and values but could not be completely directed or controlled by older and adult institutions. Thus the young became more independent and newly dependent: independent of strict adult supervision but dependent for longer and longer periods upon the adult world that made peer groups necessary and upon the peers who made a transitional independence possible. But while peers helped to effect responsible behavior among the young, that behavior appeared radically irresponsible, since it did not correspond to what was either traditional or adult. Peers neither uphold tradition nor mimic adult behavior, and they do not provide a smooth transition in a period of social change and cultural upheaval. They do, however, make possible an effective change in norms in just such a period. This quite understandably produced consternation among adults, who understood neither the role of peers nor the changes they were effecting. Thus an adult world stood aghast as the young were suddenly caught up both in a new institution and in a new set of values and behaviors for which neither family nor school was responsible but to which each had contributed.

I

The changes in the family can be most immediately and directly captured in demographic terms; demographic trends at once measure family patterns and set the structural basis for family changes. And the demographic indicators for the period are not only large but dramatic.

The birth rate in the United States had begun to decline by the first half of the nineteenth century. As the decline began to accelerate, the birth rate, together with the general rise in life expectancy, resulted in a significant shift in the age structure of the American population by the early years of the twentieth century. The proportion of the population under 15 years of age dropped from 34.4% in 1900 to 29.3% in 1930. The median age of the population rose in response from 22.9 years in 1900 to 26.5 years in 1930. The proportion of youths 15 to 24 years of age declined less sharply, from 19.6% in 1900 to 18.3% in 1930.[4] This was a natural result of the continuing downward trend of births, which made the younger groups continually smaller in relation to the older.

The age group 15 to 24 was thus becoming *larger* relative to the younger group. One-half as large as the age group 0–14 in 1870, it had become almost two-thirds as large by 1930. The effect of this shift within the youth population should be taken into account in any explanation of the growing awareness of youth and the increased concern with adolescence in the late nineteenth and early twentieth centuries. Certainly many factors were involved—scientific investigations of changing physiology at this time of life, psychological studies of the stresses accompanying sexual maturation, community concern with delinquency—but the basic population statistics should not be overlooked as part of the rediscovery of adolescence.[5]

At the same time, the proportion of youths 15 to 24 years of age relative to the sector 25 years and older was declining. The proportion of youths to adults in the population declined steadily from 1870 to 1930. Whereas in 1870 there were two persons 24 to 64 years of age to every one 15 to 24 years, there were three older persons to every one youth in 1930.[6] In effect, there were more adult caretakers per youth. With more mature adults to care for the youth group, there was more room for an elaborate nurture and for a more leisured pace of development preparatory to full adult status. From the perspective of the larger society, there was not so much pressure on the young to undertake the social and economic tasks of adulthood. So too, advances in industry and the effects of technological progress in labor-saving procedures made this conservation of youthful energy socially feasible. The labors of the young were not immediately needed for social survival or progress, and concurrently, more complex industry demanded a better educated work force.

Underlying these broad shifts was the shrinking size of the family unit. The steady decline in family size is evident from the United States census. The median size of all households in the United States fell from 4.7 persons in 1900 to 4.5 in 1910 and further to 4.3 in 1920.[7] But the actual effect of this decline on the urban middle classes was far more significant than these overall figures suggest. The specific pattern can best be understood by comparing two generations of families, the first completed in 1890 and the second in 1910 (Table 1).[8]

In 1890, there was a broad range in the size of families in all occupational groups, and more than one-half of the families in each group had three or more children. But the professional and business groups already had a significantly higher proportion of families with 1–2 children than did others. In addition, the professional class had a vastly higher proportion of families with no children than did any other class. By 1910, the pattern among the middle-class groups had become pronounced, and the difference between them and the other classes had sharpened. The proportion of professional and business families with five or more children had declined precipitously to 8% and 11% respectively. Thus, while very large families were becoming less common for every group, large families were becoming least consistent with the needs and family organization of the professional and business classes. These two groups experienced a corresponding trend toward families with one to three children. While the trend toward smaller families between 1890 and 1910 had affected all groups (each class had fewer children on the average in 1910 than in 1890) and all urban groups saw a pronounced increase in childless couples, the most significant tightening in the range of average family size occurred in professional and business groups. By 1910, these groups were clearly limiting themselves to families of from one to three children.[9]

The Plastic Age

TABLE 1-A

Percentage of Completed Families with Specified Number of Children in 1890, by Occupation of Husband (women 60–64 years of age, 1910)

Total # of Children Born	Occupation of Husband				
	Professional	Business	Skilled	Unskilled	Farm Owners
0	14.7	9.6	8.8	4.4	9.0
1	13.3	14.0	13.3	12.4	8.8
2	19.8	21.1	16.7	12.4	11.8
3	15.5	16.7	15.5	16.8	14.8
4	14.1	13.0	12.2	13.1	12.7
5 or more	22.7	25.5	33.6	40.8	43.2
Total %	100.1	99.9	100.1	99.9	100.3

This pattern among the professional and business families, taken along with the sharp increase in all families that had only one child or were childless, points to the use of effective birth control methods. Moreover, the pattern suggests that families were consciously effecting an ideal norm in family size. Contraceptive techniques were clearly not limited to the middle classes, for there was a very high proportion of both skilled and unskilled labor families without children. But while these groups began to approximate the percentage of middle-class families with no children, the middle-class groups led the trend toward small and medium-size families. In one generation a pronounced and significant pattern emerged among the middle classes—smaller size and consistent choice in numbers of children born.[10]

The families from which college students came in the 1920's experienced these changes with striking consistency.[11] Not only was there very little variation in the average size of families from which college students came, but their families had experienced similar demographic changes in the span of a single generation. Thus at the University of Wisconsin (students largely from the

TABLE 1-B

Percentage of Completed Families with Specified Number of Children in 1910, by Occupation of Husband (women 40–44 years of age, 1910)

Total # of Children Born	Occupation of Husband				
	Professional	Business	Skilled	Unskilled	Farm Owners
0	19.8	17.9	17.4	16.3	10.6
1	19.6	21.5	17.0	14.9	10.1
2	24.5	22.9	18.0	16.1	16.6
3	18.4	17.1	16.2	14.4	16.4
4	9.6	9.7	11.0	9.9	13.2
5 or more	8.2	10.9	20.5	28.4	33.1
Total %	100.1	100.0	100.1	100.0	100.0

Source: Frank Notestein, "Decreasing Size of Families," Table 2, p. 184.

Midwest), the average number of children in the students' families was 3.3 compared with 5.4 children in parents' families, a decline of more than two children per family. At the University of California (Far Western sample) the pattern was similar—an average of 3.3 children in the students' families and 5.2 in the parents' families. In the students' generation, unlike that of the parents, there was little variation around a stable norm in family size. The stabilization of a norm was even more explicit in a sample of Northeastern college students' families (Mt. Holyoke College), where the trend toward smaller families and the consistent choice in number of children born is documented in the experience of three generations. The average number of children in students' families was 3.2; in mothers' families, 5.1; and in grandmothers' families, 6.2. The number of children had literally been halved in the course of three generations, with the sharpest decline between the students' and the parents' generation. As importantly, the clustering around a norm had become really significant only in the students' generation.[12]

TABLE 2

Percentage of Students' Families with 1–2 Children by Region and Occupational Group, and the Percentage of All Students' Families with 1–2 Children by Region and the Percentage of Parents' Families with 1–2 Children by Region

Regions	All Occupations	Agri-culture	Managerial Trade Professional	Skilled	Parents' Families All Occupations
New England	35.9	20.7	37.7	21.4	18.9
Mid Atlantic	36.2	25.2	38.3	34.9	14.1
E. N. Central	33.2	19.5	38.6	30.3	9.9
W. N. Central	25.2	9.6	32.2	33.9	7.8
S. Atlantic	16.5	6.8	22.9	22.0	8.5
E. S. Central	18.8	10.3	25.1	19.2	7.2
W. S. Central	19.2	9.1	25.8	31.3	9.5
Mountain	31.9	14.5	39.1	33.8	11.8
Pacific	33.3	22.7	37.3	37.5	11.4
U.S.	27.5	12.4	33.7	30.1	9.9

Source: Warren Thompson, "Size of the Families from which College Students Come," Table V, p. 494.

There continued to be some regional variation even in the size of college students' families (Table 2). In the South and newer Midwestern states (both largely rural), families were larger than elsewhere. The average number of children in the families of one large sample of Midwestern and Southern students was 4.3, while the size of parents' families was 6.5. The decline between the generations (more than two children) was, however, similar to the experience of students from other regions. So too, even among students, there continued to be significant differences between occupational groups, most notably between students from agricultural families and those from business and professional groups.[13]

Overall, however, the similarities are more notable than the differences. In every region there was a significant concentration of small families (1–2 children) within the managerial, trade, and professional classes, and within one generation every region had experienced an increase in the number of families with one or two children (compare first and last columns in Table 2). In the course of a single generation, the proportion of all students' families with one or two children compared with parents' families of this size had trebled on a nationwide basis.

College students in the 1920's not only came from families of remarkably consistent size, suggesting basic similarities in at-home experience, but within one generation their families had undergone very similar demographic changes, suggesting important similarities in family decisions (Table 3). The pattern among college students underscores two basic facts of middle-class experience: families were small, and parents were planning consciously and carefully. Parents could now aspire to specific goals for each child. The possibility of advanced education for one or more children was one result. But more than specific material benefits were at stake. With fewer children in the household, each child could expect to receive more attention at home for longer periods of his life. Although most middle-class children still came from homes where other children were present,[14] the smaller size of families permitted each a degree of care and attention unavailable or impossible in a larger unit. Where children in large families would find parents' attention repeatedly focused on new arrivals, they could potentially receive ongoing attention in a smaller unit. Older children, who might be required to care for younger ones in a large family, would be less apt to do so in smaller families, in part because the oldest might be little older than the youngest. Large families required more regimentation and careful disciplining with specific allocation of chores and responsibilities, and parents with many children are likely to categorize children by age and sex and assign responsibilities and privileges on the basis of both. Smaller families could, however, be more democratic, with each child treated according to personal qualities and individual needs rather than his position in the family.

TABLE 3

Median Number of Children in the Families of College Students and in the Families of their Parents, and the Per Cent Decline within One Generation, by Student Sample

Study & Population Base	# of Children Students' Generation	# of Children Parents' Generation	Per Cent Decline
University of Wisconsin (Midwest, native)	3.35	5.44	38.5
University of California (Far West, native)	3.34	5.21	35.9
Mt. Holyoke College (New England, native)	3.15	5.09	38.1
Thompson sample * (Midwest and South, native and foreign)	4.32	6.51	33.6

* This sample is based on students from a large number of institutions in the Middle West and South.

Smaller families reflected a trend toward more care and solicitude for the interests of each child and in turn allowed for it. The marked change in family size in one generation and the consistent decision of the middle class by the first decade of the twentieth century to limit family size to two or three children suggests very real changes in family organization and implies a broad range of qualitative changes in roles and relationships within the household.

II

These changes were bound up with other dimensions of family experience, particularly with the changing roles of women in a refashioned marriage relationship. A new latitude in marital roles is implicit in the careful application of birth-control procedures. The very fact that decisions could be made and goals set indicates a wholly new scope for interaction and reciprocity between husband and wife. Decisions demanded the understanding and cooperation of both partners in determining birth patterns and family plans. The problem of family limitation thus opened up and reflected a new set of possibilities in marriage relations that required both husband and wife to become more self-aware and attuned to questions of family organization and purpose. Each partner could become at once more responsible and more self-interested, but women especially could grasp a new measure of control over basic family order and aspire to having their needs more readily taken into consideration within the family.

Two demographic indicators, one related to education and the other to marriage age, are especially suggestive of the new role women played in deciding family size. It is not surprising or unexpected that the number of children in families should be related to educational level among parents.[15] It is surprising, however, that the relationship between the mother's education and family size should be stronger and more significant than that of the father's education and family size. But this was precisely the pattern among the families of students at the University of Wisconsin and the University of California in the 1920's. In both cases, the number of children born declined sharply with the rising education level among women, much more so than with that among men. Moreover, this relationship appeared for the first time in the students' generation. In the parents' generation, the pattern for women was exactly the same as for men. Thus within one generation (married *circa* 1890, families completed by 1910), the educational level among women appears to have become newly related to decisions about family size. It may be true, of course, that educated women simply married later because of the delay caused by education and therefore bore fewer children. It appears unlikely, however, that this alone explains the differences.[16] The effect that education has in reducing fertility would be important only if the better educated women married significantly later because of the delay caused by extended education. In fact, however, middle-class women of every educational level married late. Education not only had delayed marriage age, but had become an independent factor affecting the conscious decisions of women in matters relating to family planning.

The patterns in marriage rate and marriage age at the turn of the century lead to the same conclusion. Family life among middle-class groups apparently reached something of a crisis just before the turn of the century. This was registered in an initial decline in marriage and a considerable delay in age-at-marriage. That crisis was resolved as contraception finally effected a readjustment which made earlier marriage possible.

The marriage rate in the United States rose between 1890 and 1920. The gross increase in the proportion of married persons in the population was, in part, a reflection of the changing age structure—as the population aged, more people were likely to be married. There was also an absolute rise in marriage, however, even if the age of the population were held constant. Proportionately more adults were married in 1920 than in 1890. More significantly, the increase in marriage resulted from the fact that more younger persons—men and women in the period of young adulthood, 20–24 years of age—were married in 1920 than in 1890. The trend toward earlier marriage resulted in an expected decline in the average age-at-marriage. Among men in 1890, the median age-at-marriage was 26.1 years and among women 22.0 years. By 1920, the median age was 24.6 years for men and 21.3 years for women. Moreover, the real decline had taken place in urban regions, for marriage age in rural areas had changed only slightly.[17]

This post-1890 trend is especially significant for the middle classes because it reverses the pre-1890 pattern in which marriage both had been less common and had occurred at a considerably later average age. This is especially curious since neither economic nor educational factors appear to have significantly affected this situation. Among the fathers of University of Wisconsin students, for example, there was only a very small difference in marriage age between occupational and educational groups. There was practically no difference in marriage age for elementary and high-school graduates, and college men married only half a year later than high-school men. Similarly, while professional men were the last to marry, unskilled laborers married later than either skilled laborers or businessmen, and clerks married almost as late as professionals. In all, there was little more than a one-year difference between any of the groups. As a whole, however, they had married considerably later than their fathers (married *circa* 1860). In the earlier generation, not only was marriage age lower within each group, but both education and occupation were more important in determining age-at-marriage.[18]

More striking still was the delay in marriage among the mothers (married *circa* 1880–1890) of University of Wisconsin students. Mothers' ages-at-marriage were much more strongly correlated with education level than fathers', a correlation similar to that between mothers' education and fertility. College women married on the average a year later than high-school women (26.10 years and 24.98 years), and high-school women married two years later than elementary school women (24.98 and 22.98). Overall, however, each group of women had married very late, long after the completion of schooling, and each group had waited considerably longer to marry than their mothers had. Of all women married around 1860, 82.5% had married by 25 years of age, but only 58.3% of those married 1880–1890 were under 25 years of age. Moreover, the age-at-marriage rose sharply within each educational group. Almost two years separated the age-at-marriage of the two generations of elementary school women, three years the mothers and daughters with a high-school education, and four years the mothers and daughters with a college education.[19] Clearly the delay caused by education alone cannot account for the very late age at which college women married between 1880 and 1890. An earlier generation of college women had married at a much younger age. Nor can education alone explain the late age at which high-school and elementary school women married. Between 1860 and 1890, education had, however, become more strongly correlated with age-at-marriage for women than it had for men, just as education had become more strongly related to fertility among women. In the course of one generation, a newly significant relationship appeared between women's education, age-at-marriage, and fertility. That new relationship resulted not from the delay caused by education but rather from the extent of education.

After 1890, both more men and women married, and they married earlier. The evidence for the age at which women with husbands in various occupational groups married in the period 1900–1905 indicates that after 1890 the mean and especially the modal age-at-marriage fell sharply. So too, after 1890 more college-educated women married, and they married earlier.[20] Why this pattern? Why was marriage delayed so long around 1890, and why was the delay especially acute among the middle classes?

These two factors, the delay in marriage and the subsequent increase in early marriage, are indications of new family patterns, and they are related to the sharp decline in family size. Changes were occurring in roles and expectations within marriages by the end of the nineteenth century. They suggest new attitudes toward the meaning of marriage, about the nature of family life, and about what was necessary for its proper development.

Initially, delay in marriage resulted from the need to put urban, middle-class family life on a viable economic basis and to provide for the health and welfare of children. Men, and especially women, delayed marriage to cut down on the number of births and to permit men to work for a time without the burden of providing immediately for a growing family. The savings accumulated before marriage could help establish family life on a satisfactory economic foundation so that the needs of the adults and the children in the family could be amply provided for.[21] The delay also permitted men to become properly established in a career. Since professional and business families were already significantly smaller than others by 1890, late marriage was thus a form of family planning, for it cut down on the number of fertile years for women and gave men time to accumulate savings and chart a career line in an urban society increasingly dependent on education and technical skills.

Contraception provides the key to the increase in early marriage after 1890, as it does to the very sharp decrease in family size between 1890 and 1910 and the clustering around a stable norm by 1910. Contraception permitted family planning after marriage rather than before. It permitted husband and wife to delay first birth and, just as important, to space subsequent births according to family goals and resources. By 1920, a low urban birth rate was positively and strongly correlated with a high marriage rate among the young. This relationship did not exist for the older population. Young people were thus more likely to marry if they were secure in the knowledge that they could postpone and space conceptions. As sociologist William Ogburn observed, the "result points strongly to the conclusion that birth control is found with early marriage." [22]

Like the sharp decrease in family size, the increase in early marriage shows the new potential for planning and cooperation within marriage. As husband and wife gained control over family life, the companionship possibilities in marriage were freed from earlier restraints. Marriage could first become a relationship between two people rather than a necessary and determinant step toward family formation. Contraception thus broke down rigid traditional roles and definitions in the family. Without the ability to affect decisions about childbirth, their most significant family experience, married women were necessarily first and foremost potential mothers, and in the context of Victorian ideology they were victimized by the sexual needs of their husbands. With contraception female sexuality could be freed from its once necessary connection with motherhood. As long as childbirth was implicit in sexual relations, sexual intercourse defined a woman's role as submission, obedience, and childbearing. Women fulfilled marital "duties" by submitting to their husbands in the effort to conceive. Contraceptives, however, permitted women to be sexual partners first and mothers second, if and when husband and wife chose that role for her. Contraception released men and women from imposed roles and permitted new choices in roles and relationships.

Women, freed from the fear that pregnancy would result from sexuality, could now permit themselves the luxury of response and recognize the legitimacy of their desires. For both husband and wife sexual relations could become expressive emotional vehicles that changed unequal duties and obligations to mutual pleasures and satisfactions. It was this material change within marriage that finally made it possible to recognize and sanction female sexuality by the 1920's.[23]

The middle classes had been intent on limiting births since at least the middle of the nineteenth century. This was reflected in the declining birth rate and probably by the initial delay in marriage. In order to effect this reduction married people had either to abstain or to practice *coitus interruptus*. Both must have created tensions and severely inhibited sexual pleasure. It is much easier to understand the sexual inhibitions of middle-class Victorians, their fear of female sexuality, and the related denial of female pleasure in this context.[24] Sexuality was fraught with frustrations for men as well as women. It was better to condemn it as demeaning even in married women than to permit its unrestrained expression. Sexual repression had a very real functional basis in a society anxious about preventing conception but without the means adequately to quell that anxiety.

Contraception thus changed the marriage relationship and women's position in the family as nothing else had or could. It made earlier marriage possible, and it expanded the area of choice in women's roles within the family and freed them from a confining maternity. Moreover, by freeing female sexuality, both from pregnancy and from nineteenth-century proscriptions, contraception helped to legitimate a new equality in marriage roles. The denial of female sexuality in the Victorian era made women the subordinate partners in marriage, first by denying women full equality of sexuality and second by confining womanhood to motherhood. Contraception freed women from that role assignment and its necessary constrictions at the same time that it permitted a fuller expression of women's total personality and emotional needs.

Marriage became more attractive under these conditions both at the outset, because it became economically more feasible, and subsequently, because the nature of the relationship between husband and wife had changed. Women, especially educated women, could aspire to a new and broader set of roles and hope to receive more kinds of satisfaction. But the new relationship permitted men to expect more as well: more emotional intimacy, more latitude for physical and emotional expression, greater companionship, and freedom from the burden of hierarchical responsibilities. The streamlined family radically revised expectations as it promised the partners new satisfactions for themselves and their children.

III

By the 1920's, family "experts" had responded to the real changes in family life by articulating a new ideal of family democracy. When they described marriage in terms of companionship, compatibility, equality of privilege and responsibility, and mutuality in sexual gratification, they gave official sanction to the new patterns. As significantly, this view of the family had become part of the attitudes of young people about their family goals and marital aspirations. The young fully and completely embraced the new family forms as a working ideal, thus helping to anchor them as normative bases of behavior. Of course, neither the conceptions of family experts nor the expectations of the young meant that marriage was or would soon realize all those ideals, but the values did help to firm up the changes that had taken place. In turn, those ideals provided a standard which challenged behavior to a more perfect imitation.

One of the most striking characteristics of the ideal was the new prominence given to female sexuality. Sex became a feature of a woman's physical integrity and an aspect of her emotional expression. And the emphasis on sexuality highlighted the new marriage ideals which equalized rights, responsibilities, and roles between men and women in marriage. The legitimization of female sexuality and the pointed sexualization of marriage were perhaps the most significant departures of the marriage literature of the 1920's, for they reflected specific changes that had already taken place and in turn implicated all facets of marital interaction.

"The happy absorption of people in and by marriage has become a newer criterion of marriage success," Ira Wile noted in a summary of the sex life of the modern adult. "A knowledge of sexual compatibility has assumed a primary value." In the twenties, a new group of self-conscious experts and professionals saw sex research as a legitimate and significant field of inquiry. Sex was a normal physical function and a crucial part of married life. That perception resulted from the experts' new sense of professional competence coming at a critical time of change in family relationships and expectations. For as studies of marriage and family life began to describe marriage in explicitly sexual terms and to judge marriage by the sexual satisfactions of each partner, the literature revolutionized women's rights. In legitimating the sexual demands of women, the marriage literature of the twenties shifted the emphasis from specific and differential obligations to mutual fulfillment. The publication in 1929 of Katherine Bement Davis' massive study of *The Sex Life of Twenty-Two Hundred Women,* the most comprehensive study of female sexuality before the Kinsey report, was an indication of the shift. Such an investigation of sexuality among normal women had, in fact, never before been undertaken in a serious way. Earlier studies of sexual behavior among women centered on the experiences of prostitutes and delinquents and by implication stressed what was deviant in the sexuality of women as a group.[25] Davis highlighted what was normal.

In the Victorian conception of female virtue, respectable women were not only chaste, they were "pure." Purity existed even in married women because it meant not merely the absence of sexual sin but the very absence of sexual appetite. Henry Seidel Canby recalled that in the 1890's "we grossly underestimated the sexual possibilities of the refined female." Men "were familiar by hearsay or experience with the sexual in every sense, yet did not think in those terms of the girls of our own class." Desire and passion were not becoming to respectable women and girls, and grown men and women of the genteel classes thus "tacitly agreed to look upon one another as sexless." [26] Because women were not supposed to possess sexual natures, their sexual demands in marriage were assumed to be negligible. They fulfilled marital roles by submitting, either to satisfy their husbands' more base instincts or to conceive. Here as in so many areas of human relations, sex epitomized more general realities. Sexuality, or the lack of sexuality, thus confirmed a woman's passive role in marriage—she submitted, she obeyed her husband, and she bore his children. Marriage is in the end a critical sexual exchange. Since women had no sexual demands, they had no marriage rights.

But in the twenties, sex for married women was no longer a matter of obedience and submission but a basic expression of personal right. Thus, in a popular college textbook on marriage and family, sociologists Ernest Groves and William Ogburn informed readers that women were now making sexual demands in marriage and even warned that their husbands might not be equal to the challenge. "Coitus," the prominent gynecologist Robert Latou Dickinson affirmed, "is an index to marriage. . . . satisfactory sexual relations are necessary to fully adjusted and successful union." Contemporaries not only paid specific attention to women's sexuality but were fully aware of the change in attitudes that separated them from the past. Phyllis Blanchard and Carlyn Manasses, who investigated the marriage expectations of young women in the twenties, noted, "After hundreds of years of mild complaisance to wifely duties, modern women have awakened to the knowledge that they are sexual beings. And with this new insight the sex side of marriage has assumed sudden importance." Groves and Ogburn firmly grasped the implications: "In the recent past in America, the sex demands of women have been negligible, but that is no longer true. At no point has what we may justly call emancipation been more significant." [27]

The perception of the sexual rights of women brought a renewed emphasis on conjugal fidelity in marriage and family literature. Like sexuality, exclusivity underscored the new equality. The primary tenet in sociologist Joseph K. Folsom's "New Code of Love Mores" was that "the essence of moral 'rightness' for a sex relationship is mutual love and monogamous exclusiveness," and sociologists Robert and Frances Binkley noted, "There is certainly in marriage a reality which runs deeper than the definitions which our institutions, or the institutions of any society, give to the marriage relationship. This fundamental reality is compounded of three elements: persons, sex, duration." Fidelity, they observed, "need not be imposed by the community; it should be the free choice of those who accept the implicit principles of marriage." [28] Free choice, mutality, and sexuality were part of a single web which, in the eyes of experts, bound men and women into a new family partnership.

As the experts described marriage not as obligation but as fulfillment, sexual exclusiveness became the capstone of expressive love. Sex, Folsom noted, was to "intensify, beautify and consecrate love." This emphasis on sex as the acme of love and on mutuality as the mark of enduring equality in marriage relations reinforced the traditional American restriction of sex to marriage. It expanded marriage while at the same time confining sex. Anthropologist Edward Sapir quite accurately observed that when Americans discovered sex, it served to reinvigorate their idealized sensations of love. In large part, the sexual revolution of the twenties was not a revolt against marriage but a revolution within marriage, and as such it recharged the momentum toward marriage as the consummation of love. It was this dual process of the sexualization of love and the glorification of sex that helped to anchor the twentieth-century American marriage pattern, the horse-and-carriage ideal. The process had other effects as well, particularly on dating relationships. Dating became sexually oriented but also sexually restrained, because dating looked toward sex *and* marriage. The result was sexual exploration without sexual consummation, with the corollary that intercourse between engaged or "serious" couples was both much more likely to occur and more acceptable.[29]

Contraception was basic to this revaluation of the sexual dimension of marriage, for the emphasis on mutual satisfaction in marriage took for granted that sex had been freed from its procreative function. Folsom noted, "The 'freedom' of love today is not simply another outburst of frivolity and licentiousness. It is not primarily a freedom of love from marriage, but from the supernatural ideology which held it in chains as an instrument of biological reproduction." Sexuality could only equalize marriage when the effects of sexual gratification were in fact the same for men and women. Before the widespread use of contraceptives this was not possible, for women could expect to suffer the consequences of sexual relations by becoming pregnant. But by the 1920's, contraception, like sexual pleasure, was in the words of

one marriage manual, "A woman's Right." "Personal liberty,"
S. J. Hayden declared in *The Art of Marriage*, "is a democratic
ideal. . . . It is a woman's right to have children or not, just as
she chooses." [30] Hayden saw quite sharply that the right not to
have children expanded the democratic ideal and made possible
women's equal participation in that ideal.

It is not possible to say how accurately the new ideal of mutual satisfaction described real changes in marriage relations.
But certain changes are suggestive. One such indication was the
newly positive attitude women had toward their own bodies.
According to Robert Latou Dickinson, many women in the late
nineteenth century declared that they "would rather die than be
examined." "No nice woman has any anatomy between her neck
and her ankles." "In the early nineties, the patient instantly
covered the least bare spot with the sheet; but in 1920 full exposure is taken for granted by the young." There are also some
scattered data to suggest an increase in the frequency of coitus
in marriage, especially among the young, but the evidence suffers from a lack of reliable comparisons. [31]

The most significant measure of the new sexual dimension of
marriage and heightened expectations among women comes to
us indirectly—from the use of and attitude toward contraceptives. Contraceptive usage ultimately implies that sexual activity is seen in other than procreative terms and potentially as a
source of satisfaction and expression. From this perspective,
marriage for middle-class women in the 1920's had become a
fully sexual experience. Of the 1000 married women in their
early thirties questioned by Katherine Davis, for example, 734
believed in the principle of contraception and almost all of these
(730) used available techniques to prevent conception. Moreover, of 1200 unmarried and slightly younger women, 84.6%
affirmed that intercourse in marriage for non-procreative purposes was justified, and 89.7% believed that birth control
should be employed in marriage. Similarly, all surveys of students' views indicate that college men and women consistently
approved of and planned to use birth control when they mar-

ried. In one large sample of students, 86% of the men and 70% of the women urged that birth control methods be made available to everyone. The question had not specified married couples. Students at schools as different as the University of Chicago, North Carolina State, New York University, and the University of Washington shared similar views. And of the young women interviewed by Blanchard and Manasses, 80% indicated that they definitely planned to use contraceptives when they married.[32]

The effort to limit birth is certainly not new. Throughout history people have used various means—natural, chemical, and mechanical—to limit births. Primitive tribes are known to employ both contraceptives and abortifacients. But the efficiency and acceptability of these means is another matter. By the 1920's there was a profusion of effective and convenient methods (condoms, pessaries, jellies, diaphragms), and contraceptive use was widespread; though not unexpectedly, middle-class groups were far more likely to use contraceptives and to use them successfully. Most studies indicate highly successful results with the available contraceptive procedures. Despite continued limitations in knowledge and application, usually related to class and education, contraceptive techniques had been brought to a fairly high level of efficiency by the 1920's. Young people especially were interested in learning about proper procedures and expected to use them.[33]

The use of contraceptives may, of course, merely indicate increased pressure by men for their wives to protect themselves against conception and may thus be yet another demonstration of a basically unequal relationship. But in view of the approval by young unmarried women and the explicit reasons women gave for using contraceptives this is highly unlikely. When Davis asked her respondents to describe the reasons for intercourse in marriage, for example, most confirmed their own sexual expectations: "As an expression of love, because it is a natural normal relation, because children might for many reasons be undesirable, because desire is strong; for pleasure, satisfaction, development; because the intimacy of married life necessitates it; for physical and mental health." In fact, many of the younger women (who were also more likely to approve of contraception) went beyond the belief that intercourse was desirable to the more extreme view that it was necessary "for complete physical and mental health." Similarly, when Blanchard and Manasses interviewed young unmarried women about their marriage expectations, a sizable majority (59.5%) specifically volunteered sexual satisfaction, a choice made much more often than the desire for economic security.[34]

It seems likely, therefore, that by the twenties both men and women had become eager to have sexual relations released from the burden of conception so that they could more freely engage in the sexual side of marriage. Moreover, whatever the initial impulse, contraceptives could enhance women's self-awareness and control and therefore their potential for sexual response. Finally, and as importantly, the official ban on sexual response within marriage could be lifted once contraceptive use became general because it freed sex from its once necessary relation to childbirth. Given the obvious desire to reduce the size of families in the nineteenth century demonstrated by the demographic trends, sexual expression within marriage must have been full of guilt and anxiety and sexual satisfactions for men and women constrained by fear. By the twenties, these multiple inhibitions on sexual enjoyment were lifted because contraception removed the most important barrier to a free expression of sex in marriage. Released from the guilt attached to sexual enjoyment and the burden of expected consequences, marital sexuality by the twenties could become an expression of intimacy and affection between husband and wife as well as a normative ideal.

In 1930, Blanchard and Manasses concluded that modern young women "ask of life not only marriage, but a new kind of marriage, one in which a man will have to do more than provide a living for his wife and children, or else fail. The modern union of man and woman is visioned as a perfect consummation of both personalities that will involve every phase of mutual living." The qualities which the young required of their prospective mates underscore this ideal, for they were largely those which emphasized personal compatibility, including disposition, personality, and intelligence. These were far more important than criteria like economic position, religion, or sexual purity, qualities that students' parents still considered essential.[35]

The young also had self-conscious expectations about their future families. They overwhelmingly wanted children but usually only two or three, and they planned to postpone the birth of the first child until after the second or third year of marriage, in order to first develop what they called the "basic companionship" in marriage, as well as to permit the family to arrive at an "adequate income." Among one group of New York University students the idea of marriage as companionship was so strong that Ben Lindsey's "companionate marriage" idea provoked scarcely a flicker of interest, even though they approved of both contraception and divorce. As one woman put it, "True marriage is and always has been companionate." Another made the point even more clearly: "I can't see where this type of marriage differs so radically from the institution we have today." [36]

Although the young strongly believed that marriage could and should provide a variety of satisfactions for each partner, they were entirely willing to accept the fact of divorce should their relationship not fulfill expectations. Of the women interviewed by Blanchard and Manasses, for example, 92.5% proposed divorce as the solution to an unhappy marriage. So did most students interviewed by George Vetter at New York University, Syracuse University, and the University of Washington. Divorce, these students believed, was justified by a breach of the marriage contract or a failure to cooperate in the life of the family. A considerable portion took the even more liberal position that divorce be granted on demand at the request of either party. Divorce, like contraception, had become part of the modern conception of marriage for most young people, and both exemplified a view of the family as grounded in personal satisfactions rather than chained to imposed responsibilities.[37]

The requirements the young made of marriage and family—their sense of the need for a certain level of economic sufficiency, the interest in limiting family size, the desire for compatibility and companionship in marriage—highlighted and reinforced the demographic patterns and trends. The young had a vision of a well-planned and well-provided-for family, and both men and women looked toward marriage with high hopes and expectations. This sense was particularly evident among young women. As Blanchard and Manasses concluded, "Girls are today demanding positive values of marriage rather than looking upon it as a way of escape from parental authority or of gaining economic security. Marriage has now become the entrance into a fuller and richer life: an opportunity for sharing joys and sorrows, with a mate who will not be merely a protector or a provider, but an all-round companion. This is, in the best sense, a romantic conception of marriage."[38]

While both young men and young women were increasingly oriented toward this ideal, it would ultimately have different meanings for each. For while men looked toward marriage as a vital part of their lives, women looked toward it as their primary and almost exclusive goal; all other aspirations became secondary.[39] And this difference, a result of continuing cultural inequality, might well have undermined the strongly enunciated views about the equality of rights and relationships in the family. Since the model of marriage was, in fact, based on a divergent set of assumptions about the part that marriage would play in the total life experience of each partner, the very ideals that the young embraced may have opened the way for growing marital tensions between the sexes.

There is little specific evidence about the sharpening of conflict within marriage, except, of course, for the rising divorce rate and the growing tendency for women to sue for divorce on the grounds of mental cruelty or incompatibility. But since this had become a divorce convention, it tells us little about the actual factors that made for conflict. Other indicators do, however, suggest a growing rift in expectations. Women, for example, tended to expect a higher living standard than men. Much more significant was the difference in the views of men and women about whether it was desirable for wives to work. Most young women expected to work during the early years of marriage in order to put the family on a stable economic foundation. Men, however, usually disapproved of their wives working and could rarely believe that their wives might want to work after marriage. At Haverford College, for example, Frank Watson found that men overwhelmingly "expected their wives to be the mother and homemaker," and only one of nine men would give the wife a choice of working after marriage. Men were willing to grant their wives partnership status in such matters as " 'authority regarding all matters affecting the family as a whole; for example, place of residence, school, and religious education of the children,' and family finances." Sociologist Clifford Kirkpatrick concluded from his own study of the marriage expectations of college men that "the abyss of disagreement between the two sexes in regard to the status of women seems to be widening rather than disappearing." [40]

Thus, by the 1920's, the young seemed to believe in complete equality for women in the home but not outside it. This ultimately restricted woman's legitimate place to home and family and denied her complete social equality and the full expression of choice and preference. Equality in the workplace would have made the new equality within the family more real because a woman's position would have been more flexible. Changing relationships within marriage and the family should not be gainsaid; they were an important feature of growing equality between the sexes. But women continued to be restricted to family life since they were defined essentially as wives and mothers, though both these roles were now more clearly grounded in choice and defined to include companionship and self-expression.

Significantly, women seemed to accept and indeed welcome this family role. In the final analysis, women indicated overwhelmingly that they would give up work and career if these conflicted with their marriage goals. At Vassar College, for example, a college poll in 1923 showed that 90% of the women asked would choose marriage over a business or professional career. In a somewhat later study of Ivy League college women, 94% of the women from these intellectually-oriented schools said that if their careers interfered with marriage, they would opt for marriage. Women questioned throughout the twenties indicated that marriage was primary. At New York University women were twice as willing to marry in college as men, even if this meant abandoning their education. As one young woman put it, "Yes, I'd be willing to marry while yet in college and pay whatever price the companionship costs." [41]

A new kind of marriage was envisioned in the twenties, one which promised greater openness and equality, but it was still for women a total commitment made at a cost. Women in the twenties considered marriage to be the primary vehicle of expression and satisfaction. Work and career were for most merely a stop-gap between school and marriage, now considered a normal part of woman's life, but neither the ultimate nor even a necessary part of her life. Thus, with the increasing stress placed on the potential satisfactions to be realized in marriage, one can begin to suggest that by the 1920's women were expecting more of marriage than men because it was for them the one arena for expression, and the only sphere for personal satisfactions. The stress on sexual rights for women in marriage both symbolized and accelerated this process, as it helped to localize completely female emotions and needs to family life. Within a severely circumscribed sense of life-fulfilling possibilities, marriage was expected to serve every channel, implicitly more for women than for men. In that sense the very expansion of possibilities now offered to women in marriage implied ultimate frustrations.

IV

The changes in marriage roles and expectations were part of a more general democratization of all family relationships. Indeed, it was the overall changes in family dynamics that made marriage not only more attractive but more common. It is well to remember that marriage decisions reflect relations with parents as well as with future mates. The changes within the family affected marriage decisions in two significant ways. First, the democratization of family life reduced the ritual significance of marriage as a critical break in family organization. Marriage became a further step in the growing independence of the child rather than a sharp interruption of hierarchical subordination. Second, the freer, less constrained relations within the family permitted young people easier access to members of the opposite sex and to their peers in general. This opening up of the family to peer intercession helped to reduce the influence of parental pressures or vetoes on mating choices and marriage decisions and in turn accelerated the democratic tendencies in those choices. A third factor might be appended to these two: in line with a growing concern for the personal and emotional welfare of children, middle-class parents may have become more willing to permit children to marry earlier and perhaps more ready to indulge their marriage choices. This last aspect of family life appears especially compelling when it is contrasted to earlier attitudes toward, and ideals about, family unity and loyalty in the Victorian family. This newer attitude, which centered on the good of the child rather than the good of the family, grew naturally from the changing nature of all relationships in the household.

One suggestive indication of the relationship between marriage and dependency is contained in the 1920 Chicago Census, in which one-fifth of all households were composed of more than the simple nuclear unit of parents and unmarried children. Almost all the multiple family units (5.1% of all households or one-tenth of all families) were made up of parents and their married children. This arrangement was most common for young clerks and professional couples who continued to live with parents as a temporary arrangement in the early years of marriage.[42] Apparently, parents did not prevent their children from marrying even when not yet fully capable of economic independence, and they assisted them through a period of economic insecurity. The tie was reciprocal, for married children in middle-class groups in Chicago also opened their homes to dependent parents. In Chicago, at least, parents felt a continuing obligation to assist their married young and, in turn, married children were willing to care for widowed parents. Marriage was not a knife to cut bonds of love and obligation on either side.[43] Of course, not all middle-class children continued to reside with their parents after marriage, nor did all children take in widowed parents, but the pattern is suggestive and the condition among some may well illuminate the relationship among the many.

The relationship between college students and their parents implies a similar intergenerational bond. At its base, college attendance describes a willing acceptance of ties of dependency between parents and children. Increased education does not automatically result from an increase in educational facilities, nor entirely from better economic circumstances and higher educational requirements for jobs. Both parents and children must be willing to accept the parent-child bond for longer periods of time and not to chafe under the terms. Parents must accept the burden of costs, but children must bear the constrictions of continued dependency. This does not mean, of course, that solicitude for children alone was involved in decisions concerning college attendance in the twenties. Social-status considerations, the rise of per capita income, and the social and economic pressure for a better-educated work force made education more accessible and desirable. But the final choice—by parents to invest in the future of their children and by children to postpone independence—is a function of the quality of family relations. It is easy to forget that there were alternatives for families with marginal means, and many students, especially those attending nearby state colleges, appear to have come from just such families.[44] An expanded view of children's welfare had become a parental obligation for many families in the 1920's; extended education was considered part of that obligation. Certainly, the decline in the size of families made this more possible for parents. But young people, too, made the choice. At an age when they might have declared their independence they chose to remain financially dependent and potentially emotionally obligated. The vastly increased enrollments in colleges and universities indicate that both parents and children accepted the parent-child tie as an ongoing bond, extending well beyond childhood and even adolescence.

This reciprocity between parents and children resulted from overall trends among middle-class families—accelerating democratization, the growth of expressive affection, and the breakdown of a rigid role hierarchy. Part of the transformation resulted from the equalization of marital rights. A good part also came from an equalization in parental roles and a parallel equalization in the treatment of each child. The family pattern that was emerging in the early twentieth century was captured in an unusually measured and precise way by a team of University of California psychologists, Wanda Bronson, Edith Katten, and Norma Livson, who neatly documented several important features of parent-child relationships in two generations (born *circa* 1900 and 1927–28). Among the several significant findings of that study were the following: authority was consistently exercised by the mother and not the father in both generations; the level of affection between mother and child and father and child was high in each generation but growing in all relations and becoming more equally expressed; there was a notable rise in the involvement of fathers with children (especially sons); there was a strong trend toward more equal involvement with and affection for each child regardless of sex.[45]

One further finding in this study warrants attention: high levels of affection did not preclude high levels of authority. Authority was apparently not the same as stern control. The dual process of stable authority and growing affection makes it easier to understand the pattern uncovered by Robert and Helen Lynd. Among middle-class families in Middletown, parents self-consciously sought to maintain authority and to avoid permissive indulgence, at the same time that they were treating their children with warmth and affection and were conspicuously solicitous for their welfare.[46] Family democracy was caught in a poised balance in the early twentieth century as it straddled older ideals of obedience and the newer trend toward sympathetic (and perhaps indulgent) affection. It was not fathers, however, who exercised authority. In fact, contrary to traditional beliefs about parental functions, the picture of fatherhood that emerges from the Bronson, Katten, and Livson study belies sharply differentiated roles for nurturant mothers and didactic fathers, as it refutes the image of patriarchal control and aloof command.[47]

Fathers were becoming more involved and intimate with children as part of the trend in middle-class homes toward an active concern with and interest in child welfare. Part of that involvement found expression in the widespread attention to expert advice on child-rearing. Middle-class men were, in fact, reading child-rearing advice to a surprising degree. One study of the early 1930's reported that 75% of the fathers in middle-class occupational groups read either newspaper or magazine articles on child care and that 15.5%, a figure only slightly lower than for mothers, attended Parent-Teacher Association meetings. So too, studies reported a high degree of concurrence between parents on the disciplining of children.[48] The growing interest of men in aspects of child care thus paralleled the growing equality in the relations between husband and wife. This does not mean that men shared equally with women in child-rearing, or even that they took an especially large part in the home regime. Rather, it suggests that the sharp separation between the mother's role and the father's role was giving way to a concept of parenthood which grew from an overall interest in the welfare of the children in the household.

The degree to which parents sought to learn about child-rearing from written sources during the 1920's and the number and variety of sources consulted is startling. One investigation found that by the mid-thirties four-fifths of women in professional and two-thirds of women in managerial families reported reading at least one book or pamphlet on child care within the year. The largest proportion in each group had read at least five books or pamphlets. An insignificant 3% of the mothers had read no articles in either newspapers or magazines. In addition to books, pamphlets, and articles, one-half of the middle-class occupational groups subscribed to specialized magazines and journals on child care.[49]

A very large proportion of middle-class parents of both sexes thus devoted considerable time and attention, as well as cost, to reading advice about child-rearing and child nurture. It is, of course, impossible to say how their behavior was affected by that reading, but the great interest demonstrates more than casual awareness and self-conscious concern with the "quality" of family life and especially the physical and psychological welfare of children. Child-rearing advice of this kind—impersonal, literary, and expert—is sought only when parents are self-critically interested in providing themselves with the best and latest information about child development. It underscores the child-consciousness of middle-class families, their orientation toward proper nurture, and a refined concern with the psychological dimensions of family life.

The interest in children and the freer, more intimate interaction between parents and children were the subject of a wide-ranging report on childhood and adolescence presented by the White House Conference on Child Health and Protection in the early thirties. The Conference discovered an urban, native, white, middle-class pattern emphasizing emotional ties and affectional unity that differed from an existing rural pattern stressing discipline, authority, and hierarchical responsibilities. The Conference reports ascribed a historical sequence to these patterns and, while this presents certain problems, there is some basis for seeing them as newer and older forms of family integration. Native urban children, for example, confided in parents much more frequently than rural children and were decidedly less hostile to parents. Children in such families were punished less frequently, and open demonstrations of affection like kissing were more common. So too, children in urban families were less often incorporated into a household work routine with specific allocation of chores and responsibilities than were children on the farm. Urban families relied on a minimal number of tasks usually related to the care of one's own things rather than active participation in a family work regime. Urban families shied away from elaborate household routines of all kinds and engaged in fewer activities as a unit. Churchgoing, for example, was a less common family activity in the city than in the country.[50] There was altogether less physical interaction and a larger measure of personal independence granted to urban children, who were given time and occasion to engage in extensive extra-family activities, especially with peers.

One indication of this double process, the freeing from strict family supervision and the expansion of time spent with peers, was the number of evenings adolescents spent at home. Less than one-half of the urban boys in the White House study spent four or more evenings at home, and only slightly more than one-third of the girls did. The average urban adolescent was away from home between four and six evenings every week. Rural adolescents, in contrast, were home much more frequently. Urban adolescents were granted a large measure of independence by the 1920's. At one high school in California, 50% of all boys had no restrictions on the number of school nights they were allowed to go out with friends. The proportion increased with school class; by senior year, 77% had no limits imposed by parents on how they chose to spend their evenings.[51]

In describing different patterns of family organization, the White House report concluded, "At one extreme is the family with harsh or stern methods of control . . . little effort on the part of the parent to understand the child or to gain his confidence. At the other extreme is the family with guidance rather than punishment as the means of control . . . and a sympathetic understanding of children." [52] By the 1920's and 1930's, middle-class urban families were clearly moving toward the latter norm with freedom and affection the basis of child nurture. It is worth emphasizing that both the disciplined, hierarchical family and the affectionate, democratic family are ideal types and that no one family or set of families fit exactly the dimensions of either didactic model. But it was the direction of change in middle-class homes that was significant, and the available data do strongly suggest that the urban middle classes were consistently and strongly developing family styles that were affectionate, democratic, and child-conscious. Children were freely and informally incorporated into a less differentiated family unit and were less circumscribed by parental dictate. Democratically integrated and emotionally bound together, middle-class families had become small, informal, emotionally intense, and private units.

A very specific kind of family style had developed among the native urban middle classes. Families were small, planned, and actively concerned with the welfare of children. The relations between husband and wife and parents and children were increasingly democratic and emotionally responsive. Fathers had become more involved with their children and more affectionate toward them. Women expected that marriage and family would provide them with a variety of personal satisfactions and scope for personal expression. There was at once an increase in the emotional bond and a decrease in the amount of physical interdependence. Children were less tied into a household routine of work and play and permitted to partake freely in peer-centered activities. The very nature of dependence had been changed as parents permitted their children personal freedoms and assumed financial burdens associated with extended education. There is moreover every indication that these patterns were becoming more and more common.

It is easier to say that these things occurred than to account for the new patterns. A number of factors appear to have been related to the change. The first is family size. The sheer magnitude of the decrease in family size, so notable among the middle classes, carried with it important implications for family order. Fewer children made strict discipline and an enforced hierarchy less necessary or desirable. The smaller family also allowed for more personalized attention and a greater degree of self-expression for each member of the family.

The decline in size resulted in a new sense of the need for family planning and a sharpened concern for child welfare in an era of urbanization and industrial specialization. To the urban family, which was to a large degree a unit of consumption rather than production, children were no asset. Rural children were usually incorporated into a work routine, where they could contribute their part to a productive enterprise. In that context, father was production director, manager, and instructor as well as parent. This was not so in the city. There he could become more of a parent and more involved with child care rather than with household management. No doubt city children were often sent to work and at an early age, especially among the working classes, where their meager salaries contributed to a subsistence standard of living and a minimum of security. The working classes did, in fact, continue to rear consistently larger families than the middle classes until the Depression.[53] But in the middle classes, children were sent to school, not to work. In an industrial society, expertise had become the necessary basis for success. The family had fewer tasks to perform, the children fewer responsibilities. There was more chance to permit the growth of personal relationships which are inherent in family life, but often, as on the farm or among the poor urban groups, subordinated to more pressing economic concerns. The middle-class family, already smaller, could permit the emotional ties to dominate, unrestrained by other roles, because personal relations in the middle-class family were much less often strained by production or economic considerations. The freeing of the emotional bond, in turn, increased the concern of parents for the nurture and welfare of their children.

Certainly this did not happen at once. The late Victorian family was also an intense and private institution, but it was still one in which unity and hierarchical responsibility remained an ideal. Unity was defined in terms of solidarity, loyalty, and morale and achieved through a mesh of responsibilities and obligations between the generations, a carry-over from a period of functional integration and specific duties. Henry Seidel Canby remembered family life in the late nineteenth century as a physical fact where the home was the symbol of family unity and the vehicle for personal identification. "In the American nineties generally," Canby recalled, "home was the most impressive experience in life." It was first in everyone's consciousness and took on an existence of its own above and beyond the members it housed. "The woman who could not make a home, like the man who could not support one, was condemned and not tacitly. . . . It must be a house where the family wished to live even when they disliked one another." [54] Close family ties were desired and effected as individual relations were subsumed in family needs. Both parents and children had an intense sense of the family good. Sons and daughters demonstrated loyalty to the family unit through respect for authority, and parents shouldered the responsibility by maintaining discipline and control.

In this kind of family, parents renounced personal satisfactions for the good of the family as a whole. Canby remembered, "We knew . . . from our own impulsive desires that the father and mother denied themselves every day, if not every hour, something for the sake of the family." Parents were concerned with the welfare of their children but conceived of that welfare as the product of a well-ordered family. In turn, the family as a whole benefited from the well-being of the children. As parents deferred to the good of the family, so children deferred not so much to the person of father or mother as to his or her role in the well-ordered household. The children thus renounced their own impulsive self-will for "the family" much as the parents did. Authority in this kind of family was thus firmly based on the sense of mutual responsibilities and deference. Canby observed that there were often sharp differences in attitudes and opinions between individuals, but those differences were repressed out of deference to family loyalty and order. "Though the family might quarrel and nag, the home held them all, protecting them against the outside world and one another." [55] This attitude affected children at home, but it also affected their ideals about their own future families which would require responsible self-sacrifice. Thus children postponed marriage in order to insure the future welfare of the family, and they renounced immediate personal needs in order to secure a future family objective.

This sense of family unity and welfare was first reflected in the decreasing size of the middle-class family unit. In turn the shrinking family finally permitted a change in roles and perceptions in the family that emphasized democracy and personal satisfaction rather than order and deference. The obsession with discipline and order had once functioned to maintain loyalty and unity in the larger family, but as the family grew smaller, what had been functional became merely formal. Relationships based on intimate personal interaction were already possible in the late Victorian family but often were consciously subordinated to hierarchical obligations.

But the mere formality in family relations soon gave way to the emotional factors. Family unity and loyalty would certainly remain important, but by the 1920's they would be differently conceived and expressed; emotional ties of warmth and amicability replaced respect and authority. Rigid and formal unity was less necessary when it became clear that emotional ties functioned to unite members of a democratic family just as mutual responsibilities had united a hierarchical one. Love functioned as sympathy and the toleration of differences rather than as respect and deference. Family affection replaced family responsibility, and greater expressiveness and permissiveness entered into the parent-child as well as the husband-wife relationship. This allowed for more personal independence while demanding more emotional reinforcement.

When this happened, it was possible for children to marry at an earlier age and with less specific parental approval. Independence did not threaten a complete break from family ties, for independence had been growing all along. So too, the needs and desires of the individual child rather than the position and good of the family could become the primary criterion in marriage decisions. As the evidence on Chicago's extended families reminds us, parents solicitous of their children's welfare and responsive to their needs were prepared to assist their children even after marriage. Middle-class parents overwhelmingly did so before marriage even when their children were grown,[56] and more and more parents willingly assumed the burden of supporting their children through years of school when sons and daughters were largely free from parental domination and control. Children were willing to accept that dependence precisely because the leash was not held so tightly and because family relationships were more free. Marriage and the creation of one's own family came not as a break but as a continuity, not as an escape from a low-man-on-the-totem-pole position for the child but as an important further step toward personal independence that had been growing within the family.

This independence within the family made possible and was paralleled by an increased interaction of adolescents and young adults with peers. Peers became especially important as young men and women, freer than ever from parental control, began to explore sexual and mating roles. Thus, as the rigidity of family relations broke down and more latitude was permitted to children and adolescents, parents at once exercised less influence over marriage decisions and made room for the intercession of extra-familial mediators. The changing dynamics of family life did not so much free young people from the need for approval as it opened the way for approval from other sources and for the patterning of norms that may not have reflected parental values. It was this dual process—the retreat of the family from exercising specific control and the entry of peers in directing mating choices—that permitted personal and emotional qualities like sexual attraction, love, and compatibility to become the dominant factors in marriage decisions. While parents tend to be status-oriented, peer groups direct the attention of young people to questions of romance, and it is romance which dominates the relationship between the sexes in the twentieth century.[57] These criteria, in turn, increased the momentum in marital relations and family life toward emotional expression, intimacy, personal compatibility, and sexuality. By the 1920's, the meaning of marriage and family had already changed significantly as the consciousness of responsibilities gave way to the search for emotional satisfaction.

Finally, changes in the larger society permitted the family to emphasize the emotional and expressive features of relationships. Industrialization, urbanization, and the breakup of what Robert Wiebe has called the culture of "island communities" [58] made

the family less important as a vehicle of status and social position than expertise and specific performance at school and work.
The family was released from its former role as an institution
that mediated between the individual and the community.
Rather, the family became more and more private, cut off from
the sources of direct power in the larger society. Marriage could
now become more than ever a matter of preference. This helped
to emphasize the roles of mutual compatibility, personal satisfaction, and sexual expression as the essential qualities making
for a successful marriage. For the children, family name and
community position had become less important than education
and professional competence. Thus, while the family counted
for less in identifying and placing the individual, it now
counted for more in providing him with an outlet for the release
of frustrations and as an arena in which he could expect understanding and could demonstrate emotion. The family no longer
mediated between the individual and the society in a direct
way. It had become less an institution that was integrated into
the mesh of other institutions—work, church, and community.
In a rationalized and depersonalized society, the family became
an agency of individual nurture and an environment for the development of intimate personal relationships.

V

This new family was subjected to close scrutiny and detailed
analysis in the 1920's and 1930's by a group of increasingly self-
conscious professionals for whom the family had become a rich
and legitimate specialty. Drawn from the burgeoning ranks of
academic sociology and psychology, social work, and clinical
psychiatry, the family experts were at once impressed by the
possibilities of a democratic, affectionate, and child-centered
family and anxious about its social implications. Few could
refrain from calling it a "crisis" [59]—a pathological crossroad be-

tween the past and the future. The sense of crisis in literature about the family tells us more about the intellectual strains of a decade in which traditional views no longer sufficed to explain observed social facts than it does about the facts themselves. The literature on the family partook of that suspended ambivalence of a decade in which hopes for social progress were still constrained by fears about social order. But the changes in the family did pose critical problems, and the views of family sociologists are particularly pertinent because they raised what remains the significant historical issue—how did the new family affect social adjustment in the new society?

The sociologists began with the traditional view that the family was the primary unit of society that assured social stability and trained individuals to socially responsible behavior, and they set about incorporating their observations about the newer family pattern into this model. The American family, experts proposed, had once been a multi-functional institution based on mutually dependent roles and a hierarchy of privileges and responsibilities. The family was stable and its members responsible because each was incorporated into a productive unit with a clear division of labor. Husband, wife, and children each had specific duties in a coordinate unit of production, education, and recreation. In turn, each had a recognizable position in a hierarchical order in which duties and obligations were matched by rights and respect.[60] Sometime in the past—no one knew exactly when, but all assumed that it was related to industrialization and urbanization—the family lost its functions. The schools took over the tasks of education, and industry those of preparing food and clothes; the farm and the workshop were replaced by the apartment and the factory. The family became merely a consuming unit which relied on the services of other specialized agencies. What happened when the family, defined and stabilized by the functions it performed as a unit, lost those functions? Would it any longer remain stable and its members responsible when husband, wife, and children were no longer mutually dependent and responsibly integrated?

The response of family experts from the Progressive period through the twenties was to insist that the family still had functions to perform, but that these were concerned less with the production of goods than with tending to the emotional and personality needs of its members. The family was indispensable to society because it provided adults with emotional satisfactions in the form of love and security and because the family remained the fundamental agency of child nurture.[61] Functionally streamlined, the family was still functionally necessary. "It is a good thing the family has got rid of its industrial functions, so that it can minister to the spiritual functions," James Lichtenberger declared. "It is the school of the affectional bonds, and civilization will be in a sorry plight when those ties of affection become limited and break down." William Ogburn's conclusion was the most efficient: "It does not seem probable that the family will recover the functions it has lost. But even if the family doesn't produce thread and cloth and soap and medicine and food, it can still produce happiness." [62]

Thus the literature of the twenties is full of this revised and updated conception of the family as a functioning social unit providing important social service. Having inherited the traditional view of the family as the building block of social order, family sociologists substituted emotional for productive functions and thought of affection and child-rearing as the functions the family retained and upon which it should properly concentrate all its energies. In their textbook on the family, Edward Reuter and Jessie Runner defined a "satisfactory family" quite simply as one which "would provide the best care for children, furnish a humanely satisfying affectional relationship, and contribute to the personality development of parents and offspring." Families were no longer hard, structural, economic atoms locked into the metal of society but emotional clouds formed on the basis of love and united through personality and emotional satisfactions. "Affection," Ernest Groves and William Ogburn announced, "rather than law provides the matrimonial foundation in which we have the right to place confidence. People do not marry with less craving for affection than formerly, but with more. The fact that there are few motives for marrying at all except this desire to join in the fellowship of love makes modern matrimony as it now exists in American culture predominantly an expression of the profound need of men and women to find their highest happiness in the close character developing experiences of marriage and the family." Families existed because they fulfilled man's most basic needs—the need to be loved and to give love. "Modern individuation," Joseph Folsom noted in his textbook on the family, "has been particularly significant in the sphere of the wish for response." [63]

Family sociologists thus greeted the affectionate family enthusiastically because it provided a rich medium for personal satisfactions. But while they wrote endlessly about individual needs, they worried constantly about social order. The experts were, in fact, proposing that the emotional family would do more than satisfy the individual. They believed that it would ensure the health of the society. The key was the concept of psychological adjustment, for by satisfying universal needs for emotional response, especially love and security, the family would see to it that all its members, adults and children, would be emotionally satisfied and socially responsible. It was this concept of psychological adjustment which linked family performance with social stability and which permeated the intellectual sensibilities of the period. In the twenties the family became, above all, a psychological environment, a nurturing unit which produced neither food nor clothing, neither education nor religion, but personal happiness and social health. The experts thus made two separate demands on the family and as a result were beset by two basic problems—was affection sufficient for family unity, or was it so fragile that it threatened social order;

and was the family properly fulfilling its social responsibility as a child-rearing institution? In other words, was the emotional family, formed in response to individual needs, truly responsive to social order?

This problem grew from two different sources: the revised theoretical model that the experts inherited and the hard social realities that they confronted daily in observations about family malfunction. For just as sociologists began to explore the theoretical consequences of the loss of family function, social workers were presenting the results of studies begun in the late nineteenth century from data accumulated in criminal and juvenile courts, prisons, hospitals, and social settlements. Here they found all the necessary evidence that social problems came from family sources; crime, delinquency, prostitution, insanity—all were associated with family disorder, generational conflict, the disorganization attendant upon urban migration, and inefficient socialization. Above all, they located the source of the problems in two related facts—the erosion of family unity and the psychological maladjustments that accompanied it.[64] Urbanization, family disorganization, social disorder, psychological debilities, and the affectionate family divested of manifest function became a cacophony of change, a dissonant orchestration of social problems and family changes. And it was precisely because so many social problems were linked to family sources that the family became even more important in the professional mind. For if the family caused the problems, then the family would have to provide the solutions.

Because they believed they had the key solution in the concept of affection, sociologists and other family experts throughout the twenties emphasized (and over-emphasized) affection, as the family was reduced to its personal services and unity and stability were pirouetted on top of emotion. As they confronted the basic dilemma of how a family which satisfied the individual could also unite the society, they were led bit by bit to reconstruct the family around the modern concept of personality and emotional satisfaction. Only when sociologists fragmented the family further, relieving it of the last remnants of function and reducing it from a basic social unit to a loose network of atomic individuals, would the family as a psychological medium replace the family as a social institution. That did not come until the 1930's.

In the meantime, most analysts consolidated the family unit around its emotional services and proceeded to instruct parents in the proper child-rearing environment with that in mind. "The experience of affection in childhood and youth," Lawrence Frank asserted, was the basis for a mature, adjusted adult personality. "The individual must learn to love and be loved, to give and receive tenderness and affection. . . . Failure to learn this will handicap the individual as a personality in all his or her activities." The family must be open, warm, and loving. It must permit each child the latitude for personality development in a nurturing and secure environment. The family must not thwart the child's ego demands. It must direct the child through reasoned persuasion, not by dogma or fiat, and allow the child the freedom to develop his inner potentials.[65] The new functionally reduced family, experts believed, had developed just those features—small size, democracy, and affection—by which this kind of child-rearing could blossom and bear fruit in emotional satisfactions and psychological adjustment.

Or so they thought, until John Watson told them otherwise. Contrary to common belief, Watson's *Psychological Care of Infant and Child* (1928) was not the definitive study of child-rearing practices in the period, nor did it represent the major tendencies in its thought. Watson had begun his work in the early years of the century, and his ideas about habit formation certainly influenced child-rearing advice during the first three decades.[66] By the late 1920's his views became extreme and aggressive as he quite self-consciously proposed a radical alternative to prevailing theory and practice. Watson's completed regime for child-rearing can only be understood against two facts of early twentieth-

century experience—the growth of the small, emotive family and
the experts' concern that affection serve social order. Watson, like
others, tried to understand the implications of the new family
forms for social order, but unlike them he neither trusted affection nor believed that it could be made socially efficient. Unlike
Freud, Dewey, and others whose thought dominated the child-
rearing advice of most family experts, Watson believed that psychological adjustment required complete conformity to social
habits and not the emotional satisfaction or self-directed unfolding of discrete egos. And with that object in mind he constructed an alternate model of personal adjustment, one that
would not need to bridge the individual and society through a
concept of satisfaction but would from the first accommodate society by denying the individual.

In one respect, however, Watson's view was completely con-
gruent with contemporary beliefs and tendencies. Watson
sought to make parenthood into a profession in which the principles of psychology were paramount. Throughout the twenties,
as the function of the family was reduced to the task of child-
rearing and personality development and as the dependence on
psychological theories increased awareness of the significance of
the early home environment, child-rearing became for family
experts a consuming passion. While child-rearing advice has a
long and secure place in American literature, never before did
marriage and parenthood appear to be such a self-conscious undertaking.[67] "The family influence is powerful," William Ogburn observed, and it "may be exercised harmfully as well as
beneficially." "In former years," psychiatrist Karl De Schweinitz
noted, "so long as parents enforced a strict discipline, any im-
perfections in the child were the faults of the children themselves. Today we have not the consolation of this illusion—and
where we make mistakes as often we do, we perhaps feel more
of the burden of failure than we should." In the twenties, child-
rearing became a veritable craze as family experts tried to make
child nurture a self-conscious undertaking and as parents turned

to the experts for advice. "Parents," sociologist Ernest Mowrer noted, "are more and more experimenting with childrearing along lines quite alien to their grandparents. . . . Application of 'psychology' takes the place of older controls." [68] For professional experts on the family, proper child-rearing meant that parents too become professional.

Most experts in the twenties welcomed this development. But even without Watson's edicts, they could not help being aware that "the cult of the child" was also a threat, both to the psychological health of the child and to the social order. Long before Benjamin Spock made a fine art of the perception, family experts worried that extreme self-consciousness was inimical to the very spirit of proper child-rearing, in which security was the principal tenet. Tension destroyed the child's sense of security, and parental self-consciousness (fed by the warnings of experts) produced tension. Ruth Lindquist, a home economist, concluded that of all aspects of household work anxiety over child-rearing was the chief worry of the family. "I try to do just what you say," reported one young mother to Helen Lynd, "but I am just a nervous wreck trying to be calm." [69]

And while the child's security suffered from parental anxiety, the social order might well be endangered by the child's tyranny. "The attitude of regarding child-rearing as a task," Ruth Reed concluded in her textbook on the family, "led many mothers with a limited understanding of the situation to an excessive concentration on the task, with the result that children in a small family are deluged with care and affection." "In middle-class homes in America, the family life tends to center about the child to a great extent." According to Ernest Mowrer, children "tend to dominate the scene, their wishes determining the policy of the family." But could this possibly be good? The lavish attention threatened to inhibit the child's maturity and might produce a generation of children who would be forever dependent upon parental care and who lacked fortitude and initiative.[70] And there was the even more perilous threat that indulgence posed for the social order—the threat of producing self-willed, demanding, unmanageable children who would become uncontrollable adults. For if the authoritarian home thwarted individual emotional needs, the family in which the child tyrannized over the family threatened social order. Incessantly advising parents to satisfy the child's needs, experts were now faced with the potential social consequences.

In the context of all these anxieties on the part of parents and experts, the beauty of Watson's advice was its simplicity. He had all the answers and an unshakable confidence. If loving parents were anxious about the details of child-rearing, Watson told them exactly what to do and when to do it. If parents did not know precisely what the personality was or what each child needed for its unfolding, growth, and expression, he assured them that the child had no individual personality, only a response mechanism. "The behaviorists believe there is nothing from within to develop." [71] If experts worried about the social effects of indulgent, individual nurture, Watson proposed to destroy individual nurture and conform all training to a single pattern. If experts worried about how to mediate between individual needs and social behavior, he described the individual as no more than the sum of his social behaviors. Above all Watson proposed to get rid of the problems of modern child-rearing behavior by getting at their source—the affectionate family. He tried to resolve the problem implicit in the family discussions of the twenties by shifting the focus from the needs of the individual to the demands of the society, by asserting that basically what the individual needed was to adjust completely to those demands. The fear and anxiety which resulted from the observations that the family was more and more centering its life on the need for self-expression called forth a counter-psychology. Its devotees hoped that the lessons of behaviorism would counteract the dangerous social implications of the affectionate family and child-centered nurture.

"Children," Watson declared, "are made not born," and he

proceeded to show parents how best to make their children. His prescription was an elaborate routine of habit training. The child's personality would be the sum result of the habits he was trained to. His security in those habits would lead to personal adjustment and social behavior. Those habits would be determined entirely by the persistence with which the mother devoted herself to the training process, undeterred by emotional reactions to the child's attempts to escape the discipline. She must not cater to his whims (a child did not express needs, only whims) but maintain a strict objective regime that she learned from Watson in accordance with the best evidence of how much, when, and how long the child was to be fed, clothed, and put to sleep. The product of the manufacture, if successful (and if parents followed his strictures, Watson assured them of success), would be a child "who puts on such habits of politeness and neatness and cleanliness that adults are willing to be around him at least part of the day; a child who is willing to be around adults without fighting incessantly for notice." Unlike Dewey's ebullient, mud-wallowing, proto-artistic original, this child would be efficient, obedient, and adjusted. In short, he would be an adult child. He would call for no special attention but would fit comfortably into the adult world of the family. Watson's answer to the child-centered family was a family of adults. "There is a sensible way of treating children. Treat them as though they were young adults. . . . Shake hands with them in the morning." [72]

In advising parents to shake their children's hands rather than kiss their faces, Watson was not being frivolous (very little in Watson's advice is ever frivolous or joyous). Watson believed that the source of social maladjustment was affection in the family. American parents, Watson declared, undermined proper socialization by their emotionalism ("Now, over-conditioning in love is the rule"), the lavishing of affection as conveyed in the parents' tone, their subservience to the child's demands, and the physical acts of coddling, kissing, and caressing. "Never hug and kiss them," Watson warned, "never let them sit in your lap." [73] As a mass of responses, the child could be trained to any model desired if only the training was consistent and the behavior became firmly fixed habits. But affection was an indeterminate variable. It permitted the child to take command. Watson's elaborate construct was an attempt to counteract the insidious effect of love in the American family, and it was as much a control on parental behavior as a regime for training children.

Watson was opposing the major trends in contemporary thought about the family and consciously rejecting the growing tendencies in the family. Social order, Watson believed, would be best achieved through bypassing the family, just as others were trying harder and harder to find some way for the family to continue to have a social function by endowing it with the supreme task of child-rearing. While most experts described the family as the only possible place for the nurture of children, while foster homes were replacing orphanages, and while states were developing mothers' pension plans to make it possible for children to remain at home, Watson proposed that all children be farmed out to orphanages.[74] At a time when most analysts tried to use the growth of affection in the family to social ends, Watson tried to nip affection in the bud during child-rearing. But Watson was really grappling with the same problem that beset other experts—the potential conflict between the emotion-based family, serving individual needs, and responsible social behavior.

What Watson's child-rearing theories lacked in humanity they made up for in shrewdness. He dedicated his book to the "first mother who brings up a happy child." Like his contemporaries, Watson was intensely concerned with personal adjustment, and to that end he proposed that the child be trained early in mechanical adaptation to the needs of social living. He proposed that happiness was a function of adjustment, of an easy rapport with the environment, and of an automatic knowledge of what was expected to receive reinforcing approval. The adjusted individual was the contented individual. He did not ask for the impossible or for special attention or self-determined satisfaction. Rather he was willing and ready to perform his part in the functioning of the world around him. He took the world as it was, content to find his place within it. There are no utopias, Watson declared, "there are only actual civilizations, hence the child must be brought up along practical lines to fit a given civilization." At the same time, the child must "learn to overcome difficulties from the moment of birth." In this seeming contradiction Watson meant to encompass the dual passwords of successful social living in America, individualism and conformity. Such training develops self-reliance within the very rigid limits set by the social environment. It enjoined that each individual learn to cope on his own with the world as it was. The individual did not expect that his every whim be realized. He set his goals by the determinants of his environment. Adjusted to the demands of the family, he would be conditioned to adjust to rules set by others.[75]

Watson's ideas were a shrewd approach to the problem of social order. With uncanny insight, he had located the crux of the problem—how does an individual nurtured in the affectionate and response-laden unity of the family, where his personal desires are given free play and his personality provided scope for expression, adjust to the impersonal world, oblivious of his needs and wishes? For Watson the answer was clear: it would be best to remove the child from the family and let the society train him from the first in accordance with its requirements. But given the family bias of American life, Watson would settle for making the family itself an impersonal setting for the training of social habits.[76]

Watson left his stamp on many American homes, but his ideas were sparingly incorporated into the family literature of the late twenties and early thirties. He could not reverse the emphasis on affection that was the dominant note among the family experts. The greatest impression made by Watson was in line with that of Freud and Dewey: that the early years of life were the most important in the formation of personality and that the family environment was its major determinant. He contributed to what Lawrence Frank called "the growing belief in the possibility of directing and controlling social life through the care and nurture of children." [77] Some family analysts were influenced by Watson's theories about stimulus and response, but rarely did they eliminate love from the picture. Watson's strictures were used as evidence that affection should be tempered by control and that emotionalism be contained so as not to deprive children of their independence. Affection might be restrained so as not to become indulgence; mother might kiss her children on the forehead rather than the lips; there might even be a sudden rash of back-patting and handshaking, but to rid the family of affection altogether was unthinkable.[78] It was also unrealistic.

While they pondered the lessons of Watsonism for child-rearing, the family experts reflected on the family's future. Even if the functionally reduced family could efficiently concentrate on child-rearing (Watsonian or other), the accumulated social data and the studies of the University of Chicago school of urban sociology were making it entirely uncertain whether it would survive. As the clinical psychologist James Plant explained, a "widely recognized change is frequently stated thus. . . . If the functions of the family are being transferred to other agencies, then there must be an increase in the 'affectional ties.' . . . Logical as this seems, it has been our own experience that persons have little ability to distinguish between phenomena . . . so that with the manifest symbols of the unifying affectional ties disappearing the affectional ties are themselves weakening." [79] But if the manifest unity of the family was being eroded through a loss of function and urban migration, then the society was threatened not only with the break-up of its basic unit but with the psychological refuse that broken families deposited on the social doorstep.

Confronted by this difficulty, most sociologists ascribed the persistent problem of family breakdown not to the inevitable effects of functional loss but to the fact that the family was an institution in transition. The new patterns had not yet been stabilized. The family could function beneficially, but it had not entirely adjusted to modern social realities, above all to the facts of urban life. Disorganization and variation were, according to Ernest Burgess, "only the symptoms in the present . . . that society is undergoing change." This institutional maladaptation to social change was usually framed in terms of some variant of the concept of "culture lag"—in a period of change, different social institutions changed at different rates, producing temporary social disorder and instability. The city especially was the *bête noire* of family and social stability. In a lineup of studies emanating from the University of Chicago, sociologists concluded that there had as yet been "no satisfactory adjustment of the family to urban life." [80]

In the city, observers noted that the family was no longer a closely tied unity. It could no longer control its members through supervision and authority, reinforced by intimate ties with the traditional community. Jostled by the pressures of urban life, individuals were torn from the family nest, exposed to the regimes of industrial plants and the lures of mass-produced recreations. At the same time, the impersonality of the city made families autonomous and anonymous, cut off from the eyes and ears of community control. No longer could community pressures insure conformity and order. "In the rural community everybody knew everybody else," Ernest Mowrer explained. "There was little which one did that was not the subject of comment and speculation on the part of other members in the community. To take too lightly the conventions and customs of the group was to be ostracized and to lose caste." Some, very few, went beyond the ingrained hostility to city life to contend that the family might actually be stronger in the city, for the individual, lost in the anonymous, impersonal city, sought refuge and comfort in the security of the family.[81] Most commentators saw the dual effect of fragmentation and lack of community control as destructive of family order and conducive to unrestrained individualism and social deviance. Cut loose from the family and the community, the individual stood alone. The dread fear of atomization and the resultant loss of social control via the family still pervaded the literature in the 1920's. The old forms of family control and stability had lost their efficacy in the new urban environment, just as the old functions had been lost in the industrializing process.

A vital, if precarious, link had been found in the concept of affection. Affection bound people together and provided them with deep emotional satisfactions. If the family could be stabilized in the new social environment, affection would become a powerful instrument of control through personal adjustment. If in the country the individual had been stabilized through an authoritative and interdependent family reinforced by a strong, censorious community, then the stabilizer of the individual in the city could be family satisfactions in the form of affection and emotional security. Throughout the twenties, this emerging view was still bogged down in inherited definitions of what the family did. What was needed was a new definition of what the family was.

With the growing concentration on issues of individual psychology and personal adjustment, it was inevitable that someone should ask the basic question, and it was left to a member of the Chicago school to pose it: "Historically as other institutions have evolved, the family has lost one by one its original collective activities," Ernest Burgess observed in 1926, "until the question may be raised whether the modern family is any longer an institution: Is it now anything more than a mere unity of interacting personalities?" It was this question, which emphasized the loss of function, that held the key to family reconstruction. Burgess' phrase, "unity of interacting personalities," permitted the urban family to be re-created around the idea of affection, and it was rapidly appropriated by sociologists and other family experts as the very essence of what the family meant.[82] Burgess started his analysis from within the tradition of family breakdown and the loss of function in the urban environment, but he transcended that view and helped to re-establish the family firmly within the social context of the city.

Burgess' phrase was completely neutral. He merely defined family life as a process that resulted from the relationships between its members. Families had no functions nor was the family a unit. Rather it was the sum of the interactions among its members. Personalities played roles which were the result of specific interaction. The family as a social network nurtured those roles and produced those personalities. Whether personalities grew healthfully or pathologically depended not on the family's physical cohesion or functions but on the quality of the multiple interactions. "The family does not depend for its survival on the harmonious relations of its members, nor does it necessarily disintegrate as a result of conflicts between its members. The family lives as long as interaction takes place and only dies when it ceases." [83]

Although Burgess' concept was neutral, it held the key to a new confidence in family life and provided a context in which affection would work, for it legitimated the shift that had taken place in family analysis from the cultural milieu and social setting, to the inner workings of family life. The family sociologists of the twenties had proposed that good families were those where there were positive emotional interactions, but they still thought of the family as a unit, as a building block of society which had to remain intact, rather than as a network of individuals and a product of emotional relationships. Now they could sunder the question of quality from the problem of manifest unity. Unity was itself not a positive quality nor was affection a function that necessarily happened in close families or disappeared in loosely united ones. Burgess' redefinition confirmed the new emphasis on emotional response rather then functional

integration with the social environment and sharpened the growing understanding that emotional bonds had little to do with
functional interdependence. The case-work technique was the
perfect method for such an analysis, for it concentrated on the
individual and his experiences inside the family, and no doubt
much of the direction of analysis during the twenties and thirties resulted from the application of that technique. The shift in
emphasis as well as the technique implied that what happened
inside the family, not the relationship between the family and
other social agencies, was what mattered. Psychological under-
standings and sociological techniques together had made personal relationships the measure of family life.

While Burgess labored on the theory which would legitimate
the new trends in urban families, Miriam Van Waters was in-
dependently coming to similar conclusions from her experience
as a judicial referee at the family court of Los Angeles. Van
Waters observed that beneficial child nurture grew from the
sum of all the relations in the family and did not reflect the
mere fact of family togetherness. For her, parenthood was more
than catering to the needs of children. In a good home, parents
were child-conscious but not indulgent, for the child was incorporated into an emotionally secure network where parents cared
for and respected each other as well as the children and where
the needs of each member of a democratically organized household were met. "In the true 'democratic' family," Van Waters
proposed, "the family where biological requirements of each
member are understood, there is neither delinquency nor conflict. There is balance, an interaction of forces, a peace between
equals." Children did not dominate in such families. They were
part of an emotional network which was tolerant and flexible
and where each member was given room for self-development.
Emotional harmony did not require complete physical inter-
dependency or preclude differences in opinion and interest. Real
self-sufficiency and independence were possible only when the
affection of parents was assumed to exist despite differences.

Good families permitted, they did not condition, indepen-dence.[84]

Van Waters met the problem of over-indulgence by redefin-ing unity. Unity was a by-product of multiple emotional in-teractions. The family did not exist for child nurture; good child-rearing was a product of a family network in which each member was emotionally fulfilled and psychologically secure. Where parents loved their children but not each other, the child was subject to tensions and anxieties. "For the welfare of the child, it is best to subject it to the influence of only one of the combating parents; two conflicting attitudes are almost certain to produce breakdown in the child, in health, sanity or morals." [85] Better a single parent than a strife-ridden home.

In the mid-thirties, the implications of the new definitions and the new ideas received something close to an official stamp of approval in the reports of the White House Conference on Child Health and Protection, the most extensive investigation of childhood and youth ever undertaken in America to that time.[86] The studies, employing wide-ranging interviews and sur-veys, climaxed the research methods of the twenties and legiti-mated the family values toward which the sociological literature of the twenties had been reaching and which Burgess and Van Waters had most clearly articulated.

The Conference studies were first of all the presentation of research findings, the sum result of a broad empirical investiga-tion of all aspects of home environment, community facilities, and family relationships. At the same time, the studies evaluated families in terms of specific criteria of what the family was ideally like and on the basis of a model of what it was ex-pected to do. Thus, while it was theoretically value-free, the very terms by which families were judged as more or less good grew out of the emphasis and direction of the preceding decade. Personal adjustment was above all the single most important and pervasive measure of family performance. The quality of relationships between family members, not unity or function, differentiated family types and made one pattern better than another. The reports took the implications of the twenties through to their logical conclusion, reversing older assumptions about the ill effects of broken homes on children and the disunity of urban families, by shifting the emphasis from social function to personal satisfaction. The Conference assumed the primacy of the individual and built a model of the kind of family that would provide the best setting for the development of healthy, adjusted personalities.

The Conference concluded that no single home pattern or child-rearing environment existed in the United States. Rather there were large differences along racial, ethnic, religious, and class lines. Again and again, the studies demonstrated that in the homes of the urban, native middle classes, a new and different nexus of conditions and attitudes surrounded the growing child and distinguished these families from other groups and sectors of the population. On all the criteria—numbers of children, kinds of discipline and punishment, involvement of father as well as mother in child-rearing, the use of child-rearing literature, educational opportunities, diet, play, and extra-familial activities—the middle-class families emerged as developing most consistently and rapidly the kinds of families in which democracy, affection, and child-consciousness predominated. And it was this pattern that appeared to produce the best adjusted, best satisfied, and most emotionally stable adolescents.

Not surprisingly, therefore, one of the major conclusions of the Conference studies was that the urban family more closely approximated the ideal than did the rural family. Throughout the twenties it was a rare commentator who resisted the impulse to condemn the influence of the city on the family. Locked in beliefs about unity and function, the twenties analyst found the urban family wanting. Few logically followed their own observations to point out that in many ways the urban family was more purely a unity of affectional interaction than was the rural family. In the twenties the city was still the enemy of order, and the American myth of rural utopia shed its light on sociological analysis. But in the Conference volume on the adolescent, under the direction of Ernest Burgess, the conclusion became unavoidable. The urban family was in the forefront of the development of those patterns which the Conference valued: non-authoritarian, affectional, intimate relationships. The Conference concluded that "the average level of family relations and of personality adjustment of the children is somewhat higher for urban than for rural children," and that "the loss of certain economic and other functions from the homes makes possible the more harmonious organization of family life upon a cultural and affectional basis." "Superficially, the rural family appears as a sociological unit. . . . Most of the leisure time is spent at home with the family. Nevertheless, the rural family lacks much of the identification of interests between members which marks the true sociological group. . . . The physical proximity of the members of the rural family apparently does not necessarily lead to psychological unity." [87] This climaxed a decade of thinking on the family. On the new psychological measures, what counted was emotional unity and not physical closeness. The twenties had labored against its own preconceptions and fears and brought forth the affectional family divested of the underpinnings of function, and the White House Conference brought forth the urban family securely based on affectionate personal relationships. It was appropriate that Ernest Burgess should act as midwife.

The Conference thus did two things at once. It documented the growing hegemony of the patterns among the urban middle classes, and it used these patterns as the standard for the good family. The experts named what they saw and pronounced it good. Ideals had finally been made to conform to observations. The small, intimate, emotional urban family had triumphed over earlier anxieties, and the urban middle classes were the bearers of the social ideal.

In 1926, after noting the changes that had taken place in the family, psychiatrist Karl De Schweinitz proclaimed that "the goal of family life" was "the liberation of the human spirit." "With all our problems we would not exchange our parenthood for the parenthood of any other age." With a grand flourish he concluded, "The family truly is not what it once was, but seeing it as it is and as it is coming to be, we parents of the twentieth century are well content." [88] By the 1930's, most analysts had reached this conclusion, for they had fashioned a new ideal that sanctioned a half-century of developments in the American family.

By the 1920's, experts observed that the once tight network of interlocking social institutions that had secured the social order had been loosened. In trying to understand how this affected the family's role in the society, experts streamlined the family from a multi-functional institution to a private agency of individual nurture. They reconceived of it as a problem of emotional relationships rather than as a unit of social organization. In the process and with the new insights of psychology, the experts reduced the society to its individual components rather than to its family units and studied individual personality rather than social institutions. They then set about reconstructing order on the basis of individual adjustment, and they redefined the family according to a new concept of human need, particularly the need for response. They thus reorganized society on the basis of individual satisfaction, fragmenting society to rebuild it around a psychology of personal adjustment.

And yet it is easier to accept their testimony about the nature of the changes in the family and to appreciate the intellectual accomplishment of rethinking a pressing social problem than to accept their beliefs about the effects of those changes. Their confidence in the new family as the molder of a stable psyche and an adjusted personality—both necessary to the functioning of society—is strained. There is, after all, a quality of rationalization about their views, a profound need to justify. While they became more sophisticated in their understanding, they became more naive in their optimism that the family would provide the sufficient instrument of socialization for the new industrial society. Family analysts believed that security and affection would result in satisfaction and adjustment, but sociologist Ernest Mowrer had shrewdly observed that when the family became the only arena for the expression of emotion and personality, it cut itself off from the rest of society.[89] Family life was emotional, life outside was impersonal and increasingly mechanical. Did such families really produce children adjusted to industrial, bureaucratic society, or did they, in the context of that society, breed potential frustration and alienation? Watson may well have been more correct in his analysis of the disabling effect of the modern family than those who invested so much hope in family affection.

Many of the experts sequestered the family from other social institutions, isolating it as the basic and almost sole unit of socialization. In this sense Watson shared the failings of other experts because like them he reduced socialization to a function of personal psychology. The experts observed that the traditional interplay of institutions had lost its grip, that the urban setting did not have the reinforcing effect of the rural community. But did the loss of the community mean that the family now carried the sole responsibility for social order or even for personality development? Most seemed to argue as if it did. In reality, there was a new network: the changes in family were accompanied by the growth of other institutions adapted to the urban environment, institutions which would supplement family nurture. These institutions, particularly the school and the peer group, would certainly not replace the family. They would, however, permit it the luxury of its development. That is where the family analysts, intent on providing the family with a basis for continued social role in the new century, over-rationalized, over-justified, and over-emphasized the adjustment potential of the emotional family. They seemed to feel that somehow emotion had to be manipulated, not to free the human spirit as De Schweinitz proposed, but for social ends; that unless the affectionate family could serve social order, it would undermine it. The family had directly and completely to serve the new society. The culture lag had to be eliminated.

If we accept the experts' observations about the new family patterns without the values they superimposed, the question of the effect of this kind of family on the new generation is not so easily circumvented. The young appear not to have received the discipline many, like Watson, believed necessary to make socially responsible and controllable adults. Rather than punishment, they had received love. Rather than chores and responsibilities, they had been given understanding and care. For parental direction, families had begun to substitute mutual confidence and understanding. Instead of demanding performance and obedience, parents had performed and responded. Could young people accustomed to security and response be turned suddenly into mature citizens who worked and played and voted, who filled their social roles without a flicker of frustration or anger? In many ways, by the twenties there *is* a major gap between family nurture and social need. The family was not socially responsible. We need not, like the experts of the 1920's and 1930's, justify the family's existence. We must, however, ask whether this nurture was sufficient. The family salvaged a certain amount of personal emotional life in an increasingly depersonalized society. It localized intimacy in the family and provided a safety valve for personal expression. But by so doing, the family helped to bifurcate the quality of social experience between the intimacy and satisfactions sought for in human relationships and the performance demands of an efficiency-directed society. By taking upon itself the task of emotional responsiveness, the family may well have ensured its future role in that society. At the same time, the family did not bridge the gap. The congealing of the pattern made necessary the emergence of other institutional mediators that could provide a transition from the personal to the social sphere.

3

The World of Youth: The Peer Society

Next to the family in childhood, and probably equally with the family during adolescence, the peer group provides satisfactions to the basic urges for security in the warmth of friendship and the sense of adequacy that come from belonging.

Caroline M. Tryon, "The Adolescent Peer Culture" [1]

Wet! What currency that bit of slang has—and what awful power.
. . . A man is wet if he isn't a "regular guy"; he is wet if he isn't "smooth"; he is wet if he has intellectual interests and lets the mob discover them; and, strangely enough, he is wet by the same token if he is utterly stupid. He is wet if he doesn't show at least a tendency to dissipate, but he isn't wet if he dissipates to excess. A man will be branded as wet for any of these reasons, and once he is so branded he might as well leave college; if he doesn't, he will have a lonely and hard row to hoe. It is a rare undergraduate who can stand the open contempt of his fellows. What horrible little conformers you are . . . and how you loathe anyone who doesn't conform! You dress both your bodies and your minds to some set model.

Percy Marks, The Plastic Age (1924)

In the widening cracks of the social surface, a dense forest was growing up in the early twentieth century. At first only a shadow between the changing experiences of childhood and adulthood, youth blossomed into a full-grown experience in the 1920's. What was still in the popular imagination a mystical amalgam of fact and fancy had rapidly become a serious undertaking for the young. A tangle of work and play, career preparation, and mating games, the practice of youth became in the twenties a fully structured, directed, and effective social act. Observers saw it as a microcosm, for good or ill, of America re-creating herself. And so it was. For youth incorporated the changes that were vividly but still strangely ushering in a new era.

Youth was, however, more than a microcosm. It was a social product made possible, even necessary, by those changes which historians have variously called the industrialization, modernization, or rationalization of American life. What the society experienced in large terms as a maturing economy, an urbanized geography, and a nationalized culture—all bewildering and threatening to those who remembered when things were otherwise—individuals born in the new century experienced on a more intimate (but no less significant) level in the changing experience of growing up. Advanced schooling, career choices, sexual anxieties, marriage decisions, political and social self-definition are all modern problems we have come to associate with a hybrid stage of life between family protection and adult autonomy, often called adolescence, but much better expressed in the elastic word "youth." Youth is an old term. But in the sense in which it means neither child nor adult but something strategically in between, it is as modern as the problems and pleasures with which it is associated.

Youth did not, of course, spring up simply because the need for it existed. It developed because the society gave it room to grow as institutions were reshaped to modern dimensions. As the family retreated to the private arena of emotion, two institutions—the school and the peer group—came to define the social world of middle-class youth. Neither was new in the 1920's, but each became more significant in the context of the changes in the family and the larger society. Together these institutions effected the transition from the family, where personal identity was formed, to the society, where social identity was expressed.[2] Between the two, the experience of youth took hold and took shape.

The role of the school in an urban industrial society is well known. Providing technical skills and training in social ideals and expectations, the school introduces the young to the material facts and social values of modern existence. Less well understood and far less commonly credited with importance in socializing the young is the adolescent peer group. But the two are profoundly related. For middle-class youths, going to school means going to school with peers and taking part with peers in a variety of formal and informal school-linked activities. A many faceted experience, modern education must be seen as a whole, as a social as well as, if not more than, an intellectual process.

Contemporary observers in the twenties rarely grasped the significant part peers played in directing individuals toward responsible adult behavior. Lay observers found them disturbing and threatening; professionals scarcely had room for them in a model of family practice which swallowed up all the significant features of child life in the concept of personality. But more recent sociological literature firmly places peer groups in the larger context of contemporary society. S. N. Eisenstadt especially has described the crucial role peers play in mediating the problems faced by individuals growing up in advanced industrial societies.[3] Unlike many sociologists in the twenties and thirties, Eisenstadt sees the transition from affectionate, responsive family life to a responsible adulthood in an impersonal, performance-geared society not as a smooth interpenetration but as a difficult confrontation. That confrontation, Eisenstadt contends, is softened through adolescent peer groups that provide many of the emotional supports of the family, especially the security of group identification and approbation, while they train the young to respond to extra-personal performance standards similar to those that function in the larger, less personal social environment. Thus, the peer group provides emotional satisfactions in exchange for responsible action. It weans the adolescent from the freely given affection of the family and gradually introduces him to the demands of social roles.

By the 1920's, peers were already facilitating the transition from family nurture to social performance for middle-class adolescents. Reared in secure affectionate family environments where performance demands were minimal and emotional security freed from role specificity, young men and women engaged in a rich peer life at universities and colleges which was helping them to adjust to a new social environment. At the same time, the structure and mores of peer life on the campus helped to create the first modern American youth culture, a culture that was fed by the larger culture but that was also distinct and separate. What was happening to college youths was, of course, only one subset of youth experiences. In high schools, at work, and on the streets, peers were helping to lead individual youths into social maturity. But peer life at colleges was dense, isolated, and middle-class. The evidence is rich here, and it permits the historian to examine varieties of experience that the street corner rarely leaves behind. It also permits us to observe closely both the process of adjustment and the effects of peer influence on attitudes and behavior among a critical segment of the population. College students were a growing elite who would graduate to work and play, marry and vote in twentieth-century style. They also established patterns that both in youth and in adulthood others would soon follow, for better or worse, throughout much of the twentieth century.

Peer influence had grown in the interstices between older institutions and in response to new industrial and social conditions. And by the 1920's, the network of peer relations on the college campus had become a youth society—a mature and complex institution that took its place along with other radical new features of twentieth-century culture. Youth life in college had congealed into a distinct and identifiable social experience, still limited to the few in the twenties but already etching a pattern which would soon bite into the experience of more and more Americans.

I

The technical requirements of industrial America had by the 1920's democratized education. The massive increase in school enrollments in the high schools and colleges influenced American life in a variety of ways: raising literacy levels, increasing expertise, changing educational policies, and fueling the economy. Extended education also changed the lives of the young men and women who congregated in unprecedented numbers in classrooms, lunchrooms, campuses, and dormitories. For them, advanced education brought a variety of opportunities and problems: expanded vocational horizons, a period of respite from the labor force ranging anywhere from one or two to eight or ten years, expectations of social mobility and higher living standards. It made necessary the postponement of marriage and childbearing and the continued dependence on adult authority in the persons of parents, teachers, and school officials. It also provided the young with a vastly extended period of remaining almost exclusively in the company of their peers. By the 1920's, the modern school had become the setting for an elaborate network of peer-group relations, the scale and nature of which was new to American life.

The school was, of course, not new in America, but hitherto its influence had been confined almost solely to the years of childhood and very early adolescence, and the grade or grammar school had provided most Americans with their only school exposure. Beginning in the decade preceding the First World War and accelerating at higher and higher rates after, the march to secondary schools and to institutions of higher education was joined by ever growing portions of America's youth.[4] Between 1900 and 1930, there was a three-fold increase in attendance at colleges and universities. During the same period, the increase in high-school enrollments was 650%. The largest absolute increase in both the colleges and the high schools took place in the decade of the twenties. At the University of Illinois alone, enrollments doubled in three years from 3000 in 1919 to 6000 in 1922, and at Ohio State University, where there were 4000 students in 1919, there were 8000 in 1922.[5] Most state schools and many private institutions experienced similar increases. By 1930, close to 60% of the high-school-age population and nearly 20% of the college-age population in the United States were enrolled in some kind of educational institution.

But more than an increase in the amount of schooling American youths received was involved. The nature of school experience had changed. In the nineteenth century the "little red school house" in a village or country district, or even in an urban center, more often than not permitted the promiscuous mixing of youths of different ages within the classroom, school yard, and playing field. The school was moreover forced to compete for attention with other agencies and institutions—work, the family, church, and the local community. Working in field or factory exposed the young to adult company. The family, especially the large, sometimes extended family, placed the individual in contact with those both younger and older than himself, as did the church and community. By the twenties, however, the schools and classrooms were organized according to strict age divisions, and an even more restricting age hierarchy was being effected with the introduction of junior high schools and junior colleges.[6] As a result, the experience of young people at school was increasingly confined to contacts with age-mates. Certainly youths at an earlier time associated with members of their own age groups; age-grouping and association with age-mates is a phenomenon familiar to all ages and most cultures. The critical difference is the degree to which this homogeneity obtains—the extent to which members of a peer group are permitted to interact largely with each other and the length of time in which such age-restricted interaction takes place. Such intense age-grouping has been effected in the modern school.

Moreover, the experience of going to school increasingly became the consuming and almost exclusive occupation for more and more youths. Work, the church, and the community became less important as attendance at school became the most engrossing experience for adolescents. No youth at any time or place is totally insulated from one or more of these contacts, and they provide a balance to his associations with age peers. Modern education has, however, tipped the balance to the aggrandizement of the peer group and away from contact with other age groups and institutions. School for many young people has become a way of life, pushing other institutional affiliations from their experience and consciousness.[7] The school and the peer groups that make up the society of the school have become so important in the maturation of the young that they challenge the family as the main agency of socialization and primary group association during long periods in the life of the individual. Depending on the degree of insulation and the length of intense exposure, they have the potential for setting up a strong counterforce to the early training of the young in the family.

The rapid increase in numbers in the high schools and colleges of the twenties is basic to an understanding of the effect of school peer societies. While many of the features that characterized the schools, especially the colleges, had existed before, the influence of the peer society had been largely restricted to a very small portion of the population, a clearly demarcated social and economic elite. In the twenties, however, we are dealing with a mass phenomenon for the first time. But the school peer society had a larger significance. One of its characteristics is to enforce conformity among its members. Peer groups helped to homogenize patterns of behavior and attitudes among increasingly diverse elements of the school population. Where once this effect of peer interaction had been limited in its influence, it now operated on a much larger scale. Peer groups helped to define sub-groups in a large heterogeneous school population, but at the same time the peer society in general increased conformity within the youth population as a whole. Ultimately, the effect of peer activity within the expanded student population was to promote wholesale conformity among ever increasing numbers of adolescents and young adults. Peer pressures and peer groups thus counteracted the individualizing and personalizing trend that had become marked in the family.

Furthermore, in the twenties this tendency toward homogeneity went beyond specific campuses, blending students into a college culture and reaching out from the campus to the general population. Age, especially youth, had become a mode of identification, and college students were fashion and fad pacesetters whose behavior, interests, and amusements, caught the national imagination and were emulated by other youths. This was made possible by the growth of national agencies like movies, magazines, and advertising which spread the influence of college fashions and styles and turned the idea of youth into an eminently salable commodity. A new genre, the movie about college life, flourished in the twenties, and a new technique for selling clothes that emphasized the prestige of the "collegiate" style was introduced. Moreover, it all happened with remarkable swiftness. In 1915, Henry Seidel Canby, then a professor of English, noted that he could interest no one in publishing a novel about college life, although it contained all the elements of a lively story. In the twenties, the college scene became a staple of fiction and movies and a showcase for the manufacturer. What once was unsalable became the focus of concern, curiosity, and big business. According to a contemporary authority on fashion economics, the interest in youth had forced the introduction of the "flapper" line, a separate category of size and style. Describing this phenomenon as one of the characteristics of a youth movement, Paul Nystrom observed that it grew from "an intense interest in youth, the dominance of ideas commonly held by youth," and the desire by others "to act as young people do . . . and to make believe, so far as may be possible, that they are young people." [8] Youth was fast becoming a national obsession.

As a result, most people knew, or thought they knew, what the "glamorous" youths of the campus were wearing, smoking, dancing, singing, and doing. College students were not oblivious to this manipulation of their styles and behavior. Noting that advertisements presaged "the future elite fads of the world," the editor of the *Daily Illini* observed that ads now made it possible "to provide the non-university man with the same advantages offered university students." The same public attention that damned youth for misbehavior also provided them with the leverage for broad national influence. An editor at Ohio State shrewdly suggested that advertisers were exploiting the publicity contemporaries were giving the student: "Colleges get enormous amounts of free advertising in the newspapers daily, and to brand a thing 'collegiate' is to reap some of the benefits of the free publicity." While college modes were becoming fashionable, some, like the editor at UCLA, lamented the resultant loss of collegiate distinctiveness: "This collegiate craze is putting a cramp in the regular college man's style. It is making him too public a specimen. . . . No longer can you tell a college man by his clothes. . . . 'Collegiate, collegiate,' everything is being collegiate. It's a fad. . . . It's being carried too far—this playing with things that really have meaning." [9]

In diluted or exaggerated form, campus youths were imitated, and the external styles and mannerisms of college youths, if not the texture of youth society, became a part of the young population everywhere in America. While traditionalists clothed youth in cultural anxieties and progressives projected them into the forefront of social evolution, advertisers and businessmen reaped the profits by making it possible for the young to identify with each other nationwide. Fads and tastes developed within the peer society were beginning to unite youth through a network of wholesale consumption. That "youth" had become an asset in selling goods is, of course, one result of the decade's latent recognition of the growing influence of peer pressure and the urge toward peer emulation newly enveloped in a mass culture. The young wanted to do and wear what (they were told) other youths were doing and wearing. Even this diluted form of vicarious association reflected the new social impulse toward age-group identification. "Modern youth" as a nationwide phenomenon was thus a by-product of the means of long-range communication and large-scale distribution of goods as well as the more intimate associations of youth groups.

In the end, the manipulation of the styles and fashions of the young also created an intense youth-centeredness in the culture. Youthfulness became synonymous with smartness, and young and old were beginning to look upon youth as models for fashion in dress, music, language. America became aware of its youth just as youth were becoming aware of themselves. Between the realities of youth behavior and youth societies, and the anxieties and excitements of a rapidly changing world, the young had come to represent modernity, the impulse toward adjustment, and even the promise of twentieth-century life. Throughout the twenties, America struggled with a torn conscience—with the fear of losing what was solid in its past and the excitement of what was new in its future. Fitzgerald understood it well, just as he knew that youth had come to represent it all. The victory would, of course, belong to the young, and in attending to their styles, their fads, their music, and their lives, other Americans would accept it too.

The consciousness of youth was grounded in reality as well as myth; in what was in fact happening to the young as well as what Americans believed was happening to the culture. One of those realities was the expansion of youth-intensive centers like schools and colleges where the young were exposed to peer requirements for identification and conformity. Another was an expanded system of communications binding together a newly national and commercial culture. Thus, in the twenties, while the schools were intensifying peer interaction and emulation, and national communications were linking up youth groups nationwide through common styles and fads, the advertisers increased the interest in youth generally and helped to spread youth styles and interests to the population at large, old and young. Between condemnation and emulation, the young had become one way for adults to demonstrate their own conscious adjustment to change.

II

But it was the schools first and foremost that gave youth a setting and a home. And it was here that the society of peers flourished, enclosing the young in a world that was theirs by right of possession. There were variations in that world, of course. The colleges of the twenties existed in a luxuriant plurality: small and large; male, female, and coeducational; public and private; denominational and secular.[10] But in each, students engaged in a similar array of academic, extra-curricular, and social pursuits. The very structure of the college environment already homogenized students' experiences. Each student had a special existence—different courses, different activities; some worked, some commuted—but each was firmly locked into a college world and a network of peer relations which were remarkably similar everywhere. While the attendance at college already underwrote a pattern of conformity for college youths, the action of peers refined the pattern into an even more specific conformity that was both dazzling in its complexity and elegant in its basic simplicity. Peer groups broke down the college community into distinct sets and sub-sets and united that same community in a single chorus of common behavior and belief. At the colleges, peer groups were baptizing the young in behavioral norms as they gained control over the totality of youth relationships on campus and off, among the young and between youth and the adult world.

The coeducational residential colleges were the most peer intensive. Here young people not only studied and played together but lived together. Cut off from home and community life, the most elaborate youth societies grew in their midst. This was also the most common student environment in the twenties, enrolling almost two-thirds of all students.[11] Most of these students attended the large state schools or large private universities that contained a number of schools within the university complex—liberal arts, engineering, business, home economics, agriculture, and education—many newly affiliated as a consequence of the expansion of college and university facilities. The Big Ten Midwestern universities (a designation for a football conference) exemplified this type of institution. Others, like Cornell and Syracuse, also fit the pattern. Growing at an enormous rate that was increasingly viewed with alarm by administrators in the twenties,[12] these large, coeducational, educationally and socially heterogeneous institutions were the most common setting for student life and provided an environment in which youth societies were most intense and elaborate.

A second type of institution was also a major focus for youth-intensive societies. Smaller, often older, the privately endowed men's and women's schools, largely concentrated in the East and almost entirely residential, were also expanding in enrollments and facilities. But they soon began to impose strict admissions requirements to hold down their size. Approximately 17% of all college men and 15% of all college women attended these schools.[13] In many ways these schools were both more intensive and less. Because they were sex-exclusive as well as age-intensive, students were dependent upon outside agencies, usually other schools, for an important feature of peer relations, socializing between men and women.

Another kind of institution, the city school, lacked the residential character of either the large coeducational university or the small uni-sex school. The non-residential schools like the City College of New York, the University of California at Los Angeles (non-residential in the twenties), and the University of Cincinnati were usually coeducational, but while students spent most of their time at the institution, they did not live there and thus remained in close touch with families and home communities. There was also a wealth of other institutions in the twenties in which the social environment differed in varying degrees from these major types: small denominational colleges, usually residential but sometimes largely non-resident, in which church control and church pressure affected the daily lives of the young; racially segregated Negro colleges; junior colleges similar to high schools in social configuration; [14] and the local teachers institutions.

Within all the colleges, however, student life had large similarities and was defined by three kinds of activities. At the top was the formal structure maintained by university authorities, consisting of classrooms, laboratories, and often chapel, where attendance was required and adult-supervised, and the libraries and university-provided living and eating accommodations. Neutral services that respected neither the personalities nor the interests or backgrounds of the students, these provided a minimal environment, adult-imposed and regulated. [15]

A second stratum of student life was the semi-formal system of extra-curricular activities. Ostensibly established to fill out the contours of students' lives, to express their interests, and to provide an arena for the profitable expenditure of energies unconsumed in the classroom, the activities brought students with like interests or backgrounds into contact with each other and formed smaller groups within the large heterogeneous and unrelated population. The administration shared partnership with the young, setting academic standards for membership in most activities, excluding students on academic probation, and providing facilities. But the organizations were student-run for student interest and were a vital center of peer standards and values.

The activities were often the focus of publicity and controversy during the twenties and a point of contention between those who believed they undermined academic interests and channeled too much energy from educational matters and those who believed that they were valuable in the educational process.[16] Usually, however, the activities received administrative blessing. The number and types of activities varied by institution, but in the largest universities they covered the whole gamut of human interests—literary, journalistic, dramatic, musical, athletic, governmental, departmental, religious, and social. The student leaders of the activities usually required certain standards of performance (standards unlike those of the university authorities) from all members, and leadership positions in most activities were highly competitive. The amount of required work varied with the school and the organization, the "competitive" standing and rating of the activity, and the individual interest and sense of obligation of the members. This variety in the amount of time, effort, and prestige demanded and conferred opened the door wide to a social system in which the activities could serve as pawns or leverage for social prominence in the peer society of the campus. Those students who accumulated prestige and recognition in activities, usually honored with election to select junior and senior honor societies, were the recognized leaders of campus life. The extra-curricular sytem was an active sphere of student life and was vital to peer evaluation. It was not, however, the foundation for the social system, nor did it provide the basic structure for that system. Rather, it was the formal arena for an underlying system based on friendship, living, and play associations.

Beneath and sometimes outside this semi-formal network lay

the third level of university life, the vast system of informal student relationships. These were the basic friendship, living, and dating associations that consumed the largest part of the leisure time of resident as well as non-resident students. The various kinds of primary associations and recreational activities of which this social level was composed varied from the formal groups of roommates or fraternity brothers and formal social occasions like dances and athletic events to informal ad-hoc eating, dating, and conversation groups. The activities around this third level of youth life were most completely within the control of the young themselves, although they were still hedged by restrictions and rules imposed by university officials. There were, for example, rules against drinking and gambling in the dorms and usually in fraternity houses, and there were parietal rules for women regulating guests, hours, and often the number of dates permitted each week. There were sometimes regulations regarding clothes worn by men and women. Most social regulations were of the thou-shalt-not variety, describing the limits of permissible conduct, and most were actively resented by students, who believed they were an invasion of their rights.[17] Beyond them the guidelines to behavior, association, interests, and the allocation of time were determined and directed by the young themselves. No requirements were set for friendship associations or recreational choices, except those they established for themselves. Their choices for dates, clothes, or conversation were their own. The values, standards, and mores developed by the young were founded in these leisure-time pursuits.[18] But these codes affected every aspect of their daily lives, spilling over into the classroom and even the chapel.

The three levels of campus life—studies, extra-curricular activities, and social relationships—effectively engaged the time and energies of the majority of college youths, and the colleges, especially the coeducational, residential institutions, were largely self-contained social environments, insulated from outside influences and other institutions. This isolation was repeat-

edly noted by contemporaries. Dean Christian Gauss of Princeton, for example, remarked that each youth lived "largely with
his own classmates," spending his time in an "exclusively adolescent" society. College students, according to Dean Davenport
of Ohio State, lived in an "artificial environment" of their own
making and associated almost exclusively with age-mates.[19] At
even the most insulated college settings, of course, variations in
individual circumstances, like home background, personal confidence, or strong religious or vocational orientations, affected
an individual's dependence on the peer system. But beyond
these individual variations there were certain factors and
counter-pressures which were more generally significant. The
most important, work and at-home residence, deserve a brief examination as potentially countervailing forces to the peer environment.

Work opened the student to the influence of a whole set of
relationships outside the peer group. It made him responsible to
a superior, usually an adult, for specific adult performance, and
it occupied a portion of time that would otherwise have been
spent in study or—as was more likely—in peer-group pursuits.
Frequently, it even took the youth away from the peer environment into downtown districts, a world dominated by adult personalities and adult values. While the youth who worked on the
campus amidst his peers might find himself vulnerable in an environment which was strongly leisure-oriented.[20]

Although about one-half of all college men and one-quarter of
all college women did some remunerative work while at college
in the 1920's—even at the most elite institutions like Yale an
estimated one-third of the students were employed—it would
be a serious mistake to believe that employment was an important counter-pressure to peer-group insulation in all these cases.
Most worked for a limited number of hours and usually for
pocket money. That they did so may well emphasize the importance of peer-group pressure, since the majority worked for
the additional cash which would enhance their status within the

campus society, earning money for extras like social events, dates, snacks, clothes, and automobiles. The vast majority of the youths on the campuses of the twenties had adequate support from home to meet most educational and living expenses.[21] Only 15% of all college students in the twenties were self-supporting. For these students, the need to work imposed certain responsibilities and the amount of time spent was considerable. For this 15%, work was an important counter-influence to peer insulation.[22] For the others, work, like family, was one element of their lives, more or less significant, but probably limited in the degree to which it could conflict with peer orientation.

All students experienced the influence of home and family to some degree. The influence resulted from financial dependence, from the possibility of support being withdrawn, as well as from the ongoing contact with the home maintained through correspondence and vacation-visiting. But the students upon whom home and family exerted the most consistent and constant pressure were the commuters to largely residential campuses. In the twenties, about one-fifth of all students at residential liberal arts schools were commuters, though the proportion varied by type of school and region, and at urban schools like Chicago, Minnesota, and Syracuse the figure was often as high as 50%. These students, like the self-supporting students—and the two groups often overlapped—were most exposed to a conflict in social orientation. Non-commuters were in an advantageous position socially. They had more time to take part in extra-curricular activities and social events. The resident student, but not the commuter, could belong to the important Greek-letter fraternities because these were first of all residence units. This initial disadvantage could lead the commuting student to one of two reactions. He could try to compensate by careful conformity and by becoming highly involved in the social and activities system or he could take up a position on the periphery of the campus social system with resignation or bitterness.[23] From such a vantage, he might be affected minimally by the general peer ethos that prevailed and be involved with a circle of associates in similar circumstances, or he might become a critic of the system. Letters to the editor often drew a painful portrait of commuter exclusion as many commuters demonstrated an unusual propensity to criticize the campus social system and its mores. At schools like UCLA where all or most students were non-residents, the social system itself adjusted to the basic fact of non-residence. Here commuting was not an incursion on peer insulation but an institutional fact of life, and most peer life was molded around daily class attendance rather than around residence.

That work and at-home residence did, in fact, weaken peer influence is suggested by the generally higher regard for academic performance among non-resident and working students and their lesser participation in peer-sanctioned activities. The peer society devalued academic performance and strongly fostered work in the extra-curricular field. For the working and commuting youth, however, the devaluation of academic work was met by equally strong pressures to achieve, either from the pressure of family attitudes or from the self-imposed pressure of working one's way through school. At Syracuse University and the University of Chicago, for example, students who were helping to meet their own expenses were more serious than other students and tended to devote more time to their studies. Working students at the University of Michigan were least involved in extra-curricular activities and least well socially adjusted to and integrated into the peer network. The situation was similar for commuting students. At Chicago, commuting students did better academic work and showed greater seriousness of purpose, and at Ohio State published grade averages showed that commuters made far better grades than residents.[24]

Other factors, like church attendance and involvement in non-college community organizations had the potential for exposing students to influences from outside the system. Many college students were regular or semi-regular churchgoers, and while the churches they attended often served the college community and associations in the church were largely with peers, the experience of churchgoing and the exposure to the pastor and his set of values and moral views could be a serious counterweight to the influence of peers. On the whole, however, the reverse appears to have been the case. The religious attitudes of the individual were strongly influenced by peer pressure and example. In an extensive study of the religious habits of college freshmen, one investigator concluded, "The most potent influences upon changes in religious attitudes and participation are to be found in the subtle and complex environmental factors peculiar to the social organization of the campus community." "Influences peculiar to the college environment," largely the result of "the contacts of students with each other through the living situation," the report concluded, changed religious views among college students.[25]

A good example of the erosion of religious sentiments by peer pressures is the case of Trinity College in North Carolina, where peer orientations overcame even the preponderant influence of church governance. Trinity, in the late nineteenth and early twentieth centuries, was a small Methodist college with very strict rules governing student conduct, required daily chapel attendance, and college-sponsored annual revivals. As the school expanded in population (nearly tripling in size between 1914 and 1929), students began to engage in more and more extracurricular and social affairs, student self-government took over the burden of overseeing campus discipline, and the religious orientation and enthusiasm of the students declined markedly. Even active participation in YMCA activities was reduced to marginal attendance by freshmen at orientation meetings or at the annual YMCA sponsored social, and the Y lost its once central position to become an object of barely veiled contempt. As early as 1921, student editors began to voice opposition to required chapel. By 1927, as Trinity became the expansive and ambitious Duke University, the early, mild calls for reform became a regular clamor for the relaxation not only of chapel requirements but of other religiously inspired, paternalistic social regulations, like those that restricted dating engagements for women, censored the movies coeds could attend, and banned college-sponsored dances. These demands were accompanied by a striking decline of religious observance and attendance at chapel and church services. In 1924 the editor of the *Chronicle* already noted the general indifference to religion which marked an undergraduate's life and remarked that "someday he may settle down to the pew and the prayerbook, the prayer meeting and the Sunday sermon. But not now. Life is too sweet and too short for him to waste it while he is still young." "The typical college undergraduate," the *Chronicle* observed in 1928, "has too much to do, both of work and amusement, to consider religion other than something 'that isn't done' in college." Similarly, while revivals were greeted enthusiastically before the twenties as a proud college tradition, the revival exercises were on the wane during the early twenties. By 1925 the *Chronicle* editor noted that the very idea of a revival "is repugnant to us" because it was no more than "an emotional debauch, an opportunity to put the feelings above the reason." [26] Revivals were finally officially suspended in 1927 and required chapel exercises significantly relaxed.

As this was happening, Duke students were actively protesting the proposed ban on teaching evolution in North Carolina schools pending in the state legislature, and editors were lauding the non-denominational and pluralistic spirit of the school, condemning the idiocies of religious fundamentalists and moral uplifters, and vigorously condemning all attempts to censor student opinion or strictly supervise campus affairs by the Methodist board of governors.[27] By the mid-twenties, religion had become an encumbrance to students at Trinity–Duke, something to be avoided or protested rather than a vital personal and social experience. Peer interests and peer pressures had become a strong counterforce to administratively supported religion on the campus.

Duke is only a particularly striking case of the situation at schools everywhere. In the lives of most undergraduates, vital religious sentiments played an insignificant part. College life tended to foster a critical attitude toward the church and made for religious indifference, if not actual hostility. Only students with a strong previous religious sentiment could withstand the bias of the peer ethos, and these were often little affected by the campus peer society and its mores.[28] The intensely religious often formed their own peer clusters on the periphery of the campus society.

Work, family, and the church, in varying degrees, affected the lives of many students in the 1920's. For the majority, however, especially those at the residential colleges and universities, school and peer-group life were the primary institutions of affiliation and influence. In the college world of the twenties, peer life demanded social and emotional commitment and preempted most other associations.

III

Life for most students revolved around peer concerns, activities, and values. Recalling his own experiences at the University of Chicago in 1919, Vincent Sheean proposed that the "social system of the undergraduate world" was made up of "a couple of thousand young nincompoops, whose ambition in life was to get into the right fraternity or club, go to the right parties, and get elected to something or other." [29] While Sheean's description of typical ambition was not far from the mark, the society he was attempting to describe was considerably more disciplined than the chaos of two thousand individual youths jockeying for position would suggest.

The actual structure of the campus society had little to do

with the divisions and definitions used by the administration, such as academic class, course of study, or competitive standing. Rather it was based on residence, organizational affiliation, extra-curricular involvement, and behavioral conformity to peer standards. The administrative structure was a kind of progressive escalator from freshmen orientation to commencement that students automatically ascended on fulfilling academic requirements. The peer society had different criteria. The peer social structure can be visualized as a large circle, at the center of which were the fraternities and sororities or, in the case of Harvard and Princeton, the eating clubs.[30] Often called the "organized," these students composed from 30% to 40% of the student body, with some variation by institution. Within this core group was a nucleus of the most prestigious and influential fraternities, usually the oldest ones on campus, and almost always those with national affiliation.

Tangential to the large mass circle were a number of much smaller circles representing closely knit groups of students with peculiar orientations or strong commitments shared by their members but generally outside or contrary to the interests of the mass of students. Usually formed around a specific interest, like religion, politics, or art, which members considered more important than being a "regular guy," these groups evolved an eccentric style different from that of the peer society.[31] Although these "fringe groups" powerfully controlled their own members, they had little influence on campus behavior, which usually responded to the centripetal force of fraternity standards. Those with strong religious convictions formed one such group on most college campuses and were normally attached to the campus YMCA and YWCA which sponsored social functions like dances and mixers, as well as church gatherings and Bible discussion groups. But while the Y's social functions were often attended by many students, the real church group was a small, highly motivated minority. At Syracuse University, for example, only about 5% of the students could be so characterized. The true

Association loyalists were not liked by the general run of campus opinion, especially by the fraternities, because Y activists were considered overly earnest, uncomfortably committed, and self-righteous. "Many of the finest men on the campus will have nothing to do with the Association," one student leader at a large university volunteered, "because of this false emphasis" (self-righteousness).[32] The religious fringes and other such peripheral groups developed standards and ethics of their own. One of these appears to have been a high valuation of industry in scholarship, and there was also some tendency during the 1920's for many students with strong religious convictions to be committed to pacifism and to demonstrate pronounced political awareness of and concern for issues like war, race, and labor, which was not characteristic of the college world generally.[33]

The heart of the peer society lay in the network of fraternities and sororities that controlled group life on the campus. Prominent in all the major campus leadership positions, fraternity members controlled and directed the network of extra-curricular and social functions and through them set the standards in clothes, speech, amusements, and attitudes that the mass of the students (often called "barbs" for barbarians or non-Greeks) emulated.

How the fraternities gained this critical role on the American campus of the 1920's is part of the story of the expansion and development of American higher education. Fraternity influence is rooted in the many factors that changed the American colleges from elite academies to centers of mass education. And the growth of fraternity power paralleled the larger social experience of which this expansion was part. It sprouted at that juncture when a culture based on parochial communities was transformed into a mass society national in scale and increasingly unified and diverse. The fraternities were a centralizing force that cut across older fragmenting forms of campus identification like school class and replaced parochial campus rituals with collegiate style and active organizational participation. Through their emphasis on personal style and institutional activity they transformed individual campuses into sub-communities of a nationwide student culture.

Fraternities had existed on the American campus since the first chapter of Kappa Alpha was established at Union College in 1825. Founded as secret societies that incurred the suspicion of the faculty, they led a precarious existence and were insignificant as social organizations prior to the Civil War. Since few had lodges of their own, they used college facilities for their meetings. After the Civil War, they expanded rapidly, and the number of chapters grew. In the 1870's they began to establish their own lodges for meetings, and a few built student residences for members as well. This expansion took place during a period of increased student freedom as faculties, emulating European attitudes that permitted students greater latitude for self-determination in social and academic matters, released students from the once stringent supervision that obtained in American academies.[34] The student social organizations took over much of the social regulation relinquished by the faculty.

In 1883 there were already 505 fraternity chapters with a total of 67,941 active members and 16 chapters of women's sororities with 2038 members. By 1897 the fraternities had an estimated $2,660,000 worth of property. As fraternities grew during the 1880's and 1890's students organized more and more extra-curricular and social functions at the university in response to the increased independence granted to them. The fraternities, as tightly coordinated organizations, began to emerge as important social centers of student life and supported the new campus activities. The fraternities sponsored inter-organizational competitions in such things as athletics and held an increasing number of social affairs, like dances, dinners, teas, and smokers for their members.[35] They were ready-made organizations that could now take advantage of the new freedom for student initiative and for student self-discipline.

The important period of fraternity expansion did not come

until the twentieth century, however, when, in response to ever larger numbers of students, fraternities grew rapidly. University administrations turned to fraternities for the housing and eating facilities which they offered and for which the schools had inadequate provision. Alumni, eager to highlight the prestige and standing of their college clubs, contributed heavily to expanding the facilities of these institutions. The most marked increase in fraternity membership and in the expansion of facilities took place in the decade of the twenties. In 1912 there were 1560 national fraternity and sorority chapters. The surging increase in enrollments during the twenties caused the number of chapters to more than double to 3900 in 1930. Fraternity building mushroomed. Fed by the worsening housing shortage on campus, the total number of fraternity houses increased from 774 in 1920 to 1874 in 1929. The value of reported property increased five-fold in ten years, reaching an estimated value of $90,000,000 in 1929.[36]

In the twenties, the demand for fraternities became so great that many local fraternities with no national affiliation were founded, and existing fraternities expanded the size of chapters. Whereas in the latter nineteenth century most chapters had from 10 to 15 members, this increased to 20 to 25 immediately prior to the war and often to 35 to 40 in the twenties. In many schools, especially the large state universities like Illinois, students and administrations consciously fostered an increase in the number of college fraternities. At Illinois, in the short period between 1918 and 1921, ten new sorority chapters were sponsored. The degree to which schools were "organized" is suggested by the fact that at Illinois, with a student population of about 10,000, there were 80 fraternities and 30 sororities. At Minnesota, with a student body of 7130, there were 67 academic and professional fraternities and 29 sororities. At the University of Michigan there were 93 fraternities and sororities.[37] The proportion of students who belonged to fraternities and sororities of the national or local variety varied from campus to campus. Usually, about 40% of the students belonged to the organizations, but the figure could vary from a scant one-third to a large two-thirds of the student body. By 1930, 35% of all students were in fraternities or sororities. In most cases there was a somewhat larger proportion of men than of women in the organizations. Considerable variation in student membership in fraternities also existed between schools in the university complex; usually more students in the newly affiliated schools like commerce and business, rather than those in liberal arts, belonged.[38]

Troubled by the lack of housing, college administrators saw fraternity expansion as a good way to increase residence space. Fraternities were also encouraged because administrators found them useful in the supervision and control of students. According to one administrator, "The University encourages the formation of fraternities. Students can be handled more easily." Fraternities, because they maintained strict internal discipline, were ready-made administrative units. This function of the fraternities was recognized in the nineteenth century when fraternity expansion was first begun. In the 1890's, the Chancellor of the State University of New York noted that "these societies largely promote a loyal and enthusiastic interest in the college or university where they are. . . . In college government and in university affairs, they can be legitimately used to promote good order and manly ambition, and honest work." Officials found that they could manipulate student behavior best, not through rigid adult supervision, but by coaxing student leaders and student organizations to enforce administrative regulations. Students complied with peer example and dictate. Well aware of the influence of organized groups on the campus, deans found it useful to set campus standards in consultation with fraternity leaders on such matters as proper dancing standards, drinking regulations, and smoking.[39] By playing on the fraternities' sense of self-importance, administrators could hope to influence the social norms of the campus. Fraternities and other residence and social units had a ready means of enforcement through peer pressure.

As significant as the expansion of fraternities in the period from the Civil War to the twenties was the progressive growth of their influence in directing and controlling campus affairs. Originally established to provide congenial companionship, especially at meal times, the fraternities had become conspicuous in campus life by the 1890's. They were taking command of an increasing number of activities and providing more and more functions of their own at fraternity lodges. Fraternity membership became more desirable as the organizations furnished opportunities and facilities for taking part in non-academic activities on the campus. With fraternities beginning to control campus affairs, affiliation became indispensable for those interested in such activities.[40]

By the twentieth century the fraternities had already accumulated the prestige of being at the center of college life. Moreover, the fraternities now offered a ready mode of campus identity. As the campuses grew in size and complexity, it was no longer possible either to know or to be known by the majority of students in one's academic class. In the nineteenth century, the primary mode of differentiating the student body socially was by class—freshman, sophomore, junior, senior. Each class had rituals and identifying clothes, insignia, and well-defined customs for relating to superiors and inferiors in the academic class hierarchy. Most social events were organized by class, and there were inter-class activities like rushes, athletic meets, and dinners. Many of the traditions went back to the early days of the college in America, and some no doubt had medieval roots. Class affiliation was the primary mark of belonging, so class traditions carried an importance which practically disappeared in the twenties, except for some remaining rituals concerning freshman initiation.[41] In the twenties, the loss of class spirit was frequently lamented in the college papers, and the academic class rituals were everywhere on the decline as real regulators of student conduct. The size of classes precluded a meaningful identification with one's academic peers and the staged rituals between classes lost their effectiveness in controlling peer relations. It was, for example, almost impossible for the sophomore class as a unit any longer to keep the whole of the freshman class under vigilant supervision so that they in turn would maintain their defined position of subservience and learn the college traditions. The same was true of the traditional relations between the other classes. By the 1920's, all that remained of a once functioning social system were some superficial rites, especially those concerning freshmen. But the substance of most rites and the significance of class affiliation were gone. There was too little initial similarity in the school population for a really viable sense of affiliation to result from belonging to an academic rank alone, and the traditions were not strong enough to create a unity out of this diversity, as was their purpose. Repeated attempts to revive the system in the name of "tradition" and "spirit" failed at most universities.[42]

The more intimate fraternity group could, however, provide just such supervision and control over the initiation of new students into college life. The spirit which had attached itself to class affiliation devolved upon the fraternities by the twenties. The fraternities, maintaining the rituals of college life that had fallen away as school populations increased, became the watchdogs of campus mores and were by the twenties most closely identified with college life and traditions. This association of college life and fraternity membership was fed by alumni, who found the lodges and their identification with the organizations a convenient means of maintaining contact with their schools and a congenial place to which to return for alumni occasions. In a changing college world, the fraternities maintained those characteristics and rituals with which they, too, could continue to identify.

Fraternities were ready-made institutions, with their secret signs, rites, and insignia, for the establishment of social identification on the campus when class membership became meaningless. Just as the fraternities were ideal agencies for continuing college traditions and enforcing them among their members, they became a primary mechanism for filtering the increasingly heterogeneous campus populations. When the classes were small, local, and drawn from a restricted portion of the general population, all students could be accepted as peers by their classmates. Students were a self-selected social and economic elite in American society. But when schools became large and heterogeneous—denominationally, economically, socially, and to a limited degree even racially—the fraternities helped to select out those students who were acceptable, congenial companions from those who were not. This does not mean that at an earlier time all students were friends but that because most were of a certain class and background, they were at least acceptable peers. By the twenties, this was no longer true. The fraternities could, however, enforce a stricter standard of social acceptability. Reinforced by continued contacts with and support from alumni, they helped to maintain for themselves a more traditional standard of social exclusiveness, a greater homogeneity than was true of the school as a whole. The fraternity standard was not based on strict social exclusiveness, but the process of selection did ensure a greater similarity among its members than obtained on the campus generally. The class system had become too rigid and dependent upon conferred academic status, and it was not plastic enough to conform to the real contours of peer criteria of acceptability.

Thus, by the twenties, to go to college no longer automatically meant to be assimilated to the peer society, once a function of the initiatory rituals of the class system. There were now specific peer-determined criteria to be met. These criteria, based on active involvement in student affairs and conformity to peer attitudes and styles, were set by the fraternities, whose members most closely approximated these standards and which, because of their prestige and campus influence, also set the norms for the campus as a whole. Students now had to mold themselves along the lines of peer sanction. Fraternity membership was a major asset in this new social world, for it was an immediate demonstration of "regularity." There is ample evidence that those who did not engage in extra-curricular activities or in the social affairs of the campus were often dissatisfied with college life and felt shut off from the real meaning of college.[43] This was exacerbated by the general devaluation of academic achievement, which meant that to be just a student no longer made one an acceptable peer. As a student, the individual was not automatically involved in the peer culture, and the good student was usually shut out from peer approbation.

The fraternities had thus become important social institutions. At the same time that they provided a ready means for differentiating a constantly growing student body, they set a peer-approved standard for the mass of students and helped to homogenize a diverse campus population. This influence went beyond a specific locale. Fraternities were national organizations that cut across campus and regional lines. Like the professional organizations and lodges that were growing apace at the time, the fraternities had a national constituency, a central headquarters, and handbooks that set guidelines and standards for local affiliates. This reduced the effect of traditional college parochialism that class rituals had once enforced. It also coincided with contemporaneous developments like intercollegiate conferences, sports competitions, newspaper exchanges, advertising, and movies. All helped to create a national basis for affiliation and identification.

On individual campuses the fraternities maintained a central position of prominence and prestige. They set patterns of behavior and belief that students emulated in the hope of being selected by the fraternities and in order to fit themselves to a recognized collegiate pattern. It was this fraternity-college pattern that now served as the basis for campus and national peer identification. Setting their standards and enforcing them carefully among their own members, the fraternities established patterns assiduously copied by most students.[44]

IV

It was conformity, above all, that was the glue of campus life, the basis for group cohesion and identification on the campus, and while it was stickiest among members of fraternities and sororities, the whole campus seemed to be molded along similar lines. Most youths were eager not to be left out of participation in every passing fad. One professor at a men's college noted, "The students are standardized and are much afraid of being called 'wets' and 'weirs' " (which was defined as "strange, queer, a genius"), and his institution was described as dominated by the "repressive influence of public opinion." As the editor of the *Daily Illini* explained, "The great college community has one standard of commonplaces." [45]

This conformity was not new in the twenties; it had elicited comment before then. But in the twenties, if only for the sheer fact of numbers, the uniformity seemed more complete and widespread. Given the growth in numbers and the increased diversity of the population, it was also the more remarkable. It was, in fact, the fraternities who helped to press the larger and more heterogeneous populations of the twenties into what appeared to be a uniform mold. As the editor of the *Cornell Sun,* in one of his more iconoclastic moods, observed, "Our Greek Gods, waddling about their campus, compel uniformity even more than the gods of the plebeians. . . . Yes, it is the fraternity that compels the goose-step and allows no murmur against itself. Before we attack the college for producing types, let us look to the fraternity and break somehow this power that crushes individuality." [46]

The fraternities controlled the campus by controlling their own members. Through careful scrutiny and direction, fraternities homogenized behavior among affiliated students, required their campus participation, and forced the rest of the campus to associate itself with both the extra-curricular network and the behavioral norms of fraternities. The fraternities did this by utilizing the major mechanisms of peer control—election, supervision, ostracism, and prestige. By effecting strong group solidarity and peer identification, the fraternities were able, in the words of a far-ranging investigation of campus life, to "control undergraduate social life wherever they are present in force." It was in the fraternity and sorority ranks that the campus "prominents," its athletic heroes and campus queens, were to be found. [47] An affiliated member, by securing election and maintaining his standing among associates, was in turn given those most treasured of possessions: personal security, peer recognition, and social esteem. [48] In the campus lingo, fraternity men and women were the "regulars," the greatest conformists, and therefore the most prestigious individuals. On the campus of the 1920's, individual merit came from group strength, personal identity resulted from rigid conformity, and social stratification bred community homogeneity. The key to this paradox was the campus peer network, a network in which fraternities maintained effective internal organizational conformity and promoted campus-wide emulation.

The control mechanisms began even before the freshman came to the fraternity house. Those who set great store by the "glamor" of college life (and few did not since it was drawing national attention) associated it from the first with fraternity membership. The fraternities were responsible for this association because of their conscious self-advertisement and their well-publicized control of social and extra-curricular activities. Often fraternity members or alumni were active in recruiting high-school students for specific schools, and fraternity members always made a point of conveying the importance of their own organizations. The incoming student knew that participation in student affairs made such membership necessary. "Many boys and girls know that their exclusion will mean being barred from most of the social life of the institution as well as from many privileges and extra-curricular activities," one investigator of campus life explained. He also knew that fraternities desired a certain "type." [49] Thus, freshmen arrived aping the mannerisms and styles associated with the college image. Conformity to what was believed to be the collegiate style epitomized by fraternity men and women was already self-imposed before a youth ever became a member.

The desire to be accepted by the inner group led to a voluntary assumption of the approved interests, manners, appearance, and behavior. Even those who would not be accepted for membership thus fitted themselves to the standard form. Indeed, many who had been rejected continued to nurture the hope of sophomore selection if they demonstrated the necessary conformity and gained a modicum of success in activities on their own. At Princeton, which had no fraternities but where social life was dominated by prestigious eating clubs, the self-imposed conformity was basic to club election. The selection took place at the end of the sophomore year, and students spent two years fitting themselves to an acceptable pattern. As the editor of the *Daily Princetonian* (always a member of such a club himself) noted, this encouraged "a barren conformity among the members of the two lower classes. By junior year this attitude is likely to have hardened into a habit of mind. The life of the underclassmen is tempered word and deed by the prospect of a day of reckoning when any peculiarities he may have will be paraded against him in the secret councils of the most high." [50]

The result for fraternity aspirants (and probably most college students entered with such aspirations) [51] was uniformity, a uniformity of manner and style that was maintained and improved upon by actual membership. A European student, after visiting a large number of American campuses, was amazed:

> In these societies you will find what is considered by them-
> selves and others as the aristocracy among students on the cam-
> pus. Here you find the typical student life. . . . The standard
> seems to be uniformity. Everyone who is different is "crazy,"
> perhaps a bookworm or the like, and only those students are
> chosen who are believed to be able to become good fraternity
> brothers or sorority sisters and that of course means that they will
> have to measure up to what is considered "good form." . . .
> They dress alike, they do the same things at the same time and
> they think and speak in the same terms and have practically all
> the same interests.[52]

There were certain definite racial and religious limits of acceptability which automatically precluded fraternity selection,
no matter what the success in cultivating the proper "style." In
the twenties, there were already several national Jewish fraternities, with many local chapters, in response to the almost universal exclusion of Jews from the other organizations. There were
also Negro fraternities and a trend toward the establishment of
Negro chapters at various schools.[53]

But this exclusion did not confine or restrict conformity. On
the contrary, it may well have accentuated the impulse toward
imitation. Vincent Sheean recalled how he had mistakenly accepted the bid of a Jewish fraternity because the editor of the
college newspaper was a member. It had not occurred to him
that the fraternity to which the editor belonged and whose
members seemed to have so much social polish and to have attained success in campus activities might in fact be restricted in
religious affiliation. Once he accepted the bid, Sheean too was
assumed to be a Jew. Much to his later embarrassment and
regret, Sheean withdrew from the fraternity.[54] The incident
points out two important features of college life: first, that certain very rigid social barriers to fraternity affiliation did exist
and were well known on campus, so that Sheean would be mistaken for a Jew; but also that an uninitiated freshman found it
difficult to recognize the difference. In some schools at least,
Jews in fraternities of their own were to outsiders indistin-

guishable from others, and they too attained campus prominence. The campus was deeply stratified but so profoundly uniform that the ripples under the surface scarcely stirred the ocean
calm. The same could not be true for blacks, whose own fraternities were often denied membership in the colleges' inter-fraternity councils.[55] Unquestionably discrimination existed on
the campuses of the twenties, and the fraternities were often at
the forefront of that discrimination because of their selectivity,
but at the same time the peer system of emulation and imitation
helped to assimilate diverse groups to a common pattern.

Beyond such limits, the criteria of fraternity membership
except for very select organizations and schools like Princeton
were nowhere so clearly defined. The editor of the *Cornell Sun*
asserted that fraternity selection was based on "certain ineffable
social qualifications," but these usually had more to do with
superficial attractiveness and personality than rigid socio-
economic class. Although family social prominence could almost
always ensure selection, those without such connections were
not automatically excluded. At Syracuse, for example, while the
majority of fraternity members believed that there should be
some financial or social requirements for admission, only a very
small minority believed that these requirements should be rigid,
and fraternity students indicated their willingness to live with
working-class students. Max McConn, Dean of Lehigh University, noted, "If a lad has an agreeable exterior, a winning smile,
and a pleasing manner, if he is a 'slick dresser' and a 'smooth
talker' and he is duly accredited as to purse, progenitors, and
preparatory school, he is sure to be taken. Nay if his 'slickness'
and 'smoothness' are exactly right, he will get in despite serious
deficiencies in one or more of the other items." [56] The criteria
of acceptability for most fraternities were attributes of manner,
dress, and style. These were certainly related to family background, economic position, and prep-school training, but they
could also be cultivated.[57]

Another basic criterion for fraternity membership concerned

what McConn called "capabilities reported or displayed, for distinction in outside activities—athletics, the glee club, the annual comic opera, or even college journalism." This was very important. In order for fraternities to maintain their prominence on the campus they had to continue to dominate and control the activities, and they were careful to choose those who showed promise in extra-curricular leadership. For fraternity aspirants the support of an alumnus, a relative, or a friend from the same town or school was also a major asset. This alumni contact reinforced the reliance on social background, but by no means did all fraternity members have such connections. The very expansion in the size of fraternities precluded the possibility that the organizations would become family castes. The fraternities maintained a solid base of continuity that depended on class, family, and prep school, but went beyond these to include members with qualities of appearance, style, extra-curricular potential, and above all personality. They emphasized, above all, personal attributes that made an individual sociably agreeable and able to mix with others. These qualities, the vital core of David Riesman's other-directed modern personality, dominated the criteria of selection. They were best summarized by a fraternity leader who described the assets most valuable to fraternity selection: "Fraternities desire men who will make a fair appearance, be athletic or interested in campus activities; be good mixers who will help the fraternity internally, and be fair students, although this is often forgotten. Wealth counts, but one cannot get in on wealth alone." [58]

The importance of money and an individual's ability to spend lavishly on himself and his fraternity chapter seems to have varied by group and school, but it was never entirely excluded from consideration. If not valued for itself as a raw qualification, it was basic to many of the other characteristics that made for campus success. Fraternity affiliation was itself expensive. Nor would it hurt to come with a full purse to spend on clothes, autos, and entertaining. Despite frequent disavowals that fraternity life was luxurious and extravagant, inter-fraternity competition for grand houses and posh entertainments put a premium on the ability of members to spend freely on themselves and the social affairs and facilities of the chapter house. Max McConn included wealth among his four criteria but made it the least important. But a careful study of undergraduate life by R. H. Edwards, J. M. Artman, and Galen M. Fisher concluded otherwise, noting that "costly clothes and a car are at times the passport to membership in a sorority or a fraternity." [59]

Attractiveness, expensive display, personableness, and extracurricular talents—a reactive mixture of personality and performance—were the qualities that counted most in fraternity selection. These were also the general solvent of peer relations on campus. "To many people," the *Daily Northwestern* observed, "the idea of being popular means that one must be good looking, have a 'line,' one must be able to dance 'divinely' and of course have money and a car. In fact, these are some of the first questions asked on inquiring about a prospective date." [60] Within the rigid limits of race and religion, popularity depended on attractiveness in style and manner and plastic amicability, aided and abetted by things money could buy rather than by rigid definitions of class, family, or social position.

The very nature of fraternity selection with its early rushing system [61] put a premium on a youth's appearance, expensive accoutrements, his ability to sell himself and be agreeable, the evidence of an already established reputation in activities like sports and dramatics, and connections with alumni. In the fraternities as on the campus as a whole, first acquaintance and superficial appearance colored future associations. Freshmen were greeted almost at the train station by representatives from the organizations. New students had almost no chance to become acquainted with the campus before they were hustled by fraternities to which they appeared attractive. And in choosing their organizations, freshmen too had to rely on alumni, friends, or the cultivated reputations that fraternities built up, the displays of wealth at the chapter house, or the visibility of fraternity members in campus organizations. "It is easy to fall in with a group because it has a fine house, or several cars hanging around, or because some of the members hold important campus offices," the Louisiana State *Reveille* warned new students.[62] In each case, the stress was on readily identifiable marks of prestige and potential for campus popularity.

"Men and women are liked who contribute most to the pleasure of their companions," Robert Angell concluded about society at the University of Michigan, "and some of these have few more substantial qualities than being easy 'mixers.' " Of all the benefits reported to be derived from club life the one most frequently appreciated by students was training in meeting and cultivating people. It is not therefore surprising that those who already possessed these qualities or had the potential for developing them were looked upon favorably. And it was precisely these qualities that were developed through fraternity association. The ability to mix was regarded by the more optimistic as the quality of civilized sociability, and some proponents of fraternity life betrayed a certain snobbish appeal to social culture. But many, like the acerbic radical journal, the *New Student*, which believed that fraternities were opposed to individual excellence and especially deleterious to the cultivation of serious intellectual interests, saw it as the ability to adapt easily to one's social environment; to underplay personal intensities and interests of any kind; to shed personal identity altogether and float in the stream of group pressure.[63] Qualities of personality thus became the quality of personableness, of the agreeable exterior and slick sociability. Personality was one of the staples of fraternity relations; expensive consumption and extra-curricular achievements were the tickets to success.

As it fostered personality, the ethos of fraternity life consciously underplayed personal commitments or individual interests in anything that did not serve the needs of the group. A fellow who was too involved in non-campus politics or literature or music was somewhat strange; his interest precluded total devotion to group goals and good fellowship. Individual excellence in athletics was the exception, for athletic achievement symbolized the victory of the group in the intensely competitive world of the campus. Eccentricity or intensity of any kind was not readily subordinated to group dictates and was a dread quality because it also had the potential for being disagreeable. The fraternities, concluded one study of student life by the YMCA (a not-infrequent critic of the fraternity type), valued "receptivity, docility of mind, conformity, regimentation," because these promised "a stereotyped result from the acceptable neophyte." [64] The qualities found desirable in a man or woman and cultivated by the fraternity explain in part the decided anti-academic ethos of campus life in the twenties. Scholarship required commitment and emphasized individual, unassisted achievement. Peers subordinated the individual to group requirements and group success. On the campus of the 1920's, the emphasis was elsewhere than on booklearning—on extra-curricular activities that demonstrated allegiance to peer pursuits and on sociability that mediated peer relations.

V

Fraternities and sororities dramatized the mechanisms of peer selection and conformity, which functioned throughout the campus world, by enveloping them in ritual formality. Initial selections were made during "rushing," which lasted from one to two weeks in the early part of the fall semester. Dined and entertained, attractive freshmen were lavished with attention and coaxed and lured to accept membership in one group over another. Choice freshmen received an inordinate amount of attention, others received only modest notice, while some received none. Deliberately aimed at building up the self-esteem of the freshman, rushing made the following period of testing, carefully planned to humiliate him, all the more profound. Once fraternity rushes were over, freshmen received "bids" from one or more organizations, one of which was accepted, and the freshman "pledged" himself to the group. He was then put to the test.

What followed was the ritual process of freshman denigration and humiliation as the novice was made to feel his humble position at the very bottom of the group hierarchy. He was, in fact, not yet part of the group that demanded that he first demonstrate his undivided allegiance by accepting personal humiliation. Set to do menial tasks for the members, often to act as a personal servant at the beck and call of the upper-classmen, the freshman thus proved his willingness to accept the commands of his superiors and to conform to the dictates of those who "belonged." Freshmen were intentionally made to "feel as low as possible in order to learn their place," according to one fraternity leader.[65] Many patterns of authority were incorporated into this ritual of subjugation. Physical punishments, most often "paddling" for disobedience or remiss performance, were only the external manifestation of a process whose emotional content was to carry the full force of humiliation and to undermine the individual's pride in personal identity. Fraternities had incorporated the system of freshman hazing that once functioned to demonstrate affiliation with an academic class.

A frequent part of the period of trial was the vow of silence among established fraternity members. This, too, was a continuation of freshman rites that prevented upper-classmen from freely associating with novices. Except when instructing them in required duties, members of the organization were not to speak to those who were being tried, for the neophyte could not feel equal to those who already belonged. The negation of his identity was complete. He was a non-entity whose legitimate existence would depend upon his membership in the group.

The length of time the freshman spent in this limbo de-

pended upon the school regulations governing residence requirements for fraternity membership. At some schools, freshmen
had to maintain acceptable grades for a semester before they
could be initiated; at others there was no such requirement, and
the process lasted only from one to two weeks. The novice was
then put through the final test of his worthiness. In what was
commonly called "Hell Week" ("Purgatory" would actually have
been a more appropriate term), each freshman was required to
perform an especially humiliating and not infrequently dangerous task to prove himself fit for membership and loyal to the organization. According to one fraternity member, "The purpose
of the punishment of the freshmen is to reduce them to a condition where they can be molded. Some of the fraternities use
tubbing and paddling. There have been a few cases of iodine
branding." [66] The variety of rituals involved, from simple demeaning commands to intense physical punishments, all partook of one essential element, that of making the initiate suffer,
thereby testing the strength of his devotion to the group and his
willing docility. The object of the process was the negation of
the individual and the inculcation of a sense of dependence upon
group approbation. No longer an individual but a loyal member
of a brotherhood, the freshman was made subservient to the organization. To receive the honor, prestige, and security the organization conferred upon him, it was his duty to subordinate
self to group. The one word that obtained in all discussions of
fraternity initiations was discipline. The initiate must be disciplined to ready adherence to the group's needs and objectives.

Having proved his loyalty and willingness to accept command, the freshman was formally initiated into the privileges of
membership. At a ritual ceremony he was told all the secrets of
the society, including mysterious handshakes and signs, known
to members only. [67] He was then fully pledged to the ideals
of the organization and welcomed to membership. The sign of
that membership was a fraternity pin, the outward symbol of
the supposedly binding inward process of spiritual affiliation.

Symbolically, the introduction to the secrets and mysteries of the group represented the deeper process of initiation, that of becoming an insider. Outsiders were denied knowledge of the group's secrets. Insiders, knowing them, were secure in their sense of belonging.

Initiation into fraternity affiliation did not, however, complete the process by which an individual was adapted to group existence and shaped to group norms. That was an ongoing process of daily association, punctuated by meetings, specific instructions, and criticism. New members especially were instructed about expectations, but all members were under constant scrutiny, for all aspects of their performance were signs of their continuing loyalty.

From the first, the new member had demonstrated the desire to conform simply by accepting the bid of a fraternity. The process of humiliation, too, had symbolized willingness to accept fraternity precepts, to take instruction from older members, and to follow their example. By the time the neophyte was initiated, he was pliable. "When a freshman finds himself at last a full fledged member of the group," one study concluded, "a long process of anticipation and preparation has been completed. Now that he belongs, he wishes of course, to become a 'regular fellow.' As a newcomer he is docile. He has been prepared in many ways to accept the group pressures which now begin to close in upon him." Once girls were rushed by sororities, a faculty observer noted, "they feel as if they had attained everything desirable . . . and begin to copy the ways and manners of the sorority . . . and settle into an unfortunate smugness." [68]

Daily group pressure capitalized on this willingness to become "regular." Edwards and his associates called these pressures "well-nigh irresistible," and a faculty observer noted that "crowd pressures control the individual" in the fraternity with the resultant "loss of the individual in the group." According to one student, "The life in each house is somewhat too intense, but it is a kind of melting pot; it knocks the rough edges off a man, polishes him, makes him responsible to and through his fraternity." This, according to the Faculty-Student Committee Report of the University of Chicago, was precisely the aim of the fraternity, which believed that "its role resolves itself into encouraging a great many forms of conduct, and into banning certain forms of conduct." Not surprisingly, students often found that "in the fraternity there is no marked individuality." [69]

The fraternity also had more formal devices for controlling the behavior of members. The most extreme, of course, though rarely needing to be exercised, was formal expulsion. All membership was conditional, and an egregious disregard of the rules, formal and informal, could be punished. But this was a last resort; the fraternity protected its members and educated them in the modes of behavior appropriate to the fellowship and prestige of the organization. According to a European student observer of fraternity life, "Each year when a number of freshmen are chosen to become members of the fraternity, they undergo a long period of education when they are told by the older students what is expected from a member and what is necessary to do in order to keep up the standard and honor of the institution. If by any chance a freshman has a personality of his own nevertheless he willingly submits to this whole standardizing because he wants to enjoy all the good things which he can only get as a member of a fraternity." [70] Simple instruction was not sufficient, however. The most popular and probably most effective educational method was known in youth parlance as "razzing." "Razzing" was not restricted to fraternity groups, but the fraternity institutionalized the process that functioned on an ad-hoc basis on the campus generally.

To razz someone was simply to deride his peculiarities and to confront him with his faults. To be razzed meant to be shamed. In fraternities, this confrontation almost invariably took place before a congregation of one's fraternal associates, especially in the presence of older and more prestigious members, often at bull sessions or at ritual weekly purgations. A good friend might subtly inform a man of his faults in the privacy of his room, but a razzing was a confrontation with the group itself; it pitted the individual and his peculiarities against the massed congregation of his peers. Razzing could be spontaneous, a sudden sarcastic remark dropped while one was in the company of one's friends, or it could be formalized in a "truth meeting" [71] whose specific purpose was to purge incipient deviation.

Fraternities, in the name of brotherhood and for the sake of the organization's campus reputation, made razzing a regular activity. It protected the group from being razzed in campus society and from losing caste. This made it more effective as a control on individual behavior. The fraternity man was informed of his responsibility to maintain the formal image of the group, which was made vulnerable because of his unbecoming conduct. One student noted approvingly, "The fraternity's group consciousness is the strongest thing. One doing wrong not only disgraces oneself but his fraternity group." [72]

This laid the basis for an actual group-specific and campus-wide conformity. According to one fraternity man, fraternities always let "you know if you have objectionable traits. They always ride your weaknessess." [73] Whether the objectionable trait was a weakness or not, it was so by group standards. An individual, in turn, accepted the razzing because he knew that it protected not just himself but the group with which he identified and which was basic to his own social confidence. Objectionable behavior was also forestalled by the razz. The knowledge that one could be called down before peers and especially before the leaders of the group would prevent potential misbehavior. Indeed, experimentation of any kind might be viewed as objectionable. Razzing was a preventive and a cure.

The return for performance of group-approved behaviors was confidence in one's ability to mix with companions without fear of criticism and the security of knowing that one was an acceptable fellow to peers. This easy relationship was highly prized among members of organized groups and on the campus generally. The statement of two students is typical: "Fraternity means more than any other group to me. It is home. It has done me a lot of good, taught me how to mix and given me confidence. I always was bashful and afraid to mix. My fraternity has knocked this out of me." "Fraternity has been the most helpful thing in my life. I have lived four years with thirty to forty fellows. The job of getting along with these very people, who change from year to year, develops one greatly." [74]

Personableness and conformity were twin handmaidens fostering peer interaction. The confidence that came with social approval was a basic drive in the whole mechanism of the peer system. The sense of confidence in affiliation was purchased at the price of conformity and renunciation of eccentric interests and styles. Campus dress, campus slang, campus fads and enthusiasms were uniform. No one stepped very far out of line. [75]

While they controlled their members, the fraternities controlled the campus by the strategic placement of members throughout the campus system. This gave fraternity members prominence and visibility in the peer society. "The fraternities and clubs [for women at Chicago] occupy a conspicuous place in the social life of the University," concluded the Faculty-Student report on student affairs of the University of Chicago, and "tie in closely with the activities which, taken together, absorb much of the time and thoughts of the average undergraduate." [76] Fraternity and sorority members were conspicuous models for imitation, and their control over extra-curricular and social functions gave them power to enforce standards. The consciously created and controlled fraternity style became a powerful influence on the campus as a whole.

Thus, while they reinforced personal qualities at home, fraternities required newly initiated members to compete for positions of power in order to maintain their grip over the campus. When members did so, they brought honor upon their group as well as upon themselves. "It is sometimes asserted that extracurricular activities have been built up largely through fraternity enthusiasm," investigators at Syracuse University reported. "Competition among students for the glory of their groups, and thus indirectly for the glory of themselves, may account for much of the zeal with which extracurricular functions are pursued." This zeal was based on peer reciprocity: an individual's success made for group achievement; the group's honors showered members with prestige on campus. It was significant that school papers, which advertised the prominent men and women of the campus system, always linked individual names with organizations, thus emphasizing and reinforcing this basic relationship. The organization to which an individual belonged helped to identify him in the prestige network of the campus at the same time that it advertised his organization. Such advertisement was crucial to sustaining the position of the organization in the campus world. Always in "search of social recognition and popularity," fraternities were, according to the Dartmouth report on campus organizations, "involved in the vicious circle of gaining more and more prestige," with the stress always on "empty group honors." "All the groups with which I have had first-hand contact," observed University of Michigan President Clarence Little, "have well-developed self-esteem and a first class organization for, and firmly-established custom of, self-advertisement before the college and the public." Imbued with a booster psychology that bolstered organizational confidence and inspired awe on the part of others, the fraternities relied upon the association between prominent undergraduates and group status. "Progress," reported one fraternity member, "is considered by us to be largely a matter of getting the group higher and higher in its standing with other male and female groups . . . on the campus." [77]

Competing for some activity became a *sine qua non* for remaining in good standing among fraternity associates, and fraternity members were pushed unremittingly to devote their time to achieve positions of glory for their organizations. Toward this end, the discipline of the fraternities was most aggressive. At the University of Chicago, "Each man's name is placed upon a large chart on which are listed the forms of activity which are most desired and into which various members should enter, and pressure is put upon the men to make them work at these activities and assistance is given wherever possible." [78] Because many of the competitions for the more important and responsible leadership positions demanded much time and energy, this continued pressure by the fraternity was often necessary for competitors to maintain the pace. Fraternity men knew that they competed for their organizations as well as for themselves and that they could expect various kinds of assistance, from completion of assignments and papers to help in "boning-up" for an examination. This permitted competitors to invest huge amounts of time. The competitions were arduous, and under-classmen vying for position were often exploited by men in power as a test of their commitment and sticking power. "The hardest thing for a man in college activities to comprehend," noted the editor of the *Ohio State Lantern,* "is what a man in business who works only eight or ten hours a day can possibly do with his spare time." [79]

The fraternities' ability to maintain tight organizational control over their members was their principal asset in securing positions on campus. "Fraternities, sororities and other compact groups," Robert Angell noted about the situation at Michigan, "exercise a power in student affairs out of proportion to their importance because of their well-disciplined organization." Individual fraternities could force members to seek positions, and they could use the leverage of the group in organizing support for their members among friendly fraternities. As the Louisiana State *Reveille* pointed out, fraternities and sororities not only "rate" better, according to the accepted opinion, if their members dabble widely and deeply in activities, but "they urge these members to join associations . . . to help 'swing an election' for the fraternity." The united votes of fraternity members would easily outweigh the fragmented support given to non-organization students. In return, a fraternity could promise united support for the candidacy of members of other groups in their bid for office, and appointments to positions which their own candidate would control.[80] The strength of organization thus enhanced the position of fraternity members in every phase of campus life—in obtaining a reserved place at social affairs like the Junior Prom, in being elected to honorary societies, and in winning key positions in the activities system.

Not infrequently, the intensity of competition led to collusion between organizations, as fraternities collaborated in dividing the arena of participation in order to cut down on the necessary exertion of members. The discovery of a secret political fraternity at the University of Illinois in 1921 was the exposé of the year. Theta Nu Epsilon, it turned out, was an organization composed of members of a number of social fraternities who manipulated campus politics from behind the scenes by delivering votes to chosen candidates. In effect, this group closed off campus politics from outsiders and from the participation of fraternities who lacked a representative. Contending parties for political office were controlled from behind the scenes by the same group,[81] and the "spoils" of political office, like appointments to social regulatory committees, were promised and delivered to the participating organizations. The situation at Illinois was only one example of what was going on in a less organized way on most campuses.

The organized strength of fraternities on the campus gave power to groups and prestige to individuals. But the fraternities more significantly legitimated extra-curricular pursuits as the recognized arena for approved peer competition and individual exertion. Thus in the twenties the fraternities had institutionalized their position on the campus, formalized peer rituals within their organizations, established bases in the far-flung social world of the campus, and by their prestige and influence turned the extra-curricular activities into a hornet's nest of social competition. More than social competition was at stake, however. Fraternities helped to redefine college work and redirect energies from an adult-controlled classroom to the peer-controlled campus.

4

Work and Play in the Peer Society

Children, as they grow up, evolve their own standards or social values by which they guide their conduct and evaluate their behavior. This is not to say that the children's value patterns do not reflect in some fashion those of the adult society which frames the particular child group. . . . But, if we were to examine the pattern of values of any group of children we would see that they were in many respects distinctly different from those of the grown-ups about them. . . . As far as we know now they emerge to a large extent out of the needs of the group and through imitation of and initiation by members of the next older developmental level.

Caroline M. Tryon, "The Adolescent Peer Culture" [1]

There are two sides in the life of every university, the educational and the recreational. The intellectual side of the life of 'an Institution of Learning' is usually very capably handled by its instructors, but the recreational side . . . (without which a college is lifeless)—is left primarily to the students themselves.

UCLA *Cub Californian*, September 26, 1922

University officials had labored hard in the late nineteenth and early twentieth centuries to create the American university. Through a process of faculty professionalization, administrative bureaucratization, and physical expansion, they had created a complex structure of classrooms, laboratories, libraries, and supervisory offices through which they hoped to lead Americans to the shores of scholarship and students through the shoals of cultural and professional preparation newly tuned to the intellectual and social needs of a modern nation. With these goals in mind, administrators and faculties began to revamp the American academies, freeing students from stringent control in the classroom and outside the classroom, expanding student choices in subject matter and subject area, and permitting them a wholly new latitude for self-determination and self-development. Certainly not all schools were equally willing or equally prepared completely to revise former goals and methods, and the freewheeling new university system had still to compete with more old-fashioned liberal arts colleges. But gradually, from institutional ambition, dedication to scholarship, or new educational philosophies, the old-fashioned American academy had given way to the modern university and college.[2] In the process, the administrations and faculties had also helped to create a new student body and a new campus culture.

The American student body had never been totally homogeneous, completely controlled, or exclusively oriented to academics, but it had been small, select, and closely watched. Throughout the nineteenth century, college faculties had to contend with a less than docile student body given to tempestuous outbursts and student rituals that had less to do with serious learning than with fun and games, as well as with intellectual performance which was half-hearted and half-baked. But not until they had created the modern institutions of higher education did administrators and professors come face-to-face with an unwieldy body of heterogeneous students and a youth culture largely dominated by leisure habits. One historian of education has described the resulting effect on education as a failure of motivation among students.[3] In fact, the result, fully effected on the campuses of the twenties, was the successful product of institutional modernization, for it permitted the young the freedom to mature in ways that were unforeseen but necessary in the context of that network of social conditions of which the modern university, as conceived by administrators and faculty, was only one expression. The student culture of the modern institution of learning was as significant as the newly embraced research goals of faculties and the utilitarian social ideals of administrators. Like a vast orchestra of different instruments, the actions of administrators, the goals of the faculty, and the activities of students came together to perform their part in re-creating the experience of education.

Certainly, formal academic innovations affected students, since they suddenly were provided with the fruits of a new scientific scholarship, new methods of instruction, and new possibilities for vocational training. Advanced education played an important part in the creation and experiences of modern youth, but their instruction in the classroom was only part (and probably the lesser part) of their experience on the campus. It is this campus experience, which the formal faculties neither controlled nor directed but which their policies had helped to create, that has not been sufficiently examined or properly appraised. It was not simply that students were anti-intellectual (which had been true of students even in the nineteenth century) or that they gave their studies less than undivided attention, but that in the youth world of the twenties campus, studies were only a small part of a social learning environment in which peers played quite as significant a role as professors. What Laurence Vesey has called the "awful chasm" between faculty and students, which he attributed in part to "the contrast between age and youth . . . (a particularly childish version of youth)," [4] was, as he rightfully observed, a function of difference in stages of life, but youth's behavior was by no means either childish or (as he implies) capricious. That behavior had real significance as part of a maturing and socializing process for which the university provided a setting and a structure but of which formal instruction was only half the story. Youth's evaluation of scholarship was quite as real and functional as that of the faculty. We must not be misled by our own parochial annoyance at youth's disrespectful and irreverent denial of the joys of formal learning. They too were learning, but (and this is most galling to academics then and since) they were learning less from their instructors than from each other. Their instructors had given them the occasion and the excuse, and they used them instrumentally and effectively as parts of their modern instruction.

As significant as the particular peer occasions that the colleges, and to a lesser degree even high schools, provided for the working out of youth's purposes was the social context within which they operated. It was a context that increasingly cut across former parochial boundaries, breaking down older forms of student integration, and effecting an age-oriented conformity that was less and less local and particular. With the expansion of school populations, students from different locales, backgrounds, and habits were brought into the vigorous campus world and put through a cultural blender that was at once age-exclusive and increasingly national in scope. This helped to create a new form of cultural stratification in which not community but a life-stage and a life-style calibrated the social mass. Students began to identify with large school patterns and finally with even more embracing national constituencies. While institutions were often extremely self-contained and internally homogenous, intercollegiate events and the national media were slowly making individual students part of a national subculture of youth.

The transformation of American education, which the late nineteenth century had initiated, played a much more critical social role than even its most far-sighted creators had imagined. Yet if the substance of their visions had been to make education and the schools part of modern society, they had succeeded better than they ever dreamed.

I

Academic work was, of course, the basis for college attendance, but the peer society neither honored nor rewarded scholastic achievement. Rather it defined both work and achievement in peer terms, making extra-curricular activities the recognized arena for peer-sanctioned work and social success the measure of accomplishment. "There are in every institution minorities of undergraduates who, for various reasons, refrain from practically all outside activities," concluded one group of investigators, "but they serve to throw into sharper relief the many who find in activities their meat and drink." [5] The young created their own standards of achievement in the schools. Although the peer society functioned within an adult-administered institution, it denied adult-supervised activities the importance assigned to the areas of campus life controlled by the young themselves. It was peer activities that were the basis for affiliation and identification on the campus as the young demanded conformity and allegiance to the society they created.

It was the norm for students in the 1920's to hope to get by in their studies and partake vigorously in the social and extra-curricular life of the campus. Most youths were mediocre students, and although women made slightly better grades, the "C" was the undistinguished mark of the average collegian. Academic work was, at best, a necessary evil, to be accomplished as painlessly as possible by an assortment of elective "snap," "crip," or "pipe" courses and through periods of cramming before examinations. For most, learning was good for the vocational, monetary, and prestige benefits conferred by the degree, and a few valued the extra dividend of a cultural veneer. [6] It would be a mistake, however, to believe that even these goals led to a serious engagement with scholarship, for even when they hoped for the pay-off, students rarely valued the experience. It would also be a mistake to conclude that the rigors of academic competition forced students to work hard even for the extrinsic benefits of a degree. Academic work was a necessary adjustment to institutional requirements—and no more. If hours spent in studies are any indication of academic commitment, then that of the twenties youth was meager indeed. At the University of Chicago, for example, the average student spent between 35 and 40 hours per week for all kinds of scholastic activities, including classroom attendance, laboratories, and preparation. A small minority spent 50 or more hours, but more than one-third spent even less than 35 hours a week in studies. Moreover, these were probably generous figures collected during a lull in campus affairs. Non-required intellectual pursuits consumed even less time. Less than one-fifth of the students spent six or more hours in serious outside reading, while the largest portion spent only two to four. In contrast, the average student at Chicago spent at least 15 to 20 hours per week working on non-required extra-curricular activities, and almost one-half spent far more. In fact, about one-quarter of the undergraduates at the University of Chicago reported spending as much or more time on activities than on classroom attendance and studies.[7]

The young thus adjusted grudgingly to the official university requirements by making minimum exertion. The inspired scholar and the goal-directed "grind" or "grub" were usually stigmatized as unacceptable "types," and college editors were careful to warn students against becoming "narrow, dry grinds,"[8] even as they urged them to study for exams. There were schools, like Amherst and Barnard, and some students everywhere, who identified with a strong and self-conscious commitment to intellectual and scholastic endeavor, but most students at most large universities would have agreed with the editor of the *Cornell Sun* that "real school life" was more than "the mere learning to be derived from the curriculum." Student life, the editor of the *Daily Illini* noted approvingly, is "divided into two phases. The phase which deals with studies and the phase which does not," and "studies after all are not the most important thing." A Trinity College editor described it as a hard choice that faced all students when they arrived at school, whether to be a scholar in "isolation from the mass of students" or "a popular man among his fellows." [9]

This evaluation of the relative merits of academic and non-academic pursuits dominated the campus ethos everywhere. "The situation in this campus today," observed the *Rutgers Targum*, "is such that the student who devotes the greater part of his time to class work and private reading is looked upon as a 'grind.' The modern American undergraduate has forgotten why he ever came to college in his admiration of the stalwart athlete and the 'big men around college.' " The grind who set himself the one task of acquiring grades had never been popular on the American campus, but in the latter nineteenth century, the grind had been carefully differentiated from the scholar. In the 1920's, such a differentiation was rarely made because academic pursuits as a whole were held in disesteem, and students subscribed to a code that denied too great an interest in studies. [10]

At Cornell, the *Sun* asserted, "A man is somehow ashamed to admit that he is in college to get an education, and that he values his education more than athletic insignia or election to an honorary society. If he does admit it he suffers in popular esteem; and few men have the courage of their convictions." One Cornell editor called studying "A Secret Vice," whose victims "carefully conceal any such heretical tendencies lest they in turn receive the brand of 'grind' which horrified them when they entered the university." Most students, he reported, "learn the precise amount of preparation necessary to fool their old foolish professors." At Trinity College editors noted that students seemed to assume that studying was a "crime," and that any student with real intellectual ambitions was looked upon as "a kind of monstrosity" by his fellows. Another Trinity editor explained that after three years of observation, he found that "the purpose of getting an education is foreign to the majority. 'Crips' and 'doing the prof' seem to be the popular hobbies

among students everywhere." Even at Barnard, it was the norm
to conceal or deny the really large amount of time and effort
devoted to studies. Students at Syracuse University who stayed
after class to discuss their work with professors were suspected
of trying to wheedle a better grade, and it was not considered
"collegiate" to take an active part in classroom discussions at
Ohio State. "Study in too enthusiastic a form has been 'bad
form,' " noted the editor of the *Daily Princetonian,* and "it is
still surrounded with unattractive associations in the minds of
many. Too constant attendance at the Library is likely to lead to
derogatory classification." And at Louisiana State, where the
blade came down hard and regularly on large numbers of failures (the "hog law" it was called at LSU), where most students
came for vocational training, and where editors never tired of
urging students to study, the *Reveille* described a similar situation: "There seems to be an atmosphere pervading the campus,
a tradition, that declares that all things come before study, that
study is the least important. Many of the upperclassmen are
thoroughly imbued with the idea, and it doesn't take long for
the freshmen to acquire it." Lest this be considered mere edi-
torializing, there is the case of the Yale class of 1922, where a
majority of students unreservedly indicated that they preferred
winning an athletic letter to earning a Phi Beta Kappa key.[11]

While extra-curricular and social success was pursued with
relish, scholarship was devalued, with the result that, as Daniel
Katz and Floyd Allport reported after a careful investigation of
student behavior and beliefs at Syracuse University, "the overwhelming majority will renounce the scholarly ideal if, in being
scholars, they must forego extracurricular and social achievements." Syracuse students admired above all the man with
grades just above passing but who participated widely in other
activities. Fraternity members especially looked toward this
ideal. It was not therefore surprising that Katz and Allport were
forced to conclude that "the most significant disclosure . . . of
the study is the subordinate value which the students placed

upon intellectual ability and scholarship. . . . The view held by professors and administrators concerning what it means to 'go to college' is so widely different from that held by those who are actually *going* that it seems to belong in a different world." Though they did not quite inhabit different worlds, students and faculty certainly had different uses for college life. For students, serious scholarship was not one of them. One obviously annoyed student, interviewed by a group investigating undergraduate mores in the twenties, finally concluded, "You might as well be at a summer resort. Nobody takes his studies seriously." [12]

Just as mediocre performance and conscious devaluation of academic work was a way of adjusting to the official university, students also found that cribbing was a powerful ally in adapting to official requirements. At all universities officials were acutely aware of the cheating problem, while campus dailies documented the periodic trials and suspensions of convicted cribbers. Each exam period brought a renewed discussion of honor systems and campus honor. While it is impossible to say how prevalent the practice of cheating was, at Syracuse only 30% of a sample of more than 4000 students claimed never to have cheated, and this may suggest something of the magnitude of the problem. Summarizing the major research findings on cheating among high-school and university students, one educator concluded that "the percentage of dishonesty of college students ranges from 34 to 66%." In some high schools the figures were as high as 100%.[13]

The ethical rationale for this systematic dependence on cheating varied as did the degree to which it was condemned or sanctioned by students. But it is significant that in adapting to university requirements, so many of the young found ways of adjusting that contradicted the very rules by which the university functioned. In part it certainly reflected the different values of youth's world and that of their mentors. Laurence Vesey has suggested that students and faculty lived in such alien universes that students could not comprehend the code of intellectual honor espoused by the faculty. But it was also more than that. Students were usually well aware that they were engaging in dishonest behavior. Cheating was one of many ways of adjusting to the given quality of their environment by their own lights, aided and abetted by their peers. Cheating on such a scale is not an individual act of defiance or desperation but a well-sanctioned group experience. For every cheater, there is another who consciously permits the cheating to take place or fails to impede it. Indeed, the main student objection to various honor systems—that they were a device used by the administration requiring students to do the dirty work of reporting on each other—reflects this understanding. So does the fact that faternity members were more active cheaters than others. The practice of using someone else's notes or copying his essays and assignments, a regular habit among students at fraternity houses and dormitories, was not a collective and social form of learning, or a refusal to comprehend the basic dishonesty of the action, but a way of "getting by," of "fooling the old foolish professor," and of adjusting to the system. It is also doubtful that cheating was related to the desire for intellectual achievement, for those students most intellectually and scholastically inclined tended to cheat less.[14]

An illuminating exchange about cheating appeared in the *Cornell Sun* in 1927. At issue was the apparently higher incidence of cheating among Jewish students than among other groups. The editor of the *Sun* asserted that it was a social problem related to the fact that the Jew had "wandered all over the earth in search of self-preservation" and had been forced to cultivate traits that would permit him to get by. A letter to the editor, objecting to the ascription of racial traits, noted that the real issue was not the amount of cheating among Jewish students but the fact that Jews were more likely to be reported.[15] The exchange underlines two facts about the situation on campus. First, cheating was seen as self-preservation, not as the road to achievement—a point that is even more striking in connection with the Jew, traditionally accused of over-concern with scholastic success—or as a blind incomprehension of alien values. Second, the correspondent perceptively reveals the mechanisms that sanctioned the whole cheating process when he noted that Jews were reported while others were not. It was, after all, peer support that permitted cheaters to get by, support more often denied the Jew than others.

The low evaluation of academic work did not mean that students never studied. Obviously, even maintaining a "C" required that students pay some attention to their studies. Classroom attendance and the associated preparation was still the mainstay of daily life and the structuring activity of university attendance. And as editors reminded readers, participation in activities required a level of scholastic proficiency. Studies were the continuing basis upon which all activities were built. Even fraternities, their eyes firmly riveted on the activities, might pledge a scholarly student for the assistance he could give to his less intellectual brothers and for the effect that his high grades would have on the general academic standing of the fraternity, for fraternities, too, were required to maintain certain academic standards to retain university certification.[16] But the amount of time and serious attention given to academic interests was small. Students usually confined their 35 to 40 hours of studying to four-and-a-half or five days each week. With eight hours to sleep and three for meals and personal duties, an average student had two free days and seven hours left each work day to spend as he pleased. This leisure time was the gift of the young at school; it was time spent in his or her own social world. His academic work was not particularly taxing; duties to home and family were minimal. Assimilating to the world of his peers, not the world of the classroom, determined adjustment to campus life. That adjustment required that he adapt to the standards of his peers rather than to the academic standards set by his superiors. As University of Michigan observer Robert

Work and Play in the Peer Society

Angell noted, "Failure in studies is not as important to college students as failure in social adjustment." Drop-out patterns usually indicated that academic failure was not so frequently the cause for leaving school as were problems of money, health, and social relations. Adjustment to the social norms of the peer society, integration into that society, relationships with friends, and rating with the opposite sex were more important to a youth's sense of stability and fulfillment than academic scales imposed by adult authorities.[17]

Toward the middle of the decade, the belligerently anti-scholastic attitude of the college papers began to give way, but it is doubtful that this reflected a genuine reversal in the campus ethos. Starting at Eastern schools like Cornell and Princeton (where it was often accompanied by an offensive snobbishness and elitism), the new appreciation of intellect spread westward and affected, to a degree, even the most sternly anti-scholastic institutions like Illinois. At this time, too, editors began to attack the once-sacrosanct fraternities. The two were related. But the shift in view often depended on the personal inclination and style of a passing editorial staff, which was checked after a year or two of self-conscious anti-Philistinism. It was a minor ebb in a general current, related to a reaction against the over-emphasis on athletics and activities, and fostered by a spirit of journalistic iconoclasm. Editors were, in part, emulating H. L. Mencken and were probably also affected by the critical spirit of the *New Student,* a radical journal which from its inception in 1922 ceaselessly inveighed against the rah-rah spirit and anti-intellec-tualism of student life.[18] Campus editors now found it more stylish to denounce their readers as boors than to belabor their lack of spirit.

It was not really until the Depression years that a notable change took place and that the esteem previously denied the scholar was more readily granted him. The thirties also saw a decline in fraternity membership and in the influence of frater-nities on campus generally. By 1933, Robert Angell, who had previously described the shallowness of intellectual life at the University of Michigan, was claiming that "all evidence seems to point to a more serious interest in academic work" at that institution, and Dorothy Bromley and Florence Britten, after interviewing students across the country about their sexual behavior, also noted the difference. Well-read students now "enjoy a new prestige, slightly challenging those former campus big men, the athletes and prom leaders." [19]

There were, of course, students in the twenties who took their academic work seriously, but their personal interest was outside the general current of campus approval.[20] The preference and norm on most college campuses was toward maximum exertion in activities and minimum adjustment to academic requirements. Mediocrity was the rule in the classroom, and while leaders of social activities were given prominent coverage in the newspapers and all new fraternity and sorority pledges were duly noted on the front page, the names of Phi Beta Kappa initiates usually found their place in small notices in the back.

The insulation of the campus sheltered youths from family and other adult influences that might have provided a counter to this devaluation of academic achievement. The one adult on campus with whom students came into regular contact and who might have breached the wall of isolation, the professor, was from the first effectively deprived of that role by the devaluation of intellectual pursuits. The professor, unlike a janitor or shopkeeper, was not peripheral to a student's life but ostensibly at the very center. Only in exceptional cases, however, was his real influence more than marginal. For most students, contact with professors was restricted to formalized classroom instruction that lasted for no more than a semester. The student accepted the necessities of that contact but did nothing to cultivate it further.

More important even than the minimal contact was the ethos of hostility toward the faculty. Certainly the structure of academic learning, the limitations of the lecture method, and the

formality of interaction between students and faculty aggravated
a situation that led to fence-building, but the situation seems to
have gone beyond a failure of communications.[21] The anti-
intellectual values of the students resulted in hostility, contempt,
and suspicion toward the faculty, who were characterized by
term like "bone-dry" lecturer and "dry-as-dust pedant." In the
campus ethic, cultivating a relationship with an instructor made
the student vulnerable to the accusation that he did so in order
to raise his grade. In January 1922, the *Daily Illini* observed
that there was suddenly an outcropping of students staying after
class to chat with instructors and that some were even to be seen
going to faculty offices. This despite the constant talk of "poor
relations between instructors and students" and the fact that
they usually "avoid all personal contact." Then noting the approach of final examinations, the editor asserted that "he who
has any knowledge of university ways knows that it is just the
old time game played twice a year just before the end of the
semester in which the student tries to wheedle a better grade
out of his friend instructor." This was not an isolated observation. As Katz and Allport discovered, a very small minority of
Syracuse students considered contact with instructors a vital or
valuable part of their college lives. On the whole, students were
suspicious of those who cultivated faculty members [22] because
such contacts both went against prevailing values and, by in-
troducing adult personalities into a youth world, threatened to
disrupt peer controls.

The potential influence that the professor might have had in
offsetting age-homogeneity on the campus and its consequent
peer pressures was made largely ineffective because it was tabooed by the culture. That proscription helped to insulate the
young from the adults with whom they manifestly shared their
word. Those who were most influenced by professors, like the
so-called "grind," resisted peer pressure and its standards in the
first place and were peripheral to the social world of the campus.
Contact with the faculty might reinforce such individualistic

tendencies, but its power to counteract peer conformity was slight. Thus, in an adult-controlled institution and with a full contingent of adult inhabitants, the young lived in a youth world. The devaluation of intellectual activities and the hostility toward the faculty helped to protect the young from the intrusions of those who governed and controlled it and provided the young with a large margin of autonomy on the campus. Dean Davenport of Ohio State was no doubt correct when he asserted that "whoever believes that the teacher exerts any considerable influence, outside his role as subject-matter instructor, simply does not know the situation." [23]

II

Participation in extra-curricular activities was the critical demonstration of peer group affiliation. It was the measure of group loyalty and the road to achievement. As Vincent Sheean observed, the activities were "the most serious part of life." [24] A youth no sooner arrived on campus than he was informed of his responsibilities: "Participation in a campus activity is working for the University," declared the *Daily Illini:*

> Who hears of a University as having a reputation for the number of hours the students study each day. The youth of America is attracted to a university which has a strong football team, a talented band; a university which has students who are willing to build up its activities, to work for it. If a college has a strong faculty, that is good advertisement among the teaching profession but it has little or no weight with the high school graduate. The candidate for college wants to know what the students are doing.
>
> The average man of whom we are speaking cannot plead lack of time. He knows that the requirement of two and a half hours of preparation for each class is a joke, and that every day he has from three to seven hours to use absolutely as he chooses.[25]

In these "epistles to the freshmen," which filled the pages of student papers at the beginning of each school year and were periodically echoed throughout the year, editors introduced the newcomers to the relative values of their world. The activities, they were told, were necessary for the college and good for the individual. The newspaper harangues were part of a larger process of freshman orientation that acquainted incoming students with campus traditions, values, and behavioral norms.

While most of the class rites had passed from the scene by the twenties, those affecting the freshman tended to persist because they functioned to initiate him into the reality of campus society. As a newcomer, the freshman was not yet molded to the values and behavior patterns that prevailed among the majority of students. He had come from the outside and had to be properly inaugurated into the society of his peers. The UCLA editor appropriately observed that freshmen were "on trial," and had to serve an "apprenticeship," and an Ohio State editor called the freshman regulations "baptismal rites." [26] Of the freshman traditions, however, the most symbolic and effective, hazing, was eliminated at school after school during the twenties, largely because of the many national scandals that resulted from what were often brutal physical trials sometimes resulting in the loss of life, limb, or sight. But hazing was not given over without nostalgia by students who saw that an important method for disciplining freshmen was being lost. "What ever may have been the evils of hazing," observed the editor of the *Illini*, "the supervision of freshmen did exert a powerful influence toward making them careful of their conduct." [27] Some schools compensated by establishing sophomore vigilance committees to supervise freshman conduct, and everywhere editors verbally abused freshmen and warned them to obey rules and regulations.

Still desirable, however, was the discipline that hazing had ensured, and most freshman rules remained for that purpose. Freshman regulations were, according to the *Ohio State Lantern*, like the army, a "powerful democratizing agency," which destroyed individual distinctions and subordinated each man to the purposes of the larger organization. Underlying most freshman regulations were two principles—humility and loyalty. The rules were first to humble the freshman and to impress him with his social insignificance. Freshmen could belong only after they proved themselves worthy through obedience. Second, the rites would foster allegiance to the university. By obeying the rules, freshmen effectively demonstrated what the *Daily Illini* called "a proper realization of their responsibilities as members of the ILLINI tribe." Traditions, according to the *Kansas State Collegian*, made a man "feel he is really a part of the institution." [28]

Three kinds of regulations and rituals were retained to humiliate freshmen and to promote allegiance to the institution. The first of these, the freshman cap bearing the color of the school, was to be worn by freshmen at all times as the stigma of the outsider. The cap thus made the freshman "a marked man," easily identifiable to all members of the community. [29] The cap kept upper-classmen at a distance as it homogenized all freshmen and identified them not as individuals but by their position in the institution. The second freshman rule was the universal taboo on the wearing of high-school insignia. [30] This cut the freshman off from all past associations and all previous positions of prestige and honor, at once stripping him of past loyalties and directing him to a new process of affiliation. He would have to earn his honors by demonstrating new loyalty. It was also a form of humiliation since it stripped the freshman of status and as far as possible of all personal identity. Without insignia, except for the cap, the freshman was reduced to the lowest position in the college hierarchy.

The third freshman rite was the rush, a physical confrontation between sophomores and freshmen, in which one class, usually the sophomores, would emerge victorious because of their spirited and enthusiastic devotion to the class. Although the shell of this rite remained, at most schools it had become a sorry spectacle. Few men seemed interested enough to attend. The rush suffered the fate of most activities that emphasized class rather than school spirit, and it was symptomatic of the decline of class events that in the twenties the freshmen, supposed to be thoroughly humiliated by the spirited sophomores, often won. "In dear dead days," lamented the editor of the *Illini*, "each underclass cherished enmity for the other. Class fights, sack rushes, and pole rushes were the horror of fond parents. Each year sophomores and freshmen spent their time pummeling each other." By the twenties, however, the school and not the class had become the important institution of affiliation, and football, not class fights, symbolized group honor. Increasingly, therefore, freshmen were forced to attend pre-game pep rallies to cheer on the team as a demonstration of their allegiance.[31]

In addition to these formalized rites, each campus had an assortment of regulations emphasizing the freshman's deprivation: prohibitions against using certain walks, congregating at designated areas, or sitting on the senior bench; regulations governing the wearing of privileged apparel like knickers or cords; and more important social prohibitions against dating women, or "queening." As the decade progressed, less attention was paid to these trivial upper-class prerogatives, and fewer restrictions were effectively enforced against freshmen.[32]

Except for social ostracism and the haphazard work of sophomore vigilance committees, however, there were really very few means available to upper-classmen to subjugate freshmen and ensure their loyalty. Unlike fraternities, which could deny a man election, the peer society of the school as a whole could not enforce initiation. Some administrations joined with students to help enforce rules. At Michigan a freshman was dismissed for failure to wear the required cap. But such official support was rare.[33] At one time, hazing had the effect of forcing compliance through physical punishment and strict supervision, but during the twenties, for lack of more effective means, the campus society made sure that the freshmen were at least aware of what was expected. The newspapers, the freshman handbook or "Bible" (note the use of religious terms for peer rituals, "Hell Week," "baptism," "Bible"), sophomore-sponsored "get-wise" sessions, and traditions assemblies introduced the freshmen to their responsibilities.[34]

Ultimately, however, the only effective demonstration of loyalty was involvement in peer-sponsored activities. Activities in the twenties became the real gauge of proper allegiance and the means for affiliation. As the editor of the UCLA newspaper observed, "In exchange for the benefits this university extends, all fair-minded students should feel duty-bound to render service to California wherever and whenever possible." The annual newspaper incantation about "going out for some activity" had appropriately become a basic part of freshman initiation. For behind the veneration of activities in the 1920's was the stress on loyalty to the school, more properly called "school spirit." The *New Student* called it the *"allerhochst gott* of the American College." [35]

As fraternities urged participation in activities for the greater glory of the organization, so all freshmen were urged to participate in extra-curricular activities for the glory of the larger fraternal organization, the school. Activities like athletics were the product of school spirit and demonstrated group morale. It was symbolic of this association between spirit and activities that the Big Ten universities sponsored a competition in 1922 for the one student who was most active in activities. Like athletics— and athletics were of course the most venerated of the activities—extra-curricular affairs were the incarnation of the peer society. Participation demonstrated the loyalty of the individual to his peers and his willingness to do his part in their "work." No one was more condemned than the slacker, or shirker, for involvement in activities was the demonstration of conformity to group norms.[36]

The intense concern with activities and the need for students to join for the sake of joining plagued the campus with a network of criss-crossing organizations that seemed to serve no apparent purpose other than to provide a means for affiliation and fodder for the empty space in the student year book.[37] "We are clubbed to death," noted the editor of the *Daily Illini,* and there were sporadic reactions against the over-organization of the campuses. But the activities had become so important that editors sometimes proposed that activities be accredited and help to fulfill degree requirements or that special grade consideration be given to those students active in student affairs. According to the *Illini,* "Student activities have become such a part of the life of the WORK of a university, that some students who participate expect and reasonably expect, that there should be some recognition for them when the degrees are handed around. They have earned a right to special consideration when the grades are being given out and when the probation lists are being made up. . . . If the University is designed to teach men to think, student activities have a more important part in the curriculum than many of the pipe courses we send our deficient freshmen to register in." [38]

So too, at most schools there was considerable agitation against the probation system that prevented students on academic probation from taking part in activities. Most papers argued that since all students were permitted to attend classes, all students should equally be permitted to take part in the extra-curricular system. The *Cornell Sun* ran a two-week-long campaign protesting the inequities and discriminations of the probation system. Other papers issued similar protests. Activities, students argued, were not detrimental to academic work; on the contrary, they helped to interest and involve students and taught them how to discipline their time. Students on probation would merely waste their time and do no more studying anyway. The opposition to the probation system, like the plea that activities be accredited, suggests how serious extra-curricular work had become in the minds of many. It was, many students believed, equal in value to academic work and should therefore become a legitimate and acknowledged part of a student's experience.[39] Since all students attended classes, they all had the right to participate, a right with which the institution should not interfere.

University administrations, too, were attempting to deal with school activities. Many officials sought to control the tendency of the system to foster over-participation by a few, and at some schools officials instituted a point system which defined how much each student could participate. In such a plan, each kind of office or membership would carry a given number of points, depending on the responsibility and burden of time involved. No student would be permitted to carry more than a certain number of points each semester. Thus the administration would regulate the participation of students in extra-curricular affairs. The point plan was rarely a success, for students resented the interference in their affairs. The law of supply and demand, they argued, should regulate student activities, and students alone should determine the extent of their own participation. University officials should neither demand nor curtail the amount of work that students chose to expend on such functions. "The fact that the responsibility was felt largely to be in the students' hands," argued Frederick Kelly, Dean of Administration at the University of Minnesota, "gave to these activities their greatest value." [40] For the young, the activities were the sphere for demonstrating loyalty. For the administration to force students to participate or deny students the right to determine how much each would participate destroyed the system as a sphere for judging performance. The activities had grown up as students were released from close faculty and administrative supervision and were jealously guarded for the power they gave the young to set peer standards of responsibility and allegiance.

Participation in extra-curricular activities was the rule among students in the 1920's. Although there was some variation by the type of school and by sex and while freshmen participated least, the majority of students were active in at least one or two activities, and some students (disproportionately distributed among fraternity members) were active in many more. The University of Minnesota is a good example of the pattern. In a population of nearly 5000, one-half of all students took part in one or two extra-curricular activities; another 15% were active in three or four, and the most active 5% in five or more. The average male undergraduate in the School of Liberal Arts spent 32 hours each week on activities, while women averaged half that time.[41]

While students everywhere were involved in some extra-curricular activity, those at denominational colleges and women's schools spent less time than those at large coeducational institutions or men's colleges. At women's schools, the average time expended was probably the lowest of all kinds of institutions.[42] At Vassar College, for example, while 90% of the women participated in some activity, the average time spent was only four hours each week. In these generally small schools the variety of activities was usually limited and the demands on students' time reduced. Student newspapers, for example, appeared only once a week at most women's schools, rather than the five to seven times that was general at larger coeducational institutions or men's colleges. More significantly, at women's schools (and for women in general), activities were less a working field for competition and for achieving prominence. There was no interlocking network of activities control and social control, no dominating sports competitions, and often no organized sororities. At men's schools, on the other hand, men vied with one another for positions because they equated success in activities with business acumen and believed that activities developed those qualities which would serve them in later life. At the coeducational schools, women spent about half the time men did and tended to participate in those areas that assisted them in social and dating relationships.[43]

Not surprisingly, while participation was general, at most schools there was an activities elite that included the most prominent men and women on campus. Prominent individuals were often put on committees and in office, "not that they shall work hard in the position, but to give prestige to the committee." [44] Prominent students were heavily fraternity and sorority members who tended to spend a disproportionately large amount of time in activities. This relationship between activities leadership and fraternity membership was recognized at most institutions. Often, editors had to reassure freshmen not selected by fraternities that this did not automatically exclude them from leadership or prominence. In general, non-affiliated students believed they were discriminated against, while fraternity members rarely admitted that such barriers existed. [45] Secure in their own sense of belonging and position, fraternity members found it difficult to understand the sense of exclusion that others might experience.

The perception of inclusion and exclusion is significant. Extra-curricular participation did give most students the critically important sense of affiliation even when they did not achieve prominence. Students who were involved in the extra-curricular system were more satisfied with college, more secure in their sense of belonging, and happier in their social relations than those who did not participate. Students who took part in the activities were both more satisfied with school as a whole and more likely to finish their course of study than those who did not. [46] But while activities gave students a sense of active affiliation, not all activities brought equal prestige and esteem, and the fraternities dominated the most highly desirable areas. Athletic participation was always at the top of the list of approved activities, and it is not surprising that at Minnesota more student leaders participated in athletics than did other students. The student head of the YMCA or YWCA, on the other hand, was rarely equally appraised, and fraternity men and women were less active in church organizations than other students. On many campuses freshmen and sophomores started out actively involved in the Y for its benefits in meeting people and because it provided an easy way to become involved in an activity. But those students who became active in more prestigious activities quickly dropped the Y. Others who did not fare as well remained because of the social opportunities which the Y offered and which non-fraternity members especially could not find as readily elsewhere. Y students and religious students, and activity and fraternity students, usually formed very different groups.[47]

Activities thus at once bound students together by giving them a sense of participation in peer pursuits and at the same time differentiated students and groups into a stratified prestige network. Activities demonstrated loyalty to the peer system, but prominence depended on involvement in an activity in which most students had an abiding interest, like athletics or campus dramatics, or which endowed the participant with power, like student government or the editorship of the student yearbook. The editorship of a usually short-lived literary magazine or leadership of the YMCA did not have these qualities. The literati and religious enthusiasts were too eccentric, too radical, too intensely issue- rather than socially-oriented. It was in the sphere of group spirit and honor and in the subtle arena of congenial group sociability that the peer society bestowed its highest accolades and awarded its most sought-after prizes.

III

The man who has taken no part in the social side of college life usually comes a very long way from having all the characteristics that the world implies in the use of the term "a college man."
Daily Illini, May 19, 1922

The world of youth also had an informal side, a life of entertainment and recreation, of "coking" and "dating," of loafing, gossip, and bull sessions. This third tier of campus activities—perhaps the most engrossing of all in the scale of youth values—included the whole range of leisure activities that punctuated the daily, weekly, and yearly round of campus affairs. This round of leisure gave to the American campus in the twenties its aura of frivolity and indulgence. "As a general rule," Robert Angell observed, "undergraduate life is pleasurable, even at times gay. House parties, 'proms,' and 'bonfire nights' are the most obvious indications of a joyous—I had almost said holiday—spirit." It was the "ocean of frivolity" that had "gained advantage on the shore of the curriculum" and elicited the most adverse criticism from observers of college life and youth generally. To the editorial writer of the *New York Times,* "a college course has come to be regarded largely as affording a leisure residence and for social advantages." [48]

The leisure side of college life was the most fertile arena for evolving mores, values, and interests. Except for parametric rules imposed by the administration, the content of this life and the standards that governed it were determined and regulated by the young. It was here that peers were most autonomous and most instrumental. When an individual broke the informal rules, he ran the risk of ostracism from the society of his peers. The fraternities had the most opportunities and the best means for enforcing group norms, and they usually set the pace for campus social affairs. But fraternity controls were only more ritualized, more explicit, and better publicized than those of other groups, and they are symbolic and illustrative of peer-group interaction generally.

Razzing, for example, formalized in the fraternity, functioned on the campus generally and was especially useful in promoting conformity among green freshmen. The *Colgate Maroon* noted, "Razzing is the official undergraduate nonconformist-recanter. If a freshman is different, razz him. . . . If he doesn't show any spirit, razz him. If he hasn't any brains, razz him. If he has more than he knows what to do with, razz him. If in any particular he is not a regular college man—whatever that is—razz him. Razzing is a good bump reducer when applied in moderation, it makes people watch their step." The "gentle razz" was a common form of social communication. According to the *Daily Illini,* "Let a man wear something peculiar, say something unusual, and the gentle razz is visited upon him. The great college community has one standard of commonplaces, a standard of dress, conduct, and speech, that cannot be departed from without the gentle razz. One's weak points then are unmercifully flaunted in one's face, peculiarities are treated with no respect at all; quickly and clearly they are pointed out to the world at large. . . . It usually works." [49]

Newspapers razzed freshmen unmercifully. They were provincial, stupidly self-assured, gauche in dress and manner, totally ignorant of the ways of the world. Freshmen were admonished that high-school rooting was not the same as college "cheering," that their clothes were the indelible stigma of the newcomer, and they were advised to follow the example of those who knew better.[50] The *Cornell Sun* asserted that the molding of the freshman to the norms of his peers was a basic part of his learning experience: "Any freshman in any university must upon matriculation begin a process of orientation from a nondescript youth into a college student. Consciously or unconsciously, he changes his manner of speech and dress, his standard of values, his ideas and ideals. This, of course, is exactly what should happen during his college career." The *Sun* also recognized that this molding often went too far, well beyond an "improvement in table manners" and "sartorial tastes"; that it tended to force the student into "accepting blindly all the conventional beliefs and opinions that a majority of his fellows" held. The acceptance by freshmen of all the approved norms protected them from the possibility of exclusion: "The simplest way for the freshman to keep from making embarrassing blunders," the Duke *Chronicle* observed, "is for him to try to appear and act in the same manner that the others do; accordingly, he adopts the style of dress of his associates, assumes their mental attitudes as far as possible, cultivates their habits, talks about and tries to become interested in the same things that he hears them discuss, and expressed briefly, he imitates a certain conventional prototype—'the College Man,' as he sees him." [51]

Conformity in attitude and manner propitiated social relations on campus and permitted that congeniality so valued in college life. On the campus, as in the fraternity, students who were personable and could mix easily were liked above all others. "My foremost impression of the American student," a visiting Chinese student observed, "is his ideal of congeniality and his jollity of life. He wants to have a 'good time'; he wishes to be a 'good fellow' . . . his judgment of the men he meets is based on their being or not being 'good fellows.' His ideal is the ideal of good fellowship, and consciously or unconsciously, he models himself accordingly." Personableness and congeniality demanded the renunciation of vigorous personal views or distinctive tastes. Extra-curricular activities were valued in part because they taught a man "how to get along with others." According to the *Daily Illini,* the activity man "can bluff . . . can persuade . . . can compromise," and "get things done. Heaven crown the fellow who can get things done. . . . Let us never forget that it is not the scholar who is to negotiate the daily transactions of the world." So too, social affairs would train a man in those qualities that would make him adjust socially. "Life's biggest problem is to know how to get along successfully with other people," asserted the editor of the *Ohio State Lantern.* "It takes football games, parties, and social contacts to help solve this problem." [52]

It was in the social sphere that peer groups exercised their fiercest control, setting and enforcing norms of conduct and value. Regulations imposed by the administration were hardly effective unless they received the tacit approval of public opinion, and students knew it. "If the 'affairs' pertain to students," asserted the *Cornell Sun,* they should be directed by students. Paternalistic social regulations were resented by students and sometimes greeted by angry student protests. At the University of Wisconsin, for example, women held a mass protest against the University's chaperone requirement. Rutgers College students were enraged when the Dean abolished the Junior Honor Society after students held an Easter weekend dance in violation of college rules, and they asked the administration for his dismissal. Commenting on the incident, the *Cornell Sun* noted that "the event stands out as a most interesting and perhaps healthy indication of student reaction to faculty control." And the Louisiana State *Reveille* applauded when Princeton's Student Council members resigned in protest against the administration's harsh ruling against automobiles on the campus. At Michigan, representatives of 60 fraternities held an indignation meeting and proclaimed that President Little had "overstepped his rights" when he appointed faculty members to police drinking regulations at fraternities. The editor at Ohio State called this "part of a system of paternalism that has never worked and that never will work," and the editor of the *Cornell Sun* protested that "permitting faculty spies to force an entry into a fraternity house at any time they may choose smacks very much of an invasion of the rights of a private citizen." [53]

Student groups and student opinion often sabotaged imposed regulations. If the consensus of opinion in a house or on the campus was against a rule, that rule was almost impossible to enforce. Such resistance usually undermined drinking regulations for men and smoking rules for women during the twenties. At Cornell, the editor of the *Sun* noted, "The matter is for the students to decide . . . from the nature of the case they [university authorities] cannot do much without the support of the students. The faculty can punish offenders, but it can hardly control drinking. . . . The only way in which the situation can be materially improved is by creating a solid opposition on the part of the undergraduates to the misuses of liquor." Administrators knew that substantial drinking took place at the houses and on the campus generally, especially at alumni events like Homecoming, and that fraternity members gave their tacit approval to the practice. But when the administration at the University of Chicago tried to prohibit students from attending out-of-town football games where heavy drinking was known to be common, students openly defied the order and continued attending such games and undoubtedly drinking as well.[54]

Anti-smoking regulations for women were met with similar resistance. At Illinois, sorority women requested rooms on the fire escape, thus conforming to official rules against smoking "in" the house and at the same time indulging the habit with the full knowledge and tolerance of the sorority. There were periodic suspensions of students for drinking and smoking, but all students and officials knew that the problems were widespread and that suspensions did not halt what from the administration's view, though not from the students', were objectionable practices.[55]

Rules requiring chaperones and governing proper dancing form were usually treated in cavalier fashion. Chaperones were invited but conveniently seated in the parlor, superficially engaged in conversation (often the chore of the freshmen), and kept out of sight and hearing of the real activity on the dance floors, entertainment areas, and unlit grounds outside. Such treatment and the slights and open or latent insults chaperones had to endure were a source of constant complaint and contributed to the acknowledged scarcity of chaperones on many campuses.[56] Rules governing curfew hours for women and regulations concerning signing-out procedures fared no better, as residence groups set their own standards and selectively enforced regulations. "As a general rule," observed the editor of the *Illini* in response to new curfew regulations, "attempts to legislate large bodies of people into morality, discretion, or 'goodness' are generally ineffective. People are simply not built in such a docile manner. They will be 'good' as a usual run only after a fashion based on long tradition and popular sentiment. . . . Students often object to being told what they can or cannot do but the majority will not do what is not popular." [57]

With varying degrees of success, students sometimes petitioned authorities for changes in rules they disapproved. A student petition by women at MIT urging that they be permitted to smoke at social functions was successful, but similar requests, which had the overwhelming vote of the student body at Vassar and Wellesley, were turned down. A vote by Yale students calling for the abolition of compulsory chapel attendance was accepted by the administration, but repeated petitions at Princeton were denied. In general, students found it difficult to overcome administrative regulations that concerned such academic matters as probation or easily enforceable rules like those that banned automobiles on campus.[58]

Peer groups also protected individual offenders. Organized groups did this both as a fraternal gesture, protecting their own, and in an effort to shield the group from adverse publicity. Critics of the fraternity system often reserved their severest words for this protection of the individual from the consequences of his behavior. To Clarence Little, President of the University of Michigan, this "pseudo-honor" divided the university into opposing camps, "university officials such as the dean . . . on one side of a fence and they, the students . . . on the other." Little concluded that the "belief of the members of the fraternity in their sacrosanct protection from investigation or interference by college authorities is at the present time so ingrained that it clearly indicates a long standing desire on the part of college executives to 'pass on the other side of the street' rather than to face the unpleasant experience of grappling with the situation."[59]

Student opinion and student leaders could, of course, assist in enforcing regulations. At the University of Southern California, for example, the Student Welfare Committee agreed to cooperate with the administration by refusing to register women who smoked. The women, naturally, were in the best position to know who did or did not smoke, and they thus became a peer watchdog agency. At the University of Missouri, fraternity men, in "collaboration with college officials," abolished drinking when "one member of each organization was appointed to see that prohibition was enforced throughout the school." [60]

The need to work with students in regulating social affairs affected administrative decisions on a host of issues. At Cornell, for example, fearful of a bloody student confrontation with the citizens of Ithaca should the freshman-sophomore rush spill over into the town's streets, the President considered forbidding the event. The editor of the *Sun* warned him to use the power of persuasion and not the fiat of regulation or to suffer the consequences by antagonizing the student body. The President followed his advice and subsequently issued a public expression of thanks for the students' restraint. [61]

Authorities were well aware of their dependence on student opinion. The dean could not personally supervise every student, and even at those functions which were supervised, the young found ready means for circumventing the imposed control. As the Duke *Chronicle* recognized, one of the main reasons for administrative support of student government was "to relieve the dean of some of his most onerous duties in connection with disciplining the students." Officials found it useful and often necessary to work through fraternity leaders and campus influentials in order to mold campus opinion along the lines of university directives. [62] Fraternity groups especially shaped the views and conduct of their members and indirectly that of the campus. At many institutions, the administration supported and encouraged non-fraternity students to organize into small affiliated groups of their own based on residence because such compact groups were useful in regulating social behavior. [63]

The strictly social side of campus life was jealously cultivated by the young for their own uses. Advising students to take care that social life be kept to a reasonable level, the *Cornell Sun* warned that failure to do so might bring that "very unfortunate catastrophe—Faculty Intervention." [64] But those chronicles of student affairs, the newspapers, suggest that such injunctions were rarely heeded, as the young partook in a round of social functions rich in variety and fertile for peer direction.

In contrast to the 1870's and 1880's, when the newspapers were largely literary and except for an occasional athletic event scarcely indicated that the campus had a social side, the newspapers of the twenties noted all the multitudinous weekly social events at the university. They gave expanded coverage to special weeks and weekends, like Winter Homecoming, which was centered on a football contest, and the spring round of celebrations, open houses, and parties that accompanied the Junior Prom. Much of the socializing took place in fraternity houses, but increasingly in the twenties there were more and more opportunities for non-organization students to take part in social events.[65] In addition, "society" affairs like engagements and the social goings and comings of campus notables were assiduously followed.[66] The opening of the school year usually brought a rash of engagement and marriage notices, and the selection of beauty queens, Nile queens, rose buds, and representative women were prominently featured in the early spring. These "honorary" selections were often accompanied by acrimony and vigorous political contention as group vied with group to have one of their own chosen. Notices of the opening of campus productions, plays, masques, operas, and sings, and the accompanying rave reviews, were a regular feature of the campus news.

The University of Wisconsin was reported to have hosted 30 college dances and 80 fraternity and sorority dances each month in 1925. At Michigan, women attended an average of eleven social affairs per month and men an average of nine. More than one-half of all Minnesota students reported attending dances and parties on a regular basis, and at Chicago only one in eight women and one in four men took no part in the social affairs of the campus. Most students at Chicago spent between one and five hours each week in formal social occasions like dances, parties, and dates, but almost half spent considerably more than five hours at such functions. Most students, organized or not, were involved in social affairs. At Ohio State, a survey by the *Lantern* found that the sign-out sheets at the women's dormitory showed that "Ohio State girls are no stay-at-home, play-at-home, eight o'clock, sleepy-time girls." The average coed went on dates four nights a week, and the more popular had a date every night of the week. Women at Northwestern University made a pact to have a certain number of dateless nights every week in order to have time to do some studying,[67] which suggests both how engrossing and time-consuming the social life of a student could be and how sharp the competition for popularity. All had to agree so that no one girl might get a competitive edge.

On the whole, women were more active in social activities than men and invested them with more significance. Men dominated the activities, women the social functions. At Syracuse, women designated "daily social contacts" as the single most important part of their college experience.[68] So too, students at certain divisions of the university were more active in social affairs than students at other divisions. This was true of schools like Home Economics and Business, while much less common at professional schools like Engineering or Science.[69] Both business and home economics were new divisions in the academic world and enrolled students who prior to the rush to college in the 1920's would probably not have attended the university at all. Women too, had only recently become a familiar addition to most large universities. The relative rise in importance of social as distinct from strictly academic concerns was certainly related to the founding of such divisions and the general expansion of education to a new and diverse population. They provided, within the arena of the university, the opportunity for attendance and peer exposure of large numbers of only semi-academically oriented youths. The academic world had become a world full of fresh faces and new goals. Whatever the utilitarian or democratic intentions of college expanders, the effect for the young had at least as much to do with providing an arena for peer socialization as it did for specific vocational education.

Social events were, of course, a beehive of sexual introductions. "When planning their houses," observed the *Daily Illini,* "most of the fraternities thought first of the facilities for social functions and secondly of conditions conducive to study." And an *Illini* correspondent noted, "It is coming to the point where the ideals and purpose of college life are being lost sight of in the senseless rivalry of competitive swagger." Much of the rivalry and swagger was meant to attract and impress eligible members of the opposite sex. All campuses were alive with peer norms and controls that mediated the relations between men and women, as youths engaged in the complexities of a "rating-and-dating" system that separated the attractive from the homely, the smooth from the crude, the good from the bad. In that game, houses, like clothes, played their vital part, and the maintenance of a high social rating was one of the assets of fraternity membership.[70]

Fraternity and sorority affiliation helped facilitate the introduction of individuals to "proper" members of the opposite sex. Fraternity house parties, mixers, receptions, and dinner dances were almost always closed affairs to which only other fraternities and sororities were invited. The organizations thus provided occasions for sexual introductions unavailable to non-affiliated students. But they provided more—a distinctive cachet. Members of sororities and fraternities in general and members of the most prestigious organizations in particular were well known as the most eligible and desirable partners in the campus social round, and organizations were careful that new members uphold their image as attractive dates. The cycle reinforced itself. One had a social reputation by belonging to a certain group long before one had a personal identity.[71]

To protect their carefully cultivated reputations, fraternity brothers tutored new members in the social graces, the proper clothes, appropriate "lines," the right manners, and the latest dance steps. Fraternities also directed their members to associate only with individuals of comparable status. Not only was it usually taboo for fraternity or sorority members to date those not in organizations, but within the fraternity nexus the object was to date members from the most elite groups. After visiting sororities on a large number of campuses, one investigator concluded, "In the majority of institutions I have visited, members of the older fraternities and sororities look down on members of the newer ones; which, within fraternity circles, and in college parlance, do not 'rate,' while sorority girls will not go out with non-fraternity men, nor will fraternity men 'date' non-sorority girls." One girl at a Midwestern institution explained that she had been " 'Put on the carpet' " by her sorority sisters for going out with a non-fraternity man and had finally decided to give up the relationship because "it wasn't worth all the row." [72]

Success with the opposite sex also enhanced an individual's standing in the eyes of his peers, and dating associations facilitated contact with members of one's own sex. As one fraternity guidebook advised members, "You should date good-sorority women in preference to non-organization women . . . because one acquaintance at a sorority house leads to an acquaintance with the rest of the group . . . who are probably congenial to the members and whom you feel free to invite to our parties . . . and you meet men there from other fraternities who are likely to be the right sort." Well might the *Daily Illini* remind readers that "A man can never escape the consequences of his selection of associates. . . . A man is judged by his companions and his organizations." [73]

By the 1920's, sex had become an important feature of campus affairs, and peers restricted associations, directed introductions, and set elaborate criteria for behavior, selection, and propriety. Fraternity and sorority groups had a specific reputation to uphold and set standards most rigorously, but the peer associates of non-organized students had the power to supervise and censure the relations of friends as well. A subtle and precarious social game was played out on most campuses. Organized groups played the game most avidly, but others too were involved in a race for dates, contacts, prestige, and competitive popularity.[74]

In that game, visibility was important. Certain events and places were the feeding ground of campus reputations. Notable among these were athletic events, campus hangouts like favored coke and ice-cream parlors, downtown pastry shops, certain cinemas, and special galas like the Sophomore Cotillion and above all the Junior Prom. The lavish University of Wisconsin Prom, which had dominated the newspaper for weeks, prompted the editor of the *Daily Illini* to observe that students too easily forget that "real success is hardly built upon foundations of polished hardwood floors." The event occasioned "no end of press-agenting of the 'great men and great women' who head committees and lead great marches," and "trumpets the social elite as the personification of achievement." The prom usually took weeks to prepare for, weeks to recuperate from, and thousands of inches of newspaper copy to document.[75] It was a veritable orgy of self-advertisement for campus personalities.

A position on the Prom Committee was a position of power because its members determined ticket distribution. As only a fraction of the junior class at most large institutions could attend, prestigious upper-classmen wielded great social power in drawing up the priority lists. Scandals over the unfair distribution of tickets occurred annually. The usual system was to reserve tickets to certain groups, often as payment for past favors, and to leave a token number for public distribution by lottery or on a first-come-first-served basis. At Illinois, after a year of protesting the political nature of ticket allotment, the newspaper finally denounced the totally democratic lot system that took its place because when the system operated on a purely chance basis it excluded most of the campus notables. The prom lost its glamor. In response, campus leaders organized a counter-prom that received the paper's support and turned out to be a great success. The glory of the official prom, probably the most important social event in undergraduate life, was considerably diminished.[76] The next year, a method was devised whereby a considerable portion of the tickets was once again set aside for preferential distribution.

Athletics were also a regular part of college life in the 1920's. At Chicago, only one-fifth of all students (17.8% of the men) reported spending no time as spectators at athletic events in the fall (football) semester. The vast majority of all students spent two or more hours regularly attending an average of one athletic competition each week. During the winter, attendance was somewhat lower, although still considerable, with 40% of all students and almost one-half of all men attending as spectators at one game each week. Attendance at athletic events was always large and enthusiastic for sports competitions were an institutionalized way of life. Athletics, like few other things in the twenties, kindled the fire of youthful enthusiasm.[77]

The existence of a variety of on-campus affairs helped to insulate the young from outside influences. Social affairs were youth affairs. There were also occasions and diversions that took the young away from the campus, but rarely did these significantly infringe on the peer group. Many were incursions on the specific isolation of a campus rather than events that exposed the young to adult institutions or influences. Such an occasion occurred when students traveled together *en masse* to an athletic competition at another school, a familiar event during the twenties, especially at Midwestern universities. Special trains were often engaged as whole caravans of students descended on a sister institution. In 1923, 4000 students out of a total of 8000 at Illinois went with the team to a game at Northwestern. Some students with meager means devised creative methods to go along, hoboing in boxcars or hiding in sleeping compartments.[78]

A similar occasion was the weekending habit that prevailed at uni-sex schools. This had been a feature at men's schools like Princeton and Harvard before the twenties, when eligible young men were invited to society affairs in the cities of New York, Boston, and Philadelphia to meet proper women or to make business contacts. During the twenties, the weekend habit took on epidemic proportions and became a regular part of the routine at women's schools as well.[79] While forays into society and well-appointed salons were still a part of the routine, more and more men went to women's schools and women to men's schools rather than to the homes of the parents. The *Princetonian* noted, "The railroad conductors are much busier than professors with students over the weekend. . . . The students no longer look forward to a weekend with friends at Princeton as they used to. They are much more interested in establishing friendly relations with Vassar, Bryn Mawr and Spence." The *Princetonian* also regularly welcomed contingents of weekending women, usually from women's schools, to the campus at the time of special social events.[80]

Women's school administrators were especially alarmed at the proportions the habit was taking. Some declared that the schools were nearly emptied each weekend. At one women's college, a senior claimed that 30 to 40% were absent every weekend. At another, an official noted that in a school of 2000 women, 15,000 weekend absence applications had been approved in three months since November.[81] As might be expected, the most active weekenders were the most social and prestigious in the campus society.

The effect of such athletic and social cross-pollination between schools and peer societies was to break down some of the provincialism of individual campuses. As significantly, the influence was contained completely within the age category, for the migration was not only to other youth centers but often in groups, a phenomenon that might best be described as taking the peer group along to a different location. The same situation

characterized the frequent inter-university conferences that occurred throughout the decade. There were conferences on athletics, journalism, curriculum, student government, politics,
and religion.[82] They provided occasions for exchange of ideas
and views, exposure to fads, collegiate mannerisms, slang, reading, and leisure enthusiasms—all within the age-group. In a
sense, the conferences provided occasions for contact between
groups and for the development of a nationwide and homogenized peer culture. The exchange of student newspapers and the
growth of a national student newspaper, the *New Student,* with
the specific aim of fostering "national student consciousness,"
also helped to break down localism and made students aware of
events and interests at other institutions. Every newpaper carried notices of activities at other schools; some set aside special
columns for this purpose. The growth of intercollegiate conferences and the beginnings of intercollegiate student federations
in the 1920's [83] were the result as much as they were the cause
of increased student interest in the common concerns of youths.
While the importance of a general youth subculture should not
be overestimated, there existed during the twenties a vital interest
among youths in what others were doing, thinking, and wearing, a breaking down of parochial patterns, and an identification with and sensitivity to youth as a special group, all of
which suggests youth solidarity and verges on "youth consciousness."

Students also partook as individuals and in groups in commercial recreations like movies and vaudeville shows, downtown
dances and restaurants that abounded in college towns. Advertisements for these amusements and notices and reviews were
prominently featured in the campus papers. The number of different theatrical and cinema events in the twin towns of Cham-
paign-Urbana in which the University of Illinois is located
was astonishing. City enterprisers had obviously found a lucra-
tive market in the college community. Most students regularly
attended one movie per week, and students were especially in-

terested in the personalities, tastes, and interests of movie stars who were given full coverage in columns, reviews, and interviews.[84]

Some schools, like Illinois, were hard-pressed to provide the large and growing student population with campus diversions, and the campus population frequently spilled over into town areas in search of amusements, just as it was forced to utilize town housing facilities. This fact did not go unnoticed or uncriticized by both officials and students. Students called for more on-campus mixers and dances, and editors urged students to patronize those campus events that were available in preference to town amusements.[85] At Illinois, as elsewhere, attempts to organize non-fraternity students into affiliated units were in part based on students' desires for such units to serve as a basis for campus entertainments. The move was encouraged by the administration as a means for keeping students on campus.[86]

On the whole, college officials sympathized with the desire for more campus social events. By keeping students away from nearby towns they avoided friction with town police and prevented town-and-gown incidents, which continued to flare throughout the decade. More important, by keeping students on campus, officials could maintain some supervisory power over the social lives of the young. They could set rules and regulations and not lose their charges to the lures and anonymity of road houses and downtown dances. Throughout the twenties, officials encouraged more and more on-campus events, and by the thirties "the college . . . had gone into direct competition with the out-of-town weekend, the road house, and the night club for its students' leisure time." [87] Despite these efforts and despite the growing abundance of campus affairs, however, students still sought off-campus events and usually found them.

Perhaps above all, the campus provided ample time for informal peer contacts in just "loafing and fooling around." Students were enthusiastic players of bridge and mah jongg (recently introduced) and listened avidly to the radio and the phonograph.

These diversions, incalculable in terms of time, were certainly important and conducive to peer interaction. It was during the time "wasted" as well as the time spent in activities, dates, and social events that college-going provided the occasion for peer grouping and peer influence. These diversions were frequently singled out by students as the most edifying aspects of student life. Non-activities, including bull sessions and gab sessions, marked the life of all residence units, fraternities, dormitories, and even rooming houses.[88] Intense group life existed in many different settings, and Robert Angell was surprised to discover "closely knit groups in rooming houses, not unlike fraternities in their sense of comradeship." For non-residents, day-to-day interaction was more circumscribed. But any ongoing social group, given time and occasion, including those of commuting students, provided opportunities for informal interaction. The campus provided both the setting and the opportunity at cafeterias, on the lawn, in the libraries, at tea rooms, in lounges, in automobiles, and even on the buses that brought the young to and from the campus.[89]

IV

Although circumscribed by rules and regulations imposed by the administration, the campus peer groups and the peer society as a whole were able to carve out a sphere of peer control and direction within the universities and colleges of the twenties. Peer conventions and evaluation of performance and behavior had become a significant influence in the lives of college youths. By devaluating academic achievement and honoring the activities that were peer-controlled, the peer system assumed the task of evaluating responsible performance among its members. Peer groups and the social leaders of the campus could be used and were used by officials to direct and control the young. But by that very dependence on peer sanction, the administration was forced to circumscribe its own power. The peer society was certainly not free of adult supervision and control, but it had substantial power in the twenties to mediate relations among the young and between youths and adult authority.

But self-contained and insulated as the peer society on the campus of the twenties often was, many youths maintained their association with that society only briefly. The number of students who dropped out annually was very large, and on the whole, only about one-third of all students who entered colleges and universities in this period would graduate. The precise proportion varied by institution. At Dartmouth College in 1925, only 35% of the entering freshmen did not graduate, and at Vassar 27.8%. But at the University of Chicago, 60% of the freshman class never made it to commencement. The highest casualty rate occurred after the freshman year, followed by that after sophomore year; it fell precipitously thereafter.[90]

It is difficult to know the combination of factors that led an individual to leave. It seems likely, however, that the very factors that were counter-pressures to the peer culture also increased the likelihood the individual would leave school. Thus factors like working, commuting, and the location of the school in a big city were among the most prominent causes for dropping out. The potential infringers on peer influence were thus real causes for peer-group disruption. They created a strain in orientations and institutional pressures. Those schools with large portions of the student population exposed to such pressures, like Chicago, had the highest dropout rates. Moreover, it is clear that academic failure alone was rarely the cause for leaving school, nor the most important single factor. Rather financial difficulties, lack of adjustment to college life, and failure to gain social recognition were major reasons for withdrawal. At Chicago, less than one-fifth of the freshmen who withdrew after the first year were dropped for poor grades.[91]

Given the high dropout rate, one is left with the difficult problem of assessing how effective the peer society could have been in socializing the young. The problem is aggravated by the fact that most of the dropouts were still green, that is, they had not been long exposed to the peer system. In fact, their lack of adjustment to that society was a major cause for leaving. In many ways, however, the problem is a false one. The peer society formed at the universities and colleges was only one among many. It has been examined here in depth because it was in many ways a model with clear-cut mechanisms of peer control. Many of the influences that have been called infringers on peer-group containment were the normal influences to which most youths were exposed. They are, after all, the usual institutions which affect the individual as he matures. It is clear, however, that these influences were subordinated to that of the peer society if and when it was powerful enough to be the primary institution at a certain period of life. In that sense, the college has served as the ideal case, sheltering the young from normal exposures and thus permitting the full impact of peer life to be explored. Undoubtedly, this "false" environment has accentuated the influence of peer associations. But one should bear in mind that college was becoming more common for youths in the twenties and that high school had become a normative experience. The increasing exposure to peer groups in insulating school environments had, in fact, become the trend for the young in the twentieth century, and the high school did to a lesser extent for the many what colleges were doing for the few. For unlike the colleges which, though expanding, were still reserved for a socially and economically privileged group, the high school could no longer be so defined. And high schools, by intensifying age-group exposure and age-group consciousness, both facilitated the homogenization of diverse populations and isolated the young from adult institutions. It is, in fact, in the nature of modern educational environments to do this, for they institutionalize the peer group and help solidify their mechanisms of control.

Prior to the twentieth century, high-school enrollment was

limited to a small, elite portion of the American population and attendance was usually reserved to those preparing for college and professional schools. But the first two decades of the century brought a major reorganization of educational institutions. High schools and newly formed junior high schools became institutions for the mass of the youth population as the age limit for compulsory school attendance was extended to older and older ages and child labor laws forced hitherto working youths into the schools. The increase in attendance at high schools in the first three decades of the twentieth century was nothing less than spectacular. By the early 1930's, 60% of America's youths of high-school age were in school. The retention of students by the schools also increased—the number of youths who entered and remained to graduate increased by more than 100% between 1924 and 1934. More youths were going to and staying in school.[92]

The opening up of the schools resulted in a massive exposure to adolescent peer groups. Unlike the college, however, the world of the high school was more circumscribed by adult supervision and regulation from within and from without the school, for the influence of peers was under constant and powerful pressure from competing institutions. Whereas in the ideal self-contained college community the peer society was the primary and dominant one for the mass of students, in the high school the school peer group was one of a number of competing influences.[93] The family was, of course, primary among these, and for the high-school youth the family did not so much check the peer group as it was itself checked by peer associates. Additionally, prior peer associations in the community—church groups, clubs like the Scouts, the childhood gang—were still present in the individual's environment and remained potential sources of influence and orientation. Some, like the gang and club associates, were partly incorporated into the social environment of the high school and reinforced the influence of the school. Others remained outside and, depending on their importance, like the family, competed for the attention of the young. Any new influence emanating from the high school had to operate on already established and ongoing relationships.

The high school did, however, largely eliminate what, next to the family, had been the most important adult institution—work. School replaced work and became, after the family, the primary institution of orientation, absorbing more and more time and attention. The school significantly affected youth in two ways: by removing them from the adult labor market and by increasing the exposure to peers.

Except for the negligible number who attended elite boarding schools, peer-group influence was mitigated at most high schools because they were not residential and the young continued to live with their families in the home community. Unlike those in colleges, students in high schools lacked an abundance of leisure time at school. Much more of the in-school time was consumed in required classroom attendance; less was self-determined and spent in unsupervised peer activities. There was less time for clubs, and the time available was delegated to a specific, structured time-slot during the day. There was also much less time for the leisure pursuits of mixing, conversation, coking, and general loafing. When these activities did take place, they did so outside the school and usually in an atmosphere of potential family veto. High-school youths did have after-school leisure; and this extra dividend of school attendance further accentuated peer influence among non-working youths.

While high-school youths participated in a wide range of extra-curricular activities, they were far less meaningful than those in college. In the twenties, school administrators and educational theorists looked positively on such activities, which they felt could direct and channel excessive adolescent energy. A major proponent of extra-curricular activities, Elbert Fretwell, believed they were the "most useful tools for that adaptive, directive, and corrective training of youth which it is now conceived to be the function of the school to provide." The activities were fostered as a field for "learning by doing," according to what was popularly understood to be Dewey's injunction. In line with a new and "better understanding of the psychology of adolescence," when "the rule of the group tends to become the rule for the adolescent," officials expected that activities would allow them to "stimulate and repress and to guide and direct these adolescent tendencies." [94] Students were thus not only encouraged to participate, but frequently bullied into participation.

The extent of student participation in high-school activities, duly recorded in a host of studies in the twenties,[95] must therefore be viewed with a proper skepticism, for they are not a good measure of student interest or in any sense a good indication of the function of the activities in the peer system. Activities in the high schools could not, by their nature, play the part they did at college, because they were neither initiated nor controlled by the young. Rather than serving as an arena for real expenditure of energy or for establishing norms of work, the activities provided the occasion for clique meetings and a ground for the expression of already formed friendship networks. Adult supervision and control undermined the potential for peer direction and approval, and as a result the young retreated to their own informal groups for self-expression. It is one of the ironies of modern educational policy that as educators recognized the potential for social learning implicit in the peer group, the young were increasingly denied the freedom that made peer activities important to them. The school thus at once opened the possibility for peer interaction and at the same time denied the young the fruits of the new opportunities.

The society of the high school was also far less well-defined than that of the college. Not only did students lack control over activities, but high schools did not have an inner core of organized students with a disproportionate control over activities and social affairs and the accompanying prestige and influence. High-school fraternities had been specifically outlawed in 17 states and by innumerable local school districts. Although Massachusetts passed such a ban as early as 1909 and Mississippi in 1912, most states and local districts enacted the legislation between 1919 and 1922. The explicit reason for the prohibition was that fraternities were undemocratic, excluding many from the privileges of the few. Actually, most officials feared their secrecy would not permit adequate supervision by adults. It was usually alleged that such secret organizations fostered sexual "immorality," encouraged alcoholic drinking, and were concerned with the social side of life only. "Any system that makes paramount the decisions of immature minds on questions of social and other distinctions, is in my opinion radically vicious," declared one Massachusetts school principal.[96] This fear of peer self-determination was the other side of the coin to the thinking that encouraged high-school extra-curricular activities. Educators sought to bring youths' interests out into the open and to expose them to the guiding light of adult authority.

Despite the laws and the fact that school officials were on the alert to weed out the secret organizations, high-school fraternities remained a problem throughout the twenties. Their illegality and secrecy makes it difficult to assess their importance in the social affairs of the high school. They necessarily held meetings outside of school on their own time and in the shadow of anonymity, but the flavor of intrigue and secrecy and the dangerous excitement of the illicit may have made them and their members very influential in the informal social world of the high school. Because of their inherently social orientation, it is likely that most were made up of just those students interested in social affairs, the social leaders. Whatever their informal influence, however, they could not control the life of the high school in the same way that college fraternities controlled that of the college. The fraternities were, therefore, no different from other youth gangs and groups that had a special sense of group identity and practiced their own variety of secret ceremonial. They were, however, more oriented toward college life and manners, which they consciously imitated, than other groups.[97]

Having deprived youths of their control of clubs and denied them the right to fraternity organization, school officials also attempted to lay claim to the informal social and recreational activities of the young in order to train them in "the right social standards." Educators asserted that schools should take "a much larger responsibility" in order to "aid in the integration of the boy and society through more adequate social education." The same was, of course, at least as true for the girl. Dancing, so much prized by the young, was to be an especially appropriate means for this "social engineering." "The formal dances," one high-school educator noted, "offer an exceptional opportunity for training." [98]

How important various school social occasions like dances, teas, and mixers really were is hard to say. It is possible that they were conduits for setting examples in conduct, manner, and style by popular students. They had the potential for homogenizing social standards and spreading the influence of popular school groups to the students as a whole. Since they were intended to provide an arena for teaching proper social behavior, there is some question, however, about whose standards were being advertised. Were they really occasions for spreading peer values or merely occasions for consciously demonstrated adherence to adult-approved norms? This is not to say that they may not have been very effective in diffusing adult standards but rather that an official dance may not have reflected the real views of a high-school peer group. It is possible, of course, that the young were pliable enough or dependent enough to adopt adult regulations as their own, but this seems unlikely. The very fact that administrators were so much concerned about controlling peer activity and so much afraid of unsupervised groups suggests that the standards of the young differed from their standards. Even the most sanguine school organizer was by no means certain that a social program carried out under the direction of the school would eliminate "sporadic outside organizations which often run under little or no control." [99] Teachers and deans generally were haunted by a specter of *sub rosa* youth life that was probably far worse than the reality.

The schools did attempt to manipulate peer pressures in the service of adult standards. One example is the dress regulations passed by Lakewood High School (Ohio). Sponsored by the Girls Student Council, a girls' social organization made up of prominent women at Lakewood, the following pledge to avoid "extravagant and extreme dress" was distributed:

> That we, the girls of Lakewood High School, bar from school dress the following: georgette, net, silks, velvet, silk hose, French heels, transparent sweaters worn without waists, rouge, lip stick, eyebrow pencil, and any inappropriate wearing apparel.
>
> Furthermore the Council recommends: middies and skirts of modest length and fullness, sweaters worn with waists, plain serge, gingham and jersey dresses, and a minimum of simple inconspicuous jewelry, and simple arrangements of hair.
>
> A girl who can carry out these regulations will be regarded as a satisfactory pupil. [100]

The pledge was to be signed by the girl and her parent.

One cannot know, of course, how effective this officially underwritten statement was in promoting the wearing of middies, serge, and gingham, but one can be quite certain that there was much peer-pressure toward wearing precisely those articles interdicted, or else the statement would have been gratuitous. The standards of the peer group were obviously having an influence on the women in dress and habits, an influence that alarmed school officials. As with college students, one is permitted to wonder how interested the ordinary high-school girl was in being a "satisfactory pupil" rather than a "regular" friend. Not the least interesting aspect of the letter is the fact that it was prominently published in the *Year Book of the National Association of Secondary School Principals* as an example for other school officials. There was an obviously recognized need among officials to encourage peer groups to check unofficial peer influence.

Deprived of the circumstances that made for the continuous pressure of daily living experience, circumscribed by school officials, and lacking a tight, well-organized central social core, the high-school peer society was school-linked but not school-centered. The high school was, above all, a meeting-ground for loosely composed networks of friendship groups, sometimes based on residential proximity, often a carry-over of previously established relations, and more frequently the result of contacts made at school.

Like a clearing-house, the high school integrated small friendship groups into a large youth society, breaking down local patterns, setting up competition between groups, and facilitating wholesale imitation. High-school students had enormous amounts of free time during the day and evening to spend in non-study activities with friends. Middle-class youths in the twenties were released from stringent parental supervision and from complex home responsibilities and given considerable latitude in how and with whom they could spend their time. While the family released the young and the school freed them from work, instruction occupied only a part of the day. It can be safely assumed that most of the free afternoons and evenings were spent by the young with their peers. This provided rather a wide area for peer-group interaction and influence. Some of this time was spent in supervised activity in community centers and clubs, but by the twenties such activity had declined in importance among older adolescents. Supervised play was replaced among fifteen- and sixteen-year-olds by informal peer activities, especially those concerned with the opposite sex, including formal dates and ad-hoc socializing. While school dances provided a limited number of occasions for such interactions, most of it was done outside school on their own time and free of supervision.[101]

Besides dances and parties, other occasions for socializing

were movies and auto-riding. These modern amusements took youths from the home and club where they might ordinarily have been forced to spend their time and put them very much on their own. Most investigations showed that youths in every social class attended at least one movie per week. Next to dancing, the activity that alarmed school officials and parents most was motoring. During the twenties, riding with friends became a major form of entertainment. At college, automobiles on campus were a bone of contention between students and officials. Among high-school youths, they were often the battleground between parents and children. Whatever their effect on family life, which is not at all clear, cars were a popular amusement for the young, and motoring gave them an opportunity for peer-group isolation. More than 40% of one sample of California high-school boys had the use of the family car whenever they wished, and almost one-quarter owned their own. As might be expected the proportion having unlimited access to the automobile increased with high-school grade. Less than one-third of these youths never had the use of the car. But this deficiency was readily made up by friends who would take them along. Women especially were able to rely upon men for their rides. According to one Middletown parent, "Our daughters [eighteen and fifteen] don't use our car much because they are always with somebody else in their car when we go out motoring." [102] The automobile was a mobile meeting place for the young.

While the high school was not the locale for most informal peer occasions, it mediated group relations and contacts and was a rich source for dating associations. Just as important, it was a medium through which the standards and behavior patterns of one group were spread to others in a snow-balling process of imitation and emulation. One had to appear acceptable to a wider network of acquaintances and potential friends. The broadening effect of the school environment and social orientation of the high school was quite visible to the Lynds in Middletown: "A fifteen-year-old son, wise in the ways of his world, protested to his mother because his sister of fourteen in the eighth grade wore lisle stockings to school: 'Well, if you don't let her wear silk ones next term when she goes to high school,' was his final retort, 'none of the boys will like her or have anything to do with her.' " The peer pressure for conformity also makes understandable the story of the Middletown girl from a working-class home who left high school rather than appear inappropriately dressed according to the standards set by the more affluent students. The high-school peer network set very clear standards of acceptability and served to increase conformity in consumer tastes in line with the effect of fads and rapid fashion changes.[103]

At the same time that it broadened the group to which one had to appear acceptable, the high school, like the college, narrowed the category of people who mattered in this consideration. The high school, by occupying the largest portion of the individual's time and dominating his daily attention, oriented youth largely to each other and cut the young off from the influences of adult patterns. The school intensified the experience of a youth world. The school became a substitute for work. But unlike the working world, school was youth-oriented. And because the school was the major occupation for the individual, it served as a gauge for the evaluation of his non-school activities and provided a base for opposition to parental demands and standards. That "everyone" at school did something, or believed something, or wore something became a legitimate criterion for evaluating one's own behavior. "I've never been criticized by my children until these last couple of years since they have been in high school," lamented one Middletown mother. Now, she complained, both her son and daughter were telling her, "But, Mother, you're so old-fashioned." [104] The high school was a reference point larger and more powerful than a friend or a group of friends. Children in grade schools undoubtedly did this too, but the grade school was smaller and more local than the high school, more community-based. Moreover, the degree of freedom granted the younger child was narrower than that given the adolescent. The parent was less willing to be bullied. The high school broadened horizons and extended the length of time during which the young were subjected to the daily influence of their peers.

High schools as well as colleges were thus crucial to the new patterns of youth socialization. They substituted youth centers for work centers, intensified age homogeneity, exposed youths to broader influences than home and local community, and provided the facilities and occasions for the homogenization of behavior and beliefs through peer-imposed conformity. At a critical juncture when a young man or woman prepared for an independent adulthood, the schools exposed him to peers rather than to adults. These four, five, or even eight years occupied a pivotal period in the life of an individual. Increasingly, the idea of patterning his life upon that of mother or father or of stepping immediately into the responsibilities of job performance receded into the depths of childhood imagination as the youth stepped further into the society of his peers and remained there for longer and longer periods of his life.

But for what were his peers preparing him? As we have seen, college students were sheltered from even the most immediate values which governed the adults of his world—dedication to scholarship and intellectual achievement. The young quite consciously insulated themselves from these adult models. In good part, the values of the youth world were those necessary for the reciprocal needs of group survival and individual security: loyalty, mutual protection, group identification, and harmony through conformity. Peers were jealous masters who sought so to connect individual habits to group standards that while the individual was sacrificed to the group, the autonomy of the peer group permitted both the group and the individual to resist internal dissension and adult penetration.

But the values peers enforced went beyond specific interests of the short-lived and carefully stabilized unit and had more long-run personal and social consequences. Many of these values grew from the leisure which the young enjoyed in abundance, and many were directed toward the approved consumption of leisure time—sports, dates, sociability, and congeniality. Qualities of personality, appearance, and style were crucial to these pursuits, and peers both valued and emulated them. The campus peer society also subscribed to specific work values: aggressive and directed competition, merit through association, and a carefully calibrated system of prestige. While these values served group and inter-group ambitions, they also bound the young into the larger social culture. For as they served their immediate interests, peers were ultimately directing the young to future adult roles and expectations as consumers, mates, workers, and citizens. In carving out a sphere for peer autonomy within an adult world, the young were themselves being introduced to a new society.

PART II

PART II

FLAPPERS & PHILOSOPHERS

This is the world: the lying likeness of
Our strips of stuff that tatters as we move
Loving and being loth;
The dream that kicks the buried from their sack
And lets their trash be honoured as the quick.
This is the world. Have faith.

For we shall be a shouter like the cock,
Blowing the old dead back; our shots shall smack
The image from the plates;
And we shall be fit fellows for a life,
And who remain shall flower as they love,
Praise to our faring hearts.

Dylan Thomas, "Our Eunuch Dreams"

5

Competition and Conformity
in the Peer Culture

We are radical—we youths. We are experimenting with life. We are radical in the sense that we are dissatisfied with some existing conditions in the world, and we want something done about it. We are radical because we disavow the old-time proprieties. We are living in a world of confusion and excitement, and we are radical because in a world dominated by machines, a world of naturalistic science and psycho-chemico-libido psychology, it is fun to be radical. . . . Those who do understand, who do share the spirit of the day, and are able "to translate timeless truths into terms of TODAY" we welcome and upon them we throw a great responsibility and a great opportunity. They will discover that we are not so radical but that we have very few convictions about anything.

Cornell Sun, February 4, 1927

Modern youth is wild and reckless and radical, we are so often told that we have almost come to believe it. Perhaps it isn't so. Perhaps it is only that the world changes, that everybody of our time is a little different from those of any other era, that youth shares in the difference instead of standing still. And after all, it is probable that the changes are not as considerable as some of us hope and others of us fear. Modern life is like the ocean—a lot of lashing and lather on the surface with miles of unmoved depths below.

Duke *Chronicle,* April 27, 1927

When the editor of the *Cornell Sun* proclaimed the radicalism of youth, he carefully defined it in historical (not political) terms as the adjustment of values and habits to contemporary conditions. Simple as that definition seems, it was in fact the vital clue to the significance of these middle-class students of the twenties. In linking the plasticity of youth to the transformational quality of the era, the *Sun* rightfully insisted on the plural "we." For only as group rather than as individual experience did the uncertainty and malleability of youth become a socially effective instrument. Group controls bound the individual to a historical process as college youth in the 1920's were drawn by peers into a strong and directed current of change.

Peer groups and the college peer society operated on two distinct levels. First, as primary units of affiliation, they fulfilled individual emotional needs for security and identity. Second, as didactic instruments, they monitored responsible social behavior. That behavior was responsible insofar as it was sanctioned by the society of peers, but it was also socially responsible because peers inducted youths into larger social realities. It was in this capacity that the college peer society became a truly radicalizing phenomenon that helped to press individual conduct and beliefs into twentieth-century directions. This was true especially as it connected four primary areas of adolescent concern to twentieth-century patterns: work and consumer habits, sexual relationships, political attitudes, and the subtle areas of style, taste, and personal choice. Above all, college peer groups directed the young to the axial facts of modern social relationships—competition and conformity. Competition within conformity and conformity in the service of competition were the structuring facts of campus life in the twenties. These bound groups and the peer network together and were the mechanisms for group responsibility. At the same time, conformity and competition were also values, values that in a specific American social context were made to read like a twentieth-century text on business success and consumer habits.

Competition and Conformity in the Peer Culture

A good illustration of how peer instruments were firmly locked into larger changes is the phenomenon of fads. Fads are thoroughly modern. Even the term is modern—describing a sudden explosion of interest in some commodity that becomes widespread and rabidly popular but then quickly disappears to be replaced by another fashion or interest equally ephemeral. The twenties is probably the first period which can be quickly identified and characterized by its fads and, not surprisingly, the fads which are associated with the twenties were youth-centered and youth-oriented. This is exactly correct, for youth as a social phenomenon and fads as a cultural fact emerged together in the period. Fads depend on the same conditions—rapid communications, cheap mass-production techniques, large-scale distribution of goods, and national advertising—that also created the national phenomenon of youth. Fads are democratic as they homogenize the population and provide everyone with easy access to fashion. At the same time, they differentiate the population through the rapidity with which they change, making some groups appear old-fashioned (or old) if they fail to adjust quickly or completely enough. They create a form of temporal stratification that depends on nuances of style just as age-grouping provides a new form of social stratification that depends on associations with the latest style.

But fads are even more directly tied to youth. Fads depend on a human factor, the need to imitate, which is most acute during adolescence. The fad is only a more extreme form of those means which peers use to solidify their control over individual behavior. Thus, peer groups traditonally bore insignia of their affiliation like fraternity pins, and schools had historically appropriated differentiating marks and colors, varsity letters, school emblems, and distinctive clothing. In the twenties, national fads competed with parochial marks of peer identification, serving the specific peer society of a campus and binding youth together nationally. The local peer groups played their part by providing the immediate basis for identification and security, encouraging imitation and enforcing conformity. But the smaller groups were now linked to a national phenomenon. Some group symbols, like athletic letters, remained. But more parochial patterns, like class uniforms and styles, which had once been as important, disappeared and were replaced by "collegiate" styles and fads that were nationwide.

The fad is a positive asset among the young because it is both widespread and temporary. Being transitory, a fad is an especially good mark of association between age-mates, for the fad can change as quickly as the population that composes the age category and can serve as a means for demonstrated loyalty to the group at a specific point in time. Because fads change rapidly, they are also the perfect means for demonstrating that constant loyalty which peers demand. But in the twenties, while fads bound students together, they also divided them along an axis of competitive advantage, as rapid conformity to the newest and the latest separated those who could keep up from those who could not or would not.

Thus, fads reflected the importance of peer groups and depended on peer enforcement, while at the same time they redefined those groups along the lines of changed conditions. Fads and peers, like youth and the new society, were mutually responsive and reactive. The fads were necessary to peer-group function. But the fads also bound the young to the realities of the society—epitomizing the rapid pace of change, making constant adjustment necessary, and symbolizing the new ethic of consumption. Fads were one effective way in which the needs of the young were being channeled into the historical conditions of a changing society.

I

"No other class," remarked a *New York Tribune* columnist in 1924, "is so entirely subservient to conservative public opinion as this same gorgeously emancipated collegiate younger generation." Conformity on campus was so general that few editors did not at some time remark on the slavish imitation that prevailed among students. "These fads," the *Daily Illini* remarked with considerable wisdom, "are absolutely necessary if one wishes to be like everyone else." In the twenties, campus fads were changing with astonishing rapidity because so much of college life was peer-dominated. "College students," the *Ohio State Lantern* noted, "can almost always be found in groups, seldom alone. They dress, they walk, they talk alike." [1] Imitation and conformity in dress, manner, and interest were basic to college relationships. They provided an immediate basis for peer identification, a continuing means for judging loyalty, and a necessary foundation of commonality. It is well to remember that students came from diverse backgrounds, with varied initial interests, habits, and beliefs. Conscious conformity overcame these differences and allowed for immediate integration which, though superficial at first, did permit associations to take place. Only after jarring differences were overcome could an association of strangers give way to primary group relations.

Because they changed rapidly, fads also provided the means for constant and repeated demonstrations of conformity. While conformity was important personally, it was also necessary socially. As the editor of the UCLA paper observed, "Cords make the man" and are part of the "collegian's creed." "It goes without saying that until he has his cords the man-about-the-campus is non-existent as far as any social standing is concerned." At Louisiana State, the *Reveille* described the ritual of the newest "secret of success to campus popularity," the polo shirt: "One is not well dressed unless a polo shirt is worn some time during the day." To go against common norms was to commit social suicide. The editor of the *Daily Princetonian* put it well in discussing Havelock Ellis' valuation of individualism: "Being young, we in Princeton do not always appreciate 'unique and miraculous persons' amongst us; instead of classifying them in the kindly terms of Havelock Ellis we too often list them in unflattering phrases of our own as 'queer birds' or 'wet smacks.' " He went on to explain, "The type most widely admired on the campus is not generally a type that stands out because of special originality but a type which, though it has undoubtedly its sterling qualities, is comparatively commonplace. We like a man to be good-looking, well-built, physically plucky, socially agreeable, 'Brooksey.' " Duke students had another term for the disagreeably different individual, "shine," and the *Chronicle* observed that to be so labeled "will destroy an individual's power more quickly than anything else." [2]

The peer society put a premium on the immediate signs of regularity—facile conformity in dress, manner, taste, and language—while deriding other qualities like abiding interest, diligence, earnestness, and inner convictions.[3] But where regularity was valued in a period of fast-changing fads, the individual needed not only to be willing to conform but to be able to afford the things which made for conformity: the niceties of dress and grooming, the expensive treats at confectioneries and florists, the automobiles and dancing lessons that gave prestige and popularity, the decorations and refreshments of the chapter house. In placing emphasis on the externals of appearance and the accessories of sociability and in demanding constant and careful conformity to all its subtleties, the peer society promoted and enforced an ethos of consumerism. It was not a question of initial cost, for expensiveness and durability, with the possible exception of "Brooksey" Princeton, was not at issue. Rather the peer group emphasized repeated buying to keep up. Consumerism in the peer group was based not so much on marginal differentiation as on continuous replacement.[4]

At the same time, the dependence on fads affected more than intra-campus imitation. Youth at one institution were interested in and aware of the changes in modes and interests at other institutions. Through the exchange of newspapers, inter-

Competition and Conformity in the Peer Culture

collegiate conferences, and interscholastic competitions, and especially by way of advertisements, the young were conscious of what it meant to be "collegiate." "Sports clothes," announced the fashion editor at UCLA, "are in," and were worn everywhere, "at Dartmouth, Yale, Michigan, Princeton, Wellesley, Cornell, Northwestern." A Trinity College editor observed that as soon as a clothing salesman announced "that the boys at Princeton or Harvard are wearing them that way . . . the article is sold." And at the University of Illinois one columnist scolded men for wearing business suits and dressing formally. In an article entitled, "Tweedies for Collegiates," Millicent the campus "cat," asked that men dress in the "baggy tweeds, knickers and great coats," popular on most campuses. "We are happy college students but once, why not be it, dress it, play the part with the distinction of the rah-rah casual collegian?" "I weep, salt feline tears for you poor commercial, old young Illini. Pep Up! You haven't a job to lose yet." [5] Clothes and manners were designed not only to bind youth together but to mark youth as a group apart, a group that could enjoy an age devoid of responsibility and old men's cares. Millicent was taking her cue from other campuses and other youths.

Clothes helped to identify an individual with peers locally and nationally. "Style" in dress separated students from ordinary mortals and gave the college man or woman a distinctive air and the group identity that enhanced a sense of personal security. Thus, youths could indulge fads which would otherwise appear ludicrous: fads for women like open galoshes ("flappers"), yellow rain slickers, and multi-colored bandannas at the head and waist; huge raccoon coats, knickers, golf stockings, and oxford bags or "Valentino pants" for men.[6] All could be worn safely, indeed proudly, and an individual could defy adult derision because the fad identified one with the group which provided support in opposition.

The continuous peer pressures within the youth community also made interest fads spread like wildfire.[7] Most of these were available to everyone, but they had a special significance to the young as they gave them a basis for common interests and sociability and a ready means for effecting group allegiance. To mention just a few is to see how interests as well as appearance changed under pressure. Dance fads set the pace for the decade and changed repeatedly and rapidly. Crossword puzzles became, in 1924, a new form of recreation that suddenly engrossed the time of undergraduates everywhere, and college papers imitated each other in publishing puzzles as signs that they were keeping up with the times. So too, the teachings of Émile Coué were the basis of a short-lived and telling infatuation with self-improvement by way of self-hypnosis. "Every day, in every way, I'm getting better and better" became an expression oft-repeated in a variety of contexts. Mah jongg became an over-night sensation, rivaling bridge as a staple of dorm and frater-nity entertainment. Ads for instruction in mah jongg, like ads for instruction in the latest dance steps, became regular features of the college newspapers. Books too, were fads. Certain books like *The Plastic Age, Town and Gown,* and *Main Street* were *de rigueur* reading.[8] The name of Freud, and the terms repression and complex, were known to all, though apparently understood by few.

Interest fads overcame differences in background and habits and provided the young with accoutrements of sociability and homogeneity. No wonder the hold-out was suspect. He denied his fellows access to his personality and impeded the social in-tegration necessary to comparatively short-lived campus associa-tions. He also placed himself beyond peer control. National fads, like campus spirit or collegiate sports, were the substra-tum for commonality at the same time that they were in-struments of peer regulation. They were also a critical demon-stration of the new attention to consumable items which because they were available to all had constantly to be renewed and reviewed if they were to remain true signs of loyalty and an ef-fective means for providing competitive peer advantage.

In the same way, fads in slang were followed avidly and imitated assiduously by the young, and expressions linked youths at one institution with those at others. At Ohio State, the *Lantern* discussed some of the differences and similarities between the slang that prevailed on campus and that at Bryn Mawr. "Fads in speech," the UCLA editor noted, are making it "positively unfashionable to speak straight, simple American." Another editor at UCLA called for the publication of "a college dictionary" to make "collegiate lingo understandable to the outsider." One would need a glossary to follow the perambulations of fashion in language. It varied by school, group, and region, but there were terms with a nationwide currency. Language quickly initiated the young into peer relations, but to be truly fashionable in slang, as in dress and interests, it was necessary to keep close watch over the changing fads.[9]

The young were quickly adapting to an ethos of consumerism in interests as well as clothes. Ideas were suddenly picked up and as suddenly dropped. Rapid adjustment became fundamental because the group needed constantly to employ new techniques for demonstrated loyalty and to define competition. Thus, easy adaptability became an accompaniment of conformity and a means of success, and the need for continuous conformity reinforced the sense of constant change. An abiding interest in an author or a composer could not compete with a facile knowledge of the latest jazz piece or the hottest book in social intercourse. This was as true of the so-called heart-to-heart bull session (a wonderful, if also contradictory, term connoting a cocky self-confidence that defines successful, competitive discourse) [10] as in superficial banter. Shallowness in thought and glibness in speech were valuable assets in a culture based on the ability to keep up. Fads reflected the needs of the young for identifying symbols of conformity and differentiation. In turn, the commercial vehicles of the culture increased the pressure on youth to relate their every action, interest, and thought to those of others.

Because the fads appropriated by the young were national, they were at once a foundation for a national subculture and at the same time vulnerable, as college youths found their clothes, speech, dances, and interests copied by others. "No sooner does a thing become popular and customary in a university," an editor at UCLA observed, "than it is immediately copied by the students at secondary schools." For other youths, college styles epitomized glamor and perhaps even an enviable privilege. But adults also eagerly copied the ways of the young. "Approximately 65% of the clothing industry in America today is dominated by college and University styles," noted a California editor with no little self-inflating exaggeration.[11] Youth had come to represent all the chaotic newness of the culture that was best expressed in consumer habits, and nothing was more eagerly consumed than youth. The young were consciously proclaiming that they were able to change and adapt, and while adults accused the young of changing too fast and of adapting too easily, they envied them for all of that. Through a complex process of vicarious association with youth styles and vicarious self-condemnation of youth's behavior, Americans used youth at once to denounce change and to adapt to it.

II

Conformity was valued in theory as well as in action by the young. The term loyalty described the ideal of group allegiance and community cohesion. Loyalty to the institution was basic to the peer system. According to the *Cornell Sun*, the two most important benefits to the undergraduate of college life were "loyalty and lasting love for his Alma Mater, and a self-confidence that will enable him to go forth and perform in the world."[12] The conjunction of loyalty and success was revealing. One led to the other.

The system of extra-curricular activities was the primary field for the demonstration of group allegiance and solidarity. Success in that system brought peer honors. Faculty honors, on the other hand, signified little. This provides at least a part of the explanation for the devaluation of academic success during the twenties. The activities were peer-dominated and peer-directed. They were the ground for approved performance, and that performance was valued not only or primarily for itself but for its effect in improving the reputation and success of the school. Students attended mass rallies and cheered on the team to show loyalty to the university and solidarity with the group. Nothing was so bitterly condemned as shirking one's duty and failing to show full support. Betting on the other team was treasonous. A man who joined activities for his own sake, editors insisted, was a selfish egotist, and the man who refrained from doing his all in support of the team, the living embodiment of the spirit of the school, was reprehensible. Editors who criticized fraternities did so because the fraternities channeled too much of the loyalty of their members away from the school rather than toward a greater expression of such allegiance.[13]

The fraternity epitomized the tendency of peer groups to demand loyalty and to enforce strict conformity. In return for the sense of solidarity provided, the group demanded two types of performance, extra-curricular participation and personal style. Members were first to work on behalf of the organization to ensure its prominence in campus affairs. Each individual was pressed into accountability, forced to activities performance. He acted on behalf of the group. But the fraternity position also depended on its distinctive style and its social rating. The fraternity pin, itself a kind of cachet, represented the social ideal in manner, dress, and social flair. Thus loyalty to the group was measured by more than work and specific performance; it was measured in terms of personal conformity in appearance, attitude, interest, and personality. At Syracuse University, Katz and Allport found what they called a distinct institutional mentality among the young, best exemplified by the "fraternity patriots." These individuals were willing to "intrust the standards and prerogatives of the individual to group control" and were "inclined to follow the mores of fraternity life . . . rather than to develop [their] own standards," because they "derive personal satisfaction from the identification of themselves with the larger group, whose prestige and standards they wish, for that reason, to maintain on a high level." [14] Individual goals were thus subservient to group interests, and individuality was replaced by group style, because individual identity was a function of group life.

The fraternities only emphasized what was true of the peer society in general. Strict performance in activities and personal conformity in nuances of style, dancing, and sexual conventions were a demonstration of belonging. But above all loyalty and spirit assured the hegemony of the group itself. Often schools distributed distinctive buttons or varsity letters to those who participated actively in extra-curricular affairs. This open sign of recognition was a public demonstration of one's loyalty and therefore a further stimulus to involvement. It set individual against individual, group against group, in a competition for greatest conformity. At Columbia, for example, such insignia were adopted to "distinguish the Freshmen with college spirit from their inactive classmates." The publication of the names of fraternity and sorority groups who had 100% subscription to the Cornell athletic association had the same effect. Each individual had to join in order to save the face of his organization and, in turn, to promote the interests of the school as a whole. [15]

Student newspapers cultivated a booster psychology of attendance at school events and student support for school activities as participants and spectators. It was the duty of students to attend every school affair from the lowliest debate to rallies for the team. But the most significant demonstration of school spirit was always reserved for interscholastic athletic events. "Probably no single factor has contributed more to the growth of the

American college than varsity athletics," according to the *Daily
Illini*. "Sports supply that college spirit in this country which at
European institutions of learning is made up in atmosphere."
Athletics were the highest expression of group life because athletics most powerfully embodied the subsuming of individual
differences to group goals. "It is an undeniable fact," the Duke
Chronicle declared, "that in the college of today athletics have
come to exert an influence and to hold a place the importance of
which cannot be estimated. . . . *Here is bred the feeling of unity*
and here are met on a common basis of thinking the ambitions
of different minds. *All thought is directed to the one aim, that of
glory for the college. . . . Self is lost in the effort to have the ideal victorious. Team-work is placed above personal distinction.*" [16] While an
athletic victory certainly expressed the urge to competition on
the campus, it was above all the symbol of group cohesion and
thus first among peer activities.

In an editorial entitled "The Supreme Joy," the *Ohio State
Lantern* summed up what football meant to college students:
"College joys cannot be duplicated anywhere. They are novel
and gleeful and forever young. But among all the bright spots
which a college man remembers throughout the rest of his life
there is none more bright than the recollection of the trips he
made with the team when it invaded foreign territory. A student who has not made a football trip has missed half his life."
An athletic contest was more than a competition between rival
teams. It was a contest between school spirits. A Trinity editor
compared the reception given a victorious team to that of "a returning army of conquest." "Above all," the *Chronicle* explained, "there is instilled into the thinking of everybody concerned the ideal, the ideal of victory in a contest of strength, the
ideal where the college in question is to triumph." When an
Ohio State student was dropped for failing grades, he wrote the
Lantern, " 'Viva Ohio State' is our cry. Let's hope she can raise
her scholastic standing, but in the same breath one can't help
from shouting: 'God bless her football team.' " [17] What were

the grades of an individual when the school with which he identified could boast a championship team?

No other interest or enthusiasm could rival athletics in the
1920's. Football was a new religion, and Dean William L.
Sperry of the Harvard Divinity School identified the outpouring
of fervor at games with the communal spirit of religious revivals. In that religion the premier dogma was "college spirit,"
the sublime and complete abnegation of self to a higher
purpose—the group. Denied intellectual comradeship and competition that would have resulted from application to a common
intellectual quest, the young endowed the football stadium with
all the symbolic attributes of their group unity.[18]

In the campus code personal interests were always secondary
to the support and encouragement of the school team.[19] Nothing so glorified a school as a successful team, and nothing was,
in turn, more honored by students. The twenties saw a veritable
orgy of stadium-building. Often dedicated to the war dead (a
fitting tribute to another victorious team), the stadia stand as
symbols of a football mania perhaps never equaled in modern
college history. Toward the end of the decade, the over-involve-
ment with sports, especially football, gave way to an inevitable
reaction. There were calls for control of what had become a massive preoccupation. But this was only part of the story. In effect, football, like many of the clothes, music, and slang fads,
had been taken from the young because of general public interest
and the game's obvious commercial value. What at the beginning
of the decade was still considered the "only form of college athletics which can be called an exclusive college sport and lends
prestige to an institution that has it" was by the end of the decade the property less of the university or of any one school than
of a broad public constituency.[20] Victory became less the result
of school spirit and unity than that of cash outlays for coaches
and team members.

When athletics and especially football are viewed as symbols
of community spirit and group identity, it is easier to under-

stand why varsity team members were unquestionably the "big men" on campus. They represented in the extreme the demonstration of peer loyalty and the subsuming of individual to group expression that was basic to the campus code. Most school papers repeatedly urged varsity team members to wear their letters so that they might be recognized by all and be given the honor which was their due. They would also serve to remind students of the personal success that came from school spirit and loyalty. The injunction was, however, unnecessary, for everyone already knew who the big men were. Indeed, wearing the letter had become unfashionable. But the false modesty often attributed to those who failed to wear the insignia was not modesty at all, but an expression of that security which team members had of their campus prestige and prominence.[21]

Activities and athletics were the major, but not the only, demonstration of the subordination of the individual to group identity. According to the *Columbia Spectator*, "Registration in the University, mechanical as it may seem, presumes a certain subjective attitude towards the traditions and customs. If a man cannot take part in them he can at least conform. . . . No university is required to continue on its rolls any man or group of men who frankly show that they are using its educational facilities in a purely selfish way." Not to take pride in one's school was to be disloyal and to demonstrate that spirit of ingratitude which the *Chronicle* called "a sin." "As a class and as an individual you have become a living part of Trinity College," the *Chronicle* told freshmen. "Any insults directed toward your college should be a cause of indignation within you. And so in the glories and honors that are heaped upon the college you too may share. While you labor ambitiously either with your hands or with your head, you must not forget the college which nurtures and mothers you."[22]

Similarly, "boosting" was a demonstration of allegiance. Before every Easter or Christmas vacation, editors urged students to "boost" or advertise the virtues of their institution; to speak of it in glowing terms to adults and other youths; to urge high-school students to attend it rather than another; and generally to demonstrate their pride in affiliation. Everyone, the editor of the *Ohio State Lantern* asserted, must "feel himself a silent member of a vast boost Ohio organization. The person who does not believe in his school to the extent of recommending it to another is not getting all that he should out of school life. Belief that one's school is the peer of all others is one of the things that goes with being a student." [23]

The result of this spirit of boosting was that every school event, major or minor, every school publication, and every school activity—all group enterprises—were publicized by the papers and uncritically applauded. One editorial staff at Cornell included in the *Sun* platform the pledge to "support whole-heartedly everything which bears the stamp of Cornell, believing that what is worthy of the name is worthy of active support." [24] By the middle of the decade, some editors did begin to adopt a critical approach to school functions. Imbued with Menckenesque iconoclasm and wary of being provincial Babbitts, they began to criticize school events and the booster spirit. This was, however, no more than a passing phase in editorial leadership. While it lasted, critical editors were bombarded by letters which informed them that criticism must be constructive and must help to improve the institution. Denunciatory criticism was self-indulgent, not loyal.

Institutional commitment was one facet of the loyalty pattern. Conformity to the collegiate style in manner and dress was another. College youths gave scrupulous attention to tidy appearance and attractive grooming. Bohemianism was condemned in dress as well as in thought. One could dress more or less informally depending on the specific school and event, but one dressed with great care whatever the prevailing mode. Even adults normally critical of the young were impressed by their care in dressing. An attractive appearance was basic to the collegiate style, which was clean-cut and neat. It was also to train them for a proper business appearance, a means for achieving success on campus and off. As one clothes ad reminded young men at Illinois, "Dress well and succeed." [25]

The young were both well-groomed and acutely fashion-conscious. Most papers carried news of the latest in fashions for men and women as prescribed in New York or Paris, and all newspapers carried fashion ads and fashion columns. The attention to fashion emphasized two major campus concerns, business success and sexual attractiveness. Thus, both sexual interests and professional achievement were measured in consumer terms, and mating and work became functions of conformity in appearance. Clothes for youth in the 1920's epitomized peer concerns and youth needs—mating, job success, and group identification.

But collegiate style was more than just fashion. It emphasized the well-rounded individual as the ideal personality type: neither a genius nor a dolt, not a social lion or a wet, not too smooth but not crude, active but not rah-rah. The man who succeeded on campus and was most admired, according to the *Columbia Spectator,* was "the balanced man, the compromise type." This man gave his all for his institution and was willing to subordinate personal interests to group needs. An eccentric or a man committed to a personal goal was purely self-indulgent. No matter what his external smoothness, the social lion, like the social outcast, was basically selfish. So was the rah-rah boy who engaged in activities for his own sake and not that of the school. Like the grind, he was lopsided in his interests, indulging his selfish ambitions to the detriment of loyalty to the institution.[26]

A tense ambivalence ran all through the emphasis on conformity among youth in the twenties, an ambivalence between those qualities that demonstrated group spirit and those that made for personal success on the campus. It was not always easy to distinguish the man who engaged in activities as a mark of institutional loyalty from the one who did so in order to succeed, especially since the approved road to success was by way of demonstrated group loyalty. So too, the attention to personal appearance and style emphasized not only loyalty to the college image of the school, but success both on campus and in the outside world. The young were not always clear about where they put their emphasis. Somehow, however, they believed that individual success would naturally grow from this kind of commitment and allegiance to the group. As the Cornell editor reminded his readers, college life taught a man loyalty and made it possible for him to "go forth and perform in the world."

III

The conflict between group loyalty and individual success was built into all peer relations on the campuses of the 1920's. It reflected the basic structural tension between competition and conformity around which most peer concerns revolved. Complete solidarity permitted groups to compete successfully. Thus, for example, a loyal following assured athletic victory. But the tension was more thoroughgoing still, for it also juggled individual interests against group actions. The individual who conformed to the nuances of campus style and the peer determinants of work would be the successful individual in the campus network. The man who conformed to fraternity criteria of acceptability was the man who achieved prominence on the campus. The outstanding athlete was a "big man" because he worked on behalf of the team. The very notion of "big man" is somehow incongruous with the subordination of the individual to the group.

That conflict is fully understandable only in terms of the different but reciprocal social functions of peer groups. On the one hand, conformity to peer standards trained individuals to accept the criteria of performance established by the peer society and provided individual security through group approval. The group and not the individual determined what was worthy and what was not. By acquiescing in that evaluation, the individual accepted social measures of success. On the other hand, the specific values enforced by the peer society were largely those of the American business culture, which emphasized individual success and competitive prestige. The concern with success was itself a reflection of that culture. So was the stress on outward displays of status, like the fraternity pin, or the consumer ideal of collegiate style. The scrupulous attention to grooming was meant to train the young to proper business appearance. The cult of sociability and the emphasis on personal congeniality were believed to be assets in the business world. Thus, by conforming to group dictates, the young were also trained to achievement in the society and taught about the ends and values of the society within which they lived. Potentially, at least, there was a possible conflict between how the young were socialized by the peer group and what they were socialized to expect. In fact, however, the tension between group conformity and individual competition was caught in a fine balance which, in the context of American society, permitted the young to adjust to changing cultural patterns as well as the requirements of the peer society.

Many of the most significant peer values reflected this dual commitment. Adjustment, for example, was valued by the young because they believed that the ability to adapt to circumstances was a prerequisite for modern living. In an editorial entitled "Find Your Place," the *Ohio State Lantern* observed: "Aside from its other obvious advantages, college offers one a complete training in adjustability—the knack of knowing just how to fit in. Truly has it been said that college students after having gone through four years of college life, can fit almost everywhere at any time. . . . Let us avoid . . . becoming square pegs in round holes. It is easy to adjust oneself if one but will. Fit in!" It was "not the scholar who is to negotiate the daily transactions of the World," the *Oregon Sunday Emerald* observed in urging students to participate in activities. His mind was too finely tuned to "compromise." To succeed, it was necessary to "strike a balance and go forward." [27] This necessary quality of personal plasticity was inherent in the value attached to sociability and well-roundedness. To conform to the demands of friends and circumstance trained the individual to succeed in American life. This evaluation was also implicit in the condemnation of the queer individualist or the man overly devoted to unyielding personal convictions. It was the man who could adapt to group pressures and compromise personal standards who was marked out for success.

College youth were so accustomed to this argument that they frequently used it to defend their behavior against those adults who accused them of immorality. "Time and conventions change," one correspondent at Illinois observed in defending coed smoking, "and if we intend to keep up one [*sic*] must broaden our ideas and viewpoints accordingly." Similarly, in an editorial entitled "Youth Versus Age," the Duke *Chronicle* observed, "a vast deal is being said by the Old Schools and the Old Fools about the fecklessness, shallowness, immorality and the lack of spiritual tendencies in the make-up of the modern student." In fact the *Chronicle* believed it was youth's great advantage that they could move forward and keep pace with a changing world. [28] But adjustment was more than a defense; it reflected the real imperatives of peer relations on the campus. The need to adapt oneself was not only an evaluation of reality but an operational necessity in their behavior. The peer culture demanded repeated demonstration of conformity and forced the young into a constant process of readaptation to new fads, styles, and attitudes, and into a rapid assimilation of commodities and beliefs. Conformity to peer criteria thus trained them at once to accept extra-personal standards and to adjust to the rapid changes that had become a part of the modern world. Both involved a subtle reorientation in beliefs about what was right and wrong, what was proper and improper.

In the 1920's, the behavior of the young was based on considerations of prudence and public opinion rather than on an inner sense of virtue or certainty. "We have very few convictions about anything," noted the *Cornell Sun,* while a University of Denver coed asserted that "there is no absolute right or wrong. Circumstances alter cases." Psychologists Alice Anderson and Beatrice Dvorak found that the critical basis for evaluating personal conduct among college students in the twenties was the acceptability of that behavior to others. In comparing the standards of behavior among students and their parents, the investigators discovered that college students were only half as likely as their parents to judge behavior on the basis of right and wrong and that their judgments were even further removed from that of their grandparents. Anderson and Dvorak concluded that "the standard of right and wrong as a basis for conduct is rapidly dying and that the standard of prudence is being set in its place." [29] Of course, this study does not tell us whether the behavior patterns and codes initially adopted on the basis of prudence did not in later life become criteria of rightness and wrongness—that is, whether they did not congeal into a rigid value orientation.

To the extent that a young man or woman was increasingly attentive to peer evaluations and sensitive to the demands of prudence, David Riesman's contention that modern youth is "other-directed" is undoubtedly an appropriate description of youth in the 1920's.[30] Still, whether this orientation is so radically different from that which governed peer relations among previous generations when they were young, and whether this orientation persisted into adult life, cannot be answered by reference to peer institutions alone. Probably youth has always been conscious of the behavior of peers. The crucial difference between modern youth and the youth of different periods lies in the degree to which they are exposed to the influence of age peers, an exposure unchecked by other influences, and in the greater opportunity available to modern youth to enforce conformity among peers.

Moreover, the effectiveness of peer exposure reflects the relationship between peer groups and other social institutions. Peer relations and attitudes establish a foundation that may or may not be exploited by other cultural pressures—at work, on the golf course, through the media. In that sense, peer influence on college students was not only newly strong but also newly significant. College peer societies existed in a larger context where peer pressures toward constant imitation could be prolonged and reinforced. Peer groups always live within a larger social universe. In the twenties, that universe first made them more dominant by expanding the institutional structures in which they could operate and then made them more effective by extending the pressures through new social agencies and cultural vehicles. The emergence of powerful peer centers during a period of rapid social development made the college campus of the 1920's a crucial new instrument for social change.

Middle-class youths in the twenties were unquestionably oriented toward peers because so much of their time was spent largely in their company. There were moreover few impediments like work or community to check that influence. The young had the leisure of prolonged dependency, the opportunity of extended education, the latitude of a permissive and solicitous family. Peer exposure could thus be more effective than ever before at the same time that it affected more youths than ever before. School peer groups not only supplemented the family but challenged the authority of the family during long periods of life. Thus the decade was witness to one of the first real youth cultures. Never before had so many youths been so insulated in a world so completely dominated by other youths and sheltered from adult example.

That exposure came just as agencies like advertising and rapid mass communications were able to exploit the peer emphasis on imitation and the need for vehicles of identification. It also came at a time when the pace of change had become strikingly modern, and peer groups, because they valued conformity and plasticity, could help the young to adjust to such rapid change.

This was not because the young were inherently more liberal or because they were particularly critical of adult values, but rather because the peer group experimented with changes and enforced conformity to those changes. The young could adjust much more easily than adults who were less leisured, more responsible, and more fixed in their values. The young accepted the basic structures of American society—the capitalist economy, the political party system, the ethos of business success—in their modern guises as consumerism, government regulation, and bureaucratic conformity. But the groups also redirected behavior in sexuality and style that represented advance positions. The peer culture thus socialized the young to stability and change; it anchored attitudes in basic social structures and directed values toward personal liberties and rapid changes in cultural tastes and styles.

IV

While conformity was valued in theory and in action, it was in no sense part of an ethos of cooperation. Very much the opposite was the case. "Competition," observed the *Daily Illini*, "is the biggest incentive to progress both in college and out." Competition, like conformity, was basic to the peer social system and eagerly embraced as a value. The success ethic lay beneath all the exhortations to conformity. To be successful in the world of youth was to conform to its dictates. But to be successful, it was just as important to compete vigorously in the tightly woven prestige network. When an individual competed within the framework of youth's approved interest sphere, he was at the same time conforming to the accepted valuation of those interests.[31] This competition dominated the interaction between individuals, organizations, and schools.

Something of the intense competition fostered in extra-curricular activities and social affairs has already been alluded to.

The testing process by which positions were obtained in the activities was appropriately called "competition." So too, it was competition that powered the social rating system and the contests between school teams. Fraternities competed for potential members who would be assets in the control of activities.[32] Fraternities and sororities competed for social prominence and tried to outdo each other in the lavishness of chapter houses, the sumptuousness of entertainments, the cachet of their styles. Sororities competed for the prestige of having the most beautiful girls by putting forward candidates in beauty contests and prom queen selections. Students, the *Daily Illini* believed, had become so serious about social success that they had lost all spirit of play. "Even the campus 'snakes' have their competitions, and dancing is a serious business to them that must be done, and done with a flourish and a swagger at least twice a week." Beyond that, intercollegiate athletics was the epitome of the competitive impulse. To own a victorious team was to reap all the fruits of a successful competition. One shared in the glory of the successful team because it represented one's identifying institution in the intercollegiate world. "Athletic events," observed the *Ohio State Lantern,* "are inestimably valuable, since they create and foster a fighting spirit that is essential." [33]

But competition, like conformity, had its own ambiguities, ambiguities that illuminate the general tensions between personal merit and group affiliation. For some, success on campus came without competition. "The Best Man will always win," observed the *Cornell Sun,* "but the Man with Fine Friends has more chances to win." No one on campus denied the importance of what was known as "drag," and no one would refuse its benefits. Although the young believed that an outstanding individual could make it on his own and that the advantages of initial prestige and status by association could be equaled by personal exertion, they also recognized that this was comparatively rare. Thus, the editor of the *Ohio State Lantern* noted that two kinds of men made good at college—the man whose way was cleared for him by friends and relatives or whose high-school reputation preceded him, and the man who "comes unheralded" and makes it strictly on his own. The *Lantern* asserted that the success which came from his own struggles was more precious: "What greater reward can there be in the strife for college honors," than to succeed on one's own merits? [34]

The young thus paid homage to the traditional canons of the American competitive system. But while the young valued competition, success normally did not depend on individual merit; neither was it based on equality. Student competitions were based on initial advantage, usually the advantage of group association and accumulated prestige. The man who belonged to a fraternity was way ahead of the unaffiliated man because he had group prestige and group support. The peer system taught the virtues of organization and the leverage that came from group solidarity. A maverick without a group behind him was usually powerless in the face of a solid organization.

Moreover, the peer system taught that often the best way to achieve success in inter-organizational competition was to avert competition through collusion, manipulation, and bargaining behind the scenes. This was especially true of political operations, but it also applied to social, journalistic, and dramatic activities. In intensely competitive situations, groups, by log-rolling, placed their respective candidates in office. This *sub rosa* cooperation ran counter to the spirit of free-enterprise competition, just as organizational leverage ran counter to the concept of individual achievement, but it taught very well the modern lessons of political and business manipulation. While most college papers officially condemned such behind-the-scenes activities, the Duke *Chronicle* was more honest: "We believe that political activity is an essentially healthful condition. . . . As training for life, student politics are invaluable. For, whether it is desirable, admirable, or not, the truth is that most affairs of our modern world are run by politics. . . . Anyone who has been behind the scenes of church government knows the enormous part played by politics. So in business organizations, Roto-Kiwanian and other country clubs, Parent-Teachers' Associations, and the Anti-Saloon League politics exist, and flourish; the only sane course is to recognize the fact." [35] And recognize the fact they did in most of their daily experience and behavior.

Although the drag that came with reputation and association was accepted as a fact of life, the drag that came with taking unfair advantage of the peer system through bypassing its formal and informal norms was severely condemned. A man who brought a corsage for a girl when the student prom committee issued a ban against flowers was not playing by the rules.[36] Competition within conformity had specific restraints. Those restraints determined what was worthy. They did not limit the degree of exertion. Conformity to group dictates did not prevent the individual from applying himself to the fullest extent of his ability. Peer pressure for acceptability did not impose mediocrity in performance. It prescribed where effort was to be applied and condemned individual eccentricity. Jockeying for position in the peer society was not, however, confined to marginal exertion, as sociologist Edward Hartshorne has implied, nor did the ethos of adjustment and conformity destroy vigorous contention. According to Hartshorne, peer pressure against "too much distinction" serves to "maintain mediocrity and to discourage effort." Hartshorne, and to a degree even Riesman, [37] mistakes distinction with distinctiveness. What the peer group controlled was the direction in which the effort was to be applied. To apply that effort toward peer concerns was highly valued, to apply it to individual and eccentric interests which added nothing to the group was not. Among college peer groups, at least, the group existed above and beyond the individual so that vigorous exertion on its behalf was demanded and expected.

Thus a grind had no place in the society of the young, not because he was a good scholar but because by being a good scholar he valued that which was not valued by his peers and diverted all his energies into channels which served no purpose in the peer society. Activities were peer-controlled and therefore served as the field for distinction. For the peer group, grades were not value received for energy expended. The young asserted that by devoting his time to "mere learning," the grind deprived himself of the real values of a college existence. By working hard within the world of his peers, the individual showed that he was willing to carry his part of the responsibility for the maintenance of the group. But more than that, the young argued that the personal benefits derived from competition in peer activities were far more valuable in the long run than the benefits derived from studies. The grind was ostracized for his disloyalty and also for his stupidity.

Thus again, as with the ethos of adjustment, the values of the peer society were based on evaluations of the real world as well as on the needs of the group itself. The individual needed to compete on behalf of the group, but the young also had a well-articulated rationale for their social values. They asserted that competition within the peer society provided functional training for adaptation to the "real world." They based their arguments on a two-pronged evaluation of that world. Studies were unreal, dry, and lifeless, while competition in youth activities and social affairs developed those qualities which made for success in life. According to the *Daily Princetonian,* "Princeton without these activities would be dull, lifeless—a fossil among universities. They are not 'tolerated' by the University—they are essential to its cultural development." "The world consistently refused to be blinded by the effulgence of a straight A average," observed the *Daily Illini.* High salaries went to activities men, not to scholars. The important question in the business world was not "What do you know?" but "What can you do?" The activities, according to the Louisiana State *Reveille,* "put the student more nearly in contact with actual problems of real life," and they teach "the participants to meet practical problems in a practical way, which is just what is required of persons in after-college life. When one leaves the portals of one's dear Alma Mater the possession of text books is of little value." [38]

Academic learning was simply not enough. "We ask for a look at life," the *Ohio State Lantern* explained, "and are given lectures illustrated with pretty colored lantern slides." The young believed that the peer society reflected the real world of business and that it fostered those qualities that made for success in that world. "American college life inevitably reflects American public life—and vice versa," asserted the *Cornell Sun,* "and competition and activity are the basic structure of business. Without this element within the walls of a university, the product of that university would be cast helpless on a world none too hospitable, the university graduate would find himself at a loss to contribute his share to the life of the nation." The activities man, the *Sun* believed, would be "several leaps ahead of his fellows when the time comes to sign the payroll." Seconding the sentiment, the *Daily Illini* explained that "The fundamental spirit which prompted students to undertake extracurricular activities was born from the desire to make their education more practical . . . students knew nothing of the world about them, and were at the time they received their degrees, wholly unqualified to compete with the situation they were forced to meet in business . . . as a result they began to enter activities where they might achieve tangible results, rather than comparatively meaningless grades and degrees." [39]

"Life's greatest problems," observed the editor at Ohio State, "are not answered in books." It was the well-rounded individual, not the bookworm, who knew how *"to get along successfully with other people,"* an absolute prerequisite for business success. Not studies but activities developed those personal qualities of compromise and personal plasticity that permitted a balance between individual and group goals necessary to business success. "The man who uses all his time learning the petty details never goes beyond the petty detail stage in success," according to a

UCLA editor. "It is the man who is versatile, the man who tries his hand at many things and understands human nature; this is the man who will succeed. The man who is too busy with his studies to think of activities will be the underdog who does the petty jobs for the activity man who will become the successful businessman of the future." [40]

To be the successful businessman of the future—that was the conscious goal, and the young believed that activities taught them about real tasks and work-a-day realities. Activities developed those personal qualities which made success possible. What the young were really talking about had less to do with training in work habits, however, than training in personality. And for that, success in the social affairs of the campus as well as in the activities was an asset because the business world depended on the ability to mix, to impress, to sell oneself. "The student who goes through college neglecting the social side of life has not obtained an education," according to the *Ohio State Lantern.* "He must learn to meet people with an absolute lack of self-consciousness. He must feel at ease in the presence of superiors, equals and inferiors. He must acquire a self-reliance that makes him at home anywhere." The well-rounded individual, not the bookworm, would make good in business, because the former knew how to handle people. The advantages of the activities man over the scholar was "the quality of being a good mixer. It means that the man knows how to get along with others . . . it means he knows how to express himself; it means that he can bluff, that he can persuade, that he can compromise, that he can get things done. Heaven crown the fellow who can get things done," observed the *Oregon Sunday Emerald.* At UCLA the editor advised readers that "Every man should some time in his life have experience in salesmanship. Selling goods is the best cure for those elements in a man that tend to make him a failure. The art of success consists in making the people change their minds . . . get out and sell goods! Hustle. Fight. . . . So the best and biggest prizes in America are open to you." It was the activities man, the man who partook in social functions, who knew how to "advertise himself," to "sell himself," and to "cultivate an impressive appearance" that would "attract the attention of the employer." "Salesmanship is an art," the *Ohio State Lantern* insisted. "It is an art that pays." "Our whole existence is built on salesmanship," a Duke editor declared, "and if we can't sell our personality and characteristics to our friends we are handicapped for the future." [41]

It was personal qualities, not work habits, that counted, and prestige, not intrinsic achievement, that the young prized. The campus was riddled by status- and prestige-consciousness. Status gave an individual a sense of belonging with his fellows and a subtle competitive edge over his fellows. Badges (best symbolized by the fraternity key), clothes, manners—all influenced success. Competitions were often won or lost on the basis of such attributes rather than active work. Competition on campus was less a competition of merit than a competition of position, and the system fostered not a high valuation of individual work but an acute awareness of the nuances of appearance, style, and personality. Moreover, individuals and groups competed less for what was really gained than for the aura of success, less for the work than for the status. Fraternities cared for their prominence on campus rather than for the training in work that activities were ostensibly to provide their members. This did not limit competition any more than conformity limited exertion. Rather it readjusted the ends of competition just as conformity limited the sphere of competition. Status, not work, was the goal of competition.

The very notion of an in-group and an out-group gave one set of students a keen sense of their own superiority not gained through individual meritorious action, except for acquiescent conformity. The most available means for individual exertion —academic achievement—was denied to students because of the devaluation of scholarship. In a sense, this was a way of excluding individual status-climbers or "polers," similar

in its intent and effect to the policy of university administrations, which were at the same time excluding out-groups like
Jews by imposing extra-scholastic personality requirements for
admissions. Social status was above all the function of the right
associations, and these associations were based on personal congeniality, appearance, manners, and money, not work.

The system had one major institutional escalator—the case of
the outstanding athlete. To him all doors were open. He had
truly achieved according to the code of the young. He had made
it on his own merits within the terms of peer success. It was the
athlete, not the scholar, who was the potential social climber
in the system of the young. He was, after all, the really legitimate competitive man, for he competed for the society and not
for himself. He gave the group status by competing on its
behalf. He was completely loyal to the group and through that
loyalty merited individual acclaim.

Whether or not the activities were indeed so like the "real
world" that they promoted business success, it is significant that
the young considered it a telling rationale.[42] Business ideals
were constantly used to legitimate peer practices, and the young
often took conscious cues from the business world. Thus almost
every paper carried news of the estimated money value of a university education, and most were concerned when some noted
businessman criticized college students as badly prepared for
business careers. The editor of the *Daily Princetonian*, which
usually emphasized the value of a broad liberal education, probably expressed the sentiment of his readers when he applauded
the development of the Harvard Business School for its "legitimization of business on par with the other professions." For as
the editor of the UCLA newspaper observed, most students no
longer came to college for a professional training, but to prepare
themselves for a business career. "The old idea long prevailing
in the South that a college graduate should avoid business has
entirely given way to the new belief that college training is
especially helpful for the businessman," observed the Duke

Chronicle in reviewing the newest curriculum changes. "Consequently, the Business Administration group in most colleges is attracting the greatest number of students." It was every man's dream, the *Cornell Sun* declared, to become "an industrial executive." But the editor of the *Ohio State Lantern* put it most simply when he explained that most students came to college not to get an education but with the one object of finding a short-cut to wealth.[43]

In 1925, the *Daily Princetonian* delivered what amounted to a Chamber of Commerce eulogy about the relationship between materialism and progress in America. The editor lauded the businessmen for their key role in American society: "What class of men is it that keeps governments, businesses, families, solidly on their feet? What class of men is it that endows universities, hospitals, Foundations? . . . What class of men are the fathers of most of us—fathers who provide decently for their families, who educate their children, who believe in order and justice, who pay taxes to support jails, insane asylums and poor houses, which neither they nor theirs are likely to occupy?" The answer, of course, was the American businessman. One could be tempted to see this as a satire or caricature of a businessman's self-promotional address were it not written in all seriousness. This blatant worship was an extreme case of what was general. The "foundation of American life," announced the *Cornell Sun,* "is business." [44] Calvin Coolidge couldn't have put it better.

Just as business success was at the heart of students' values, competition and conformity were the ligaments of the peer social system. The structures and the values ran a parallel course. Together they welded the American campus into the American market better than any curriculum. Even more significant than the manifest business orientation, the evaluation of academic and non-academic training in business terms, or the specific emphasis on success and competition were the latent effects of the campus social structure. It was the very tensions between individual success and group conformity which provided these middle-class young with a variety of critical lessons: the relation between prestigious association and individual achievement; the importance of personality and the nuances of style and fashionable interest in work competition; the subordination of the individual to group goals as the means for personal success; the tie-in between consumption and status. Not only did the peer society admire the American businessman, but the realities of peer life helped to orient the young to the critical needs of the modern corporation.

V

In 1924 a Cornell editor speculated that economics was the favored subject among male undergraduates because they believed it would help them in business careers.[45] He was probably right, for the students of the twenties quite consciously aspired to successful adjustment to the system of American economic enterprise. The twenties was, of course, the heyday of the businessman, of Wall Street glamor, and of the Chamber of Commerce hero. And college students saw themselves as part of the charmed circle. In so doing, they were much like contemporaries for whom the big sell had become synonymous with America's contribution to Western civilization.

But the young had the edge. And the edge was, ironically, a function of the radicalism of their nurture. That radicalism was two-pronged. On the one hand, their families had emphasized indulgence and not denial. On the other, their peers directed that indulgence into specific social channels. To be wholly part of the economic life of the new society, the young had to be not accumulating entrepreneurs but at once workers and consumers. And it was as both that middle-class youths became modern economic men. Not only were commercial products appropriated by peer groups as instruments of group life, but the rhythm of commercialism and the constant attention to nuances of style and repeated replacement were a necessary part of peer integration and cohesion. At the same time, the ethos of consumption—the need for conformity and for competitive advantage—duplicated the governing spirit of peer relationships. Similarly, the peer network rang with the cadences of corporate enterprise—enforced personal subordination to group activity, sharp competition on behalf of the group, and success through group conformity.

The parallels are striking, but the cultural effects were more thorough still. For through both consumption and corporate association, the young placed a supreme emphasis on style while denouncing eccentricity. Eccentricity is deeply individual and usually based on the rejection of large-scale patterns and the contortions of mass consumption. But style uses those very contortions as a means of identification. As a form of status, style can function only within a democratic mass where differences are small ripples on an ocean of sameness. Peer relationships on the campus were oriented toward just such differences, so that these styles were caught in a time grid that depended upon rapid change and small innovation. It is little wonder that youth, which is above all a time-linked status, should suddenly have become associated with fashion. In a consumer society, only youth is depleted as quickly as styles. Youth is associated with the fastest-paced fashion changes because it can most easily adjust to those changes. The young of the 1920's identified with a time-specific status (youth) and with styles that were increasingly also time-linked. A consumer society began to look to both, quite correctly associating youth with change and with fashion.

Work, like style, was also redefined by the young as a function of their peer relationships. Effort was first of all deflected from individual channels, academics, into corporate enterprises, extra-curricular activities and social relationships. This at once oriented the young to the group and to the pay-off of group success, prestige. For if a high valuation of work as a means toward personal position results from individual effort, prestige, which measures self in relation to others, results from group accomplishment. When it is enmeshed in corporate activities, work is drained of intrinsic content because the precise boundaries of the individual contribution are obscured. Through a subtle jockeying between individual and organization, what remains is a sense of relative status that is measured in terms of prestige. This happened because group goals were ultimately competitive, not cooperative. Cooperative work could give each member equal recognition (as on a kibbutz, for example), but competitive group effort led to a severely stratified and hierarchial order of merit, a merit that was never wholly a product of one's own effort but never completely the expression of coordinate activity.

It was, of course, the structure of peer activity in an American social context that gave the tension between conformity and competition its specific meaning. Style, personality, prestige, and corporate enterprise were explicit lessons of the college network, and through that network American middle-class youths were brought into the twentieth-century marketplace. But youth's radicalism did not stop there. While college peer groups helped youth to adjust to a new set of social conditions, college youth also used the new conditions for their own ends and purposes to become a strong and independent force for social change.

6

Sexual Mores in the World of Youth

Whatever the partial satisfactions and partial abstinences that characterize premarital sex life in various cultures—whether the pleasure and pride of forceful genital activity without commitment, or of erotic states without genital consummation, or of disciplined and devoted delay—ego development uses the psychosexual powers of adolescence for enhancing a sense of style and identity.

Erik H. Erikson, "Youth: Fidelity and Diversity" [1]

"Most of 'em pet, I guess."
"All the pretty ones."
"Some do one night and don't the next—goddam funny."
"ALL of 'em pet. Good women. Poor women. All of 'em."
"If a girl doesn't pet, a man can figure he didn't rush 'er right."

Lynn Montross and Lois Montross, Town and Gown (1923)

Students of modern sexual behavior have quite correctly described the twenties as a turning point, a critical juncture between the strict double standard of the age of Victoria and the permissive sexuality of the age of Freud. Too often, however, the sexual revolution of the twenties has been described exclusively in terms of scattered data suggesting an increase in premarital sexual intercourse on the part of women. One is tempted to picture investigators hunting for that special morning between 1919 and 1929 when 51% of the young unmarried women in America awoke to find that they were no longer virgins. Instead, of course, investigators are forced to deduce revolutionary changes from small, though important, increases in what remained a minority pattern of behavior.[2] This kind of thinking, not unlike the Victorian concept of all or nothing, overlooks the fact that changes in sexual habits, as in most other areas of social relations, are evolutionary and take place through a gradual accretion of behavioral and value changes. These changes must be located not in sudden reversals of traditional beliefs and habits but in adaptations to new circumstances and in a reorientation to new social groups that set the standards and establish the patterns which most individuals imitate.

By concentrating so exclusively on the incidence of premarital coitus, analysts have overlooked the most fruitful area for understanding the changes in sexual patterns among the majority of the middle-class population. For it is to the behavior and attitudes of young men and women in the twenties, who had to deal with emerging sexual impulses and had the least vested interest in maintaining older norms, that one must look for the readjustments that underlay the process of change. From this perspective the post-war decade was indeed critical for the evolution of modern sexual patterns. The young, reared in a moral standard in which all sex was taboo, redefined that standard according to their own needs and laid the basis for a change in the standard itself. The college campus, especially, provided a fertile social environment for the new mores concerning the relationships between men and women. On the coeducational campuses of the 1920's (matrimonial bureaus, they were sometimes called),[3] sex was a perpetual peer concern.

College youth of the 1920's redefined the relationship between men and women. In good part this resulted from a simple rediscovery—love is erotic. The remainder drew on an old assumption—that the goal of relations between men and women was marriage. Together the new insight and the old tradition resulted in a significant restructuring of premarital forms of sexual behavior as relationships were charged by a new sexual dynamism and a vigorous experimentalism. Sex for middle-class youths of the 1920's had become a significant premarital experience, but it continued to be distinctly marriage-oriented and confined by stringent etiquettes and sharply etched definitions. In the process of defining their future roles in the new society and within the context of already potent changes, the young helped to create the sexual manners of the twentieth century.

I

The norms established by college youths had a dual purpose. They provided room for the exploration of immediate sexual interests, and they facilitated mate selection for future marriage. The result was a sexual revolution: not, however, as often implied, a revolution erupting in a sudden and drastic increase in sexual intercourse among the unmarried young, but a revolution growing out of new patterns of sexual play. The young evolved a code of sexual behavior that was, in effect, a middle ground between the no-sex-at-all taboo officially prescribed by the adult world and inculcated by their families, and their own burgeoning sexual interests and marital aspirations. To this dual purpose, youths elaborated two basic rituals of sexual interaction— dating and petting.[4] These behavior patterns accompanied and emphasized several important value changes: more tolerance for non-normative sexual behavior, the recognition and approval of female sexuality, and a positive evaluation of emotional response and expression in relations between men and women. This nexus of behavior and value was the heart of the sexual revolution of the 1920's.

Dating was something definitely new in the ritual of sexual

interaction. It was unlike the informal get-togethers that characterized youth socializing in the village or small town of the nineteenth century, for at such events there was no pairing early in an acquaintance. It was also unlike courting, which implied a commitment between two people. Dating permitted a paired relationship without implying a commitment to marriage and encouraged experimental relations with numerous partners. Dating emerged in response to a modern environment in which people met casually and irregularly, and in response to new kinds of recreations like movies, dance halls, and restaurants, where pairing was the most convenient form of boy-girl relation.[5] Moreover, it developed as youths were increasingly freed from the direct supervision of family and community and allowed the freedom to develop private, intimate, and isolated associations. Dating opened the way for experimentation in mate compatibility. The lack of commitment permitted close and intimate associations and explorations of personality, and isolation and privacy laid the ground for sexual experimentation, both as a means for testing future compatibility and as an outlet for present sexual energies.

With the isolation of relations, the young were forced to rely on their own judgment in determining the degree and limits of permissible eroticism. It was this latitude for self-determination that produced the haunting fear of sexual promiscuity in the jeremiads of the twenties. The fear was unfounded. The young were thrown back on their own resources, but they were not free, either from the influence of childhood training or, more immediately, from the controls and sanctions of their peers. Basing their actions on an unyielding taboo against sexual intercourse and an elaborate network of peer norms and standards, they proceeded to open up the possibilities of sexual play without overstepping the bounds of family prohibition and peer propriety. After investigating female conduct in the late twenties, Phyllis Blanchard and Carlyn Manasses concluded that "very many girls draw a distinct line between the exploratory activities of the petting party and complete yielding of sexual favors to men." [6] In the behavior of young men and women in the twenties, this charting of distinctions was as important as the exploration. The two ran a parallel course, for the young experimented with eroticism within a clear sense of limits, thus tasting a little of the fruit and enjoying the naughtiness of their bravery without seriously endangering the crop.

"Petting" described a broad range of potentially erotic physical contacts, from a casual kiss to more intimate caresses and physical fondling. Even such limited eroticism would have automatically defined a woman as loose and disreputable in the nineteenth century. To the Victorians, who divided good women from bad, revered ideal purity, and were suspicious of female sexuality, all forms of eroticism on the part of women could be equated with total submission. Even in the twenties, it was not unknown for reformers to introduce legislation that would prohibit petting and define it along with fornication as illegal as well as immoral. [7] But the young drew distinct boundaries between what was acceptable erotic behavior and what was not. Petting was the means to be safe and yet not sorry, and around this form of sexual activity they elaborated a code of permissible eroticism. As a result, while there remained two kinds of women among college students in the twenties, the difference was not between sexual women and non-sexual women but between sexual women who lived by the rules and those who did not. A Trinity College editor put it well when he asserted, "There are only two kinds of co-eds, those who have been kissed and those who are sorry they haven't been kissed." And he later added just the right note about the group norms that carefully tailored female behavior: "Although a girl will not always let you kiss her when you ask her, she usually appreciates your asking her, often so much that she has to tell her friends." Blanchard and Manasses described this new "attitude toward sex behavior" as "a compromise between the old manners and the new." But in fact the youth of the twenties were incorporating

dating and petting into a wholly new ritual of graded relationships. A casual first date might thus entail a good-night
kiss, but greater intimacies and a certain amount of erotic play
were permitted and expected of engaged couples. "Erotic play,"
as Ira Wile rightfully observed, had "become an end rather than
a means," and the strong "distinctions made in petting recognize that erotic activity may or may not have coitus as a goal." [8]
The young first sanctioned eroticism and then imposed degrees
and standards of acceptability.

College youths were fully aware of, and highly sensitive to,
the criticisms that petting evoked from their elders. But the editors of college papers were quick to deny any widespread evil in
the behavior or intentions of the young. They did not, however,
deny the existence of petting or its importance in the social relations between the sexes. What they denied was the adult evaluation of such behavior as promiscuous or immoral, as in fact it
was by an earlier standard. Peer norms, which deviated from
adult attitudes, were now legitimate criteria for evaluating conduct. By the standards of the young, petting was not immoral.
It was inappropriate when abused and when the rigid boundaries the young imposed on their own behavior were overstepped.
In decrying the inordinate amount of attention that youth's
morals were receiving from the public, the *Daily Illini,* for example, illustrated how out of touch older people were with the
life of the young by referring to a recent questionnaire where the
term "spooning" had been used. A sure way of antagonizing
youth, the *Illini* noted, was to be so removed from the realities
of their lives as to use an expression as archaic and wholly unreal as "spooning." [9]

In view of the strength of peer-group influence, youth were
unlikely to bypass the restrictions and staged ritual associated
with sexual behavior. But neither was petting restricted to only
a small minority of wildly experimental youths, for petting had
become a convention and a necessary demonstration of conformity. One investigation of coed behavior found that 92% of all

women admitted petting at one time or another. Indeed, "Those rejecting all sex play feel that they are on the defensive," Ira Wile reported, "their ethical concepts endanger their social success and their peace of mind." One observed the restrictions on petting in order to remain respectable to peers, but given the occasion and the desire, one could and did pet because it was commonly accepted behavior. There was undoubtedly also considerable pressure to pet at least a little in order to remain in good standing in the eyes of peers and to assure that future dates would be forthcoming. One result of this peer compulsion was that experimental erotic exploration was often a group phenomenon. The petting party was probably the major contribution of the twenties to group sex, and it was in such groups that the first hesitant initiations into erotic play were often made. As sociologist Ernest Burgess noted, "The pattern of behavior, the code of conduct, the actual undertaking of the experience, appear often as phenomena of group determinism." "One factor has remained constant through the fleeting years," Blanchard and Manasses noted. "Popularity with boys has been and still is close to the heart's desire." But, they concluded, "the technique for achieving popularity is very different." [10] In the twenties, to maintain one's position with peers, petting was permitted but intercourse was not. The group restricted conduct but also freed it from the greater restrictions that had been imposed at home. Again the petting party is illustrative. It both forced erotic exploration and controlled the goal of eroticism. It was a self-limiting form of experimentation.

This does not mean that there was no increase in the incidence of premarital sexual intercourse generally and among the young specifically. There undoubtedly was, but premarital intercourse was still the behavior pattern of a small minority of women and had probably not substantially increased among men. On the college campus the discovery of a sexual indiscretion on the part of a coed was still a potential cause for scandal, and it was infrequent enough to be disturbing news. Burgess observed that it was still the going assumption that a coed was virtuous. It is always possible that there was considerable *sub rosa* activity or that college administrations were effective in suppressing such news, but given the social system of the campus world, it is doubtful that there was much sexual intercourse with campus women.[11]

The rating system by which social connections were made and by which eligibility was established and maintained worked within a tight system of gossip, reference, bull-session discussions, and careful conformity to standards. A correspondent to the *Daily Illini,* in defending *Town and Gown* as an accurate portrayal of college life, asked pointedly, "At what fraternity house will you not find sooner or later just such a discussion of 'Girls Who Pet'?" If a woman could be criticized for the way she wore her hair, for excessive reliance on the paint box, or for overly suggestive dancing, and when it was generally known whether she was "a first-night petter," how much more would her reputation be affected by an imputation of officially and unofficially proscribed behavior? One study of undergraduate life noted, "Men are very dependent on one another's estimate of a girl. Some fraternities blacklist a girl for being obviously 'a speed,' too giddily dressed, or lacking sex attraction." There was a very clear differentiation between positive sex appeal and offensive behavior. For the majority, "a petting party is the right thing to do," [12] but a really "fast woman" was disreputable. Sexual irregularity on the part of coeds, as one investigator of campus ethics discovered, was universally condemned by men and women as the worst of all possible offenses on the campus. Significantly, women still condemned such irregularities more consistently than men, and since it was women who usually regulated sexual behavior, there was still a tight lid on intercourse with campus women. Despite an easing of the double standard and an erosion of distinctions between virtuous women and sexual women, students still clung to a double standard in their own behavior and described illicit sexual behavior as far worse for women than for men.[13]

The vigorous competition that existed on campus among women was certain to produce adverse comment should an individual be suspected of overstepping the limits of the petting standard to gain unfair advantage. It is well to recall that women at Northwestern University entered into a compact to have a number of dateless nights. One can only guess how fierce was the fear and the resultant ostracism by campus women of a promiscuous sister. The majority of women and men still considered sexual intercourse too risky for a variety of reasons, pragmatic as well as moral, and it was the rare individual who could hazard an indiscretion and hope to maintain her status.[14]

Dating and petting were, moreover, distinctly marriage-oriented in the twenties. Since mating was one of the chief aims of both rituals, immediate sexual satisfactions had to be carefully weighed in view of long-term goals. And while virginity in a bride was no longer an absolute prerequisite for most men, it was still considered desirable. For men, female chastity appears to have taken a back seat to considerations of compatibility, but there was still some ambiguity on this point, and the devaluation of virginity in the bride was probably related to a growing acceptance of intercourse among engaged couples rather than to a tolerance of casual promiscuity. Women too continued to display considerable anxiety about the consequences of lost virginity.[15] These multiple ambivalences reinforced the sense of acceptable limitations on sexual indulgence.

For most youths, this meant an acceptance of eroticism with very clear limits of permissible expression. Petting established a norm that deviated from that of the family but was still not antagonistic to its basic taboo. The majority could pet because it filled the need for response in a specific relationship, and in filling that need they believed they had the security of peer-group opinion. Of course, many ambivalences remained. But by the 1930's these sexual definitions had congealed into a dependable norm, a norm which, in the words of one investigation, provided ample room for "spontaneous demonstrations of affection." In their study of sexual behavior on the thirties campus, Dorothy Bromley and Florence Britten discovered that the fact "that a girl should feel she can give within limits or permit exploratory intimacies without compromising her essential virginity is one of the phenomena of the contemporary younger generation's mores." During the twenties, peer pressure to pet was still strong, and behavior patterns were, as a result, less stable, more inhibiting, altogether more full of anxieties. Probably many youths petted less to express personal needs than to conform to group standards and to demonstrate what Ernest Burgess called "the outstanding attitude of modern youth"— their "self-consciousness and sophistication about sex." [16]

Experimentalism and bumptious sophistication characterized the sex lives of college youths in the 1920's. Both were significant for the development of the new patterns of sexual behavior of the twentieth century. For while sex was certainly not new in the twenties, sanctioned sexual indulgence as a regular feature of premarital relations was. In opening up the sexual possibilities in the relations between the unmarried young, some degree of compulsion was almost a preliminary to a loosening of taboos. The petting party demonstrates this tension between freer sexual expression and group compulsion, for here sexual activity was manifestly regulated by the group. As a result, a certain aura of intrigue and "naughtiness" hovered around this semi-illicit behavior in the twenties. This was especially true among certain sets found on most campuses for whom a reputation for petting, like a reputation for drinking, was a form of braggadocio, a mark of smartness. [17] On the whole, however, the promiscuous petter attained what his affectation desired—notoriety. He was a strained by-product of the more moderate experimentalism and self-consciousness that characterized sexual behavior among the youths of the twenties. Group compulsion and tantalizing bravery made these youths disturbing to contemporaries who attacked them as immoral, licentious, and decadent. "Flaming Youth," one novel of the period called them, and the epithet has remained to obscure our understanding of the realities of their lives.[18] Perhaps, however, the description was appropriate, for they did spark out in new directions and glow with a fresh sense of excitement.

By the 1930's the strains of innovation, the naughtiness, and the compulsion wore away. What the college youth of the thirties inherited were the innovations of their predecessors without much of their self-consciousness. The difference was summarized by sociologist Theodore Newcomb when he noted that there was "less social compulsion upon the young to go as far as they dare." What was left was an acceptable, though limited, means for expressing emotions between young men and women. According to Newcomb, by the mid-thirties there was "more widespread acceptance, particularly by females, of the 'naturalness' of sex intimacies, with or without coitus; less extreme 'petting' on first or early acquaintance; and more 'steady dating' with fewer inhibitions as to sex intimacy following long acquaintance." Petting was no longer an issue during the thirties. It did not provoke the kind of attention and apprehension common just a decade before. As petting lost its notoriety, the sexual issue seemed to melt away. In fact, however, premarital sexual activity of all kinds became probably more and not less common. Bromley and Britten found that despite the fact that things appeared to have "toned down from the hectic postwar decade, current reports still give no indications of a return to the prewar age of innocence. . . . The terms necking and petting are already obsolete in a few colleges. The custom signified persists, however, on every campus and under many new names." [19]

The innovations of the twenties had been solidified so that by the thirties the sexual mores begun by the college youth of the twenties were already a widespread and casual feature of behavior. "We smoke with more abandon and we kiss with more restraint," was how one college student described the difference. "That doesn't mean that we are better than we used to be. Only that flaming youth has lost its novelty." It was a "sign of the times" that, as Bromley and Britten concluded, "our study turned up so few girls to whom the adjective inhibited could be applied. . . . While numbers may have been brought up to consider sex shameful . . . we have observed that young people have an emancipating effect on each other in the formative college period." Perhaps even more significantly, the college behavior of the twenties appears to have filtered down to the high schools by the thirties. Bromley and Britten believed that college norms had become a widespread standard and that this reflected the peer emulation that had become general among American youths. "The college population might be said to represent the advance guard of the younger generation. It gives prestige to mores that are already in the making." Other studies confirm this wave-like influence radiating from the colleges. In one study, for example, Walter Buck found that the liberalization of attitudes, especially about things with a sexual connotation, that took place between freshman and senior year in college in 1923 was already effected among college freshmen in 1933. In 1923 college seniors were significantly more tolerant about sexual matters than freshmen. But by 1933 freshmen were far more tolerant than a decade before and there was little difference between freshmen and seniors, suggesting that the liberalization had already taken place in high school.[20]

The controlled ritual of petting had opened up the possibilities of intimacy and response in the relationship between young men and women. At the same time, it also restricted complete spontaneity and laid the basis for the emotionally inhibiting cat-and-mouse game of staged seductions and "scoring" that continued to govern sexual relations among the young throughout the first half of the twentieth century.[21] It was a first and necessary step toward modern patterns of sexual behavior, for the youths of the twenties redefined sexuality in erotic and emotional terms. But in ritualizing a process of personal and cultural experimentation, the youth of the twenties had also placed bonds on individual expression and behavior quite as real and determinate as those which ruled in the heyday of Victorian morals.

II

The mass of college women appear to have been guided by these group-established and sanctioned mores. Personal circumstances, strong religious convictions, or family pressure could, of course, counteract peer pressure and prevent a woman from indulging in even mild forms of petting. Conversely, a woman little involved in the peer network might believe she had nothing to lose by over-stepping the bounds of group sanction and indulging in promiscuous petting or intercourse in order to become popular, having completely misunderstood the mechanisms by which popularity was achieved and maintained. In addition, certain fringe groups of literary or political radicals may have developed mores of their own, in conscious opposition to the prevailing norms, both of the young and of adults, or in imitation of the Soviets or the Greenwich Village bohemians. Although such deviations were not common, they could account for variations.

The most important factor that could and did undercut the systematic limitation of sexual expression was engagement. The engaged couple was outside the mainstream of peer-group life, and an engaged woman no longer had to maintain her competitive position in the peer network. So too, the influence of family precepts faded as she gained a new sense of maturity and looked forward to the creation of her own family. Now secure in her future role, another aspect of the moral code of the young became effective—the sanctification and legitimization of sex by love.

One of the main tenets of youthful morality was that love made sex right. "Many of the girls have advanced in their thinking so far beyond their early training," Blanchard and Manasses observed, "as to draw a distinct line between promiscuity and premarital intercourse with the man they expect to marry." One young woman, when reminded that men might better respect women who did not pet, quickly remarked, "I would rather be loved than respected," and another asserted, "I disapprove of promiscuous relations on moral grounds; not, however, between a man and woman in love." Even when a group of women at the University of Southern California formed an "anti-petting" league, they reserved a coed's right to sexual favors in a serious relationship, noting that "she must kiss and squeeze and be kissed and squeezed by only a man to whom she is engaged." By the 1930's, almost two-thirds of the women interviewed by Bromley and Britten affirmed that they would willingly engage in sexual intercourse in a relationship marked by much affection.[22] In the sex code of the young, intercourse could be sanctioned in a specific marriage-oriented relationship.

The young thus placed great emphasis on the cogency of sexual involvement in a love relationship. This, of course, highlighted the already prevalent theme that sex in marriage was desirable and necessary to complete fulfillment. The young merely took this ethos a step further, extending its implicit morality to the period before marriage. The young thus accepted and in turn accentuated the prevailing marriage-love-sex syndrome. Sex for them had become a part of love and helped to define a relationship where love prevailed. It was emotional commitment above all that legitimated eroticism, for the young were true romantics who believed strongly in love. Unlike the saccharine sentimentalists of the nineteenth century who idealized marriage and dissociated love from physical passion, the young were romantic realists, who considered an accusation of sentimentality to be "a striking indictment" against their character. But their devotion to candor and reality and their high valuation of sophistication and "smoothness" did not make them hard-nosed cynics or any less devoted to love.[23] Rather they rejected idealized notions of love that shunned physical realities. "Formerly the people prided themselves on an outward front of righteousness," mused the editor of the *Daily Illini*. "The youth of today rather prides himself on being a good enough sport to be not 'too good.' . . . Where the ancient rules have been foolish he has scoffed, and rightly so; but where the ancient code has touched a vital principle he has hesitated to overstep its bounds." [24] Such reflections were a commonplace in the college papers of the twenties. On the whole, they express the philosophy of the young very well indeed: honesty in the face of the facts and a tempered respect in the face of fundamental principles. Sex was a fact. Love was a principle.

By merging sex and love, petting became a *modus operandi,* permissible and even honorable in a relationship marked by a certain amount of affection. Sexual intercourse, while less practical, became possible in a relation where love was clearly demonstrated, as in engagement. In removing the curtain that had earlier separated sex from love, they made love the very basis for response.

That the young had not entirely worked out their conceptions of love and romance is no doubt true. Many of youth's anti-romantic poses were more bravado than sincere belief. Their self-conscious modernism, with its iconoclastic views of old-line sexual hypocrisy, betrayed a lingering uneasiness in the service of sexual love. The veneer of hard-boiled realism was more than a little the demonstration that sex had not yet been fully integrated or harmonized in their views of love and marriage. But by the very loudness of their protestations and by their daring, they laid the ground for a true assimilation of sex in love. When sex was no longer news, then it could comfortably become part of love.

Although solid data on premarital coitus among young women in the 1920's scarcely exist, certain statistical guidelines are available that confirm the vitality of this dating-engagement pattern in the sex lives of the young. For this evidence, however, we are forced to look beyond the 1920's. Surveys of the sexual behavior of young women during the twenties are virtually nonexistent. Fearing that the questionnaires would implant immoral thoughts in the minds of young women, school administrators effectively kept such surveys away from their college and high-school charges. Questioning young men, on the other hand, was not potentially dangerous, and so some studies are available. Even by the late thirties, however, investigators met hostility when they approached school officials with requests to survey their students, and Bromley and Britten found only one college authority, the president of a progressive women's college, who willingly endorsed the inquiry. The only unaffiliated women accessible for study were the sexually deviant: the prostitute or delinquent brought to the courts or counseling agencies. Data collected on the basis of their experience are hardly representative of the morality of most young women.[25]

The earliest reliable evidence available on sexual behavior among college men and women comes in the 1930's, and the most useful is contained in two complementary studies, one by Bromley and Britten on undergraduates, and the other by Burgess and Wallin on engagement among college students.[26] Together these describe an upper limit on sexual activity among youths of the twenties, for the patterns established during the twenties continued to define and organize sexual relations for some time thereafter. Bromley and Britten found that one-fourth of the women and one-half of the men in their extensive sample had experienced premarital sexual intercourse. In general, men had their first encounter earlier than women—in high school at a median age of 17. Women had their first experience in college, at a median age of 18. Among engaged women, the incidence of coitus rose considerably. According to Burgess and Wallin, almost one-half (47%) of the women were not virgins at the time of marriage, but of these three-quarters had restricted their sexual activity exclusively to relations with their future spouse.[27] It is thus probable that sexual intercourse was at least two to three times as likely to occur between couples who were engaged as between those who were not.

Together the Burgess-Wallin and Bromley-Britten studies serve well as evidence for an outer limit of the prevalence of sexual intercourse among college youths in the twenties. The picture they present is fairly clear: probably something less than one-half of all college women in the 1920's experienced coitus prior to marriage, and considerably more than one-half of these had restricted that activity to a serious, marriage-oriented relationship.[28]

Undoubtedly there was a liberalization in sexual ethics during the twenties, but it was a liberalization with very clear limits. The young had evolved a new standard and developed a new code to govern the relations between men and women. These defined a new sphere of possibilities. As important as the new possibilities were the new definitions. The revolution in sexual morality went on within the rules of the game. Those rules defined petting as an appropriate form of eroticism for the unmarried young and intercourse as an acceptable demonstration of love for those committed to marriage.

III

The acceptance of erotic love by the young in the twenties made tolerance of the actions of others possible. All studies of attitudes note a sharp increase in tolerance among the young. In one such study, Walter Buck reported a consistent decline in the number of things disapproved of by young people, especially in relation to sexual matters, and a "consistent liberalizing of opinion," which he suggested resulted from the liberalization in "mores or systems of morals and manners of the society in which these young people lived." Among the women questioned by Blanchard and Manasses, only one-third disapproved of friends who had extramarital sex experience, and only 13% would break their friendship on the basis of that disapproval. Noting a marked difference between the behavior that these women chose for themselves and that which they would accept in others, the authors concluded, "Meticulous as are their personal standards, most of the girls who answered the questionnaires evinced a tolerance toward others whose ideals might be less exacting. They would not pass judgment upon friends whose behaviors deviated from their own code of conduct." Men registered a similar liberalization in their attitudes toward virginity in a wife. Three-quarters of the men interviewed by Bromley and Britten were prepared to marry a woman who was not a virgin.[29]

There thus remained a notable distinction among youth in the twenties between behavior and attitudes, a latent hypocrisy in a generation that was contemptuous of hypocrisy. Ernest Burgess remarked on this disjunction when he observed that the decline in importance of premarital chastity had significantly affected attitudes but not yet permeated behavior patterns. Others were similarly impressed by a profound liberalization in views that had far outdistanced norms of conduct. The young seemed to have been caught in a time-lag, the effect of what Talcott Parsons has called "a slow, uneven, and often painful process," [30] by which norms are adapted to new conditions and behavior is permitted to effect expectations. The young had become more permissive sexually, but their actions were neither so pronounced as many historians have long assumed nor so courageous as the ideals of self-expression toward which they had already committed their views.

Yet the implicit values and attitudes were significant. The young were enunciating an ideal of sex as a private matter to be determined by personal needs rather than by moral prescriptions. The college newspapers reflected this view in their cynical disdain for all moral reformers, whom they condemned as self-righteous usurpers of personal freedom. The young were unswerving in their contempt for moral intolerance, whether by the disciples of the Eighteenth Amendment, blue-law advocates, or the members of various leagues for moral purity.[31] They condemned them on the abstract grounds of personal freedom and often even more strongly on grounds of impracticality. Morality, the young insisted, could not and should not be imposed. This sexual attitude was only one part of a much larger world view that affected youth's views and behavior in manners as well as morals and in politics as well as private styles.

The new code of permissible eroticism and the liberalized attitudes toward sex relations had a large effect on mate selection and on the roles of women. Once petting became an acceptable form of behavior between men and women who "dated," then the whole double standard became vulnerable. The standard was not destroyed in the twenties but, by sanctioning petting and legitimating sexual love, youth had opened the door to increased sexual permissiveness. It was still not part of the code to permit or to encourage premarital sexual intercourse, and most women did not elect it for themselves, but it was now an indiscretion and not a moral outrage.

As significantly, young men and women came to deny that the double standard had a basis in fact or in abstract morality. As a result, in word if not in deed, they voiced their opposition to an inherent need to differentiate between the behavior of the sexes. The editor of the *Wisconsin Daily Cardinal* expressed it well: "The new woman is not of the clinging vine type. . . . She has elected to discard many of the feminine wiles and tricks which were formerly supposed to be her chief stock in trade. . . . But after all, what has the present age lost? If man has lost his ideal, he has gained a pal; if woman no longer exists on a pedestal where man may kneel in worship, she at least meets him on a common level and in fair comradeship offers her counsel and aid." [32] Men had gained not only a pal but a sexual partner as well.

The behavior and attitudes of the young emphasized the ideals of compatibility and mutuality that have been discussed elsewhere. Female virtue became less important than affection and response. Relationships were less hedged by traditionally ascribed roles, of which female purity had been the most important, and there was now more possibility for personal expression and the growth of fuller affectionate relations. Within limits, emotional and physical demonstrations of affection had been at least partially freed from traditional inhibitions. The young were seeking satisfactions and gratifications of all sorts in the relations between the sexes, both before and after marriage. So too, parentally reinforced status attributions became less important as young people judged each other on the basis of peer definitions that emphasized personality, attractiveness, and sexual allure. [33]

IV

Not surprisingly, the new attention to sexuality colored a whole range of related behavior. Language became more candid and conversations more frank as the fact of freer association between the sexes was accompanied by a basic commitment to freedom of expression. As women became companions to men in work and play, it was easier to see them as "pals" and partners, and the informal access between the sexes radically affected ideas of *de facto* equality and the manners that reflected that equality. At the same time, this access encouraged a pronounced attention to sexual attractiveness and to the cultivation of styles that operated on a purely sexual level. [34]

What is at first glance enigmatic in the fashions and manners of young women in the twenties—the apparent conflict between those modes that emphasized her boyish characteristics, her gamin quality, and those that consciously heightened her sexual piquancy—must be understood in terms of the two distinct but related consequences of this new access between the sexes. They express not conflict but a well-poised tension between the informal boyish companion and the purposefully erotic vamp. They served at once a symbolic and a functional role in the new variety of relationships between the sexes. Bobbed hair, for example, which was the prevailing style for women on all campuses, was enthusiastically defended on the grounds that it was carefree and less troublesome to care for than the long ponderous mane, which was *de rigueur* in the prewar period. It facilitated indulgence in ad-hoc and informal activities like sports and made it easier for women to remain well-groomed during an increasingly busy campus or work day.[35] It was indeed liberating, as it emphasized the woman's more informal existence and behavior. It allowed her to feel equal with men and unencumbered by a traditional symbol of her different role.

At the same time, the short hair was carefully marcelled, a process that occasioned no end of campus humor. The well-sculpted head was, in fact, in the context of the twenties, more self-consciously erotic than fluffy long hair that was girlish and young. Long hair was often inimical to real sexual allure because it was necessary to wear it carefully tied in a bun or chignon. Hair worn loose had for a long time been restricted to very young girls. Older girls, forced to compose it because it was improper to wear hair so informally and because it was unmanageable in an active day, often appeared staid and sedate. Short hair, on the other hand, could be worn freely and the possibility of prudish compactness averted. Bobbed hair was often attacked as a symbol of female promiscuity, of explicit sexuality, and of a self-conscious denial of respectability and the domestic ideal.[36] Once we suspend absolute definitions of sexual attractiveness, we can begin to see the sexuality implicit in bobbed hair in the context of the period. It was not mannish but liberating, and that liberation implied a renunciation of sexual stereotypes.

Moreover, the short hair gave an air of sophistication in keeping with the image projected on the movie screen. The fact that Gloria Swanson, for instance, was wearing her bob sleekly pressed around her head and not carefully curled was well-noted and imitated. Interest in the fashions of the glamor queens of the cinema was great, and bobbed hair was glamorous. To be deemed attractive by campus society, one subscribed to the going definition of fashion and sophistication.[37]

Short skirts, which became increasingly abbreviated as the decade progressed, were defended on the same grounds of comfort and practicality. Again, women could feel less encumbered and freer to engage in all the purportedly male activities. But the provocation of bared calves and knees was not overlooked. One outraged observer, a divinity student at Duke University, was so repelled by the bared knees of coeds that he was provoked to write a disgusted letter to the school paper. What really offended him, more even than the fashion, was the women's manipulation of the fashions. The coed, he observed, "would look every now and then to assure herself that they [her knees] were exposed to the nth degree." He went on to explain quite accurately that the girls did it because it drew the boys' attention and approval.[38] The sexual provocation of shortened skirts was further increased by wearing open lacework stockings and rolled hose that often bared flesh as well as contour. Silk stockings had become a necessity for the new-fashioned woman and an object of gift-giving and male attention, and the sheerer models were overwhelmingly favored by the young whatever the increased expense. Surely mere utility would not have dictated silk rather than lisle nor made the sheerer models more desirable. An enormous variety of colors, patterns, and degrees of opacity were displayed for the young woman's market—all helped to draw attention to the leg.[39]

In addition, women wore less and less clothing during the twenties, discarding corsets, garter belts, layers of petticoats, and waists. Facetious male editors, perhaps as a line of defense against their own provoked responses, were prone to speculate on the number of garments women still wore and to take a paternal interest in the coeds' vulnerability to cold winds and raw weather. While the editors decried the fashion-consciousness of young women, they gave latent approval by their obvious interest.[40] Men were obviously intrigued, surprised, and maybe even a bit worried. But except for an occasional Victorian-minded sister, women rather liked the attention evidenced by the concern. No doubt the shedding of layers of under- and over-garments freed women for more lively and uninhibited participation in various activities, but it was also intentionally provocative. To accompany the trend in skirt lengths and form-revealing silhouettes, there was a keen calorie-consciousness among young women. Dieting became so popular that newspapers often cited the calorie value of foods and gave nutritional advice about the amount of food intake that would help to sustain or shed weight. Young women were conscious of the new vamp silhouette and sought to imitate the lean, honed-down proportions of the movie queens.[41]

The defense of the new clothes and hair styles on the grounds of practicality had a solid basis in reality.[42] The loosened and dropped waistline was more functional than the tightly-bound middle that demanded strong, often painful, corseting and large expenditures of time in dress. Women felt freed from the necessities of such formality and inhibition and preferred the non-restraint of the loosened waist. The symbolic importance of the freedom must not, however, be overlooked. Women increasingly denied that they wished to be placed in restraints when they were engaging in the same activities as the men at their sides. The campus, as well as the white-collar professions of secretary, typist, and salesgirl, now provided a host of occasions for men to work with women.[43] Why should her clothes not reflect the woman's new status?

Significantly, women made the most of the occasions provided by these business and school contacts, and the clothes that were defended as practical also enhanced sexual attractiveness. The form de-emphasized at the waist was compensated in bared legs and arms; and the sculpted waist of the nineties certainly met its equal in the bared shoulders and backs and the clinging fabrics popular in the evenings.[44] For while provocation was tempered in daytime wear with its loose lines and straight proportions, evening dress was emphatically sophisticated. Sleek and neat, far more erotic than feminine flounces, it emphasized the new sexual maturity of the young woman.

There was little practical reason but much self-conscious sexuality in the open and unabashed use of cosmetics by young women in the twenties. After a short period in the early twenties when, like bobbed hair, it produced humorous male comment (not on moral but on aesthetic grounds), makeup became an acceptable female prerogative. The vanity case and the powder puff were never far from the young woman's reach, and powdering in public became a favorite subject for editorial comment and male derision, as well as the bane of school officials.[45]

The cosmetics most popular with young women emphasized artificiality and tended to draw attention to their use. Face powder was indispensable. It smoothed out an uneven surface and covered a shiny nose, giving the face a smooth, whitened finish. Rouge and lipstick then added the necessary color. The result was a heightened contrast between pale skin and rouged lips and cheeks. There was nothing natural about the effect. Rather it contrasted surface contour and color sensuality. The plucked brow further accented this effect, as the uneven line of the natural brow was replaced by a precise arch. Lips too, were sometimes artfully bow-shaped. Each feature stood out against a smooth white surface. It was an artificial scheme that produced a doll-like painted look when cosmetics were used to excess.[46]

Cosmetics were used to increase attractiveness, but they were more than that—they were provocative. The use of cosmetics symbolized the woman's open acceptance of her own sexuality.

Whatever the long history of cosmetics and their general use, the reference point for women in the twenties was not ancient Egypt or India but the America of the late nineteenth and early twentieth centuries. And by the mores of that period, cosmetics were immoral. They were associated with prostitutes.[47] By appropriating the right to use such sexual aids, respectable women proclaimed that they too were endowed with a sexual personality. They had taken on themselves as potential wives all the characteristics of lovers. The two kinds of women were no longer separate and distinguishable at first glance but one and the same.

Young women did not generally abuse their new-found cosmetic allies. They used powder, rouge, and lip color in moderation with an eye to increasing allure without offending propriety. The moderate use was in conformity with the standards and expectations of their peers, who had incorporated cosmetics as a permissible part of fashion. That the peer group that encouraged the use of cosmetics also limited its over-indulgence was lost on adults. The adult world, its eyes still fixed on an older standard, stood aghast. But among the young the moderate use of cosmetics was encouraged and recognized for what it was, an attempt to increase physical attractiveness and to score points in the game of rating within the rules set by the peer group. As Ernest Burgess noted, "Youth in this day and generation are rated in terms of sex appeal." [48] Cosmetics were part of that rating scheme. In a value system where sexuality was recognized as a fact and sexual attractiveness was an asset, it demonstrated conformity to group standards. The use of makeup was a mark of respectable conformity and not the contrary.

Adult critics tied to an older standard failed to understand how cosmetics could make one respectable. One seventeen-year-old girl complained, "If a girl wears short skirts and just a little rouge, mother thinks she is indecent, when she really is a nice girl and dresses as all the others do." For girls living at home, clothes and cosmetics were a frequent point of contention between parents and children. A young woman, Blanchard and Manasses observed, was often forced to conceal things from her parents "which might worry the parents but which really do not expose her to any great degree of danger." College administrators similarly misunderstood the meaning of cosmetics and accused coeds of being bold and brazen.[49]

The young were quick to defend the new woman as not immoral, only more free. Her clothes, her hair, her attention to her sexual self were badges of that freedom. At Duke University, a young minister's attack on coeds' clothes and rouged cheeks was greeted with jeers from the editor: "It is just such outbursts as this that label the country preachers 'old fogies' and do much harm to the ministerial profession." The editor went on to make a statement about women's rights to personal choice with which most contemporary youths would have agreed. "We believe that for the most part woman's dress is her personal affair. Personally, we do not believe that rouge enhances a beautiful woman's beauty, but not all women are beautiful. But we fail to see why a man should have any more right to prohibit a woman from wearing rouge than she has to prohibit his smoking cigarettes, wearing loud 'collegiate' sweaters and balloon trousers or using Stacomb on his hair." It had all become a matter of personal preference, which described a new latitude in behavior and helped to release young women from older moral definitions and inhibiting stereotypes. At Ohio State, the editor answered a similar attack on women by noting that men were not making immoral demands on women, nor were women immoral in order to be popular with men. Rather, the critics did not understand the changed nature of relations between men and women: "We concede, of course, that our deference and chivalry are of a later model than yours. . . . We do not go to the ludicrous extremes of chivalry you might have when you were young. Our girls understand our freedom, not because of the demands we make upon them, but because they are themselves freer. . . . This freedom really does no harm. And you mistake something fine for something degrading because it is different from your way of thinking." [50]

The campus social system in a coeducational school provided young women with the best opportunities to develop the dual role of "pal" and sexual partner. [51] Women who attended uni-sex colleges were notably different in their informal dress. While daytime dress at coeducational schools was attractively casual, the dress of women at uni-sex schools seemed deficient in attractiveness, more rugged when sporty, more staid and tailored when formal, less sexually enticing. Some of this resulted from traditional dress regulations carried over from the more formal prewar years. At Barnard, for example, specific permission had to be granted by the dean before women were permitted to go hatless when walking around the campus or in Riverside Park. The lady-wears-a-hat rule was still, however, in effect for walking on Broadway. In 1933, Eunice Fuller Barnard noted that where women in coeducational schools wore French heels and silk stockings and the latest dresses, women at older uni-sex schools sported oxfords, socks, and sweaters. [52] The reason for the difference was clear: there were no men around during the day. At social affairs, the differences in dress melted away.

Although sexual suggestiveness in the dress and manners of women bore the brunt of criticism, young men were not untouched by the increased valuation of sex appeal. The attention given to grooming aids, hair creams like Stacomb, pomades for luster, colognes, and the careful appreciation of the right clothes provoked a good deal of commentary in campus papers. Whereas women were accused of borrowing from men in their boyish styles, men were said to be effeminate in their attention to appearance. The *Daily Illini* noted that there was a tendency toward "little distinction between the fads for both sexes." Women were wearing male costumes like knickers, vests, and ties, while men had become more "choicy" in their selection of fancy perfumes. An article in the Louisiana State *Reveille* described men as spending hours in front of the mirror getting every strand of hair in place and finally resorting to the powder puff should their complexion betray any trace of shine. "The only difference was that the girls do it in public and the boys are ashamed to." At Trinity College the editor of the *Chronicle* noted that in many ways former roles had been reversed as men became more enslaved to fashion than women, while the "co-ed stands meekly by and casts envious glances toward her rival, yeah even her better, in dress, women's own natural gift." The men, like the women, were concerned to increase sexual attractiveness and followed the lead of glamorous models. The slicked-down hair and the baggy "Valentino" pants reflected the conscious effort to emulate movie idols noted for their sexuality. "Makes a Young Man Better Looking," announced one college ad for an after-shave complexion lotion.[53] For men as for women, better looks meant better opportunities.

When carried to extremes, as it was among the notoriously "smooth" types who applied themselves excessively to social concerns, this fashion- and style-conscious male was criticized as a "lounge-lizard," a "tea-hound," a "cooky-pusher," or a "sofa-moth"—a man who devoted his time to the cultivation of female company. While he was in a distinct minority on the campus, some of his modes and manners were imitated by the majority of the men, and he represented in the extreme the concern with sexual attractiveness general on the campus. In extreme form, the type verged on the effete, but in combination with more rugged clothes like the omnipresent sheepskin jacket and the fashionable leather coat and in the context of an intense interest in athletics, it represented a touch of decadent allure that heightened sexual appeal.[54]

So too, the male "line" was a conscious extension of the cultivated attention to sexual manners. A line was a well-rehearsed and oft-repeated set of phrases used by men when introduced to women. The line was a mark of sophistication, a demonstration of worldliness, a touch of cynicism that made a man more attractive by making him more dangerous. "As for the co-eds," remarked a solicitous Trinity editor, "don't the young sweet things know that the senior law students have a line so long and slippery that it can't be caught?" But it was the very slipperiness that made the line effective. It was a staged ritual, a self-conscious and even self-protective form of sexual aggression in the new and potentially dangerous sexual explorations in which the young were engaged. It was well known that the line was not spontaneous but used as a staged approach in meeting and cultivating female company. It identified a man as experienced, so the approval of the line reflected the desirability of "experience" in meeting respectable women.[55] A man without a line was an innocent, basically not savvy in the ways of the world. Like a woman without her cosmetics, a man without his line went out naked into the frightening wilderness of a newly sexual world. With its barely veiled sexual naughtiness, the line pointed up the ways in which conscious sexuality had been incorporated into the rituals of attack and protection that governed male and female interaction.

V

Various factors came together in the 1920's to heighten interest in sexual matters and to produce a basic change in the sexual manners and mores of the young. The family had become more and more concerned with responding to the emotional and personality needs of the children, and affection in the relations between all members of the family was now more openly and informally demonstrated. It is not surprising that children reared in such an atmosphere should eagerly expect to demonstrate and to receive emotional reinforcements in relations that looked toward marriage and family life. Nurtured in an atmosphere of emotional intensity, the young could more easily express emotion in their relations with others. Personality, too, had been cultivated in the family, and the young believed that their dating relations should encourage more uninhibited personal expression. Most campus relations, sexual or not, were oriented toward personality, congeniality, and compatibility.

At the same time, the family had granted the young more freedom within the home and more time to engage in a variety of relationships outside the home. This gave youth more opportunities to cultivate and to be influenced by peer example and peer pressure. The school especially provided the occasion for such exposure. During adolescence, sexual concerns became urgent, and peer opinion and example relieved the individual of responsibility for his own decisions on a matter so important and so weighted with taboos and fears. Peer example and the insulation of the young from other institutional pressures and family supervision were especially effective at the coeducational colleges, where the most opportunities existed for experimentation in sexual manners. The campus thus became an ideal locale for the exploration of sexual interests, sanctioned by peer opinion. Petting became a campus ritual, permitting such experimentation without contravening family standards about the immorality of premarital coitus. Both the family and the peer group became less important, however, among engaged couples when the need for response often over-rode social considerations and intercourse became a legitimate form for expressing affection. This was in line with the new evaluation of sex in general and of erotic love in particular. The trend toward intercourse in engagement reinforced the already powerful association of marriage and sex and the desirability of sexual satisfaction within marriage. Sexual relations thus expressed the urge toward marital compatibility among the engaged and epitomized the marriage-love-sex ethic prevalent in the culture.

The changes in social environment reinforced these factors. In the city there were few ritualized patterns for association between men and women, few community- and group-supervised activities. Dating and pairing, which had once been reserved for late stages of courting, now became the usual mode of association from the beginning of a relationship, and they opened the door to greater personal intimacy and the testing of mutual compatibility. So too, the movies and marketing techniques increasingly exploited sexual themes that heightened sexual awareness and emphasized its basic function in attractiveness. Popular symbols of glamor gave legitimacy to once forbidden subjects.[56] The young, insulated in peer environments, could and did turn to these models as standards for their own behavior.

The young were more and more orienting their behavior to non-traditional institutions—peers rather than parents, movies rather than the local community. New institutional moderators and new values forced changes in mores and norms to take place. Those changes were not total, for family and community opinion certainly continued to count, but that opinion was now checked and often over-ridden by new signals. In the twenties, these institutions and values had taken on a momentum and an importance that made them for the first time effective regulators of conduct. The Jeremiahs believed that in the twenties all controls on the behavior of youth had been eroded. What they failed to see was that older controls were being supplemented or supplanted by newer controls. The seeming chaos of the twenties was not anarchy but a culture re-creating itself. In that process and at that point, the young, beset by sexual anxieties and preparing for future roles, grasped a new measure of control over their own behavior. In so doing they not only freed themselves from the past but became independent agents in a changing society.

7

Symbols of Liberation

To me the Jazz Age signifies an age of freedom in thought and action. The average young person of today is not bound by the strict conventions which governed the actions of previous generations.

University of Denver coed [1]

The word flapper to us means not a female atrocity who smokes, swears, delights in pictures like "The Sheik" and kisses her gentlemen friends goodnight, although there is no particular harm in any of the foregoing. We always think of the flapper as the independent, "pally" young woman, a typical American product. Frivolity . . . is not a crime, and flappers, being young, are naturally frivolous.

Any real girl . . . who has the vitality of young womanhood, who feels pugilistically inclined when called the "weaker sex," who resents being put on a pedestal and worshipped from afar, who wants to get into things herself, is a flapper. . . . The flapper is the girl who is responsible for the advancement of woman's condition in the world. The weak, retiring, "clinging" variety of woman really does nothing in the world but cling.

Letter to the editor, *Daily Illini,* April 20, 1922

Youth's exhilarated self-awareness and delight in the expansive possibilities of a changing world can easily be confused with a sense of freedom, and indeed the youth of the twenties often talked as if they were a newly free generation. In fact, however, to describe them as free would be to misunderstand the reality of their lives and, more significantly, to lose sight of their historical role and influence. They were bound—tightly bound—to family, to school, to each other, and to the many social conditions that held them fast to a specific time. Still, their sense of liberation was quite real. So was their sense of themselves as liberators, for they helped to free a whole range of behaviors and beliefs from older constraints, traditional prohibitions, and conventional assumptions. This was the case in sexual behavior, for example. It was true as well in such areas as smoking for women, dancing and music forms, and social drinking. We think of these today as trivial matters concerned with manners or style. It is easy to forget that not so long ago they were issues weighted with moral taboos and sexual proprieties. It was from these older associations that the youth of the twenties liberated these (to us) minor indulgences. For them, each carried a large burden of history and convention, and in separating them from the old assumptions they also helped to rip apart an older world view. As they adopted these behaviors, first as part of their own lives and then as part of the culture they were helping to create, the young carved out a whole new territory to be governed by personal style, preference, and taste. Ironically, in so doing, they transformed the consequential into the trivial. But they also redefined the public and the private. And part of their historical significance lies precisely in the fact that by differentiating custom from morality, taste from propriety, the youth of the twenties set the stage for a new pluralism in behavior and the rhythm for rapid change in cultural forms.

I

Smoking was perhaps the one most potent symbol of young woman's testing of the elbow room provided by her new sense of freedom and equality. Prostitutes and women in liberated bohemian and intellectual sets had been known to flaunt their cigarettes publicly and privately before the twenties. But in respectable middle-class circles, and especially among young women, smoking, like rouging, was simply not done. Throughout the twenties, smoking could still provoke heated commentary, and for many young women, to smoke in public was a welcome form of notoriety. Although young women in college did not initiate the smoking habit, they increasingly took advantage of the cigarette as a symbol of liberation and as a means of proclaiming their equal rights with men. More importantly, within the college community they had the support of peer-group opinion. Among the young, smoking for women became widely accepted during the twenties, and while smoking remained an issue, as the decade wore on it became an acceptable and familiar habit among college women.[2]

Smoking is not a sexual activity in itself. In the abstract, it is morally neutral. In the context of the specific values of American society, however, it was both morally value-laden and sexually related. Like cosmetics, smoking was sexually suggestive and associated with disreputable women or with bohemian types who self-consciously rejected traditional standards of propriety and morality. College administrators objected to smoking because it undermined an ideal of proper female behavior and decency. As the Dean of Women at Ohio State University noted, smoking was simply not "done in the best circles," and it was, in the words of the Dean of Rhode Island State College, "an unladylike act." In 1920, when four girls were dismissed from a female seminary in the Midwest, the administration admitted that smoking did not make them "bad girls" but claimed that such behavior would undermine commonly accepted standards of decency and might lead to other socially objectionable practices.[3] The implication was clear. The objection to women's smoking was based on traditional criteria of proper conduct for women; once one of these was questioned, all of them would be questioned.

The right to smoke was denied to women as part of the double standard of morality. The implicit fear was that smoking would have an immoral effect on women because it removed one further barrier from the traditional differentiation of the roles and behaviors of the sexes. Smoking implied a promiscuous equality between men and women and was an indication that women could enjoy the same vulgar habits and ultimately also the same vices as men. It further eroded a tradition that held women to be morally superior to men. Moreover, the kind of woman who smoked in the period before the twenties was disreputable or defiant, and smoking was therefore associated with immorality. Thus, one correspondent to the UCLA paper objected to popular cigarette ads featuring women smoking because they lowered the moral "tone of the paper." Those who objected to smoking could give no specific moral definition to the habit. They were forced instead to argue that smoking was simply "unladylike." [4] The opponents of smoking were ultimately helpless when the young rejected the insincerity and dubious distinctions of such conventions.

These associations and conventions underlay the almost unanimous reaction to what became a *cause célèbre* in the twenties, the lifting of the no-smoking ban at Bryn Mawr College. That action brought the issue out into the open and reflected the growing acceptance of smoking in the college community. When in 1925 President Marion Edwards Park, in response to pressure from the student body, opened smoking rooms at various points on the campus, the day of the smoking young woman had dawned. The Bryn Mawr gesture was, of course, more symptomatic than revolutionary, but it was important nevertheless because it provided official sanction to what had been unofficially countenanced by the peer group and because it came in response to community demands. That it occurred at Bryn Mawr, one of the bastions of prestige and respectability, made the action all the more powerful in the public imagination. Bryn Mawr was, in fact, not the first school to permit women to smoke on campus, but President Park had done her deed with a flourish of publicity and well-poised liberality. Similar requests for smoking rights by Vassar and Wellesley students and by women at Brown had been rejected by school officials.[5]

Moreover, Park's action came at a time when most schools had strong anti-smoking ordinances. At Mt. Holyoke and Smith, for example, the penalty for smoking on or near the campus was suspension. At Nebraska Wesleyan Teachers College women who smoked were refused certificates of teaching. Indeed, some schools that did not have such regulations because the issue had not heretofore been raised began to impose them in the twenties. Rules have no rationale when the behavior they are meant to control does not exist, and smoking had not been a problem. Vassar College, which had no anti-smoking rule before, imposed one in 1925, and in 1926 so did the University of California at Berkeley.[6]

Park's liberal gesture provoked consternation among deans of women throughout the country. In effect, she had given official recognition to the prevalence of the habit among college women. The reactions were predictable, for they reflected the disparity between traditional perceptions and newly accepted habits. Administrators reacted by linking custom to morality. The young severed custom from morality and regarded the antipathy to smoking for women as a meaningless convention, long overdue for revision. At Kansas State Teachers College, President W. A. Brandenberg reacted with anger: "Nothing has occurred in higher education that has so shocked our sense of social decency as the action at Bryn Mawr." At Northwestern University, the Dean of Women announced that should a girl be found smoking anywhere on the campus, in town, or even at her home, she would be summarily dismissed for immoral behavior. In her view, "nice girls" did not smoke. "Any girl I catch smoking anywhere and at any time will not be permitted to remain in college," declared the Dean at Rhode Island State College after dismissing two girls who were caught. When the

Dean of Women at Minnesota heard about the action at Bryn Mawr, she quickly formulated a policy: "Smoke and leave school." When asked whether she would ever follow Bryn Mawr's lead and permit women at the University of Minnesota to smoke, Dean E. E. Nichols answered unequivocally, "Never." So pressing did the urgency of the issue now appear that in 1925 the presidents of the Eastern women's colleges met to discuss smoking rules.[7]

But the young rejected the standards of propriety that governed the actions of the administrations. They overwhelmingly accepted the right of women to smoke in the 1920's, and smoking received the approval of most college papers. It was probably not true everywhere and among all youths: women at Coe College, Iowa, for example, were still shocked when a female guest lecturer smoked publicly and with abandon.[8] But it became increasingly true at the larger non-denominational schools for women, in coeducational universities, and even in high schools. Starting first in the East and then becoming general on the West Coast, the new freedom penetrated to the heart of the Midwest, and even into the South where women were probably viewed more traditionally than elsewhere. At the University of Texas, for example, between 1920 and 1925 there was a marked increase in smoking among coeds and an important liberalization of opinion among male and female students about whether smoking was wrong for women. By 1927, North Carolina's Duke *Chronicle* carried a large ad for Old Golds in which two young women were portrayed eagerly enjoying their smokes. By the end of the decade, smoking for women had become legitimate. When women were given permission to smoke at Stanford in 1927, the editor of the UCLA newspaper noted that only six years before the women's editor at Stanford had caused a scandal and was nearly dismissed for even suggesting that women should be allowed to smoke.[9]

It is impossible to know how many young women smoked habitually or occasionally during the twenties. Precise statistics are unavailable, but it is clear that smoking was becoming more popular among college women. At Ohio State one-third of the coeds admitted smoking at least occasionally, and an ad-hoc survey of weekending women at Bowdoin College revealed that there were as many women who smoked one brand, Luckies, as all those who did not smoke at all. One knowledgeable fraternity leader at Rhode Island State College declared, "Practically all the girls smoke." [10] But this seems unlikely. In many ways, knowing how many women smoked is unnecessary. Smoking is no more a necessary expression of female freedom than sexual intercourse alone is a gauge of sexual activity. More important than the extent of smoking was the increasing sense that women could smoke if they chose to and the breaking away by the young from traditional proscriptions governing female behavior and connecting smoking with immorality. In 1925, noting that the Dean of Women at the University of Texas was surprised and outraged to find that coeds were smoking, the editor of the *Daily Illini* chided, "The girls are beginning to smoke! Good Gracious, Annabelle! They have been smoking for months and years. One only has to be a boy and answer the continued demands for 'a drag' or a cigarette to know that smoking has with the fair young co-eds long ceased to be a practice. It is an art, and one of their most perfectly practiced ones. All co-eds at the University do not smoke but neither do all the boys." He explained that women who did not smoke failed to do so either because they did not like the taste, or because they did not yet consider it "quite lady-like," but certainly "morals never came in for consideration on this score. It is taste, social and olfactory." Furthermore, those girls who did not smoke themselves rarely "score anyone else for smoking." [11]

Women and men on the campuses of the twenties proclaimed that women had a right to smoke if they pleased: "If a man can enjoy his coke more by smoking as he drinks it, why isn't it logical to assume that a woman can enjoy hers more when it is accompanied by a cigarette?" asked one woman correspondent at Illinois. "Why shouldn't a woman have a taste for cigarettes just as a man has? It is not the smoking that breaks down the bonds of convention between men and women . . . a woman can command just as much respect with a cigarette in her mouth as without." At New York University women claimed their rights by announcing that they would hold a smoker rather than a traditional tea. The Dean was outraged and prohibited the event, but the women went ahead with their plans anyway. Blanchard and Manasses found that 80% of the young women they questioned approved of smoking for women. In marked contrast, only 26% of the parents approved.[12]

Except for occasional facetious comments about lost male prerogatives, women's smoking generally received the approval of college editors on two grounds. In the first place, the papers took a critical attitude toward all attempts to reform or regulate conduct in the name of moral uplift. Invariably hostile to the pseudo-reforms that abounded in the twenties with the prevailing fears about moral degeneration, editors thus defended the rights of men or women to smoke as an expression of their right to self-determination in morals and behavior. Editors were quick to point out that those who objected to drinking would soon find in smoking another fertile realm for regulation. Smoking for men and women was for the young a personal issue of preference, not morality. The editor of the *Daily Illini* rebuked those who would regulate smoking among women and asserted that the silly "anti-smoking attempts of moral guardians, usually self appointed, to paint the nasty weed in crimson stain of immorality are a great joke." "Smoking by women," the editor at Louisiana State observed, "is entirely a question of attitude, of personal taste, and possibly of hygiene." The coed, he noted, "reasons quite logically that there is nothing in cigarette smoking which is degrading or immoral, and that, in the final analysis, there is very little difference between a man's smoking and a woman's smoking." Attempts to legislate this form of behavior, like all moral reforms, he continued, were "worse than useless," because they would only be an added inducement for women to flaunt their defiance.[13]

Second, the specific question of women's smoking was defended on the broad grounds of female equality and a woman's inherent right to indulge her tastes just as men had always done. "In this day," one Illinois correspondent asserted, "one has a perfectly good right to ask why men should be permitted to smoke while girls are expelled for doing it." In this, editors and correspondents went beyond the smoking issue to object to discriminatory regulations of all kinds that restricted women's freedom to a larger degree than men's. "Paternalism in colleges," the editor of the *Ohio State Lantern* announced, "is nowhere as pronounced as maternalism. It seems that in nearly every coeducational college in the country, the regulations affecting co-eds are far more drastic and far more circumscribing than the regulations for men. . . . Is this 'new freedom' and 'equality of the sexes' a chimera? Are men really better able to take care of themselves than women? Is the co-ed an inferior sort of person who must have a guardian as if she were feeble-minded or insane? Almost every coeducational school in the country answers 'No' in its classrooms but 'Yes' in its regulations." The double standard, not completely dead even among the young, was quickly losing its theoretical rationale and with that its efficacy as a guide to behavior. The *Barnard Bulletin*, always quick to defend women's rights and equality in intellectual matters, made clear the relationship between intellectual and social equality. Noting that "instructors in any state normal college in Nebraska will be refused leaves of absence to study or attend the Universities of Columbia, Chicago and Northwestern hereafter, because the testimony of those who have been students and the news items in the daily press show that cigarette smoking is common anong women in these institutions," the editor announced that although women had not yet been spanked and sent to bed, "they were being cloistered from tobacco and research." [14] The editor had made a telling point. How could one hope to separate the classroom from the campus?

Women in the twenties had appropriated the right to indulge

in a previously tabooed behavior. Noting the revolution in women's behavior that had taken place in the span of ten years between 1920 and 1930, Blanchard and Manasses observed: "The 1920 co-ed, if her spirit was bold, may have tried a cigarette or two, surreptitiously, but she certainly could not have risked her reputation by smoking in public, and such a gesture would have been considered serious enough to have secured her dismissal from the halls of learning. To expel women students for smoking in this year of grace would sadly deplete the college and university enrollments. . . . She does not even need to feel defiant about it, it is no longer a sign of adolescent rebellion against authority, but a piece of completely commonplace behavior." By 1933 Eunice Fuller Barnard found that cigarettes had already become "outdated" as symbols of woman's new freedom.[15]

Youth in the twenties denied that certain kinds of behavior were worse for women than for men and they rejected the notion that smoking involved a question of morality or propriety. Undoubtedly, many women began to smoke in the twenties because it was a glamorous affectation and somewhat naughty. They thus welcomed the sexual connnotation that lingered around smoking and incorporated such sexual suggestiveness as part of their right.[16] By the end of the decade what had been risqué became merely another sphere of permissible behavior and, like the rights to sexual expression, it had been appropriated by women in their newer sense of freedom and the expanded concept of social equality.

II

In the twenties, young men and women danced whenever the opportunity presented itself. Unquestionably the most popular social pastime, dancing was, of all potentially questionable and morally related behaviors, the least disreputable in the view of the young. For most youths dancing was not even questionable but a thoroughly respectable and almost compulsory form of socializing. Even at denominational schools, where dancing continued to be regarded as morally risky by officials, students clamored for a relaxation of the older bans as they asked officials to give up outdated "prejudiced feelings" and respond to "the bending of current public opinion." [17] A dance was an occasion. It was a meeting ground between young men and women. It was a pleasurable recreation. But above all it was a craze.

The dancers were close, the steps were fast, and the music was jazz. And because popular forms of dancing were intimate and contorting, and the music was rhythmic and throbbing, it called down upon itself all the venom of offended respectability. Administrative officials as well as women's clubs and city fathers found the dancing provocative and indecent and tried at least to stop the young from engaging in its most egregious forms, if not from the dances entirely. [18] But the young kept on dancing.

They started during the war years, and they danced through the decade. Dancing would leave its stamp on the twenties forever, and jazz would become the lingering symbol for an era. But whatever its symbolic value during the twenties and thereafter, dancing and jazz were forms of recreation, even a means of peer-group communication, that youth appropriated to itself. [19] Dancing was, in the words of one survey of student life, the "chief social diversion of college men and women," and school officials unanimously acknowledged that it was the most popular and universally indulged social activity. Almost all fraternity and university social affairs revolved around mixed dancing. Advertisements for dancing instruction appeared in most college papers. At the high schools, too, dancing was a prime occasion for socializing. One simply had to know how to dance to be sociable, and to be popular one had to know how to dance well. The ability to dance was both a sign of belonging to the world of youth and a necessary accomplishment if one wished to take part in the activities of that world. "I adore to dance" was a common remark among high-school girls. When asked what her favorite recreation was, the Vice-President of the Associated Women Students at UCLA answered quickly, "Of course, I adore dancing, who doesn't?" The fact that a man was a "divine dancer" made him an attractive date and added much to his social reputation, whatever his other possible assets or liabilities.[20]

The dances the young enjoyed most were the ones most criticized by adults. The shimmy and the toddle, which had become popular during the war, started the decade and the young on their dancing way. They were followed by the collegiate, the charleston, the black bottom, the tango. The dances brought the bodies and faces of the partners too dangerously close for the comfort of the older folks. Dimmed lights added to the mood. Because of the novelty of the rhythms and the "indecent" motions involved, most of the adverse comments came at the beginning of the decade. As the era progressed, less was said, but not because the dancing stopped. The dancing went on, probably becoming more and not less popular and certainly more hectic.[21] While the steps changed in fad fashion and increased in variety, they remained basically the same—exciting, sensuous, and always to the accompaniment of jazz. The older generation was no less opposed, but by working through the public opinion of the young they found a means of controlling what they considered its most indecent extremes. The young tempered the extremes to meet the adult criticism, but they were really calling the tune.

In the early twenties, college papers, noting administrative opposition to the dancing forms, advised students to reform themselves to forestall administrative interference. Student organizations, especially women's leagues, put the most offensive steps under interdict. But while the editor of the *Daily Illini,* for example, called the shimmy "that insult to our whole moral code," he was careful to distinguish it from the less extreme toddle, which he, like the Women's League and the Student

Council, endorsed.[22] Above all, no editor was willing to condemn dancing in general or the jazz music that accompanied it. These they approved as wholesome pastimes.

Some letters to the editor in the early period took issue with the whole mode of dancing and observed that the toddle as well as the shimmy undermined respectability. Such dancing, critics noted, and jazz music generally, had once been known only in the "Black and Tan districts of Chicago or the East Tenderloin in New York." A college professor called jazz degenerate because it "expresses hysteria, incites idleness, revelry, dissipation, destruction, discord and chaos." [23] In the long run, those who believed all kinds of jazz dancing were offensive proved the more perceptive, for once the rhythm of the music was accepted and approved as it was by the young, the dancing forms appropriate to the music logically followed. By accepting the sensuous and exciting rhythms of modern jazz and its well-known association with the least savory parts of the cities, the young accepted as respectable what their elders logically could not, the excitement and those very qualities of indecency that they formally disdained.

The young made jazz music and jazz dancing a part of their social world and identified with the jazz medium. It became not dancing itself that demonstrated conformity to the peer group but a certain kind of dancing. As a would-be versifier put it,

> Jazz and the bunch jazz with you
> Dance and you're by yourself,
> The mob thinks its jake
> To shimmy and shake,
> For the old fashioned stuff's on the shelf.

"How many men," asked a *Daily Illini* correspondent, "would take a modest, sedate looking girl to a dance and brook the comment of his friends, 'Does Miss Innocence Toddle?' " In an editorial entitled "Heaven Protect Jazz," the *Illini* observed: "A college existence without jazz would be like a child's Christmas without Santa Claus." "Jazz conglomerates are second nature to us now. We have them after every meal in every fraternity and boarding house, on scores of phonographs during the off hours of the morning, at the movies in the afternoons and evenings, at the game, in the music shops, at the dance halls. . . . Without the assurance of jazz from September to June it would be folly to matriculate." College students, the *Ohio State Lantern* noted, were "jazz inebriates." [24]

As with the use of cosmetics, there were within the larger approval of jazz music and jazz dancing limits and standards of respectability consciously set by the young. "Students as a whole do not tolerate dances that savor of the indecent," an Ohio State editor declared. Reinforced by continuous administrative threats, the young carved out a realm of propriety within the jazz medium which only the ultra set on campus dared bypass. At the University of California at Los Angles, the student editor noted that there were no rules or restrictions on dancing imposed by the administration: "Student sentiment is the only restriction we have, but it has never thus far failed to maintain a very desirable plane of conduct. Of our own accord, through several years of custom, we have built up a tradition for thoroughly snappy, thoroughly wholesome dance." The editor went on to warn students not to jeopardize this self-control: "Let's plan to make all measures unnecessary." After chaperones at Louisiana State caused a rumpus by condemning the favored dancing forms, the administration decided that they would no longer "bear the responsibility of censoring improper dancing." In response, students successfully formed a "committee of representative students . . . to formulate a set of 'self-chaperoning' rules, thus making each student the other's chaperone and responsible for his own actions." And when the editor at Duke University urged the Methodist board of governors to ease regulations and approve university-sponsored dances, he promised that students would responsibly patrol themselves: "Dancing is not degrading. . . . To be sure there are steps which could never inspire poetry, or music or grace, but they can be removed. A standard could be set and anything that fell below the standard could be removed." [25]

By agreeing to regulate themselves, the young defined the medium within which that regulation took place. They did not conform to the administrative view of what kind of dancing and music was aesthetically attractive or morally wholesome. They took upon themselves the task of defining the sphere, and within that sphere they imposed regulations of their own. At the University of Minnesota, for example, couples who were dancing in an objectionable fashion were given a card, distributed by the Women's Self-Government Association and the Association of Minnesota Upperclassmen, which read, "We do not dance cheek-to-cheek, shimmy or dance other extreme dances. You must not. A second note will cause your public removal from the hall. Help keep us the Minnesota Standard." Occasional disregard of the rules on the dance floor was noted and condemned in the papers with the wise warning that should such behavior continue and become general the whole enterprise would be endangered. At Ohio State, an editorial entitled "Watch Your Step" made this clear: "Recent rumpus over dancing should make clear to students that they are being watched, constantly, closely and critically." [26]

The administration had not left the young unguarded. Rather, they gave them the freedom to censure their own behavior. At Illinois, officials responded to allegations of indecent dancing by imposing a tight chaperone system, which the student newspaper, noting "Authority's Debut at Dances," condemned as "little more than a police system," but which it wisely recognized was a drastic measure to be followed by even worse unless the young took stock of their own conduct. "If the first show of authority does not impress itself sufficiently to throw the right amount of scare into the few who have made its interference necessary," then there would be a move to abandon all dancing. Even those few who would effectively reject all standards had to conform if this most prized of social sports was to survive. At Louisiana State, the editor similarly warned students that the system of self-regulation was by no means "the last resort" and that "a desperate faculty" would find other means "to make its naughty students behave." [27]

By agreeing to impose rules against extreme varieties of dancing, the young had, however, approved what authorities could not logically approve and what, consistent with an older standard, most denominational schools continued to resist—the jazz medium that was offensive to traditional concepts of decency. The young had, in effect, redefined what was proper according to their own tastes. Dancing for the youth of the twenties was not merely a pleasurable recreation; it was a way of assimilating to their own uses one of the truly new artistic forms of twentieth-century America. It was a form that expressed the uninhibited quality of the new century, its accelerated pace and attention to sensuous movement. The young were surely not alone in their approval, but in identifying with jazz, they both expressed their right to make the choice and as significantly (and symbolically) gave respectability to the content. What was involved was style and sensibility, not philosophy or ideology, but it was a profound redirection all the same. In the name of decency the young mellowed the rhythms and smoothed out some of jazz's more raw passions, transforming the rude into the stylish. But the jazz embraced by the young in the twenties was also an expression and an outlet for the new tempo of American culture, its heterogenous sources, and its more open sexuality.

III

One young woman at Ohio State University refused to hedge the facts in deference to a respectable adult opinion when she summed up the sense of freedom and exhilaration that accompanied youth's indulgence in petting, clothes, dancing, smoking, and drinking:

Are we as bad as we're painted? We are. We do all the things that our mothers, fathers, aunts and uncles do not sanction, and we do them knowingly. We are not young innocents—"we've got the dope" at our finger ends and we use it wisely for our own protection. . . .

The slogan of the present college generation is "getting by" or "getting away with it." We are "playing the game" and flattering ourselves that we are "doing it well" in all these things— smoking, dancing like Voodoo devotees, dressing decolleté, "petting" and drinking. We do these things because *we honestly enjoy the attendant physical sensations.* There is no air of ultra smartness surrounding us when we dance the collegiate, smoke cigarettes, and drink something stronger than a claret lemonade. The real enjoyment lies in the thrill we experience in these things. And even tho [sic] our tastes may appear riotous and unrestrained the aspect of the situation is not alarming. The college girl—particularly the girl in the co-educational institution—is a plucky, coolheaded individual who thinks naturally. She doesn't lose her head—she knows her game and can play it dexterously. She is armed with sexual knowledge. . . . She is secure in the most critical situations—*she knows the limits,* and because of her safety in such knowledge *she is able to run almost the complete gamut of experience.*

The girl with sport in her blood . . . "gets by." She kisses the boys, she smokes with them, drinks with them, and why? because *the feeling of comradeship is running rampant. . . . The girl does not stand aloof*—she and the man meet on common ground, and yet *can she not retain her moral integrity? The criticism of immorality directed toward her is undeserved and unjustified.*[28]

Most striking here is the redefinition of morality. Morality, or moral integrity as the young woman put it, has been reduced to pretty much one factor, chastity. There is also implicit an opening-up of possibilities, emotional and physical, a freeing from the restraints of traditional inhibitions on propriety, and a corollary emphasis on the naturalness of all these things. So too, there is the belief in female equality, comradeship, mutuality in interest and pleasure, and the very real sense of security based on facts and the knowledge of those facts. Finally, there is what might be best described as the emphasis on taste, on personal style in matters of behavior, which in some ways reflects what being young was all about in the twenties.

The article provoked considerable controversy and incensed school officials, but the young woman had brilliantly crystallized what was happening in the lives of most of her compeers, especially her sisters: the opening-up of permissible experience. Even the critics of the article did not deny the facts she claimed; they were outraged at the unquestioned joyousness with which she welcomed the new sense of pleasurable indulgence. One young man refused to believe that women actually enjoyed the freedom that accompanied their new behavior: "The girls at this school as a group are wholesome and sensible, for *beneath the veneer* of modern dress, cosmetics, dancing, and such, is found a woman who is as conscious of the real values of life as her mother." [29] He acknowledged the changes but denied the implications of the changes. The young woman had recognized in a clear-eyed fashion the effect that accumulated changes, denied by few, were having on a woman's self-definition.

In the twenties a young woman was freer to engage in a variety of physical and mental experiences than ever before because the group that needed to approve of her behavior was not the tradition-oriented adult world of family and community but the experimental peer group. There was, of course, originally some compulsion to engage in these behaviors by the peer group itself, but once they were established as viable behavior patterns, that compulsion could give way to more freedom. The quantity of what was given in her life was more restricted, and the number of things that a woman could now choose in creating her life's roles had grown enormously.

To say the least, young women's appropriation of freedoms

hitherto denied them by the tenets of adult morality was not properly understood by the public. It was no longer easy to attribute traditional roles to a young woman who refused to be confined by traditional definitions. The confusion resulting from the expansion of possible roles caused frenzy. A college professor observed that once "one might with safety say this woman is good, this one is bad. That was in the days when the bad woman was known by her extreme clothing and her artificial aids to excite the sex impulse. But when a large portion of our 'respectable' women adopt the same methods and (shall we say it?) achieve the same result, a man is scarcely to be blamed if he occasionally makes a mistake in judgment." Noting the "bobbed hair, stream-line eyebrows, plastered cheeks, rouged lips, form-exposing skirt, and throaty voice," and the fact that the "spirit of imitation" was running rampant, he observed, "This is the ruinous condition in which the women have placed themselves. Those who are not in it feel out of it. . . . There are few, if any, out-and-out vampires on the campus. The trouble is that somewhere, somehow, the women have got the idea that they must dress and act like vampires before the men will fall." [30]

The statement expresses very well indeed the sense of confusion resulting from the insufficiency of old definitions of women's behaviors and manners. This confusion goes a long way toward explaining the twenties' haunted sense of rampant promiscuity. Contemporaries were often befuddled by what appeared to be a massive breakdown of behavioral conformity. Ironically, of course, the very same critics condemned the massive conformity that prevailed among the young. The reality lay not in the breakdown of norms of behavior but in the change in the norms. The twenties was marked not by breakdown but by redefinition. It was a period that saw the emergence of new roles, particularly for women, and the reorientation of behavior to new groups and institutions, like the movies and the peer group. It was an era no less criss-crossed by controls; only the locus of those controls had changed. The young were not free, and yet they had been liberated. For in binding themselves by a new set of controls, they had liberated each other from the past.

IV

Drinking for youth in the twenties was unlike sex, smoking, or dancing, because the young labored under a specific legal ordinance forbidding alcoholic indulgence of any kind. Prohibition was an anomaly in an age of increasing freedoms. Students had been permitted to drink at least off-campus before the passage of the Eighteenth Amendment and the Volstead Act, and beer drinking had been a regular form of celebration and socializing among male students. Prohibition cut off a former freedom. Moreover, unlike the other moral issues of the twenties, drinking was a male-centered problem that secondarily involved women. Drinking had always been a male prerogative. Respectable women were effectively barred from indulgence by tradition. Drinking among youths during the twenties therefore involved a number of distinct issues: the attitude toward the moral code, the attitude toward the law, and the question of female roles.

Drinking on most campuses in the twenties was clearly a problem. Student editors and administrators admitted that there was drinking, especially at homecoming time, but also generally at fraternity houses, mixers, and other social functions. Administrators, eager to defend Prohibition, played down the extent of drinking on campus in the public press, hoping thereby to prove that Prohibition was justified. But rarely did they deny that the problem existed. Students were suspended for drinking throughout the decade, and fraternity houses were frequently raided. At the University of Michigan, for example, the problem was so severe that President Little instituted a patrol system whereby a faculty member could enter a fraternity house at any time should he suspect that students were drinking or stocking liquor.[31]

It is difficult to determine how many students actually drank during the twenties and what the significance of their behavior was. By the end of the decade, the polls of the Congressional Hearing on the Repeal of the Prohibition Amendment presented overwhelming evidence that men and women students drank in a proportion close to two drinkers to every non-drinker. This was the case in all parts of the nation. Thus at the University of North Carolina, of the 944 students who voted, 67% admitted drinking to some extent. At Yale, 71% of the students admitted drinking; the favored beverages were overwhelmingly whiskey and gin. At Williams College, 65% of the students admitted drinking. And even at Rutgers College, which reported the lowest proportion of students drinking of all colleges investigated, 41% of those polled admitted drinking. At Purdue and Michigan, located in the Midwest where Prohibition sentiment was strongest among the general population, the percentages of students who drank were 59% and 67% respectively. Of the total number of ballots cast in the nationwide congressional poll, 29,794 in all, only 34% of the students claimed not to be drinkers.[32] By 1930, at least, drinking appears to have been very common among the majority of all students.

Coming at the end of the decade, the Congressional survey reflected the campus situation when anti-Prohibition sentiment had reached a peak. But the college newspapers suggest that there were changes over the course of the decade in the amount and style of drinking. Drinking among the young appears to have been greatest at the very beginning and again in the second half of the twenties. There was a short period between 1921 and 1924 when the amount of drinking was kept to a minimum, the result of initial attempts by the young spurred on by the administration to control drinking, especially at official university parties and at fraternity dances. At this time, the papers, after important events like proms and homecomings, were filled with self-congratulations on the commendable way in which the students were controlling the drinking problem and enforcing the national and school anti-drinking laws. In 1921, the *Cornell Sun*, for example, which noted that the previous year had been especially wet, observed, "The low point has been passed in regard to the liquor situation, and the upward swing is beginning. All evidence, at least, points to a slowly growing public sentiment against drinking at dances—which is the crux of the whole matter. The parties in the last three or four weeks have had a different tone from those of a year ago." Even homecomings, usually the wettest weekends of the year because returning alumni brought liquor in abundance, were reported to be relatively dry. At Madison, Wisconsin, as at most schools, there was reported to be "a determined effort . . . to stamp out drinking." [33] In the second half of the decade, however, there was a marked increase in the agitation for repeal or modification of Prohibition and a general decrease in the commitment with which the now formal injunctions against drinking were issued. This happened first at the Eastern schools, which appear to have had a shorter dry spell, and gradually affected the Midwest.

In the early period, some editors observed that Prohibition needed time to prove its efficacy and that slowly the public would be educated toward a self-imposed abstinence. On this assumption, students were urged to give Prohibition a chance. But most arguments supporting Prohibition were based on the law rather than on the social or moral objection to drinking. The injunction that the law should be obeyed was a constant aspect of the formally expressed attitudes toward drinking. This remained true throughout the decade. At Cornell, where editorial comment was consistently hostile to Prohibition and to all attempts to impose morality, the editor of the *Sun* nevertheless maintained that in respect to the law, there was but one answer, "to enforce the law . . . it is one thing for a citizen of the United States to be in doubt on the question of prohibition and it is another for him to be in doubt on the question of the dignity

and power of the Constitution." The editor of the *Daily Princetonian* noted, "We do not regard indulgence in drinking to be,
per se, a sin. . . . We do not approve of Prohibition in its
present form. . . . But we do most sincerely feel that failure to
comply with the law of the land constitutes the repudiation of
the first principle of citizenship. . . . The wide-spread and
flagrant disregard for this law by college and university students
is a dangerous state of affairs." [34] At first, editors urged students to obey the law. Later, they agitated to have the law
changed or repealed. Whatever the feeling about Prohibition
and the attitude toward drinking, officially at least, students asserted that the law must be obeyed. Moreover, editors were
quick to criticize public officials for inadequate enforcement.[35]
This was true even as they were urging that the law be changed.
The spokesmen for the young officially voiced their approval of
law enforcement.

At the same time, students were openly contemptuous of the
kind of moral reformers who had succeeded in passing Prohibition. Self-righteous moralists trying to impose their own standards on everyone were the butt of derision. The *Daily Princetonian* struck just the right tone of contempt: "If the projects of
the crusaders for virtue and purity are realized . . . once more
the tottering world and western civilization will be made safe
for unsullied virgins and old ladies above sixty. The absurdity of
such efforts is second only to the presumption with which they
are undertaken by . . . certain self-styled upholders of public
morals. . . . To presume that one can define decency or legislate virtue is folly." The young dismissed the idea that morality
or propriety could be imposed from above. Even in the early
period, when editors urged students to give Prohibition a
chance, it was based on the belief that an anti-drinking ethos
might evolve from the people themselves and not on the principle that such an ethos could or should be imposed from without. "No law which makes criminal a thing which has not,
hithertofore, found an analogous condemnation in the code of

morals common to all men, can look for the popular accord necessary to its enforcement," observed the *Cornell Sun,* which went on to predict that law-breaking would become a normal pattern because Prohibition rested solely on the righteous conviction of the few and not on the sentiment of the many.[36]

These two very distinct and clearly articulated attitudes—the strong sentiment supporting the law and the hostility toward the idea of Prohibition—were accompanied by a less clearly enunciated ethic that made drinking an unofficially sanctioned peer activity. The editorials reflected this view. While always serious when denouncing law-breaking, editors were rarely serious about drinking. Usually drinking and Prohibition were fair game for humor and "smartness." The informal approval demonstrated by making Prohibition a joke cannot possibly have done other than undercut the effectiveness of the formal injunctions to obey the law contained in the very same papers.[37] In this sense the spirit of Prohibition, if not the letter of the law, was officially denied. Drinking jokes were a staple of the humor columns and, more insidiously, of the side comments of the purportedly serious editorial columns. Even when intending to scold, editorials came off as shoulder-shrugging at the antics of college youths. Thus in 1920, the *Daily Illini* officially disapproved of drinking but remarked that the homecoming had spread joyful wetness throughout the university community: "A healthy slice of all the local male element was caught in the sudden alcoholic torrents and was completely drenched, although it is true that some escaped with slight foot-wetting; precious few succeeded in keeping wholly high and dry." The editorial went on to observe with casual unconcern that "bootleggers and whiskey speculators had a field day." This was a very different kind of disapproval than that contained in a frenzied letter from a town resident condemning the actions of students. The writer was "revolted" by students "staggering and reeling down the street" in open defiance of both a university ruling and a federal law.[38]

Prohibition was everywhere called a joke and considered a failure. At Cornell, the editor called it a "stock joke," with a *double entendre* on the word stock. To make this yet more explicit, he noted that students were already "stocking" up for Junior Week, and that the smuggling made the activity all the more enjoyable. In commenting on the claims of success for Prohibition made by enforcement agents, the editor at Ohio State commented, "Yes, for the bootleggers." At Trinity College, the editor casually suggested that the most considerate senior gift to the college might be "a large room about the size of the new gym, with several hundred beds in it, where the Saturday night drunks might go when they come in Sunday morning so that they might not disturb their roommates," or failing that and "if the class wanted to make money, it could erect a still on the campus . . . with the proceeds going to the college." The result would be that the hoped for seven million dollars needed by the school "would soon be a reality." And an Ohio State editor mildly chided students for drinking on the train to a University of Michigan game, which brought adverse publicity in the national press, by noting, "We know that prohibition is considered funny by the average man," but, "lay off the stuff boys. It gets neither you nor the school anywhere." If this was not enough, an editorial comment in the same issue undercut the urgency completely with the quip, "There's many a slip 'tween the hip and the lip." "In our bootleggers we trust," read the tag on an empty bottle found on the Trinity College campus and appreciatively recorded by the college editor. Everywhere drinking was treated about as seriously as galoshes and bobbed hair. "Liquor violation," noted the *Cornell Sun*, "is in the category of an indoor sport." [39]

Editors noted from the beginning of the decade that Prohibition was a failure, that people still drank, that in fact drinking and drunkenness appeared to be on the increase, and that students were not only drinking but proudly affecting drunkenness and bragging about their drinking sprees. It was the attitude of braggadocio and the changing ethos about how much, where, and when one could drink that most clearly reflected the reaction of youth to Prohibition and the emergence of a new peer-supported ethic that considered drinking "smart." [40]

In the early twenties, there was a clear code of limitations on drinking that reflected traditional attitudes toward propriety in drinking. Thus, drinking at athletic events and with other men was permissible, but drinking at dances and in the presence of women was not. When editors denounced drinking with alumni or at athletic events, for example, they usually invoked the law rather than the moral code. But the same editors were disturbed by drinking at dances, where it was believed to be improper because it was public and in the presence of women. The *Cornell Sun* called such drinking "an offense to good manners and against decency," and the *Sun* noted that while there was never a time in Cornell history when students did not drink, "there are times, when it is considered bad manners." So too, at the University of Wisconsin 2000 women students signed a pledge to boycott any social function where men were under the influence of liquor. The action reflected the prevailing ethic that drinking in the presence of women was improper. [41]

The code also drew a fundamental distinction between drinking and drunkenness. In 1921, the editor of the *Daily Illini* noted that "The number of persons who object to an individual taking a drink of intoxicating liquor is probably in the minority," but that the student public strenuously objected to drinking to the point of intoxication. The editor concluded his message by advising that drinking "must not become open or offensive to student society." [42] When the young drank according to these self-limiting rules, they were, in effect, conforming to the traditional standard of adult society that operated in the days before the Prohibition law went into effect.

During the twenties, however, the young increasingly deviated from these unofficial codes of conduct. There was a subterranean ethic developing that worked counter to these self-limiting rules. In this ethic, one drank to become drunk or, failing that, to appear drunk. Thus the *Cornell Sun* noted that where once it had been the aim to see how much one could drink without appearing drunk, it had now become part of "the game" to get as drunk as possible on whatever drink was available and to see who "can get the Greatest Publicity while in a state of Pseudo Ginification." "Contrary to the rabid assertions of matronly sewing circles and pessimistic male reformers," the *Dartmouth* declared, "the college student of today is sober ninety-nine one hundredths of the time. When he does drink, it is usually to parade his drunkenness—at a football game, at a dance, during a vacation, at a social gathering—and it is on such occasions that a shocked older generation is most liable to see youth in action." In addition, one drank in the company of and together with women.[43] It was not until the middle of the decade when this new ethic began to jell that drinking among women became an issue. Before then it was considered a strictly male-centered problem. Drinking at dances, with women, and to excess had become, by the latter twenties, a new code of permissible behavior among college students because it was sanctioned by peer opinion.

"Terpsichordian tippling," as the *Cornell Sun* called it, had become commonplace on most campuses and the editor explained quite accurately why this was so. " 'Is it the smart thing to be drunk at a college function?' 'Yes,' reply the undergraduates by their indulgence in liquor consumption at dances, house parties and the like, and by their tolerance of it by others. Right there we believe lies the solution of the drinking problem at colleges in general. . . . Campus leaders set the style by drinking openly and laughingly approving the drunken actions of fellow students." A similar situation prevailed at Duke, where "a dance among the younger set can hardly be called a success nowadays unless most of the boys get 'high,' not to mention the occasional girl who cannot be outdone by her masculine companions. Banquets, teas, and other social functions are usually the centers of these orgies of the followers of John Barleycorn." Thus the editor of the *Daily Texan* concluded that while the amount of alcohol consumed on campus may well have diminished during Prohibition, the new drinking code was more insidious: "It cannot be said that prohibition has done much for the morality of college students when the one-tenth consumption of illicit liquor partakes largely of a form of putting a 'kick' into college dances. The situation is in no wise improved when the male tipster no longer hesitates to share his meager pint of potent spirits with a girl, an act which would have been visited with social ostracism in the pre-prohibition days." [44]

This new drinking spirit was peer-sanctioned, and drinking was, in general, most prevalent in the fraternities where peer pressure was most intense. At one school a coed noted, "Some fraternities won't pledge a man unless he carries a flask," and the freshman handbook at the University of Chicago noted that "in order to be collegiate, one must drink." Bootleggers, according to the *Daily Illini*, made regular calls on fraternity houses, and there were more fraternity dances with drinking than without. Furthermore, many men now regarded "fraternity formals as an occasion upon which to get drunk." A former Duke student similarly blamed the fraternities for setting the drinking standard. The fraternities "have got more money to spend, more of what is called 'social position,' and hence greater temptations and a greater opportunity to play the part of gilded youth." He went on to declare that "if the leading men in the Greek letter fraternities . . . took a genuine, sincere stand against the use of alcohol, drinking would immediately cease to be a problem." That drinking was most common in fraternities was generally acknowledged by school officials, who usually tried to control drinking on the campus as a whole by working through fraternity leaders. In 1928 the President of the University of Washington tried to do just that by calling together a large gathering of fraternity and sorority members. They were "the chief sinners on the campus," and "six times as bad as non-fraternity members." [45] The positive attitude toward drinking in fraternities and the power of fraternity leadership in the drinking issue illustrate the potent influence of peer sanction in regulating drinking behavior. Drinking was most common in fraternities because peer sanctions were most immediate and effective. At the same time, the fraternities helped to make drinking smart on the campus as a whole. University officials knew that fraternities alone could effectively control it because they set the standards that condoned it.

By the second half of the decade most of the energy of student editors was expended not to urge that Prohibition be enforced but to have the law repealed or modified. There were no more mass meetings like that at Wisconsin calling for a boycott of functions where there was drinking. Peer opinion had effected a change in drinking habits and attitudes. Social drinking had become acceptable, and the cocktail or hip flask shared by men and women had replaced the beer consumed by men at an inn or surreptitiously in the stadium. This does not mean that all men drank, and certainly not all women did, but the peer society now sanctioned a new kind of drinking behavior. Students applied themselves to having the law changed so that they could drink legally. In 1926, in a poll at Yale in which 2500 ballots were cast, students voted four to one that Prohibition had increased rather than decreased the amount of drinking at school and that Prohibition had been a failure. [46] By the latter half of the decade, the call for modification or repeal became more or less common at all schools, and most schools began to sponsor student referenda to ascertain the attitudes toward Prohibition.

The agitation was earliest and most intense at the Eastern schools where wet sentiment among the whole population was strongest. As early as 1920, the *Harvard Crimson* had called for the modification of Prohibition and the legalization of wines and beer. By 1925–1926 schools across the country registered the opposition to Prohibition. At Cornell more than three-fourths of

the students and at Yale 80 % of the students called for modification or repeal. At Princeton in 1926 a poll showed the overwhelming majority (87%) in favor of repeal or modification,
with most students in favor of complete repeal. In 1923 a similar poll had given only 54% in favor of changing the law, with
a much smaller turnout for the vote. Clearly, anti-Prohibition
sentiment was growing. At Illinois 60% of the students voted
for repeal or modification, and at Ohio Western Reserve a poll
taken in the chapel found only 40% of those voting who wanted
to see the law remain as it was. When students from Midwestern and Southern schools met in 1926 to discuss common
campus concerns, the delegation made a point of registering
students' opposition to abstinence at the same time that it condemned the excessive use of liquor.[47] Whenever Prohibition
polls were sponsored, students turned out to vote in large numbers, much larger numbers in fact than in similar polls that
called on students to express their views on politics, the League
of Nations, or the World Court.

By the end of the decade, the poll on student attitudes toward Prohibition presented at Congressional hearings showed
that students overwhelmingly opposed the law. At the University of North Carolina more than two-thirds of all students
favored repeal, and 85% favored repeal or modification. At Yale
students favored repeal five to one; at Michigan 76% of the
students opposed Prohibition, and at Princeton 87.7%. In a
later poll of ten schools conducted in 1932 some 95% of the
10,027 students voting opposed Prohibition.[48]

Youth's attitude quite clearly ran counter to the officially
prescribed behavior of the 1920's. Most students believed that
Prohibition had not stopped drinking and some that it had, in
fact, increased the incentive to drink by making it dangerous
and exciting. In 1926 the *Daily Princetonian,* which had earlier
advocated an experimental policy for Prohibition, began an all-
out campaign to repeal the law, based on its observation that
Prohibition had been demoralizing and that drinking and drunk-

enness had increased among students. Agreeing with the Yale dean who had concluded that the "law is not only unpopular, but is violated on a large scale," the paper went on to describe the new forms of drinking. "It is in the change in the manner of drinking that Prohibition has affected college life. It has substituted hard liquor for beer. Worse than this it has seriously threatened the best traditions of the colleges. Whereas undergraduates once confined their drinking to the Nassau Inn, liquor is now taken and kept in the room or sought in roadhouses. There is but little respect for law." The *Princetonian* noted that since the beginning of Prohibition, the polls of senior class views showed that with each succeeding class students drank more and disapproved of drinking less. The editor of the *Wisconsin Daily Cardinal* asserted, "Without doubt, prohibition has been an incentive for young folks to learn to drink. . . . The expense of the Volstead experiment has been an exploitation of youth, and a general breaking down of respect for national law in the minds of the people who are law abiding citizens at heart. Briefly, we feel that the Eighteenth Amendment has accomplished nothing but the ruination of our gastronomic organs, our taste, and our one time respect for federal law. The Volstead law has been an ineffective weapon to stop drinking. Its failure shows that it is impossible to legislate morals." [49]

Some editors asserted that the law had been a stimulus to drinking. The editor of the *Daily Illini* believed that "Ever since prohibition was first passed, many misguided individuals who were not in the habit of drinking anything stronger than tea took to liquor probably because of the instinct to be contrary or because moonshine was popularized in song and story." Many editors noted that conspicuous drinking had become popular because it permitted the young to flaunt their disregard for traditions and conventions. According to the *Wisconsin Daily Cardinal*, "Students drink in the spirit of braggadocio. It is the natural reaction of youth to rules and regulations." Most also observed that students drank because others did, for it was popularly regarded as a demonstration of conformity to peer norms and a criterion of smartness and sophistication.[50]

It is difficult to describe youth's behavior as simply a reaction or rebellion against adult behavior patterns. Prohibition was a legal injunction, and while it was official it did not necessarily reflect the view or the behavior of most adults. Editors frequently remarked on this fact and often claimed that there was in fact less drinking among students than among the population as a whole.[51] In part, therefore, youth's behavior and attitudes reflected what was a common unofficial standard among adults in the twenties, especially among certain smart or glamorous sets frequently portrayed and described in the movies and the literature of the period. John Barleycorn, a Trinity College editor noted, had been driven "from the saloons and the vulgar cabarets into the social circles and the dance halls of the five hundred. . . . The enterprising bootlegger does not waste his time with the scum that infest the slums of the city; instead he moves and sells among the prominent society leaders." [52] Imitating the liberated society leaders was certainly in line with the affectations of smartness approved by the young in the twenties. Anti-Prohibition sentiment was strongest where drinking was most fashionable, as in the East, and where there was the least moral opposition to drinking both before and during the Prohibition era.

What was important, however, was not just that the young imitated adult models but the kind of models they emulated. These were the models not of conventional conduct or propriety but of glamor and liberated behavior. The young ridiculed righteous moralists who urged a return to traditional standards and conventions and turned instead to modern or deviant pace-setters. If the young were merely following traditional forms in spite of the contemporary law, they would have restricted their drinking to conform with the traditional code which prevailed on campus in the pre-Prohibition days—that is, occasional and minimal drinking among men. But the drinking code had itself changed. Thus the young were deviating not only from the law but from traditional canons of propriety.

Drinking was both imitative of adult society and a rejection of conventional patterns. Drinking was less a sign of generational rebellion, however, than an attempt to update conventional forms of behavior. Law-breaking did not in and of itself make drinking more attractive to the young. Rather the law appears to have gotten in the way of their adaptation of traditional mores to conform to their own standards of modernity. Law-breaking was a by-product of and not the stimulus to change in drinking patterns. Probably the legal prohibition accelerated a change that would have taken place anyway. It exacerbated the affectation of drunkenness, if for no other reason than that the young were forced to substitute whiskey for beer, and when liquor was available the tendency was to drink more of it. Drunken displays became a sign of the fact that the young were flouting the drinking conventions. It was, however, the old moral association, rather than the law, that was the chief target of such bravado. The young came to associate Prohibition advocacy with old-fogeyism and with the illiberal moralism for which they had a profound distaste. They dissociated drinking from morality altogether by denouncing both the traditional moral code and the social regulators who enacted the morality into law.

To some extent drinking like smoking or petting became a necessary demonstration of conformity, but this should not obscure the fact that the young believed that drinking should be left to the taste of the individual. It was a personal preference that should not be denied on the basis of law or convention. Drinking, like smoking for women and dancing, was a way by which the young adjusted traditional standards of morality to express their sense of freedom to engage in various kinds of behavior and their self-conscious modernity. All of them were linked to sex, because the traditional sensibility saw them as indications of promiscuity and a further demonstration of a growing license in moral behavior. Prohibition got in youth's way because it was, in fact, an anachronism that made the young law-breakers in spite of themselves.

V

Was youth's flamboyant behavior and flouting of convention merely capricious or did it function to express individual and group needs? To pretend that the behavior of these youths can be neatly squeezed into a streamlined functionalism would be to miss much of its petulant naughtiness and spirited frivolity. "It takes nerve to rise in collegiate circles," remarked a Trinity College editor; "the freshman who stopped by the English office and asked for a match to light his fag is assured of any position he wants." [53] Part of their excitement and vitality lay in youth's self-conscious naughtiness, their dare-devil antics, and their conspicuous modernity. But by the same token to deprive their behavior of regularity and direction would be to confuse what was contingent in that behavior with what was vital and necessary. It was not caprice that made the moral reformer seem the malicious fool on their cultural horizon, nor was it caprice that made them question traditional proprieties in sexual morality and in such areas as smoking, drinking, and dancing. These the young defined as the private sector, as a sphere for personal expression to be governed by need and taste rather than by law and morals. This differentiation was clearly enunciated in their view of Prohibition—the law had no business regulating personal tastes. It was also implicit in their views on music, dancing, and smoking, which they saw as arenas for expressive style and not for moral absolutes.

In these areas the standards of the young deviated from conventional canons of propriety. That deviation was sanctioned by group approval and as such functioned to unite age peers. It provided the young with a much needed area of self-regulation and served as a mild form of generational differentiation. The young knew that their patterns and attitudes provided a margin of difference between them and their elders, and this gave them a vehicle for group cohesion. It is not insignificant that many of these conventions were sex-linked, for sex is probably the most self-conscious form of adolescent expression and, as Erik Erikson reminds us, the most powerful source for adolescent ego development. In the twenties, personal ego-needs took on group proportions, and thus sexuality became a fertile arena for group direction and identification.

The ego-needs of the individual adolescent may be more or less constant. What changed in the twenties was the availability of group support for experimentation and expression. It was this sudden group interest in and consciousness of sexual subjects that seemed so threatening to contemporaries. Contemporaries rightfully linked the young to sex. Every new generation seems to rediscover sex. When it is an individual adventure, it is amusing, but when it is a group experience, it looks alarming. Adolescent sexual concerns did not suddenly appear in the twenties; rather the emergence of intensive adolescent centers, the availability of leisure, and the postponement of adult pursuits turned an individual concern into a generational experience. In this the decade was revolutionary, for it ushered in a century of acute sexual awareness, as each youth group rediscovers sex for itself with the resultant rapid changes in sexual norms and the cultural forms with which they are often associated.

Sexuality and sex-linked behavior came readily to adolescent groups because they were pressing personal concerns in an altered social environment. They called for new rules, new conventions, and new techniques. They were also a particularly cogent form of generational identification in a culture barely teetering off the edge of Victorian prudery. Sexual norms and manners provided peer groups with a significant sphere for regulation. These regulations were functional, but because they deviated from those of adult conventions, they were also provocative and offensive. Failing to recognize the significance of peer groups in the twenties and the particular urgency of sexual subjects to such groups, historians have been misled by an offended contemporary public and by their own image of the youth of the period. The young did not discard sexual regulation; they decried the existing adult conventions.

Did the young use sex and morals as a basis for conscious generational revolt? On the whole the answer would appear to be no, although their sexual attitudes and practices did distinguish them from their elders and made them appear rebellious. They welcomed the lingering naughtiness of which they were accused, but more in the spirit of play than with any serious display of anger. As eager capitalists, the young were anything but rebellious in social and political questions. They emphasized style in personal matters and severely demarcated the personal from the social sphere. In so doing they were in the advance guard of twentieth-century American culture. Their behavior signaled the growing divergence between permissible expression in the personal and cultural sphere and necessary conformity in the political and social arena, and they accelerated the process in their conduct and beliefs. This does not mean that they did not enforce conformity among themselves. They did and with vigor, because it served the peer group and its needs. But by enforcing a deviant standard, they helped to transform uniform norms into pluralistic styles and made preference and change, not tradition and morality, the guide to private behavior.

8

The Politics of Cultural Liberalism

We are almost the only section of the population which has the leisure and opportunity to study the controversial questions of the day without bias and to act accordingly. The power of today is in our hands.

But do we study the industrial, economic and international questions and explain them simply to the man on the street, which would seem to be the natural function of the student? We do not. And largely because we are too immature to see this as our role. We have the power but we do not use it.

The New Student, March 10, 1923

Amidst rapid institutional changes and full of new values and norms, the twenties is a decade notorious for its conservatism. A false image of stability continues to dominate our perceptions of a period barren of political vibrancy. Worse yet, reform in the twenties is remembered as a species of moral fanaticism intended to capture the imagined virtue of a bygone day. The result is a witches' brew of narrow, self-righteous reaction emerging from deep within the American social psyche to stir the smooth surface of stuffed-shirt complacency. It was in the 1920's that the thwarted visions of the Ku Klux Klan, the

Women's Christian Temperance Union, Blue Law Leagues, Purity Leagues, Immigration Restriction Leagues, the Palmers and Bryans finally came together to impose their reform package under the benign non-leadership of Presidents Harding and Coolidge. Ultimately, of course, it was no reform at all, only the convulsive last gasp before the enveloping waves of an urban, heterogeneous, permissive society swallowed up what was left of the old America.

It was easy for the young to be on the side of the angels. They were required only to stand opposed to such efforts. This they did. For the young were not traditionalists, but neither were they radical. They valued freedom of expression, but also the American capitalist system. The political behavior of college youth in the twenties is in the nature of a paradox. To favor change, they had only to stand firm. On the whole, the young were politically apathetic. Little interested in political or economic issues, they neither pressed for change nor partook actively in political discussions. Nevertheless, in the context of the period, they were an intensely political generation. So the young were political without meaning to be—forward-looking and conservative at the same time.

The paradox grew out of the political definitions of the decade. A wide range of cultural and moral issues in the political arena dominated platforms and discussions. Political and economic questions in the narrow sense were treated casually, almost cavalierly, but Prohibition became a way of relating to candidates. Problems of cultural style, symbolic of deeper social cleavages,[1] diverted attention from pressing economic and social problems. Not that specific political questions did not exist; they did. But in an era of social transition, gilded by prosperity, cultural questions were uppermost.

The young were not terribly concerned with the details of political life. Their conversation was barren of political and social topics;[2] their political participation limited to a weak responsiveness on questionnaires and polls; their political excitement restricted to transitory enthusiasm at election time along strictly traditional partisan lines. Editors often berated readers for lack of knowledge and interest in political affairs, but usually they too were guilty of the charge. When the young were moved to declamation or enthusiasm, it was not on economic or political questions but on those involving personal freedom. They reacted against the reforms of the period and registered their strong opposition to attempts to control and repress self-expression and self-determination in behavior. In this sense, they were active political liberals, although they had little interest in changing political or social structures. In their own minds, cultural questions were not political but private. Thus they stood at the opposite pole from those who put a political gloss on every moral and cultural quirk.

Finally, the behavior of youth is understandable only in terms of those tensions that make the decade a cluster of paradoxes: radical social change and political quiescence; rapid cultural transformations and frantic reaction; expanded personal freedom and rabid intolerance. Because they were heirs of new institutional patterns, the young were forced to political positions in order to defend their way of life. But because they were also the heirs apparent of American industrial capitalism and the political party system, they quite casually assumed the political and social attitudes that came with the role. They were thus able in their beliefs and actions to separate political conservatism from cultural liberalism, and to become businessmen and jazz hounds, Republicans and flappers.

I

The issue that had the greatest potential vitality as a political cause and might have set off a chain of political activism among the young was World War I and the associated problems of internationalism and disarmament. For a small minority of politically active youths, it was the war that became the focus for agitation and organization. For the mass of the young, however, these questions provoked no more than a gentle spasm of interest.

The image of youth in the twenties as disillusioned, iconoclastic, and cynical is associated with their purported reaction to the Great War; their bitterness and hedonism represented a recoil from fumbled idealism. Like so many images of the period, this too is a distortion. The immediate post-war reaction of youth was a mixture of apathy and tempered enthusiasm. It is amazing how little national or international news appeared in campus papers in the years after the war and how little comment accompanied those items that did appear. The first half of the decade reflected in the extreme the self-sufficient provincialism and isolation of the campuses. From 1919 to 1924, self-satisfied boosterism flourished, and football and activities manias spread. These years were also most emphatically patriotic and nationalistic.

When editors did take note of important national events, there was neither cynicism or iconoclasm. At the time of Wilson's death in 1924, not one paper demurred in the general outpouring of praise for his noble idealism and exciting leadership. The editors were unanimous in their belief that history would grant Wilson the laurels tragically and unfairly denied him by contemporaries. When Wilson retired from the White House in 1921, the *Daily Illini* proclaimed, "President Wilson has engraved his name with deeds that will keep his name alive as long as the United States endures. His many and great accomplishments are temporarily being forgotten because so much fuss has been made over his few mistakes." In a similar vein, the *Cornell Sun* applauded the new professionalization of the diplomatic corps and took the occasion to note that the " 'renaissance' of political idealism which Mr. Wilson forecasts gives us the temerity, at least, that the political horizon is not always a grey one, and that, while the course of democracy is undulating, the waves have their loops as well as their nodes." [3]

Editors and students, especially in the East, displayed confidence in the rightness and ultimate triumph of internationalism and cooperation. The young repeatedly voted their support for the League of Nations in various polls, and active students organized conferences to mobilize students behind their commitment. Some of the earliest national student organizations, notably the National Student Committee for the Limitation of Armaments, were formed around the issues of disarmament and international cooperation. [4]

But the early interest in peace and internationalism was already tempered, not by cynicism but by apathy. The turnout at straw polls was rarely large. At Ohio State, for example, students took time to vote on campus questions but failed to register an opinion on the League, although both questions were contained on the same ballot. Students, like their elders, appear not to have bothered to learn much about the issues as they floundered on a sea of confusion about the Wilson League, the League with reservations, the Peace Treaty without the League, and the Wilson plan with compromises. [5] Mildly interested, the young were not profoundly moved. There was little editorial comment and no outpouring of resentment when the League issue died. Typical of the attitude was the *Daily Illini*'s casual observation that Harding had apparently turned the League down and that only time would tell whether it was the wisest choice. Only with the election of 1924 was the issue seriously raised again, when some editors began to ask faintly what had happened to the war issue. It had quite literally been suffocated by the more interesting questions of football, petting, drinking, dancing, and fraternities. No one rioted when the League was turned down, but in 1919 at Syracuse University 2000 students went on strike and rampaged through buildings when the administration denied them a holiday to celebrate an athletic victory, and in 1923 at the University of Wisconsin women turned out in large numbers to organize a mass protest against chaperone requirements.[6]

The young were mildly interested in proposals to prevent future wars, but they never really took student initiative seriously. And while they voiced their opinions in response to adult invitation, a student political movement never got off the ground. There was some attempt at mass organization to demonstrate youth's interest and concern. But when the *Daily Princetonian* proposed that students organize a disarmament conference, it was in response to President Hibben's suggestion that youth show their enthusiasm for internationalism. The proposal elicited the following comment from the editor of the *Cornell Sun:* "The suggestion of a student conference to urge international disarmament has a fine sound. There would be something rather inspiring in the sight of the youth of the nation rising to demand that war be made 'an unthinkable thing.' But have not the sponsors of the scheme let themselves be carried by it a little beyond the realm of the practical?" A youth concerned with considerations of practicality could never be really idealistic, or really cynical.[7]

The editor of the *Daily Illini,* commenting on the same issue, discounted student idealism completely when he observed that student opinion on disarmament was of no value. Most students would not vote out of conviction but only because they were afraid of being shot. Everyone was in his heart of hearts for disarmament, but that sentiment was meaningless. He had managed to convert an anti-war sentiment into a soft non-issue: "For all the individual thought that resolution will provoke, it might as well read: 'Please Mr. Conference, we students like to live. In fact, if we can emphasize our desires we will resolve that we want to live, and be happy, and play.' " [8]

By 1924, the responses to the peace proposals sponsored by the organizers of the Bok Peace Prize, an attempt to rejuvenate the League issue, were considerably less than enthusiastic. A rather strong interest was provoked on the campuses by the World Court, again resulting in conferences and committees, which resulted in the formation of the first major national student organization. But it was once more in response to a call for student views, not a surge of indigenous feeling growing from an intense concern with a dying impulse for world cooperation. It was not that students became tired of the issue with time but rather that from the beginning the war and the peace were never really vital concerns. As early as 1922, at a student conference called in support of the Washington disarmament talks, the student statement noted, "The average student does not take an active interest in questions pertaining to the public good." [9] When asked, the young usually came out on the side of enlightened internationalism.[10] But the level of their commitment was very low, and the issue by no means dominated their world view or their sense of themselves in opposition to an evil or even a bungling older generation.

In 1925, Oliver La Farge, representing himself as a spokesman for youth, asserted in *Scribner's* that youth was bitter at their elders, "that boys in college gasp at the terrible things our elders are busy inventing and preparing for our delectation." The young, La Farge proposed, were appalled at the prospect of a future war, a war "not vaguely and unreally in the far future, but imminent, actual, and most important." If this was the case, there was precious little sign of it on the surface of college life. La Farge himself amended the observation that "between the horror of the next war and our disgust with the last, most of us have come not to think about war at all. Most boys at college accept the general thesis that war is an abomination, that they detest it and that they will fight only when desperately necessary; beyond that they do not go. They repeat words, but do not meditate at all." [11] Whether, as La Farge claimed, students refused to think about war because they were stunned into silence, or as seems more likely, because they did not care to think too much about the issue, very little political meditation about war was in evidence among America's college youth.

II

Small vocal elements existed within the student population. There were a few intensely controversial pacifist groups, many of which were Christian groups who linked pacifism with the principles of Jesus and world brotherhood. One such group found its focus among Christian theology students and its voice at the Indianapolis Student Volunteer Convention in 1923–1924, where 500 students pledged themselves not to support war under any circumstances, and many others affirmed a tempered pacifism, an abhorrence of war, and a commitment to education for world cooperation and understanding. Another group of 105 pacifists emerged at a meeting of 500 Methodist students in 1924, and still another group at an Interdenominational Student Conference at Evanston, Illinois, where 165 took the pacifist pledge. At Northwestern, 38 Garrett Bible School students pledged themselves to pacifism in 1924, as did 49 students at the University of Missouri. Small groups of students organized meetings and discussion groups, like those at Northwestern and Chicago who met in 1923 to discuss "Youth and the Warmakers." All through the decade such groups and individual students caused controversy by their opposition to military training and their pacifist or semi-pacifist affirmations.[12] But they were a distinct minority.

Political radicalism in the twenties was very often a Christian phenomenon, and the most sustained impulses toward internationalism and national reform were connected with denominational or inter-denominational conferences, like those of the Student Volunteers at Indianapolis and of theology students at Evanston. Students singled out by school officials for disobeying compulsory military training rules were often pre-ministerial candidates. At the Des Moines Convention of the Student Volunteers in 1919 (a division of the Young Men's Christian Association) students challenged the adult organizers for failing to provide them with really vital political and social issues to discuss and for continuing to concentrate on traditional questions of missionary work. The young asserted that students needed to concentrate closer to home and not on far-off socie-ties. This demand led to a major reorganization and reorienta-tion of the Student Volunteer Movement and its conferences. In response, the next convention, at Indianapolis, saw greater input by the young themselves in organizing the discussion and far more time devoted to political and social problems. This trend continued at the Milwaukee conference in 1926–1927, which was now sponsored by the YMCA and YWCA rather than the Student Volunteers, which had reorganized to concern themselves exclusively with missionary work. The topics dis-cussed at Milwaukee emphasized the religious impulse behind the conference: "International Problems and the Christian Way of Life"; "Racial Relations and the Christian Ideal"; "Economic Problems and the Christian Ideal." But by the second half of the decade, general student interest in the conference had declined. Des Moines and Indianapolis proved to be the high point of en-thusiasm for relating Christian principles to international and national questions.[13]

The conjoining of Christian impulse, especially missionary work, and political activism underscores that the ideals of these activist youths were traditional Christian concerns—equality, mutual understanding, and brotherhood growing out of per-sonal commitment. These concerns lay in the realm of what one YMCA historian has called "Christian sociology," and another observed that it was a part of "the growing concern among college students during the last few years for the application of Christianity to social and international problems."[14] The movement was based not on a revolutionary program aimed at a fundamental restructuring of American institutions, but on an enlightened revitalization of basic Christian ideals applied to modern economic and social problems. Frequently, the attack was two-pronged. On the one hand, the young discussed problems of their own soul-searching to achieve a sense of personal reform and recommitment in individual behavior. On the other, youths were urged to organize voluntary groups to ameliorate conditions. The whole impulse was person-centered, very much in line with the missionary traditions from which it grew. It is in this light that the pledge to pacifism among so many religiously-oriented students must be understood, for it affirmed this subjective sense of world reformation.[15] This organized radical thrust was a call for each man to recommit himself to his ideals and for all men together to effect those ideals in society through education, mutual understanding, and private action.

Another kind of political activism was manifested in the *New Student,* organ of the National Student Forum. The Forum was formed in 1922 by the merger of the National Student Committee for the Limitation of Armaments and the Intercollegiate Liberal League, the latter growing out of a series of conferences at Harvard, Princeton, and Chicago.[16] Based largely in the Eastern elite universities, these organizations evolved from older socialist groups. The Forum represented political clubs and speakers organizations at approximately 25 campuses, many on the East Coast. The *New Student* might be best described as a left-liberal journal that expressed views and interests similar to those of the *New Republic* and the *Nation*. Herbert Croly and Freda Kirchwey at various times served as editorial advisers to the journal, as did others from Eastern liberal periodicals. The student editors of the journal were usually drawn from Eastern universities, and articles from established left-liberal intellectuals like Bertrand Russell, John Dewey, Robert LaFollette, and A. S. Neill were interspersed with news from the college campuses and expressions of opinion from students.

Some of the student contributors like Talcott Parsons and Justine Wise would some day leave their own mark on American intellectual life.

The *New Student* was politically activist rather than radical. It conceived of the issues of war, peace, and internationalism as the foundations upon which to build a youth insurgency, an organized student movement that would attempt to effect changes in national policy and ameliorate social conditions. In addition, it looked forward to promoting international understanding and increasing friendship between students throughout the world in a vision of a united youth movement.[17]

But the *New Student*'s political push quickly relapsed into the fashionable emphasis on cultural philistinism and the issue of freedom of expression. Starting as a voice of student political and international action, it soon concerned itself largely with condemning moral intolerance, fanaticism, materialism, Babbitry, and repression. It ended by condemning the students for the selfsame provincialism. It still served as an organ of student opinion, sponsored polls, and promoted conferences, but it had failed in its original objective—student mobilization. The *New Student* demonstrated the basic paradox of politics in the twenties: the dissipation of potential political action by the need to stand opposed to backward-looking repression. As early as 1923 the National Student Forum asserted that it had "only one plank in its platform: freedom of speech." [18]

These were minorities. In general, students disdained extreme political commitments like pacifism. Letters poured into the offices of campus newspapers condemning the cowardice of the pacifists and their sympathizers. Most editors fell into line. The editor at Illinois took an aloof attitude: "It must be remembered that these students are far in the minority and that most of them will lose their delightfully invigorating radicalism as soon as they get out in the world and start earning a living in a bond house or real estate firm." At Cornell, the editor of the *Sun* called pacifists "adherents of this doctrine of aloofness, of indifference to human welfare at times when national service may be rendered to best advantage." And another *Illini* editor noted, "There may come a time, as there came in 1917, when war in defense of the principles of peace is more honorable and righteous than insane devotion to peace." While most editors opposed pacifism, they unanimously supported the right of pacifists to speak their mind. "Pacifism is . . . cowardly, unmanly and dishonorable," noted the *Daily Illini,* but "free speech still exists." Here, as on so many of the political issues of the twenties, was the clear position of the young: we oppose radicals of all kinds, but we uphold their right to be heard. A Trinity student, returning from the Indianapolis Convention of the Student Volunteers, was impressed by the openness of all the student representatives. While he was opposed to the pacifists, he praised the open discussion and free expression on a wide range of subjects, including race: "The majority of the students . . . were perfectly willing to hear and consider another's point of view. . . . This was in direct contrast with the attitude of some of the older generation, who were on hand with some of their old fashioned prejudices." [19]

The young of the twenties were intensely nationalistic, but at the same time they strongly opposed the narrow nationalism that often coated patriotism with intolerance and fanaticism. "We are not defending pacifism," explained the *Daily Illini.* "We are against war and eagerly seeking a way it may be abolished as the biggest wrong in the world. But the hasty and unfair methods of militarists with the 'firing squad' mind will never solve the problem. . . . The attempt to throw men into prison or to silence them for words with which the majority does not agree is not free speech. Men certainly should not be shot for having a mind of their own and for being willing to stand up and say what they think." Similarly, an Ohio State editor noted that the hysteria that the pacifist pledge among students at the Garrett School for Bible Study had produced among administrators and in the national press was laughable. But he ended on a practical note: "Let the pinks sign their pledges. If this country ever becomes involved in another war—God forbid—these students will soon forget their juvenile idealism, and along with the rest of us, be among the first million or so to enlist and try once more to make the world safe for democracy. If they don't—well, the government didn't have much trouble dealing with conscientious objectors during the World War." [20] It was this balance between tolerance and pragmatism that defined youth's attitude throughout the twenties. It is inconceivable how such attitudes could be confused with bitterness over an American idealism betrayed. American youth in the 1920's were nationalistic and practical; they had a humanistic concern with international cooperation, [21] and were keen on the preservation of personal liberty and freedom of speech. They opposed war in a generalized way, but that opposition provided neither a faith nor a basis for generational identification.

III

The issue that came closest to stirring campus political consciousness in the twenties was related to war but was more directly a campus concern. The issue of compulsory military training in the Reserve Officers Training Corps made the campuses come alive at mid-decade. At the City College of New York, the question of compulsory military training became a *cause célèbre* when a student poll in 1925 brought out a strong vote of opposition to compulsory drill, and the student editor was censored for a strongly worded anti-ROTC editorial. The student radicalism that the event seemed to portend caused administrators and the public to have nightmares about sedition and "pink" sentiment. Military drill became an issue at institutions all over the country, and students at school after school, especially at state institutions, began to voice their opposition to compulsory military training.[22]

When the ROTC question first emerged around 1922, editors took their stand solidly on the side of the necessity and efficacy of military drill. Editors generally believed that the Morrill Act (1862), which had been the basis for the land grant colleges established by states after the Civil War, made military training a compulsory part of the education of all male undergraduates at state schools. In fact, the Morrill Act called only for schools endowed under its provisions to provide facilities for such drill. But editors seemed to acquiesce in the necessity for some kind of military training as a demonstration of patriotism.[23] The letters-to-the-editor columns, however, were full of the debate over ROTC, with many supporting but others condemning the drill as both unnecessary and pernicious. Occasionally students withdrew from school rather than participate in a requirement which inducted them into techniques they considered dangerously militaristic.[24] Gradually, as the discussion over the issue gained momentum, and with the example of CCNY before them, editors began to voice their opposition to the compulsory aspect of the training.

The ROTC issue really involved two different questions. The ideological issue was associated with student pacifist sentiment and involved the question of training for war and obedience to paramilitary authority. The more cultural issue centered on the question of compulsion and the complications that resulted when administrators censored editors and students for expressing their opposition to military drill. The editor of the Louisiana State *Reveille* put the issue squarely for students' consideration. After first paying due homage to the worthiness of the campus battalions, he informed students that "This University and its student body cannot completely ignore any movement which has achieved such momentum of late as has the agitation against compulsory military training." He then carefully drew the necessary distinction. "The target of the antagonism is not, it must be clearly understood, military training as a course, but military training as a compulsory course." Moreover, as the *Daily Illini* suggested, the ROTC question had resulted in actions against students which stirred the college world into making a sharp point of the right to freedom of opinion: "First and foremost, neither the *Daily Illini* nor its editors subscribes to the pacifist stand; it does, however, unalterably believe in the right to free speech." [25]

Editors did not agree on the details of their opposition to compulsory drill, but all objected to it because it was compulsory rather than because it was militaristic, and all strongly rejected the actions of administrators who censored college editors and suspended students for their views. Editors at Ohio State and Louisiana State came closest to taking an ideological position when they variously noted that drill undermined the American tradition of civilian control, led to Prussianism, or conditioned a servile mentality,[26] but both shied away from attacking ROTC itself, confining their critiques finally to the compulsory character of the drill. Most recognized the implicit connection between opposition to ROTC on ideological or moral grounds and the urge toward pacifism, and many, like the *Daily Illini,* explained that "Impractical idealism should not be made an excuse for demanding the abolition of military training. Supporting of the present military system will serve as protection while better international relations are being worked out." ROTC should be put on a voluntary basis, the *Illini* argued, because such training would be more effective, improving the quality of the corps.[27] No editor took the position that military drill had no place on the campus.

Most students, like these editors, took issue with ROTC on the basis of its compulsory character. One correspondent at UCLA started out with a strong anti-war position—"We, the youth, [are] the first to bear the burden in time of war"—but finally demanded only that drill be made voluntary. At Ohio State, one-third of all students turned out to vote on an ROTC poll. Of these, 61% voted to make drill elective while 39% wanted to see it remain compulsory. More than 80%, however, asserted that there was need for some kind of military training on the campus.[28]

Throughout the controversy, even editors opposed to compulsory drill remained skeptical about the depth of student sentiment. The editor of the *Daily Illini* asserted, "ROTC, the *Illini* believes, is fairly popular. Students object to it more as a matter of ceremony than of conviction." At Cornell the following observations by a correspondent were printed under the paper's editorial mast: "A large majority of students, I believe, would prefer military drill at Cornell made voluntary. But, I do not for a moment believe that more than one out of 20 of them object on the grounds of high moral principles—that he is opposed to killing his fellow man, and so forth. He is opposed to drill because of what he considers a dull and comparatively useless monotony."[29]

What is most impressive about the various opinions expressed on the drill issue, as well as on the larger issues of war and pacifism, is the refusal to take youthful idealism seriously. The young of the twenties appear to have been cynical less about the older generation than about themselves. When students at CCNY, where the issue had first drawn national attention, were finally given the option to elect military or civilian drill, they chose the former, four to one. The editor of the *Cornell Sun* noted with barely veiled derision that "purse pressure has thrown pacifists' propaganda for a fall." Students, he believed, chose military drill because the Navy supplied the uniforms that civilian drill required each student to supply for himself.[30] When the young chose to make a stand on a political issue in the twenties, it was usually couched in highly practical terms. Neither the war nor compulsory drill was seen as an issue that involved moral or abstract commitments pitting youth against a ruthless older generation.

The ROTC issue had not quite created student solidarity, but it had produced action and in many cases results. Not really awakened to political consciousness, the young had at least been roused by the ROTC issue. Despite the immediacy of the issue, however, the youth of the twenties were not ready to oppose their society on the high ground of political idealism.

IV

Nor is there any indication that youth were dissatisfied or angered by domestic policies. Rather, it appears that the young were basically conservative, that they voted as their fathers did and held similar views on economic and political matters. Their attitudes were not even controversial, and on the whole the youth of the twenties were a politically stable generation. The presidential election choices of the young are perhaps the best measure of their complacent conformity to the mainstream of American political life. The election of 1924, coming in the middle of the decade and providing a Progressive candidate as an alternative, is a significant barometer.

A nationwide straw poll sponsored by campus groups like newspapers, student government organizations, and the YMCA and YWCA was taken on October 26, 1924. Of the 550 institutions solicited, 120 reported. One hundred thousand students had been given the opportunity to vote at these schools. The turnout was about 50%—a considerable showing as student polls go.[31]

From the beginning of the tallying, when only a few schools had yet reported, it was evident that President Calvin Coolidge was way ahead of the Democratic candidate John W. Davis or the independent candidate Senator Robert W. LaFollette. Schools of all kinds, from all parts of the country except the South, followed suit. The final results gave Coolidge more than a two-to-one lead over Davis, and a four-to-one lead over LaFollette. The vote was Coolidge 30,141, Davis 13,825, and LaFollette 7491. The Democratic and Progressive candidates together had received just two-thirds of Coolidge's total vote. Coolidge had swept the colleges by an even wider margin than in the national election. The *New Student,* which supported LaFollette, observed sardonically that they were finally "in a class by ourselves" and questioned whether students even knew who LaFollette was.[32]

The regional returns demonstrate how consistently the young voted as their elders did. Of all regions, Davis had carried only the Southern schools, just as he carried only the South in the general election.[33] Coolidge carried every other region. His strongest showing was in staunchly Republican New England, where he carried every school reporting with majorities of between 60% and 80%. Only at Clark University and at Dartmouth College was his vote less than 50%. Coolidge also made a strong showing in the mid-Atlantic states, where he won at most schools with from 50% to 70% of the vote. LaFollette carried only Hunter College and Wise Theological Seminary, both in New York City and both exceptional because of a large Jewish constituency. At Barnard, also in New York and with a similarly heavy concentration of Jewish students, Coolidge got less than one-half of the vote, the other half splitting evenly between Davis and LaFollette.

LaFollette carried his home-state University of Wisconsin by a slim margin with 39% of the vote. So too, he made a good showing in the California colleges, where he usually took a two-to-one or three-to-one lead over Davis.[34] In a number of Midwestern institutions, LaFollette ran ahead of Davis, and in some, like Reed College in Oregon and Bethel College in Kansas, LaFollette won. The college results were remarkably similar to the national election returns, where LaFollette was to lead Davis in several Western states, to leap ahead of him in California, and to carry his native Wisconsin.

In 1921, when he was Vice-President, Coolidge had written a series of articles in the *Delineator* accusing the Eastern women's colleges of being hotbeds of radicalism and Bolshevism.[35] But the election returns of 1924 belied that accusation. Coolidge carried every one of these Eastern colleges, most with impressive margins, while LaFollette made a consistently poor showing in each except Barnard. At Wellesley, for example, LaFollette received only 6%, while Coolidge had 76% of the vote; at Smith, LaFollette 5%, Coolidge 73%; at Vassar, LaFollette 15%, Coolidge 54%; at Bryn Mawr, LaFollette 14%, Coolidge 54%. Like so many accusations against the young in the twenties, Coolidge's heated diatribe fell wide of the mark.

That the young were neither a war-angry generation nor seriously concerned about the failure of internationalism is suggested by the returns at Princeton. Princeton was a school with a strong urge to organize conferences on disarmament and the World Court. The faculty, the student newspaper, and even President Hibben, a staunch Republican, had openly supported Davis, because Davis promised increased international cooperation. But Coolidge won the student vote easily with a margin of two to one: Coolidge 1072, Davis 501, LaFollette 66. The faculty, on the other hand, eager to rejuvenate the League issue, gave Davis the edge.[36]

Despite the usual political apathy among college youths in the 1920's, the campuses were the scene of considerable political organizing and agitation as groups formed around candidates and debated each other.[37] Thus college students could and did respond to political issues. They, like their parents, were sparked into action in a political year, but the interest did not outlast the election.

There is "a striking tendency . . . for the entire group of students to vote as their fathers vote," sociologist Gordon Allport concluded after studying the political attitudes of "liberal" Dartmouth College students. This was true of radicals and conservatives alike, although radicals voted as their fathers did somewhat less frequently than conservatives. But Allport reported that at least half the time even the talking radicals were voting conservatives, and that they voted contrary to their pro-claimed views. Moreover, in the group he studied the conservatives "stand closer to the mass" of students than did the radicals. In the election of 1928, Dartmonth students went 79% for Republican candidate Herbert Hoover; only 19% for Democratic candidate Alfred E. Smith.[38]

There were activist groups on most campuses who were concerned with economic and social problems. On every campus, speakers came to address groups of interested students, often under the sponsorship of waning socialist or liberal clubs. There were also attempts made toward intercollegiate cooperation in the formation of leagues and organizations with political interests. Often, again, active students and groups converged around the YMCA Student Volunteer Conventions, like those at Indianapolis and Milwaukee, and the smaller Interdenominational Conference at Evanston. Usually these groups worked with the pacifist groups; in many cases, the memberships of the two overlapped or were identical. But on the whole these social-issue groups, concerned with labor, socialism, government regulation, racism, and other political questions, caused less interest in the campus world than those concerned with the pacifist and international issues. Like the youths active in the latter causes, they tended to be fringe groups, unassimilated to the general campus society. They were groups with little leverage in the campus scene, largely isolated, intensely involved, and peculiar.

In the twenties, youth were not self-consciously political because they acquiesced in most of the policies embraced by the nation. That acquiescence is clear from their voting record. It is also clear from their expressed views when these were investigated and from the opinions of student editors.[39] The young did not get below the surface of American political life to engage in a debate with America's leaders or to challenge her basic institutions. They did not agitate for change. They did, however, oppose repression and they reacted against attempts to suppress the possibility of change. They believed that freedom was basic to the American political system and that its politics should be flexible and responsive, and so most of their political consciousness came in reaction against attempts to return American life to an earlier day or to undermine freedom of personal expression.

Most surveys of youth showed students to be generally conservative on economic and political matters. Their "leading bias," according to Gordon Allport's investigation of Dartmouth students, was "anti-socialism." This is supported by George Vetter's large-scale study of students at New York University, Syracuse University, and the University of Washington. On the question of government ownership, the majority of students at each university leaned toward the conservative view that "Only such enterprises as cannot be made to yield a profit under private ownership and are necessary to the nation, should be under government ownership or control, such as young forests, parks, canals, or the mails." The position generally reflected prevailing government policy. Most students came out strongly for the protection and inviolability of private property. On questions of hereditary wealth, most youths advocated a reasonable tax but not confiscation or a ceiling on the size of fortunes. On medical care, students urged the retention of the system of private care for those who could afford it with some provision to assist those who could not. On the question of the equality of incomes, students concentrated heavily around the position that a graduated income tax should not affect those with incomes below $5000 and should never reach the point of confiscation. Students favored minimum-wage requirements but opposed other pro-labor regulations. In a similar study, G. A. Lundberg found that students overwhelmingly opposed government ownership of industry or the confiscation of private property in other than emergency situations. The young were generally optimistic about the possibilities of improvement within the capitalist system, slightly more than half favoring increasing government regulation of industry but not control.[40]

Student editors reflected this general approval of capitalism and the American economic system. In commenting on a speech by labor leader Paul Blanchard, Secretary of the League for Industrial Democracy, the editor of the *Ohio State Lantern* observed, "Quite a few of the students present, including the editor, disagreed heartily with the idea that we should have a society in which no one will make a living by owning. It seems to the editor that any person who is frugal and thrifty and brainy enough to accumulate a fortune should be permitted to enjoy that fortune." The editor of the *Cornell Sun* evoked a similar sentiment when he voiced his strong approval of the address by State Senator George Cartwright of New York, praising the American system and denying the urgency of a more equal distribution of wealth: "His keen observations on what he termed 'the price of success' as well as his sincere and eloquent exhortations against the sullen, feverish, dissatisfaction and hatred of the ubiquitous malcontents, made his talk acceptable, profitable and wholly good. . . . Briefly the senator suggested that much more could be accomplished by the process of helping the low fellow rise than by knocking the high fellow off his perch. And there's a lot in that." [41]

The disaffection in which the young held socialism and political radicalism of any kind did not mean, however, that they were willing to defend those who used the issue of a red menace to control and suppress speech and action. In 1919 the editor at Cornell asserted that the IWW's claim that the "Centralia outrage" had been a frame-up was as absurd as the doctrines of the organization. But the editor noted that America, as a country of law and order, "must not allow mob spirit to handle guilty I.W.W.s." The same editor condemned vehemently the attempt by the state of New York to purge socialist and Communist teachers from the schools: "Has the panic caused by Bolshevism and socialism so befuddled the college graduate [in the state legislature] that he can urge the investigation of the beliefs of every member of the Cornell faculty, and the discharge of every man whose views do not coincide with his own? Since when, may we ask, has any group of citizens been granted the power of determining what a man may think in order that he may secure a livelihood?" A Duke editor similarly condemned the American Legion for its part in securing the dismissal of two Pennsylvania normal school teachers for radical views. And when the state of New York's Lusk Act threatened to restrict the freedom of teaching by requiring all teachers to subscribe to a loyalty oath, it was vigorously condemned at school after school. Some schools, such as Vassar, Barnard, and Wells, drafted petitions reflecting the near unanimous sentiment of the student bodies, and sent them in protest to the legislature.[42]

At Duke University in North Carolina, students took a vocal and vehement stand in opposition to proposed legislation that would have banned the teaching of evolution in state schools, as they and students at the neighboring University of North Carolina organized mass meetings and circulated petitions in opposition to the pending Poole bill. As the issue emerged, the Duke newspaper saw fit to take as its motto the statement by alumnus Walter Hines Page, "It is the Duty of Every Community to Encourage, Even Enforce, Free Speech." In one of its many condemnatory editorials, the *Chronicle* noted, "Such a move recalls quite vividly the age of intolerance," and concluded, "In the final analysis, our civilization is at stake." The editor of the North Carolina *Tar Heel* made a similarly strong defense of the freedom of instruction: "The University does not seek to prohibit the teaching of contrary doctrines to the evolution theory, and it likewise cannot take a stand to prohibit the teaching of evolution. It does take a decided stand for the freedom of thought and liberty of conscience that is so vital a part of our national principles of individual freedom and liberty." And when an anti-evolution bill was actually passed in neighboring Mississippi, the Louisiana State *Reveille* lamented, "The grand old Magnolia state has made a backward step," and hoped that the "spectacle of a legally blind-folded, legally crippled and legally laughable system of timid half-way instruction" would be fair warning to prevent Louisiana's own "Puritanical self-righteous" reformers from attempting a similar move. "Anti-evolution laws," the *Reveille* declared, "are but a form of that intolerance which has been the scourge of the world from the beginning." [43]

Even when they opposed specific views, editors readily defended the rights of others to hold and express them. Thus, despite their own pro-capitalist, anti-socialist sentiments, students were outspoken defenders of those who openly opposed American policies. "Free speech is one of our most precious inheritances," asserted the editor of the *Cornell Sun* when he protested the State Department's refusal to grant passports to two alleged Communists. The situation, he observed, smacked of "Czarist Russia." "We can ill afford the slightest infringement of this right. . . . The charge that Countess Karolyi and Saklatvala are Communists is not a thing already proved, anyway. And even if they are Communists, what of it?" At Duke, on even so explosive an issue as miscegenation, the editor struck out for freedom of expression. When the Dean of the School of Religion was wrongfully accused of voicing approval of inter-racial marriage, the *Chronicle* called it a slander but added that even if he did say it, "every man has a right to say what he thinks in a college community." When the editor of the *Daily Illini* was attacked for voicing deviant views, he found it appropriate to quote H. L. Mencken's retort to the accusation of being un-American: "Perhaps I am. I believe in liberty and I advocate honor." The *Illini* editor could at one and the same time condemn pacifism but also "chauvinistic and jingoistic contumely." [44]

The young in the twenties were spirited into defense by the reversals of traditional American values and policies, demonstrated by political repression. They did not, however, pay much attention to those issues which, while reflecting similar repression, had not normally been seen in that light. On racial matters, for example, the attitude of the young reflected the complacent acceptance of American policies, while in Southern schools, like Louisiana State, conscious racism remained a point of honor. The problem of racial justice was always among the topics considered by active students at intercollegiate conferences, and was sometimes the subject of special meetings like those at Swarthmore and Duke,[45] but it rarely played a role in campus papers. When the issue did emerge, Northern students self-consciously took a liberal stand, while Southern students, quite as consciously, took the opposite.

This is best illustrated by the split that took place in 1925 at the organizing session of the National Student Federation at Princeton. Northern students made a pointed gesture toward racial equality by electing a black woman from Howard University as the representative for the Southern region. The action drew a clamorous protest and finally caused the withdrawal of the Louisiana State delegation when the majority refused to rescind the action. At Louisiana State the *Reveille* lauded the action of the school's representatives and called the election of a black woman "a direct slap in the face of the South" and an attempt by Northerners to "cram the insult down the Southern throat." The North, the *Reveille* noted, "cannot understand the reasons why the South, knowing the negro, refused to discard racial distinctions." [46]

The Princeton affair is a good example of the prevailing student views. Northern students made an overt and public stand for racial justice, while Southern students, in turn, refused "to be represented before the world by a member of an inferior race." Both sides were, in effect, mouthing and acting according to the respective etiquettes of their regions. Actually, the Princeton action was little more than a gesture and the Louisiana State reaction a quite foreseeable response. The issue of racial equality was hardly a vital student concern. Of course, an especially egregious instance of racial bigotry, such as the refusal of a school team to compete against one with a Negro member, usually provoked Northern editors into denouncing this blatant affront to the principles of democracy. Occasionally, even in the South, letters to the editor contained outraged observations about racial insults and deviations from respectful treatment of Negroes.[47] But the interest in racial matters in Northern schools was usually restricted to the specific instance. And it was completely appropriate, if also ironic, that not so long after the Princeton incident, Louisiana State officially played taps at the death of an old and trusted black servant (the *Reveille* referred to him as a kinky-haired "old darkey") and students organized a fund for his widow. Like racism, anti-Semitism also occasionally became a subject for discussion in the campus papers, often in association with admissions restriction policies and especially in response to the Harvard debate on quotas.[48] But college students rarely paid much attention to either problem. They were content to stay clear of the issues.

On the whole, college students in the twenties were strongly bigoted, but Northern students, at least, were not consciously racist. Rarely did they openly subscribe to the innate inferiority of one group or the superiority of another. Rather they limited themselves to the question of social acceptability.[49] In one survey, for example, the strong normative response of students was, "All races are of very nearly equal worth, each making its own peculiar contribution to civilization. No race should assume itself to be the elect," and few considered the "Nordic race" superior to others. At the same time, editors and students usually urged strict immigration restrictions and welcomed the choking off of Oriental immigration. The usual rationale for these actions was the difficulty of assimilating so many people at one time. At the same time, racial incidents flared on the campuses throughout the decade, and surveys of youth revealed that college students were prejudiced against a whole range of ethnic, racial, and religious groups.[50] Again, the issues were social rather than racial.

Although political interest among the mass of youth was minimal all through the twenties, politics did begin to play a larger role in campus affairs around the middle of the decade. This was a time when the national election, the ROTC issue, a student referendum on the World Court, and the beginnings of a large student organization, the National Student Federation,[51] stirred up political interest and concern. Editors for the first time paid attention to campus groups who identified with political causes, and at a normally quiescent school like Illinois the editor even bemoaned the sad fact that no such groups existed on campus: "Illinois, they tell us, is the one institution in the middle west that has no radical group or even no noticeable liberal group among the student body. At other institutions, we are told, these groups congregate." Noting that readers were probably "gasping" at this departure from normal policy, he went on to assert, "they are saying that such a group has no place in a University such as ours but we think that it might well have, although it has not in the past. The world is changing, our old prejudices and beliefs, and fears and tremors are slowly being ironed out in the face of facts and new ideas. They are talking about doing away with war, of a new brotherhood of mankind, of a new youth movement and it is not all idle talk. Illinois, we think, might well foster such independent and forward thinking." [52]

More significantly, by mid-decade, accumulated instances of repression, particularly as they resulted in the dismissal of students or in the censoring of college editors, provoked students to a new political awareness. Thus at Duke, where politics had long been a dead letter, the evolution issue and the censoring of various North Carolina publications effected a new political consciousness among students and editors alike, ushering in a considerable amount of student agitation that spilled beyond evolution to incite students to protest American policies in Nicaragua and to sign petitions condemning increases in naval appropriation bills. The *Chronicle* now urged students to become "leaders in various types of thought" and advocated a new radicalism in thought and action.[53]

Radical groups which had hitherto received scant attention in the newspapers were suddenly interesting. At Cornell, the *Sun* congratulated those who gathered at Evanston to discuss political and social problems like war, racism, fundamentalism, labor unrest, and nationalism: "How many Cornell undergraduates, for instance, could be found to subscribe to such opinions? A mere handful, perhaps; no more because no more ever thought much about the questions at all or else are dictaphone records of what somebody said in 1907, 1913, and 1920." [54] Editors at mid-decade seem to have suddenly awakened to the problems that small groups of students and the *New Student* had been discussing for some time but that had passed the mass of students by.

There was also a general liberalization of views on political and social matters among editors at this time. This resulted largely from the repeated attention focused on repression and the consistent position opposing such repression. Thus, from their opposition to intolerance and illiberalism, the editors were forced into political awareness. Political consciousness grew from reaction rather than from initiative. So too, small vocal minorities appear to have provoked some thought and interest in matters that usually lay beneath the threshold of youth's conscious concerns. It was not that the young were naturally apathetic or unthinking in the twenties, but rather that there were few vital issues that stimulated them to political involvement. The young lived within the context of adult interest, and in that context their attention was focused on cultural questions. And because so many of the cultural issues were concerned with intolerance, their political consciousness was usually stirred by the attempts at repression. They did not dredge out the issues that lay beneath the surface.

The political questions, where they caught fire, were part of a "persuasion," to use an apt conception, a nexus of views and beliefs best described as "modernist," and which looked toward increased self-determination in behavior. It was strongly practical and flexible rather than moralistic and rigid. "It doesn't take a philosopher to understand that the tendency in college life today is freedom," observed the Duke *Chronicle;* "unlimited, unrestrained freedom." Here youth took its stand. The editor of the *Daily Illini* denied that students were radical and described them instead as tolerant: "This tolerance, which to our mind is the greatest blessing of education, is mistaken for radicalism. It isn't." [55] In the cultural politics of the twenties, the young, raised in families that encouraged self-expression and exposed to peer groups that challenged traditional proprieties and denied that morality was an unchanging verity, reacted to those situations that challenged the freedom to choose. That in the end was the real political issue of the twenties, and the young expressed their political sensibilities by opposing the pseudo-reforms of the period. Most of the issues that aroused youth were cultural, and all involved the right of the individual to make personal choices on the basis of new experience and altered circumstances.

V

"The only subjects that are getting any attention from the 'political minded,' " noted a UCLA editor in 1926, "are Prohibition, Birth Control and the Bible Issue, none of which are in the least related to politics or political wisdom." [56] He was wrong, of course, for they were all related to politics, and if not to wisdom, then at least to sensibility. On these cultural questions, the young were aware, active, and committed. They turned their energies into channels in which neither the League nor socialism was at stake, but instead their own styles and preferences.

This was the dominant note among the young for the entire decade. In 1920, the *Cornell Sun* made a plea for "downpullers." "The American public is weary of persons who seek to better the world . . . and sometimes wishes that among all the efforts at uplift and betterment some comfortable souls would get together and organize a society of down-pullers, to even things up a little." This was not cynicism based on warweariness or exhausted idealism. It was a perfectly practical response to the specific texture of reform in the twenties. "The old maids of all three sexes who are wont to attest to their own virtue by being very much interested in the wickedness of others is [sic] only too familiar to us," the editor of the Duke *Chronicle* remarked. In 1927 the *Cornell Sun* pleaded with reformers to "let the world and morals alone." [57]

The *Sun* had asked for "comfortable souls" for those who could accept the changes in the society and especially in morals and values without discomfort and without feeling that it was a distortion of a purer and better self. The young were not irritated by the world in which they lived. They were not idealistic, but neither were they despondent. Their attack was a negative attack—against the suppressors and all those who would impose the standards of an older day. Although the papers became slightly more politically alert and involved as the decade progressed, and while it was not until 1925 that the issue of the period, ROTC, started a mild contagion, uplifters, moral reformers, super-patriots, and suppressors of free speech had received the condemnation of the young from the beginning of the decade. Even the issue of military training provoked concern over the question of freedom of choice rather than over that of militarism or war.

In rejecting the idea of an authoritarian control, the young found an ally in H. L. Mencken, and in discovering Mencken they turned mildly upon their own foibles, their own mediocrity and conformity, their illiberalism and rigidities. The young appropriated Mencken because he was eloquent and devastatingly charming. They learned his techniques and his style, but the impulse was their own. The merely borrowed was easily recognizable, unnaturally high-browed, artsy, and elitist. The vital issues that concerned them were issues of freedom and personal expression, adjustment and fact. Where these were denied by the "Booboisie" and the Kiwanies in the administration or the government, Mencken was a useful friend.[58] But they were little interested in the Mencken of Nietzsche and German Kultur.

The young called first of all for facts, for the opening up of knowledge that would permit appropriate choices and adjustments to be made. The editor of the *Ohio State Lantern* congratulated his school for the size and vigor of its sociology department, noting that "persons who understand the problems of their fellows must make proper allowance for them, and then there must be less bigotry, less intolerance, less Ku Klanism."[59] They then demanded what they considered to be their right to personal preference. This may sound strange in view of the conformity and group restraints they imposed on themselves, but it was not. Their norms were out of phase with the mores and values of the self-proclaimed defenders of traditional standards, and as a result they were under constant attack on grounds of immorality. Their behavior and interests were, they believed, a matter of preference, not morality. These preferences reflected a necessary adjustment to modern conditions, and as such they were open-ended and would change with those conditions.

"Youth," the editor of the *Ohio State Lantern* noted, "has new standards of conduct and decency, he believes that 'sin' has been stricken from the new code. 'Goodness' and 'sin' have become phrases to the new generation to which all of life is a challenge

to experience and expansion. . . . A certain moral squeam-
ishness and affectation has disappeared, facts, rather than romantic fallacies, govern youth's outlook more and more . . .
today youth . . . looks beneath the respectable traditions of
conduct and tries to see life whole." The college student has
been called "immoral, immodest," the Tulane *Hullabaloo* observed. "Is it because he is frank? True, his moral code is no
longer conventional. . . . His is the reasoned balance of good
and evil in the terms of practical life. . . . His philosophy of
life is a practical one. For social conventionalities he cares very
little but, nevertheless, he knows what to do and not to do."
The connection between the youths of Germany and those of the
United States, the *Cornell Sun* declared, was their mutual allegiance to the "spirit of rational inquiry. . . . Youth also
knows that to continue the regime of the 19th Century also is
impossible." Self-expression based on the facts was the proclaimed code of the young.[60]

In attacking the immutability of eternal verities and romantic fallacies inherited from a dead past, the young found a
large variety of targets in the America of the 1920's. There was,
from the beginning, the issue of suppressing speech. The sup-
pressor might be President W. W. Atwood of Clark University
disrupting an address by Scott Nearing, a case that called forth
the unmitigated ire of editors and students at Clark and elsewhere. The suppressors might be the administration of the University of California preventing a debate on birth control or an
open discussion of the future of marriage. They might be the
states of Kentucky and Tennessee, Bryan, and the fundamentalists leagued against the process of evolution; the administration of Denison University ousting S. I. Kornhauser
from the zoology department because he was a Jew teaching
evolution at a Christian college; the state of New York against
socialist teachers and legislators; the states of Michigan and
Washington against private school education; the federal government against the IWW's and leftist visitors; the Palmers and

the red-baiters. They were movie censors and theater censors
and book censors. They were the uplifters, Senator Volstead,
"Pussyfoot" Johnson and the WCTU, which spearheaded the
decade and the reaction against which epitomized the young's
views. They were the petty administrators, the city fathers, and
the women's clubs who denounced jazz, penalized bobbed hair,
screeched at smoking women, and despaired of the automobile
while they imposed curfews and enforced compulsory chapel.[61]
They were, one and all, the opponents of self-expression and
social change, and in so being they were the chosen enemies of
the young.

The young opposed these reformers of American life for their
intolerance, their repression of personal expression, and their
stupidity. Moral righteousness could not be imposed. But more
important, they asked the implicit question, what was morality? Was abstinence from drink, smoke, and sex morality? And
if so, whose morality was it? Surely not their own. They rejected the imposed morality of an older day because it was no
longer in harmony with their own value system and attitudes.
Their socialization process, which had stressed self-expression
and personality, rather than duty, had been "modern," and in
so being it repelled, like antibodies, the older virtues. It was
this modernity that defined the youth of the twenties and
welded them into a kind of generation. Moreover, ironically,
while it was not a generation formed in opposition, it was
united in opposition. It was not an opposition to the war-mak-
ing generation of the Progressive period or to the capitalist society in which they found themselves. It was an opposition to all
those who tried to stop change and who, failing to see that the
young were adjusting to a new environment, accused them of
being radical or immoral. Their politics was defined by the
necessities of their nature.[62]

There was no specific youth movement in the twenties, despite abortive attempts to start one. Necessarily, there were
often political issues that emerged from attempts at suppression

and control, and when that happened the young reacted on the side of liberalism. When editors were censured and papers suppressed and students suspended for airing their views on pacifism, the church, ROTC, or Prohibition—and there were many such suspensions and suppressions during the twenties [63]—the young took the side of freedom, not because they took sides on the issues but because they believed in the right to believe in them. When the cultural issues of the period were brought to the fore, the young reacted. The spark that failed on international issues and domestic politics flamed on cultural concerns.

The young could identify in terms of jazz and dress, birth control and Prohibition because these were important in their peer culture and because they defined the impulse to modernism. They charted the path toward permissive pluralism in the private realm. In the public realm, on issues of economics, internationalism, or political structure, peer norms were themselves conformist. Neither political activism nor political radicalism was important on the campus, for political subjects were outside the attention and interest of the campus society. A political radical was strange or eccentric, but a man who drank gin, shimmied, and petted was fashionably "naughty."

The young did not feel either the need or the desire to change their political system. They were optimistically and very consciously the beneficiaries of that system, and they aspired to succeed on its terms when it came time to assume their full roles and responsibilities. [64] Neither angry nor idealistic, neither anxious nor displaced, they were at the very center of a sociopolitical order that they would soon inherit. Peer norms and values were already preparing them for that estate. They were, at the same time, the heirs of very real changes in the family, sex, school, and recreations, and they understandably called for freedom in these areas. They embodied the social processes that many reformers hoped to contain or reverse. The moralists necessarily attacked the young, because youth represented everything they feared in American life. They turned to politics to halt the contagion. And the young never tired of defending themselves. In the end, it was this commitment to the cultural processes, articulated in their opposition to reaction and repression, that made the young of the twenties into a political generation.

CONCLUSION:
CHANGE & STABILITY

We who number ourselves among the so-called wild and wicked youth, already flaming, would prefer to go out with drums beating and bugles blowing if it is necessary that we go. Slow funeral marches are not sweet to the ears of youth. We want to have strength enough left to make one last convulsive kick. We want to be young before we are old.

Ohio State Lantern, October 7, 1925

Doubtless a generation from now, the youth of today will look at its own human product and say with a sigh and a pessimistic countenance: "What is the world coming to. It surely wasn't so bad as this in our day" and so forth ad infinitum.

Duke *Chronicle*, December 19, 1923

"We are all more or less self-centered residents of Main Street," remarked a Trinity College editor. And truly, much remained about the lives of college youths in the twenties that bound them securely to their time and place. Fraternities were imbued with the same boosterism familiar to the lodges and clubs which dominated the social lives and cultural horizons of the contemporary middle classes. Indeed, more often than not, Kiwani or Rotarian met collegian at the same athletic events and matched him cheer for cheer. And the self-advertisement of universities was not so very different from the efforts of many small-city Chambers of Commerce out to put their towns on the map. Students eagerly read Lewis' *Main Street,* carelessly imitated Mencken, and often cultivated worldly airs sorely belied by the facts of their lives. The provincial still tainted the modern, and beneath the brushed-up and sophisticated exterior of most collegiate fraternity pins beat the sterling heart of a Babbitt. "George F. Jr. is going to college," an Ohio State editor noted, "and he is even more secure in college than in the world of business, if we are to believe our eyes and ears and the college papers." [1]

It would have been strange had it been otherwise. The young lived in the world and most emphatically of it. Their reading matter was of a piece with the fare found in most middle-class living rooms, with the possible difference that they read fewer newspapers and more humor magazines: the *American, Saturday Evening Post, Life* (a humor magazine in the twenties), *Ladies' Home Journal, True Romance, Cosmopolitan.* Occasionally, they attended to an article recommended to them in the *Atlantic* or *Scribner's;* much more rarely they read the *New Republic* or the *Nation;* and sometimes, the *American Mercury.* They saw the films their parents saw and admired the same actors. They voted for the same politicians, with perhaps more skepticism and less general approval, but with the same overall majorities supporting Harding and Coolidge and Hoover. "As the colleges go," the *Ohio State Lantern* accurately reported about the elections, "so goes the nation." [2]

Living in a culture that valued business success and denied intellectual endeavors the laurels granted the creative geniuses of the Chamber of Commerce, the young had no desire to reorder priorities. Very few were interested in emulating the lives of their professors or in caring intensely for books or ideas. While the social structure of the peer system had adjusted the success myth to twentieth-century dimensions with its valuation of style within conformity and its dependence on prestige and association, it still enthusiastically embraced the business ethic and the American system. Although mating choices, sexual expression, and cultural forms had been newly tuned to an emerging American life style, they were still very much within the main line of the culture. Marriage was for the coed what business was in the imagination of her male partner. The young had liberated many behaviors and values from a conventional morality, but they had not separated themselves from the roles and responsibilities that they would soon assume. They had no reason to doubt that the future held anything but opportunities. They could not have foreseen, nor would they have believed, that it would be otherwise. Because they were secure in their present freedoms and in their future hopes, they were neither lax nor cynical. They were malleable, practical, and profoundly oblivious of the defects of American society, except for the superficial way in which they decried corruption in government, the existence of which was daily shouted at them from the headlines. It was, after all, for the roles of worker, wife, citizen, and consumer that youth was a preparation.

And yet, there was a difference, and it was a difference in substance as well as tone. In good part, that difference was a new latitude in experience; in part, it was also a broadening in attitude. The young had experienced an increase in personal freedoms, a newly expressive nurture, more schooling, more room for experimentation, and a greater sensitivity to the need for personal expression within themselves and for others. At home, they had enjoyed a person-oriented nurture; among peers, they were encouraged toward group-supported experimentation. And they had leisure. Thus at a time when values were not yet fixed and when youth could most readily test the limits of freedom, they were responsible only to each other.

They were more tolerant in attitude as well as freer in behavior, and in this the schools played their part, for education had exposed them to the relativism of philosophers, writers, and scientists who had long been preparing the ground for youth's beliefs and values. Not that the majority of college youths studied hard, but rather they necessarily were in contact with thinkers and innovators who colored their world view and their view of each other. Every college newspaper was unyielding in its denunciation of isolationism, fundamentalism, anti-evolutionism, censorship, and repression. Every editor took issue with the cult of moral reform. "College is the place to broaden out and to assimilate ideas from the classroom and the campus which tend to widen the scope of conception," Berkeley's *Daily Californian* proclaimed. "It is the place to balance old ideals against new experience; to test the value of former principles in the light of recent knowledge." And while students often complained that their studies were all too irrelevant to their lives, their lives had become more related to their studies.[3] For it was their experience which made the difference, and that experience made the tolerance so urgently contained in their books more meaningful and real.

This new latitude in experience separated the young from their parents and from the American past. Moreover, like the widening circles in an agitated pond, it was reaching farther and farther into the society. For the experience of the youth of the twenties was becoming increasingly institutionalized as more families became smaller, more youths were sent to school rather than to work, and more adjustments were required at a time when older attitudes toward sex, religion, and manners gave way to newer habits, to dating, movies, corporate work patterns, and Sunday golf. The young turned readily to what was new in the culture, and they did it with a delight and excitement that could only have made their elders both fearful and envious. The young could adjust, were forced to adjust, and were eager to adjust. And as they did so, they drew the culture with them.

They were a generation in tension. In a culture slowly moving toward the future, they were caught between those encroaching Main Street roles that they would soon assume and those innovations that had twisted their lives into new directions. So they were optimistic about business and naughty about sex. They could tolerate latitude in the behavior of others but most prudently guard against suspicion in their own. They could sneer with the cynic but harbor bright hopes for their own future success. The women smoked and the men drank, but neither were in any doubt about their decency and respectability. They could pet and denounce repression but carefully guard against too great indulgence in instinct. They were flamboyant about their rights and careful in their dress. They had charted the course for the new century as they prepared to assume adult lives in Zenith, U.S.A., *circa* 1929.

The peer group and the college peer society helped to direct the young both to effective stability in their own lives and to vital change in the society. At its most elementary level, the peer society provided company for young men and women freed from the need for work, released from obligations to the families from which they came, not yet engaged with families of their own, and endowed with energies unconsumed by the assigned work of the classroom. Though simple, this function of the peer group is basic to its very existence. Without leisure and without the formal structure provided by the schools, youth would have had neither so much time nor so many occasions for intense peer-group interaction. But the peer culture did more than provide fellowship for the individual. It developed an intricate set of work and play relationships, provided a sense of solidarity and identification, and asked in turn for obedience to its rules and conformity to its standards. The peer group had adapted the individual to a society largely of its own making and carefully protected from adult interference.

Ultimately, of course, it was the specific relationship between the youth society and the larger culture that was most crucial. At a time when affectionate person-centered nurture was growing in the family while other social relations were more and more governed by impersonal roles and performance demands, youth peers socialized individuals to accept group standards and thus provided a necessary transition from childhood to adulthood. From individuals reared to expect unqualified love and security just as a result of being, peers demanded performance and made approval and affiliation contingent on active behavior. Peer groups redirected expectations, providing the primary emotional security of group belonging in return for approved performance. Campus peer groups had thus become part of a new network of socialization in which schools and peers bridged the gap between family and marketplace.[4]

But once peer groups are granted this important social function in the 1920's, we must guard against a tempting deduction that a strict functionalist view such as that of S. N. Eisenstadt implies. This deduction concerns the congruence between the specific standards, behaviors, and values that peer groups embrace and those of the larger society. Peers do enforce performance standards, but those standards can as easily deviate from as support more general social norms. Peer groups vary among themselves.[5] All campuses in the twenties contained "fringe" groups—circles of literati, political radicals, religious enthusiasts, and scholars that were as effective in enforcing alternative styles and interests as the dominant fraternities were in promoting business values.

More significantly, a strictly functionalist view provides no basis for understanding why even dominant peer groups like fraternities could and did deviate from adult standards. Too dependent on a perfect fit between the social microcosm and macrocosm that circumscribes the range of youth's behavior to strictly future-oriented roles, a functionalist view reduces the young to puppets responding to social need by some kind of teleological necessity. It binds youth into a static universe, provides them no role in promoting changes in behavior or redirecting values, and cannot account for many of the tensions evident among college youth in the twenties—tensions between stability in certain areas and change in others. Finally, it overlooks the independent momentum which peer standards develop in the process of adapting to adult norms. College youth in the 1920's were not helpless dependents but active re-creators in a changing social world.

When youth in the twenties changed adult standards of respectability in sexual behavior and when they expanded the possibilities of women's behavior, they were effectively directing individuals away from adult norms and creating and approving new social patterns. When they opposed Prohibition and drank liquor, they were at once denying the urgency of adult norms, rejecting the notion of an unchanging standard of morality, and questioning the validity of adult laws. In adjusting to adult standards, they thus became by those standards immoral and law-breakers. They moreover asked for a latitude in behavior to be determined not by impersonal criteria but by personal preference. If peer groups trained only to an acceptance of standards, then youth groups in the twenties should not have denied that in certain areas there should be no standards. To explain such major variations in terms of deviancy, especially in relation to a generation in other ways stable and responsible, is not useful. The theory of direct and functional adaptation through peer-group mediation does help to explain the orientation of youth toward the basic structures of American society, the business and political world, and the valuation of success and status in that world. In this sense and in others, Eisenstadt's hypothesis is extremely helpful, but it is not sufficient. Socialization to social needs and adult norms is only one aspect of the peer-group experience.

The tensions in youth's behavior can be understood only if we recognize that in many ways college peers in the 1920's continued the person-oriented conditioning of the family. In certain areas, the young believed that personal expression, style, and need—not objective standards—should govern conduct. This was especially true in moral matters and was very effective as a value in sexuality and mating. But beyond the enunciated ideal of preference, many of the actual criteria of acceptability in the peer society were largely those of personal congeniality. Each group selected congenial associates within certain broad racial and class limitations and then proceeded to instruct members in those qualities which would increase that congeniality. Many of the tasks that members were required to perform concerned sociability. Personal conformity and not work performance was most highly valued. Despite the emphasis placed upon active competition in extra-curricular activities, it was personal rating, prestigious association, and collegiate style that dominated the social world of the young. Those values were latent in the whole network of peer relations. Amiability, sociability, congeniality, personal plasticity, these and not objective products were prime assets in the youth society, which was highly leisure-oriented. Many of the personal qualities were directed toward mating, but they were also valued as a means for business success.

But what exactly are the universal criteria of merit that govern performance in an impersonal bureaucratic world and which peers, according to Eisenstadt, socialize the young to expect and accept? If these criteria come down to the mechanical performance of assigned tasks, then personality would be disfunctional in that performance. If, however, personality is itself one of the criteria of merit, was the family as disfunctional as Eisenstadt would have us believe? Eisenstadt's model is too differentiated as to function; there is not enough overlap between the different agencies in the social universe. We know too little about the actual mechanisms of success in the business world of the twenties or thereafter to say conclusively, but Riesman's analysis of the importance of personal manipulation and status nuances in a consumer- and service-society suggests that subtleties of personality and style are far more significant than a rationalist model implies. Eisenstadt's model is too clear-cut, his categories too sharp, his functions too uni-directional. The evidence from the youth of the twenties suggests that family nurture and peer socialization were not so sharply differentiated and that the new middle-class family may well have been far less of an impediment to success than an active assistance.

Moreover, deviation from adult standards was built into peer relationships in the 1920's. One of the things the peer society on the campus encouraged was experimentation and partial socialization to a variety of minority ethics. This is a result of the comparative freedom that prevails during adolescence. Unhindered by responsibilities and obligations except to his own needs and isolated from adult values, the individual is during this period least required to conform to adult standards and freest of adult control. Youth is a period of manifest irresponsibility that Kenneth Keniston has called "belligerently non-adult"; a period when, according to Erik Erikson, a youth is at once directed toward future roles and intensely engaged in immediate enthusiasms.[6] Contradictions abound as the individual becomes intensely critical of previously respected adult models, oriented toward new ones, and uneasy about his own future. Youths in the twenties embodied many of these contradictions. The peer group permitted the individual to experiment without making him personally responsible for all his decisions. Devotion to the group and group enthusiasms mobilized an individual's energies, fulfilled his need for direction, and relieved him of personal responsibility for bad choices. The group as a whole, rather than the individual, provided models for imitation that filled the need for experimentation and commitment and assisted the process of self-definition. The peer group thus encouraged irresponsibility or impropriety as the adult world defined it. The individual was able to experience the freedom of anti-parental value choices without losing the security of group support.

In the twenties, this experimentation with values and behaviors was fostered by what David Matza has called the "subterranean traditions of youth." Matza has identified three major subterranean tendencies in youth societies—delinquency, radicalism, and bohemianism.[7] And this concept of youth's traditional choice of anti-social models of behavior can help to illuminate certain tendencies among the young of the twenties, despite the fact that I have stressed that the young in the twenties were both anti-radical and anti-Bohemian and although I have been concerned with normative and not delinquent groups.

There was among the mass of college youths in the twenties a very real infatuation with playing naughty-boy roles, an inclination toward affectations of sophistication and worldliness. It was not quite bohemian, but it was not quite respectable either. In this attitude they were amply provided with adult models. To name just a few is to recognize the varieties of the cultural history of the twenties, especially as it demonstrated disaffection from normative values and provided romantic alternatives: H. L. Mencken, Randolph Bourne, Emma Goldman, Floyd Dell, Edna St. Vincent Millay, F. Scott Fitzgerald, Scott Nearing, Theda Bara, Rudolph Valentino, Clara Bow. The list is endless. Each represents in a different way the possibilities of unconventional conduct and values. Each served as a well-advertised model upon which to base a tendency toward non-conformity. On the whole, these tendencies were developed to an important degree only among small minorities, but their influence as potential models for imitation was general, and all youth appear to have felt it to some degree. The "deviates" in adult society gave youth a host of patterns that could and did affect the tone or style of youth life. This variety expanded the possibilities of approved experimentation, now supported by active peer mediation, and was a way of assimilating change to the generally conservative (but not traditional) standards that prevailed. These models were, of course, available to adults as well, and no doubt they influenced the behavior of some. But the young in the 1920's were more vulnerable to their example because during a period of search and experimental role-playing, when values were plastic and imitative, the young had group support for experimentation.

There is another potential peer-group function that does not seem on the whole to have affected college youth in the twenties. The peer group can encourage or condone self-conscious conflicts with adult society and adult authority. The potential of adolescence as a period of hostility between adults and youth, parents and children, was well known in the twenties. The more sanguine critics used the age-old conflict of the generations as an explanation for what they interpreted as the rebelliousness of youth. The young also used the generation gap as a convenient way of countering criticism. Since that time, others, notably Kingsley Davis and Lewis Feuer, have used the basic conflict between youth and age as explanatory models. Davis' hypothesis about "parent-adolescent conflict" hinges on an irreducible difference between youthful idealism and maturing practicality exacerbated by the accelerating rate of social change in modern culture. Feuer's model is based on a psychological theory of Oedipal conflict aggravated by permissive family patterns and traumatic generational experiences.[8] Neither is very useful for understanding college youth in the twenties.

The young in the twenties were rather more optimistic than idealistic, and they were also notoriously pragmatic. With a shrewd eye for the limits of acceptable conduct and belief, youth rarely provoked adult authority on the high ground of theory. When they were idealistic, it was about very specific issues not as a general orientation. They could argue against the stupidities of war or denounce the inanities of censorship. But they condemned pacifism and radicalism and were bigoted and nationalistic. The young were plastic, but this is not the same as being naturally idealistic. That plasticity simply made them more vulnerable to change. When the young believed their vital interests were at stake, they became flamboyantly idealistic, but it was idealism that always betrayed their sense of what was convenient as well as what was good. Moreover, even when they were idealistic in theory, very few indeed were willing to pledge themselves unreservedly to pacifism, or to claim that Prohibition laws should be disobeyed, or, regarding the double standard of sexual morality, to test the limits of equality. Indeed, the young were, if anything, consciously hard-nosed, prudent, and pragmatic. No doubt, the young adapted more easily to the rapid social changes that were transforming American society and culture than their elders. But they did so not from some primary idealism directed toward a more liberal future but because peers were helping to liberate each other from the greater confines of parents and past and because peer groups were using the very instruments of the new culture, like fads and movies, to effect new social controls on behavior.

The college youth of the twenties were not a generation that deliberately denied the moral or intellectual competence of its elders. They were "naughty," not angry. They knew that they lived in a changing world that demanded new understanding, new conventions, and constant readjustments. And they conceived of their behavior and attitudes as positively responsive to these conditions. They were sometimes accused of ignoring adults and of denying them an influence in their lives. If this was so, it was because adults did have less influence in their lives and not because they chose to deny them authority. The college papers show an avid concern with adult opinion, and students usually cared enough to attempt to explain themselves. Acutely aware of being observed and criticized, the young would often artfully accentuate certain qualities to which they knew adults would react, usually with horror or outrage. As a form of self-defense, the pose itself was serious, but the implications usually less than wholly sincere. And it all betrayed a wispy self-mockery which belied their cocky self-assurance.

The *New Student* had been intent on developing a youth consciousness grounded in political commitment that would confront the adult world and contend with it on the basis of generations. There were moves to mobilize youth on political matters throughout the decade, best illustrated in the student conferences and leagues, but they affected a minority of students and found no real momentum. The one area in which the young seemed to find a voice was in cultural matters, or rather in matters of style. They conceived of themselves as modern in dress, manners, and interest, and they were proud of it. They opposed all attempts to return American life to an impossible past that would condemn their new liberties in sex, thought, and interest. This was a diffuse kind of sentiment, a tone, an inclination, but it was strong enough to lend a certain self-consciousness to the college youth of the twenties.

There was no hostility toward the world of the elders, only a sense of difference. The problem with cultural differences is that they are vague and easily appropriated. And so it was with the youth of the twenties. Their identifying symbols—their clothes, their music, their athletics, and their slang—merged into the consciousness of a decade. The adult population hounded their every step, and where some came to condemn, others stayed to imitate. For many, the path of the damned had become the way of the beautiful.

NOTES

The following student newspapers have been used for the period 1914–1932:

Barnard Bulletin (Barnard College, New York, N.Y.)

Columbia Spectator (Columbia College, New York, N.Y.)

Cornell Sun (Cornell University, Ithaca, N.Y.)

Daily Illini (University of Illinois, Champaign–Urbana, Ill.)

Daily Princetonian (Princeton University, Princeton, N.J.)

Ohio State Lantern (Ohio State University, Columbus, Ohio)

Rutgers Targum (Rutgers University, New Brunswick, N.J.)

The Normal Outlook, The Cub Californian, The California Grizzly, The Daily Bruin: cited as UCLA Daily (University of California at Los Angeles)

The Reveille (Louisiana State University, Baton Rouge, La.)

The Trinity Chronicle, The Chronicle: cited as The Chronicle (Duke University, Durham, N.C.)

CHAPTER 1

1. See John and Virginia Demos, "Adolescence in Historical Perspective," *Journal of Marriage and the Family*, 31 (1969), 632–638, for the emergence of the concept of adolescence in the late 19th and early 20th centuries. G. Stanley Hall's monumental two-volume work, *Adolescence*, which appeared in 1904, seems to have given symbolic legitimacy to adolescence as a scientific concept as well as a convenient mode of perception. But see Natalie Zemon Davis, "The Reasons of Misrule: Youth Groups and Charivaris in Sixteenth-Century France," *Past and Present*, no. 50 (1971), 45–75, who argues persuasively that adolescence as a cultural role and definition has a long history and dates back to the Middle Ages.

2. The whole subject of youth was discussed incessantly in the journals of the twenties. According to Goodwin Watson, *Youth After Conflict* (New York, 1947), pp. 48–49, there had never been a more written-about generation. His study of the entries in the *Reader's Guide* from 1918 to 1930 showed two peak periods, 1922 and 1926. At the height of the discussions, the number of articles listed was twenty times the number for 1918–1919. Significantly, "Youth" as a separate listing in the *New York Times Index* first appeared in 1920.

3. James Truslow Adams, "Our Dissolving Ethics," *Atlantic Monthly*, 138 (1926), 577.

4. See, for example, "Uprising of Youth," *The Survey*, 44 (1920), 400; R. E. T. Ernle, "The Revolt of Youth," *The Nineteenth Century and After*, 88

(1920), 925–934; "Why Youth Is Cynical," *Literary Digest,* 94 (August 6, 1927), 32.

5. "Modern Youth and Its Ways," *Living Age,* 307 (1920), 45; John F. Carter, Jr., "These Wild Young People," *Atlantic Monthly,* 126 (1920), 302, 303 (italics in original).

6. See, besides Carter's *Atlantic* article, the evidence presented by self-styled spokesmen for youth: Don Marquis, "Youth's Questionnaire Submitted to the Older Generation by the Intelligent Flapper and Her Boy Friend," *Outlook,* 149 (1928), 177; "Good-bye, Dear Mr. Grundy," by "Last Year's Debutante," *Atlantic Monthly,* 126 (1920), 645. Also, M. B. Stewart, "Youngsters vs. Oldsters," *Scribner's,* 78 (1925), 125–127.

7. Mary Borden, "Manners," *Harper's,* 160 (1929), 78; "They Want To Know," *New Republic,* 49 (December 29, 1926), 150, 151.

8. Mary Agnes Hamilton, "Where Are You Going My Pretty Maid?" *Atlantic Monthly,* 138 (1926), 298; "Elder Not Better," *Atlantic Monthly,* 130 (1922), 571. See also Thomas Arkle Clark, "The Passing of the Chaperone," *Atlantic Monthly,* 129 (1922), 516–519.

9. Mary Agnes Hamilton, " 'Nothing Shocks Me,' " *Harper's,* 155 (1927), 155; Avis Carlson, "Wanted: A Substitute for Righteousness," *Harper's,* 154 (1927), 148, 149, 152.

10. "The Release of Youth," *Nation,* 110 (May 22, 1920), 674. See also Annie Winsor Allen, "Boys and Girls," *Atlantic Monthly,* 125 (1920), 796–804, who laments the fact that most young people were just marking time and that this wastage threatened to be turned into socially deviant channels. Especially notable is the emphasis on sexual energy, which is seen as the most potentially disruptive feature of adolescence.

11. "The anti-Puritan revolt is much more than a revolt against sex repression alone," observed anthropologist Edward Sapir. "It is a generalized revolt against everything that is hard, narrow and intolerant in the old American life, and which sees in sex repression its most potent symbol of attack"; "The Discipline of Sex," *American Mercury,* 16 (1929), 416. Sapir was here referring specifically to the literary and intellectual attack on sexual mores, but the observation was also intended for and is appropriate to the way in which the revolt of youth was interpreted, as a rejection of sham and hypocrisies.

12. Ann Temple, "Has Youth Deteriorated?—Reaping the Whirlwind," *Forum,* 76 (1926), 22; Borden, "Manners," 77. "When people talk about 'morals' they nearly always mean one limited department thereof—that governing the relations of the sexes"; Hamilton, "Pretty Maid," 300. Columnist Reese Carmichael in the *Ladies' Home Journal* asked, "Why, when two or three elders are gathered together, does the conversation invariably turn to such topics as the way young girls dress nowadays, the dissipation of young men,

the way the young people dance, their frank speech, their general and horrific wildness?" The answer was obvious: it was an anxious concern over sexual irregularities which these behaviors implied; "Those Dreadful Young Persons," *Ladies' Home Journal*, 38 (May, 1921), 18.

13. Ellen Welles Page, "Flapper's Appeal to Parents," *Outlook*, 132 (1922), 607; "Mr. Grundy," "Polite Society," *Atlantic Monthly*, 125 (1920), 610; Eleanor Rowland Wembridge, "Silk Stockings," *The Survey*, 52 (1924), 28–30; Hamilton, " 'Nothing Shocks Me,' " *passim*; Charlotte Perkins Gilman, "Vanguard, Rear-guard, and Mud-Guard," *Century Magazine*, 104 (1922), 349–350.

14. Editorial, *Ladies' Home Journal*, 38 (November, 1921), 24; John R. McMahon, "Unspeakable Jazz Must Go," *Ladies' Home Journal*, 38 (December, 1921), 116. For the condemnation of jazz as Negroid, see Beatrice Forbes-Robertson Hode, in Kate W. Jamison and F. C. Lockwood, *The Freshman Girl, A Guide to College Life* (New York, 1925), pp. 162–166.

15. John R. McMahon, "Back to Pre-War Morals," *Ladies' Home Journal*, 38 (November, 1921), 13, 108.

16. An especially venomous attack on the young woman of the period was leveled by the feminist Charlotte Perkins Gilman in "Vanguard, Rear-guard, and Mud-guard." She asserted that youth was engaged in a cult of "shallow self-indulgence" marked by an "unchecked indulgence in appetite and impulse; a coarseness and looseness in speech, dress, manner, and habit of life" (349–350). Women, the arch-feminist contended, were made to be mothers, "and not, as seems to be widely supposed, for enjoyable preliminaries" (351). Modern women should devote themselves to mastering the techniques of eugenics in order to "cleanse the human race of its worst inheritance by discriminating refusal of unfit fathers," rather than "mastering birth control and acquiring 'experience' " (353). The hysterical ascription of immorality and irresponsibility to the behavior of young women found in Gilman's remarks was characteristic of the reaction of not a few old-line feminists to the young women of the twenties.

17. Dorothy Dunbar Bromley, "Feminist—New Style," *Harper's*, 155 (1927), 552. For the stabilizing role of women in the nineteenth century, see Barbara Welter, "The Cult of True Womanhood: 1820–1860," *American Quarterly*, 18 (1966), 151–174.

18. Bromley, "Feminist—New Style," 558, 559 (italics in original). See also Harriet Abbott, "What the Newest New Woman Is," *Ladies' Home Journal*, 37 (August, 1920), 160.

19. "Polite Society," 609. For the affect of choice on marital stability, see, for example, Joseph Collins, "Woman's Morality in Transition," *Current History*, 27 (1927), 33–40. The rising divorce rate seemed to many a clear conse-

quence of women's new latitude for choice. It also indicated that they were making new demands in marriage. "Those many things which her position forced her to suffer and tolerate yesterday she refuses to suffer and tolerate today"; Bejamin P. Chass, "The Alarming Increase in Divorce," *Current History,* 22 (1925), 792.

20. Alyse Gregory, "The Changing Morality of Women," *Current History,* 19 (1923), 299; "A Warning for Country Girls," *Literary Digest,* 83 (December 13, 1924), 33.

21. See, for example, "Elder Not Better," 570–572, which argued that the changes reflected only the old conflict of generations; Winifred Kirkland, "Grundyism," *Outlook,* 127 (1921), 509–510, who argued that it reflected usual cyclical changes in tastes and fashions; Mrs. Henry W. Peabody, "Woman's Morality: A Light Through the Ages," *Current History,* 19 (1924), 584–589, who believed that the same division between pure women and immoral women still obtained; also, Frances Mathilda Abbott, "As Seen by an Old Maid Grundy," *North American Review,* 212 (1920), 648–657.

22. Regina Malone, "Has Youth Deteriorated?—The Fabulous Monster," *Forum,* 76 (1926), 29. See also Bromley, "Feminist—New Style," 558. According to Alyse Gregory, "The Anglo-Saxon attitude toward the chastity of woman is undergoing a distinct change"; "The Changing Morality of Women," 295.

According to sociologist Ernest Burgess, "In speech, in manner, and in attitude, boys and girls still in the teen age show heedless disregard for convention; a contempt for the advice of their elders, or worse yet, a smug indifference to it; a sublime faith in their own opinions about life and conduct; and a cynicism for 'The sacred things of life' . . . that shock the older generation and render its occasional efforts at intervention futile, if not absurd." Burgess continued, "It is not so much what young people do, but the revolutionary and outrageous things they say, and the smart and smug way in which they say them" that exasperated and appalled the older people. See "The Growth of the Romantic Impulse," in Edward B. Reuter and Jessie Runner, *The Family* (New York, 1931), pp. 125–126.

23. George A. Coe, *What Ails Our Youth?* (New York, 1924); Judge Ben Lindsey and Wainwright Evans, *The Revolt of Modern Youth* (New York, 1925); V. F. Calverton [George Goetz], *The Bankruptcy of Marriage* (New York, 1928); Floyd Dell, *Love in the Machine Age* (New York, 1930). For a fuller discussion of these books, see the author's doctoral dissertation, "The Fruits of Transition: American Youth in the 1920s," Columbia University, 1974, Chapter 2.

24. See, for example, William E. Leuchtenburg, *The Perils of Prosperity, 1914–1932* (Chicago, 1958), pp. 84, 120–139; Richard Hofstadter, *The Age*

of Reform (New York, 1955), pp. 272–301; Eric Goldman, *Rendezvous with Destiny* (New York, 1956), pp. 220–227.

25. Lindsey, for example, wrote that his book was a "pledge of my abiding faith in the ultimate and inherent goodness of mankind and in a divine destiny for the human race"; Lindsey and Evans, *Revolt*, p. 19.

26. Coe, *What Ails Our Youth?*, pp. 90, 93.

27. Lindsey and Evans, *Revolt*, pp. 21, 122, 88, 157.

28. Calverton, *Bankruptcy*, p. 331, preface; Dell, *Machine Age*, p. 103.

29. Calverton, for example, referred to the war as chalking "a turning point in the disintegration of the ethics and ideals of the ruling class"; *Bankruptcy*, pp. 33–34.

30. Adams, "Our Dissolving Ethics," 577–578.

31. A good summary and introduction to the various facets of the industrial transformation considered important to progressives is found in Coe's *What Ails Our Youth?* These included: technological innovations and scientific discoveries; changes in the status and role of women; urbanization and the decline of community; the displacement of craftsmanship by mechanization; and the attendant urge to fulfillment and satisfaction through leisure-time pursuits.

For Lindsey, modern youth's revolt was lodged in the overall transformation of material environment: "Youth has always been rebellious; youth has always shocked the older generation. That's traditional. . . . But this is different. It has the whole weight and momentum of a new scientific and economic order behind it. It has come in an age of speed and science; an age when women vote and can make their own living; an age in which the fear of Hell Fire has lost its hold. In the past the revolt of youth always turned out to be a futile gesture. It never brought much change. But now the gun's loaded. These boys and girls can do what boys and girls never were able to do in the past. . . . The external restraints, economic restraints that were once so potent, have gone never to return" (p. 54). "Modern youth," Lindsey noted, "is growing up under the wing of science"; *Revolt*, p. 157.

32. Carlson, "Wanted: A Substitute for Righteousness," 150; "Polite Society," 608; Irma Voight, Dean of Women, Ohio State University, quoted in "The Case Against the Younger Generation," *Literary Digest*, 73 (June 17, 1922), 58, 63.

33. William Lyon Phelps, "The American Home and the Younger Generation," *World's Week*, 48 (1924), 640; "The Case Against the Younger Generation," 51.

34. Lindsey and Evans, *Revolt*, p. 127.

35. Lindsey and Evans, *Revolt*, pp. 18, 17 (italics in original). For companionate marriage, see Lindsey and Evans, pp. 164–176, 201–218, 244–255

and *passim;* also, Judge Ben Lindsey and Wainwright Evans, *Companionate Marriage* (New York, 1927).

36. Hamilton, "Pretty Maid," 297. See also Henry Seidel Canby, "Life in the Nineties: Home and Parents," *Harper's,* 169 (1934), 270–282.

37. Calverton, *Bankruptcy,* pp. 22, 47, 117.

38. Calverton, *Bankruptcy,* preface. For Calverton, the young had emerged from the war with one thought, "to live, to live intensely, to live furiously, to seize from life its every thrill" (p. 17). Jazz was an "intoxication," the great "delirium of escape" which nightly flung the young "upon the edge of nervous ecstasy" (pp. 11, 12).

39. Dell, *Machine Age,* p. 56.

40. See Dell's account of his conversion to love and fidelity through intensive psychoanalytic treatment in "An Autobiographical Critique," *Psychoanalytic Quarterly,* 1 (1932), 715–730. Dell had earlier been the naughty boy, free love advocate of the Greenwich Villagers, and his "conversion" was notable. See the author's doctoral dissertation, "Fruits of Transition," pp. 75–87.

41. Malone, "Has Youth Deteriorated?" 30; quoted in "Courting Danger in the Automobile," *Literary Digest,* 82 (July 5, 1924), 35; Phelps, "The American Home," 642.

42. S. K. Ratcliffe, "The License of the Youngsters," *Century Magazine,* 102 (1921), 392; Carter, "These Wild Young People," 303.

43. Katherine Fullerton Gerould, "Reflections of a Grundy Cousin," *Atlantic Monthly,* 126 (1920), 162, 163; Carlson, "Wanted: A Substitute for Righteousness," 150.

44. Kenneth Irving Brown, "The Religion of the New Renaissance," *Outlook,* 139 (1925), 186. See also "Challenging Questions of Youth," *Outlook,* 139 (1925), 482–483; essay-contest winners in "The Mind of Youth," *The World Tomorrow,* 10 (1927), 4–22; Coe, *What Ails Our Youth?,* p. 55; "Good-Bye, Dear Mr. Grundy," 645.

45. Christian Gauss, *Life in College* (New York, 1930), p. 18.

46. Gauss, *Life in College,* p. 16. For the various student types, see Richard Burton, "Why Go to College?" *American Mercury,* 3 (1924), 481–487; F. M. Abbott, "As Seen by an Old Maid Grundy," 655; Gerould, "Reflections of a Grundy Cousin," 158; Wilbur Abbott, "The Guild of Students," *Atlantic Monthly,* 128 (1921), 621; Eleanor Rowland Wembridge, "Petting and the Campus," *The Survey,* 54 (1925), 393–395. There seems to have been a general fear among traditionalists that these lower-class young people, who had not received the "right" and moral upbringing of their betters, would infect the habits and attitudes of their betters.

47. Gauss, *Life in College,* p. 30; Robert Cooley Angell, *The Campus* (New York, 1928), pp. 2–9, 25, 210–211.

48. Wilbur Abbott, "The Guild of Students," 619, 623, 624, 625.

49. W. H. Cowley, "Explaining the Rah Rah Boy," *New Republic*, 46 (April 14, 1926), 242–245; Coe, *What Ails Our Youth?*, pp. 14, 23; Willard Thorpe, "This Flapper Age," *Forum*, 68 (1922), 643. See also Max Mc-Conn, "Tired Business Men of the Campus," *North American Review*, 226 (1928), 545–550; Gerald W. Johnson, "Should Our Colleges Educate?" *Harper's*, 155 (1927), 723–727; Henry Pringle, "Young Men on the Make," *Harper's*, 158 (1929), 149–157.

50. "How Wild Is Wild Youth?" *New Republic*, 46 (May 5, 1926), 318–319.

51. "Good-bye, Dear Mr. Grundy," 644. "Nobody seems to know what to do about the younger generation except to be rather shocked and pained," Florence G. Woolston observed in the *New Republic*. "So much has been said, so much written, that boys and girls are fully aware that they are a problem, and they enjoy the role. The 'flapper' of fiction, plays, movies and newspapers offers a vivid pattern of modern young life and creates a certain bravado and the necessity for living up to current opinion"; "Girls and then Some," *New Republic*, 30 (March 15, 1922), 79.

CHAPTER 2

1. Bronislaw Malinowski, "Parenthood, The Basis of Social Structure," in *The New Generation*, ed. V. F. Calverton and S. D. Schmalhausen (New York, 1930), pp. 113–168.

2. Nationalization is an important concept and should not be confused with either the nationalization of capital goods or nationalism as patriotism. It means, in this context, the development of cross-regional institutions and affiliations which stratify and unify people and groups on the basis of national culture and translocal organizations. Thus, colleges were national organizations by the twenties, not only because they drew students from diverse localities, but also because they were increasingly similar regardless of region, just as industries were increasingly national because they distributed goods nationwide and because there were affiliated plants in different locations. For nationalization as a social phenomenon, see Robert H. Wiebe, *The Search for Order, 1877–1920* (New York, 1967), especially Chapters 1, 2, 5.

3. For an excellent summary of the role of peer groups in advanced industrial societies, see S. N. Eisenstadt, "Archetypical Patterns of Youth," in *The Challenge of Youth*, ed. Erik H. Erikson (Garden City, N.Y., 1965); Eisenstadt, *From Generation to Generation: Age Groups and Social Structure* (New York, 1956). For a discussion of Eisenstadt and peer groups generally, see Chapter 3 and Conclusion herein.

4. U.S. Bureau of the Census, *People of the United States in the 20th Century*,

by Irene B. Taeuber and Conrad Taeuber (Washington, D.C., 1971), p. 142, Table VIII-1, pp. 356–357; Alfred J. Lotka, "Modern Trends in the Birth Rate," *Annals, American Academy of Political and Social Science*, 188 (1936), 1–13 (all references to this journal will hereafter be cited as *Annals, AAPSS*); Robert E. Chaddock, "Age and Sex in Population Analysis," *Annals, AAPSS*. 188 (1936), 185–193; Newton Edwards, "Youth as a Population Element," *Annals, AAPSS*, 194 (1937), 6–17.

5. See John and Virginia Demos, "Adolescence in Historical Perspective," *Journal of Marriage and the Family*, 31 (1969), 632–638; Anthony M. Platt, *The Child Savers: The Invention of Delinquency* (Chicago, 1969).

6. The following table describes the shifting proportion of each specified age group in the population between 1870 and 1930 (reprinted from Edwards, "Youth as a Population Element," Table 1, 7):

TABLE A

Percentage Age Distribution in U.S. Population, 1870–1930

Year	Age Group 0–14	15–24	25–64	65 & Older	Ratio, Youths 15–24/1000 Adults
1870	39.2	20.2	37.6	3.0	537
1880	38.1	20.1	38.3	3.4	525
1890	35.5	20.4	40.0	3.8	509
1900	34.4	19.6	41.7	4.0	470
1910	32.1	19.7	43.7	4.3	450
1920	31.8	17.7	45.8	4.6	387
1930	29.4	18.3	46.9	5.4	389

7. Mildred Parten, "A Statistical Analysis of the Modern Family," *Annals, AAPSS*, 160 (1932), 31.

8. This sample was compiled by demographer Frank W. Notestein from the original enumeration sheets of the 1910 census and is based on native white women north of the Mason-Dixon line. The women were 40–44 and 60–64 years of age for the two generations, thus assuring that the families selected were all substantially completed by the census date. The sample was very large—59,149 women in 33 cities (100,000 to 500,000 population) and 43,352 women from adjacent rural counties. For a full description of the sample, the sources, and the findings, see Frank W. Notestein, "The Decreasing Size of Families from 1890 to 1910," *Quarterly Bulletin of the Milbank Me-*

morial Fund, 9 (1931), 181–188. See also Notestein, "Class Differences in Fertility," *Annals, AAPSS*, 188 (1936), 26–36, and Xarifa Sallume and Frank W. Notestein, "Trends in the Size of Families Completed Prior to 1910 in Various Social Classes," *American Journal of Sociology*, 38 (1932), 398–408.

9. The following table highlights the significant pattern by concentrating on the proportional increase in small families (0–1 child) and the proportional decrease in very large families (5 or more children) among various groups. It is reprinted from Notestein, "Decreasing Size of Families," Table 3, 187:

TABLE B

Increase and Decrease of Small and Large Families, 1890–1910, by Occupational Group

Class	% With 0–1 Child				% With 5 or more Children			
	1910	1890	Diff.	% Diff.	1910	1890	Diff.	% Diff.
Professional	39.4	28.0	+11.4	28.9	8.2	22.7	−14.5	65.2
Business	39.4	23.6	+15.8	40.1	10.9	25.5	−14.6	57.3
Skilled	34.4	22.1	+12.3	35.7	20.5	33.6	−13.1	39.0
Unskilled	31.2	16.8	+14.4	46.1	28.4	40.8	−12.4	30.4
Farm	20.7	17.8	+ 2.9	14.0	33.1	43.2	−10.1	23.4

Table B puts the pattern among the professional and business groups in sharp relief: the professional class showed the least increase in very small families of all urban groups, partly because this group already had the largest proportion of small families in 1890. But it also emphasizes the fact that the decline in large families in the professional (and business) class was largely effected through an increase in medium-range families (2–3 children). Table B also highlights the sharp decline in very large families in these groups (a 65% decline among professionals and 57% among business families). Together, these two patterns describe the demographic experience of middle-class groups.

Another significant feature of these demographic trends is the pattern among the unskilled laborers. This group showed a startling increase in very small families but no comparable decrease in large families. In fact, the trend was strongly bimodal—either very large or very small families. Within a generation, families of unskilled laborers had begun to show a peculiar trend, different than any other group. It would be interesting to speculate on the reason for this development. One strong possibility is that with the growing knowledge of birth control, unskilled laborers were faced with a choice—either severely limit family size so that one child could be adequately provided for or continue to rear large families and retain the pattern of all children assisting with family finances. Whatever the explanation, the pattern is certainly significant and provocative and warrants full investigation.

10. By the early 1930's, a survey by the White House Conference on Child Health and Protection found that three-quarters of a largely middle-class sample of native, white children from an urban environment came from families with only one to three children at home. In contrast, almost one-half of all rural adolescents came from homes with four or more children. See White House Conference on Child Health and Protection, *The Adolescent in the Family*, ed. Ernest Burgess (New York, 1934), p. 325. It should be borne in mind, however, that this finding concerned only children living at home and not all children per family and may therefore have underestimated family size because children away at school or already married were not counted.

The trend in family size continued after 1920. The best evidence for this comes from Day Monroe's examination of the 1920 Chicago census, *Chicago Families, A Study of Unpublished Census Data* (Chicago, 1932), Table 24, p. 94. In 1920, 34.1% of all professional and 30.4% of all executive families in Chicago had no children, and 49.8% of the executives and 43.0% of the professionals had one or two children only. Only one-fifth of these groups had so many as three or more children. In part the explanation for this large increase in childlessness is due to the lesser completeness of the families sampled (wives 35–45 years), but more importantly it may record the specific pattern in a large metropolis. There is evidence that metropolitan cities had more childlessness than smaller cities; see William F. Ogburn, "The Family and Its Functions," in *Recent Social Trends in the United States, Report of the President's Research Committee on Social Trends*, one-volume ed. (New York, 1933), pp. 687–688. It is also likely that middle-class families with children, or at least those with larger numbers of children, were moving to the suburbs, which were growing rapidly during this period; see George A. Lundberg, Mirra Komarovsky, and Mary Alice McInery, *Leisure: A Suburban Study* (New York, 1934). But whatever the variations due to these factors, it is probable that the trends among middle-class families continued and that even families of three children were becoming less common after 1920.

The continuous decline in the birth rate between 1880 and 1910 is documented in Table C below, which measures numbers of children per 100 wives according to age and occupation of husband (1910 Census Report):

There is a steady decline in the birth rate within each class, but the most marked decline took place among wives of professionals, where the difference was 122 births per 100 women. This meant that within 25 years professional wives bore on the average 1.2 less children than their mothers had.

TABLE C

Number of Children Born per 100 Women, 45 Years of Age or Older by the Census of 1910, According to Husband's Occupation

Occupational Group	Age of Wife at Census of 1910				
	45–49	50–54	55–59	60–64	65–69
Professional	251	263	295	295	372
Business	255	277	309	320	347
Skilled Worker	308	347	366	372	378
Farm Owner	401	419	430	438	444

Source: Xarifa Sallume and Frank W. Notestein, "Trends in the Size of Families," Table 1, 402.

This table also emphasizes the increased differentiation between classes. Among the older women, the difference between classes is only 72 children per 100 women; among the youngest group, the difference is twice as large—150 children per 100 women. The change is even more striking when we compare the professional and skilled classes. In the oldest group there was only a 6 per 100 difference, but in the youngest, the difference was 57 per 100. This demonstrates that the professional and business classes were finding smaller families increasingly more consistent with their needs. The absolute change in family size is also of interest. Among wives of professionals, the decline was from an average of 3.7 children per family to 2.5 children per family.

11. College students came overwhelmingly from middle-class occupational groups. See Table D. See also, Edward F. Potthoff, "Who Goes to College?" *Journal of Higher Education*, 2 (1931), 294–297, based on a sample of students at the University of Chicago in 1924. In Chicago, proprietors were far more over-represented than professionals. This may illustrate the special circumstances of an urban university. Thus, while 7.8% of all men in Chicago were proprietors, 42.3% of the students' fathers were proprietors. On the other hand, while 5.1% of the city population was professional, 18.6% of the students' fathers were professionals.

At the University of Wisconsin in 1921–1923, the following occupation distribution was recorded by Ray Erwin Baber and Edward Alsworth Ross, *Changes in the Size of American Families in One Generation*, University of Wisconsin Studies in the Social Sciences and History, No. 10 (Madison, Wis., 1924),

TABLE D

Percentage of Males 45 Years of Age and Over in Each Occupational Group in the United States, the Percentage of Fathers of Students in Each Occupational Group in 55 Colleges and Universities, 1923–1924, and the Ratio of Students' Fathers to All Fathers

Occupations	% in Each Occupation 1920 Census	% in Colleges and Universities	Ratio Students' Fathers to All
Professional	3.8	18.4	4.8
Proprietors	8.0	24.2	3.0
Managerial Service	7.2	10.2	1.4
Commercial Service	3.9	7.0	1.8
Agricultural Service	28.5	23.3	.8
Artisan-Proprietors	—	1.4	—
Trades (Building, Machine, Printing, etc.)	27.3	5.9	.2
Transportation Service	5.0	3.8	.8
Personal Service	3.7	.4	.1
Public Service	1.6	.7	.4
Miners, Lumber Workers	.8	.4	.4
Common Labor	7.2	.5	.1
Unknown	—	1.8	—
Total %	100.0	100.0	

Source: O. Edgar Reynolds, The Social and Economic Status of College Students, Contributions to Education, Teachers College, Columbia University (New York, 1927), Tables 4 and 8, pp. 14, 18.

Table 2-C, p. 44: professional, 20.6%; business, 32.7%; clerical, 7.7%; farm, 25.6%; skilled labor, 10.9%; unskilled labor, 2.5%.

12. For Wisconsin, see Baber and Ross. Sample composed of 2500 white, native families of students from the Midwest (largely Illinois, Iowa, Kansas, Ohio, Wisconsin) and students' related families for the present generation, and 750 families of students' parents for the earlier generation.

For California students, see S. J. Holmes, "The Size of College Families," Journal of Heredity, 15 (1924), 407–415. Holmes' data were calculated on the basis of only native families in the present generation, but include native and foreign families in the parents' generation. The number of children in students' families was 3.66 as compared with 5.21 in the parents' generation, a decline of 1.5 children per family, or 29.8%.

For New England students (Mt. Holyoke College), see Amy Hewes, "A Study of Families in Three Generations," *Journal of the Association of College Alumnae,* 13 (1920), 5–9.

13. Warren S. Thompson, "Size of Families from Which College Students Come," *Journal of the American Statistical Association,* 20 (1925), 481–495. In the South as a whole, families were 44.1% larger than families from the Northeast, 25.7% larger than the Midwest, and 24.7% larger than in the West. Thompson also found that farm families had an average of 1.05 more children than professional families (483); Baber and Ross (Wisconsin) found that rural families averaged 1.19 more children than professional families and 1.33 more children than business families (Table 7-C, p. 82).

14. The distribution of only children and children with other siblings in Chicago in 1920 is shown below:

TABLE E

Percent of Only Children, Children with One Sibling, Children with Two or More Siblings, and Children with One or More Siblings, in Unbroken Families, by Occupation of Father, Chicago, 1920

Occupation	Number of Families	Number of Children	Only Child %	One Sibling %	Two or More Siblings %	One or More Siblings %
Unskilled wage earner	5,300	11,789	9.1	17.8	73.2	90.9
Skilled wage earner	4,537	8,859	11.8	21.3	66.9	88.2
Low & medium salaried	3,449	5,294	16.3	26.5	57.1	83.6
Independent businessman	2,753	6,532	9.0	18.3	72.7	91.0
Professional	1,133	1,295	23.5	30.1	46.3	76.4
Executives & officials	784	1,018	20.7	33.6	45.8	79.4

Data based on Monroe, *Chicago Families,* Tables 22 and 23, pp. 92–93.

15. For the relation between literacy level and fertility as early as the 1850's and 1860's, see Maris A. Vinovskis, "Socioeconomic Determinants of Fertility," *Journal of Interdisciplinary History,* 6 (1976), 375–396.

16. Table F below relates level of education among men and women in two generations to number of children born. The data are from Baber and Ross, *Changes in the Size of American Families* for University of Wisconsin students; Tables 5-A, 5-B, 5-C, 5-D, pp. 64–77:

TABLE F

Average Number of Children in the Families of Students and Their Parents, by Sex and Education, University of Wisconsin

Sex	Generation	Total Number	Educational Level			
			Elementary	High School	College	Graduate
M	Parents	621	5.65	5.02	5.20	5.48
M	Students	1420	3.55	3.24	3.31	3.27
F	Parents	629	5.85	4.57	5.05	—
F	Students	1183	4.03	3.19	2.95	3.64

For a similar relationship for families of students at the University of California, see Holmes, "Size of College Families," 410.

For age-at-marriage and fertility among college women, see Willystine Goodsell, "The Size of Families of College and Non-College Women," *American Journal of Sociology*, 41 (1936), 585–597. According to Goodsell, college women made up the "lost time" caused by schooling by bearing children at closer intervals.

17. The percent married in the population was 55.3% in 1890, 55.7% in 1900, 57.3% in 1910, and 59.9% in 1920. Keeping age structure constant, the absolute increase was 1.5%; Ernest Groves and William F. Ogburn, *American Marriage and Family Relationships* (New York, 1928), p. 134.

The following table compares the percent of single men and women in two critical age groups, 20–24 and 30–34, by decade. It shows the constant decrease in the proportion of single men and women in the 20–24 year group. Although the decline is not consistent for the 30–34 group, this only reflects the fact that fewer persons in their twenties were married between 1890 and 1900. But the long-term trend is similar in each group. Both point to more and younger marriage:

TABLE G

Percent Single in Population at Age 20–24 and 30–34

Year	20–24		30–34	
	Male	Female	Male	Female
1890	82.6	53.7	26.8	15.5
1900	79.7	53.5	28.4	17.1
1910	76.7	50.3	26.5	16.8
1920	72.6	47.5	24.4	15.4
1930	72.6	47.8	21.3	13.6

Source: People in the U.S. in the 20th Century, p. 284.

For declining age-at-marriage, see, also, Paul C. Glick, *American Families* (New York, 1957), p. 45. For rural-urban differences, see Groves and Ogburn, *American Marriage,* p. 154.

18. See Baber and Ross, *Changes in the Size of American Families.* Tables 1-A, 1-C, 2-A, 2-B, pp. 33–42.

19. Baber and Ross, *Changes in the Size of American Families,* Table 1-F, p. 38.

Table H below gives the age-at-marriage of mothers and grandmothers of University of Wisconsin students, by educational attainments:

TABLE H

The Age at Marriage of Women, by Education and Generation

Generation	Number	Elementary	High School	College	Graduate	All
Married 1880–1890	1,191	22.98	24.98	26.10	31.64	24.18
Married *c.* 1860	698	21.05	21.91	22.08	—	21.34

Source: Baber and Ross, *Changes in the Size of American Families,* Tables 1-B and 1-D, pp. 34, 36.

20. See Frank W. Notestein, "Differential Age at Marriage According to Social Class," *American Journal of Sociology*, 37 (1931), 35; Pauline R. Feldman, "The Size of Families of Graduates of Certain Colleges for Women," Master's essay, Columbia University, 1927; Mable Newcomer and Evelyn Gibsen, "Vital Statistics of Vassar College," *American Journal of Sociology*, 29 (1924), 430–442; Amy Hewes, "Marital and Occupational Statistics of Mt. Holyoke College," *Quarterly Publication of the American Statistical Association*, 12 (1911), 771–797; Louis D. Hartson, "Marriage Statistics for Oberlin Alumnae," *Journal of Heredity*, 19 (1928), 225–228.

21. For relationship between fertility and ample living standard in England, see J. A. Banks, *Prosperity and Parenthood: A Study of Family Planning Among the Victorian Middle Classes* (London, 1965).

22. Groves and Ogburn, *American Marriage*, p. 269.

23. Carl Degler has recently argued that Victorian wives were not so sexually inhibited as we have long supposed and that they both expected and experienced pleasurable sexual relations. He may be right, but before we have more evidence of the kind he has exposed in one questionnaire, the Victorian woman still stands in full armor before the gaze of the historian. See Carl Degler, "What Ought To Be and What Was: Women's Sexuality in the Nineteenth Century," *American Historical Review*, 79 (1974), 1467–1490.

24. For the fear of female sexuality, see Ben Barker-Benfield, "The Spermatic Economy: A Nineteenth-Century View of Sexuality," *Feminist Studies*, 1 (Summer 1972), 45–74. The latest scientific studies of *coitus interruptus* suggest that success is often related to physiology and that many men may be incapable of withdrawing successfully; Elisabet Sjovall, "Coitus Interruptus," in *Contraception*, ed. L. Langley, Benchmark Papers in Human Physiology (Stroudsburg, Pa., 1973), pp. 13–17. If this is so, then the frustrations implicit in the procedure may have been especially acute for those couples who tried without success.

25. Ira Wile, "Introduction," *The Sex Life of the Unmarried Adult* (New York, 1934), p. 44; Katherine Bement Davis, *Factors in the Sex Life of Twenty-Two Hundred Women* (New York, 1929). This was a truly seminal study, but others did begin to appear throughout the twenties, though none was so complete or is so valuable for the historian. See also G. V. Hamilton, *A Research in Marriage* (New York, 1929), popularized in another version by Hamilton and Kenneth MacGowan, *What Is Wrong with Marriage?* (New York, 1929); Phyllis Blanchard and Carlyn Manasses, *New Girls for Old* (New York, 1930), which investigated sexual behavior and attitudes among young unmarried girls; Robert Latou Dickinson and Lura Beam, *A Thousand Marriages* (Baltimore, 1931) and *The Single Woman* (Baltimore, 1928), the records of a prominent gynecologist from the 1880's through the 1920's; Isabel Daven-

port, *A Study of the Trends of Sexual Interest and the Status of Knowledge of Young Women in Their Late Adolescence* (New York, 1923); Paul Strong Achilles, *The Effectiveness of Certain Social Hygiene Literature* (New York, 1923). These last two studies were concerned with attitudes rather than behavior, although Achilles has some data on sexual activity among men. These studies, while interested in female sexuality, do not take it for granted. Thus, Achilles asked men *how frequently* they felt sexual desire, but women, *if* they ever had such needs (p. 75). By the time the later studies, like those of Davis, appeared, sexual interest and desire by women are assumed. See also Ruth White Beebe, "The Sex Questions of Undergraduate College Students," Master's thesis, Columbia University, 1936; and the studies of men at Amherst College by M. W. Peck and F. L. Wells, "On the Psycho-Sexuality of College Graduate Men," *Mental Hygiene,* 7 (1923), 697–714, and "Further Studies in the Psycho-Sexuality of College Graduate Men," *Mental Hygiene,* 9 (1925), 502–520. Interest in sexual delinquency did not disappear in the twenties: see, for example, Mabel Seagrave, "Causes Underlying Sex Delinquency in Young Girls," *Journal of Social Hygiene,* 12 (1926), 523–529.

26. Henry Seidel Canby, "Sex and Marriage in the Nineties," *Harper's,* 169 (1934), 428, 433. For female purity, see Barbara Welter, "The Cult of True Womanhood: 1820–1860," *American Quarterly,* 18 (1966), 151–174. See also Floyd Dell's devastating remarks about the idea of free motherhood espoused by the followers of Ellen Key in *Love in the Machine Age,* pp. 148–152. Dell sharply observes that the desire for children without a husband was a continuation of the concept of female purity, because maternity was thus even more radically separated from normal sexuality.

27. Groves and Ogburn, *American Marriage,* p. 37; Dickinson and Beam, *Marriages,* p. 56; Blanchard and Manasses, *New Girls,* p. 196. According to the psychoanalyst Lorine Pruette, "only a few decades ago no lady or good woman, even though married, was thought to have a sex life"; "Some Modern Portraits and Their Interpretation," in Wile, *Sex Life,* p. 291.

28. Joseph K. Folsom, *The Family: Its Sociology and Social Psychiatry* (New York, 1934), p. 408; Robert C. Binkley and Frances Williams Binkley, *What Is Right with Marriage* (New York, 1928), pp. 48, 218.

29. Folsom, *Family,* p. 408; Edward Sapir, "Observations on the Sex Problem in America," *American Journal of Psychiatry,* 8 (1928), 519–534. For the effect of this ideal on premarital relations, see Chapter 6 herein.

30. Folsom, *Family,* p. 230; J. F. Hayden, *The Art of Marriage* (High Point, N.C., 1926), p. 41.

31. Dickinson and Beam, *Marriages,* pp. 12–13. Folsom contended that there was "strong evidence for a general increase in the frequency of the number and the intensity of intersex contacts within marriage," *Family* (p. 231), but real

evidence for such a far-ranging statement is very thin. See Raymond Pearl, *The Biology of Population Growth* (New York, 1925), p. 187; Dickinson and Beam, *Marriages*, pp. 56–59; Davis, *Factors in the Sex Life*, pp. 21, 75; O. L. Harvey, "A Note on the Frequency of Human Coitus," *American Journal of Sociology*, 38 (1932), 64. These studies suggest that the average frequency was two or three times per week, but the range was from every day or oftener to never. The problem with all the studies is the lack of a really good comparative base. Where comparisons are made they are done by age of respondent, but age is simply not a good basis upon which to judge the frequency of sexual activity, and memory in these things is notoriously unreliable.

32. Davis, *Factors in the Sex Life*, p. 356; G. A. Lundberg, "Sex Differences on Social Questions," *School and Society*, 23 (1926), 598 (Question 38); G. B. Vetter, "The Measurement of Social and Political Attitudes and Related Personality Factors," *Journal of Abnormal and Social Psychology*, 25 (1930), 153 (Question 7); Gwyn Moore and Karl C. Garrison, "A Comparative Study of Social and Political Attitudes of College Students," *Journal of Abnormal and Social Psychology*, 27 (1932), 206; Hilding B. Carlson, "Attitudes of Undergraduate Students," *Journal of Social Psychology*, 5 (1934), 203, where contraception received the most overwhelmingly positive response of all attitudes tested; Blanchard and Manasses, *New Girls*, pp. 182–183.

33. See Norman E. Himes, "Birth Control in Historical and Clinical Perspective," *Annals, AAPSS*, 160 (1932), 49–65. For contraceptive methods and effectiveness, Regina K. Stix and Frank W. Notestein, "Effectiveness of Birth Control," *Milbank Memorial Fund Quarterly*, 12 (1935), 172; P. K. Whelpton, "Causes of the Decline in Birth Rates," *Milbank Memorial Fund Quarterly*, 13 (1935), 237. At a New York City birth control clinic, contraceptive usage lowered the chance of birth by 73.6% (a measure of effectiveness) and Whelpton, a demographic specialist, asserted that the available methods could, in fact, be 90% effective.

In his summary of the experiences of 100 married couples, G. V. Hamilton (*What Is Wrong With Marriage?*) concluded that probably 99% of all Americans used some form of contraception (p. 98). This seems way out of line, however, and is especially suspect in the light of Hamilton's skewed sample (businessmen, artists, and professionals). Much more realistic is Raymond Pearl's estimate that between 55% and 60% of all American women used contraceptives, with large differences by class and education. See Pearl, *Biology of Population*, pp. 213, 231. Pearl found that of women 25 to 29 years of age with one child, 80.6% of the well-to-do, but only 35.7% of the poor used contraceptives. The rate increased to 86.0% and 52.2% for those with two children. The differences between educational groups were similar, 34.6% with an elementary school and 71.4% with a college education used contraceptives. Of those 35 to 39 years of age, 57.9% of the well-to-do and none of the poor used contraceptives. This suggests that while the middle classes were using contraceptives before the twenties, the poor only began to do so then. See also the Lynds' more impressionistic assessment of the differential use of contraceptives by various classes in Middletown; Robert K. and Helen Merrill Lynd, *Middletown* (New York, 1929), pp. 123–126. For the class differentials in contraceptive success, see Pearl, *Biology of Population,* p. 215. For interest in contraception among young women, Davenport, *Trends of Sexual Interest,* pp. 20–21, 23–24; Blanchard and Manasses, *New Girls,* pp. 91, 93.

34. Davis, *Factors in the Sex Life,* pp. 357, 336–337. The unmarried women in Davis' sample, who were on the whole younger, approved more strongly of contraceptives than the older married women (89.7% and 74.4%); Davis, *Factors in the Sex Life,* pp. 13, 17, 20, 79, 372. See also Raymond Pearl, *The Natural History of Population* (New York, 1939), pp. 192–197; Blanchard and Manasses, *New Girls,* pp. 178–179. On the whole, the younger, more recently married couples appear to have been somewhat more active sexually than older couples; see Harvey, "Note on the Frequency of Human Coitus," 64.

35. Blanchard and Manasses, *New Girls,* pp. 179–180. For mate preferences, see Wayne C. Neely, "Family Attitudes of Denominational College and University Students, 1929 and 1936," *American Sociological Review,* 5 (1940), 512–522. In this study of denominational college and university students, sampled in 1929 and again in 1936, there was some difference in the rankings of mate preferences between those students who went to the smaller, more local colleges and those who attended the universities. Men in the colleges tended to start out with a more traditional hierarchy of status considerations, while the university men were earlier and more consistently eager for personality factors in their future mates. By 1936, however, the college men's rank order resembled that of university men in 1929. The college men had become more "modern." More significantly the difference between the two groups indicates that the criteria were neither stable nor traditional, but rather that mating ideals and marriage goals were changing rapidly. Among women, the change between 1929 and 1936 was even more striking. The women in 1929 were far more traditional in their preferences than men, selecting health, education, ambition, honesty, and personal appearance above disposition. But by 1936, even the women were dropping other considerations and elevating personality qualities. For a comparison of the criteria of mate selection among students and their parents, see Ray Erwin Baber, "Some Mate Selection Standards of College Students and Their Parents," *Journal of Social Hygiene,* 22 (1936), 115–125.

36. See Stuart A. Rice, "Undergraduate Attitudes Toward Marriage and

Children," *Mental Hygiene,* 13 (1929), 788–793; Mary Field Parton, "Youth Speaks for Itself," *Woman's Home Companion,* 56 (August 1929), 30, 56 (based on study of New York University students); Neely, "Family Attitudes," *passim.*

37. Blanchard and Manasses, *New Girls,* p. 180; Vetter, "Social and Political Attitudes," 155–156 (Question 9). For similar findings at other schools, see K. C. Garrison and Margaret Mann, "A Study of the Opinions of College Students," *Journal of Social Psychology,* 2 (1931), 168–176; also, Lundberg, "Sex Differences on Social Questions," 598.

38. Blanchard and Manasses, *New Girls,* p. 179.

39. Rice, "Undergraduate Attitudes," *passim;* Parton, "Youth Speaks," *passim;* Lorine Pruette, "What's Happening in the Daydreams of the Adolescent Girl?" *Journal of Social Hygiene,* 19 (1924), 419–424, and the expanded version, "Day Dreams of the Adolescent Girl," in *Women and Leisure* (New York, 1924), pp. 153–190; Eunice Fuller Barnard, "The College Girl Puts Marriage First," *New York Times Magazine* (April 2, 1933), p. 8.

40. For the growth of "cruelty" as a ground for divorce, see Paul Jacobson, *American Marriage and Divorce* (New York, 1959), p. 122. "Cruelty" as a plea in divorce actions had grown steadily from 1860 when it was first introduced. By 1890 it had overtaken adultery, and since 1922 it has remained in first place as the most common basis for a divorce suit.

For women's expectations, see Parton, "Youth Speaks," 30; Lundberg, "Sex Differences on Social Questions," 597; Blanchard and Manasses, *New Girls,* p. 151; and the study of Ivy League college women by Barnard, "College Girl Puts Marriage First," p. 8.

For men's expectations, Frank D. Watson, "What Some College Men Want To Know about Marriage and the Family," *Social Forces,* 11 (1932), 240; also, Blanchard and Manasses, *New Girls,* pp. 215, 216; Clifford Kirkpatrick, "Student Attitudes Toward Marriage and Sex," *Journal of Educational Sociology,* 9 (1936), 550.

41. William H. Chafe, *The American Woman: Her Changing Social, Economic and Political Roles, 1920–1970* (New York, 1972), p. 102; Barnard, "College Girl Puts Marriage First," p. 8; quoted in Parton, "Youth Speaks," 30. See also Blanchard and Manasses, *New Girls,* pp. 175–177, and Pruette, "Daydreams," in *Women and Leisure, passim.*

42. Monroe, *Chicago Families,* pp. 29, 49–60.

Long an article of faith, Talcott Parsons' hypothesis about the "fit" between nuclear families and industrialization has recently come under attack by historians as well as sociologists. See Talcott Parsons, "The Kinship System of the Contemporary United States," *American Anthropologist,* 45 (1943), 22–38, and "The Social Structure of the Family," in *The Family: Its Function and Destiny,* ed. Ruth Nanda Anshen (New York, 1959). For the argument that there is no such complete fit and that nuclear families may have emerged concurrently with industrialization rather than in response to it, see William J. Goode, *World Revolution and Family Patterns* (New York, 1963), pp. 19–26. For a historical evaluation of the structure of pre-industrial families, Peter Laslett's summary of the Cambridge Group for the History of Population and Social Structure Conference for 1969, "The Comparative History of Household and Family," *Journal of Social History,* 4 (1970), 75–87, is useful. Also Richard Sennett, *Families Against the City: Middle-Class Homes of Industrial Chicago, 1872–1890* (Cambridge, Mass., 1970), who argues that nuclear families may have been disfunctional for social mobility.

43. It might be well to contrast this attitude to that of the colonial patriarchs of Andover, Massachusetts, who prevented their grown children from marrying by withholding property which would have made marriage possible. Philip Greven has demonstrated how effectively stern control and hierarchical obedience prevented children from freeing themselves from the grasp of paternal authority. In contrast, Chicago fathers appear willingly to have opened their purses to allow their children to marry young when they were not yet fully independent economically. See Philip J. Greven, Jr., *Four Generations: Population, Land and Family in Colonial Andover, Massachusetts* (Ithaca, N.Y., 1970), Chapters 4, 6.

44. There is a substantial body of data demonstrating that this was true for many of the families of college students in the 1920's. Most college students, for example, went to school in their home states, which may well reflect the financial considerations of lower in-state tuition costs at state universities; see George F. Zook, "The Residence of University and College Students," *School and Society,* 21 (1925), 415–422. Women were especially likely to attend in-state schools and usually the school closest to home. A dual factor may have been involved, reflecting a hesitancy to invest much money in a daughter's education and moral views which kept women closer to home; see Mary Ledge Moffett, *Social Background and Activities of Teachers College Students,* Contributions to Education, Teachers College, Columbia University (New York, 1929), pp. 18–31; Walter C. Eels and R. R. Brand, "Student Opinion in Junior Colleges in California," *School Review,* 38 (1930), 176–190. For the general residence patterns of students, see O. Edgar Reynolds, *The Social and Economic Status of College Students,* Contributions to Education, Teachers College, Columbia University (New York, 1927), pp. 52–53. In a sample of 55 representative universities and colleges, one-fourth of all students lived at home, but this varied by region and by the kind of institution attended. The least likely to live at home were students from elite women's or men's schools. Women, in general, were much more likely to live at home than men.

At state schools like the University of Minnesota, as many as 50% of the students lived at home. See F. Stuart Chapin, *Extra-Curricular Activities at the University of Minnesota* (Minneapolis, 1929), p. 22. At private coeducational universities like Syracuse University in New York, there was also considerable at-home residence. At Syracuse, 41% of the students indicated that they chose this institution because of its geographic proximity to home, and the economic advantage of living at home was one of the primary considerations. See Daniel Katz and Floyd H. Allport, *Students' Attitudes, A Report of the Syracuse University Reaction Study* (Syracuse, N.Y., 1931), p. 22.

45. Wanda C. Bronson, Edith S. Katten, and Norma Livson, "Patterns of Authority and Affection in Two Generations," *Journal of Abnormal and Social Psychology,* 58 (1959), 143–152.

46. The Lynds recalled, "A prominent banker and a prominent physician agreed in a dinner-table discussion that there must be once in every child's life a brisk passage-at-arms that 'will teach them where authority lies in the family. You have to teach them to respect parental authority. Once you've done this you can go ahead and get on the best possible relations with them.' " Lynd and Lynd, *Middletown,* p. 143. See also pp. 131–152.

47. This description of paternal roles contradicts Talcott Parsons' theory of role differentiation in family socialization. Parsons believes that two different kinds of relationship, one instrumental and one expressive, are necessary for socialization. This may well be true, but his hypothesis that these two are sharply localized in the person of father and mother in the modern family seems unwarranted. See Talcott Parsons and Robert F. Bales, *Family, Socialization and Interaction Process* (New York, 1955), Chapter 2.

48. White House Conference on Child Health and Protection (hereafter cited as WHC), *The Young Child in the Home, A Survey of 3000 American Families,* John E. Anderson, Chairman (New York, 1936), pp. 78, 83. See also Mildred Thurew, *A Study of Selected Factors in Family Life as Described in Autobiographies* (Ithaca, N.Y., 1935), p. 9.

49. WHC, *Young Child,* pp. 73–80; see especially Tables 29–33.

50. WHC, *Adolescent,* pp. 133, 138, 160–161, 357, and *passim.* The conference also found considerable differences among urban adolescents from various ethnic and racial groups. In general, the best relations between parents and children existed among native, white, urban groups (pp. 74–89).

Any theory about a historical sequence which is based on contemporaneous sources runs into a critical analytic problem: in this case, how do we know that the rural families investigated by the conference had not themselves changed over time? The problem is similar to the difficulty that the evolutionary school of anthropology had when it posited primitive tribal organization as an "earlier" form of society. Of course, the problem is nowhere so acute when we propose that rural families in the twentieth century are much like

rural families in the nineteenth century, but it is still not an entirely warrant-
able assumption.

See WHC, *Adolescent,* Appendix 1, Tables 28 and 29, for the kinds of tasks
that adolescents were expected to perform. On the average, urban boys had
5.6 tasks to perform per week, rural boys had 8.6; urban girls had 4.9 tasks
while rural girls had the most, 9.2. For at-home duties, see also Ada E. Orr
and Francis J. Brown, "A Study of the Out-of-School Activities of High
School Girls," *Journal of Educational Sociology,* 5 (1932), 266–273; and Eugenie
Andruss Leonard, *Problems of Freshman College Girls: A Study of Mother-Daughter
Relationships and Social Adjustments of Girls Entering College,* Child Development
Monographs, No. 9, Teachers College, Columbia University (New York,
1932), p. 49. Among urban families the most frequent family activities were
visiting, 70%; shopping, 64%; going to the movies, 63%; automobile riding,
62%; and taking walks, 49%. For rural families, visiting, 75%; automobile
riding, 71%; shopping, 54%; playing games, 52%; singing or playing music,
50%. (The percentages indicate proportion of families engaging in such activities.) The Conference found no correlation between the extent of family amusements and family harmony or emotional intimacy; WHC, *Adolescent,* pp. 163,
164. Thurew found that eating meals together was the most common activity
(pp. 24–28). She found that rural families generally made churchgoing and
family religion a part of their routine. But the factor most closely associated
with family religious observance appears to have been size. The largest families
were more likely to attend church and have home services than small ones. See
Thurew, *Selected Factors in Family Life,* pp. 20–22.

51. Table I below describes the distribution of evenings spent at home by
urban and rural adolescents, by sex:

TABLE I

Evenings Spent at Home by Rural and Urban Adolescents, by Sex

	Urban Boys	Rural Boys	Urban Girls	Rural Girls
Every evening	4%	16%	5%	17%
4 to 6 evenings	42%	61%	33%	56%
One to 3 evenings	40%	18%	57%	27%
Every evening away	14%	5%	5%	—

Source: WHC, *Adolescent,* p. 167.

See also, Frederick T. Shipp, "Social Activities of High School Boys," *School
Review,* 39 (1931), 767–774; Lynd and Lynd, *Middletown,* p. 135, n. 10, for
evening spent at home.

52. WHC, *Adolescent*, p. 139.

53. See Howard G. Burdge, *Our Boys* (Doctoral dissertation, Columbia University, 1921), for a systematic investigation of the social backgrounds and occupations of working boys aged 14 to 19 in New York State. For declining working-class fertility in the 1930's, see Committee on the Study of Social and Psychological Factors Affecting Fertility, *Social and Psychological Factors Affecting Fertility*, ed. P. K. Whelpton and Clyde V. Kiser (New York, 1946–1958).

54. Henry Seidel Canby, "Life in the Nineties: Home and Parents," *Harper's*, 169 (1934), 271, 272.

55. Canby, "Nineties," 278, 272.

56. In Chicago, for example, most unmarried children continued to reside in their parents' homes. Of all dependent children, one-third were sons and daughters 16 years and older; 14.7% were 16–21; and 19.2% were 21 years or older (Monroe, *Chicago Families*, pp. 100–101). In Chicago, 85% of all youths 16–21 lived at home with parents. As would be expected, the proportion of those who were employed declined sharply with rising occupational class of father. Where 87.7% of the grown children of unskilled fathers were employed, only 53.7% of the children of professional men and 68.5% of the children of executives and officials were employed. Undoubtedly many of those who did not work were going to school. Most of the working-class youths were probably contributing to family income.

57. For the relationship between peer groups and romance, see Talcott Parsons, "Youth in the Context of American Society," in *The Challenge of Youth*, ed. Erik H. Erikson (Garden City, N.Y., 1965), pp. 134–135 and William J. Goode, "The Theoretical Importance of Love," *American Sociological Review*, 24 (1959), 38–47.

58. Wiebe, *Search for Order*, Chapter 3.

59. "No problem in modern life so challenges the attention of thoughtful students of society as does the family crisis, if one may interpret the tenor of recent writings upon the subject," noted Ernest Mowrer, one of the most important commentators on the family in the twenties. He continues, "One group heralds the present situation as the beginning of a new day in which all the old restraints of family mores will be thrown aside; the other group is alarmed lest the most treasured of institutions may disappear to bring havoc upon modern civilization. Both, however, agree that the family in America is at a turning of the way." Ernest Mowrer, *The Family: Its Organization and Disorganization* (Chicago, 1932), p. 3.

60. See Ruth Lindquist, *The Family in the Present Social Order* (Chapel Hill, N.C., 1931), pp. 3–25; William F. Ogburn, "Social Heritage and the Family," in *Family Life Today*, ed. Margaret E. Rich (New York and Boston,

1928); John Dollard, *The Changing Functions of the American Family* (Doctoral dissertation, University of Chicago, 1931); Mowrer, *Family,* pp. 11–24, 45–63. The model of the traditional family was posited as an ideal form, an idyllic order which represented stability in family life and in the society. It provided a point of stability from which sociologists could explore the process of change. This function was served by the image of the multifunctional family of role interdependence. Whether such an order ever existed is open to serious question. The sociologists of the twenties and thirties appear to have believed that it had. William Goode has given this model of the traditional family the memorable and felicitous name "the classical family of Western nostalgia." See Goode, *World Revolution and Family Patterns,* p. 6.

61. The most elegant exposition of the family as specialized for child nurture is James P. Lichtenberger, "The Changing Family in a Changing World," *Mental Hygiene,* 17 (1933), 573–589. See also Groves and Ogburn, *American Marriage,* pp. 17–29, 78–105. For the restorative influence of the family for its adult members, see especially Ruth Reed, *The Modern Family* (New York, 1929), Introduction. Reed notes that the family "performs valuable and highly regarded services for adults. . . . It assures security of personal relationships and the opportunity to withdraw from the more complex forms of social intercourse to a simpler and less taxing milieu."

62. Lichtenberger, "Changing Family," 585; Ogburn, "Social Heritage," pp. 38–39.

63. Edward B. Reuter and Jessie R. Runner, eds., *The Family* (New York, 1931), pp. 8, 140; Groves and Ogburn, *American Marriage,* p. 29; Folsom, *Family,* p. 229. For a discussion of the changing emphases in textbooks on the family see Hornell Hart, "Trends of Change in Textbooks on the Family," *American Journal of Sociology,* 39 (1933), 222–230. The texts increasingly emphasized problems of interpersonal relationships and the emotional qualities of family life. The texts were almost unanimous in observing that affection rather than role allocation was the basis of family organizaton and that families were becoming more democratic and oriented toward personality development.

64. For the classic study of the effects of family disorder, see W. I. Thomas and Florian Znaniecki, *The Polish Peasant in Europe and America,* 2nd ed., 2 vols. (New York, 1927).

65. Lawrence K. Frank, "Some Aspects of Education for Home and Family Life," in *Papers on Parent Education Presented at the Biennial Conference of the National Council of Parent Education,* November 1930 (New York, 1931), p. 47; also, Folsom, *Family,* p. 205 and Karl De Schweinitz, "In Familia—Then and Now," *Family,* 7 (1926), 115.

66. See Daniel Calhoun, *The Intelligence of a People* (Princeton, N.J., 1973), p. 24.

67. "The important place which children occupy in the goals of family and the effect which they have upon countless aspects of family life," home economist Ruth Lindquist noted, "make education underlying the growth and guidance of children paramount"; Lindquist, *Family in the Present Social Order*, pp. 95–96. Child-rearing was only one part of a larger program of family training which was espoused by many of the experts of the twenties as both remedy and preventative for difficulties experienced by the modern family. Sociologist Ernest Groves was the most vocal spokesman for such education and established the first courses of this kind at the University of North Carolina. Groves frequently summarized the developments in the family for the *American Journal of Sociology*, in which summaries he always included notes on the progress of family education. See, for example, "The Family (Changes in 1928)," *American Journal of Sociology*, 34 (1929), 1099–1107. For a discussion of parent education courses, though largely confined to developments in the 1930's, see Laura Winslow Drummond, *Youth and Instruction in Marriage and Family Living* (New York, 1942). Also Helen Merrill Lynd, "Parent Education and the Colleges," *Annals, AAPSS*, 160 (1932), 197–204; Jessie H. Newton, "The Role of the Public School in Parent Education," in *Papers on Parent Education*, pp. 79–92, and Lindemann, "Conference Summary," in the same volume.

68. Ogburn, "Social Heritage," p. 34; De Schweinitz, "In Familia," 115; Mowrer, *Family*, p. 275.

69. Folsom, *Family*, p. 206; Lindquist, *Family in the Present Social Order*, p. 43; Lynd, "Parent Education," 198.

70. Reed, *Modern Family*, pp. 97, 94; Mowrer, *Family*, p. 275. It is worth noting that American Freudians, especially A. A. Brill, were at this time adjusting psychoanalytic theory to the American emphasis on independence and self-reliance. As the first popularizer of Freudian ideas in America, Brill's major contributions were his studies of the only child, who he believed suffered from overindulgence and became emotionally dependent upon his family. While Freud never paid much attention to the problems of developing independence or of training children to cope with their environment, Brill believed that this was extremely important. Teach the child, Brill asserted, to "give up the phantasy; accept reality and adjust yourself to it." See A. A. Brill, *Fundamental Conceptions of Psychoanalysis* (New York, 1921); "Determinism in Psychiatry and Psychoanalysis," *American Journal of Psychiatry*, 95 (1938), 597–621. For a more extensive discussion of the adjustments that Brill made of psychoanalysis to the American value system, see the author's "A. A. Brill: Pioneer and Prophet," Master's essay, Columbia University, 1968.

71. John B. Watson, *Psychological Care of Infant and Child* (New York,

1928), p. 40. Watson singled out Dewey for specific attack: "Professor John Dewey and many other educators have been insisting for the last twenty years upon a method of training which allows the child to develop from within. This is really a doctrine of mystery."

72. Watson, *Infant and Child,* pp. 7, 10, 81, 82.

73. Watson, *Infant and Child,* pp. 79, 81.

74. Ernest Groves, who was especially concerned that the family remain a basic social unit, observed, "Civilization has been family-based. The home has been without rival in its influence on social thought and practice . . . especially in regard to the responsibilities of citizenship that have in the past been definitely tied to the family"; Ernest R. Groves, *The Marriage Crisis* (New York, 1928), pp. 45–46.

For the shift to family care, see Sheila M. Rothman, "Other People's Children: The Day Care Experience in America," *The Public Interest,* 30 (Winter 1973), 16–17; Dollard, *Changing Functions,* pp. 33–34; Watson, *Infant and Child,* pp. 5–6.

75. Watson, *Infant and Child,* pp. 185, 84, 44.

76. "The home," Watson declared, "we have with us—inevitably and inexorably with us. Even though it is proven unsuccessful we shall have it. The behaviorist has to accept the home and make the best of it." Watson, *Infant and Child,* p. 6.

77. Lawrence K. Frank, "Childhood and Youth," *Recent Social Trends in America,* p. 798. Watson's strictures could not really reverse what Urie Bronfenbrenner has identified as the tendency among middle-class parents since the twenties to a less strict style of child-rearing and "greater tolerance of the child's impulses and desires, freer expression of affection," and more reasoned appeals to conscience; "Socialization and Social Class Through Time and Space," in E. E. Maccoby, T. M. Newcomb, and E. I. Hartley, eds., *Readings in Social Psychology,* 3rd ed. (New York, 1952), p. 72. Also, Mary Wolfenstein, "Trends in Infant Care," *American Journal of Orthopsychiatry,* 23 (1953), 120–130.

78. William Ogburn, for example, was able to incorporate Watsonian conditioning into his schema of family affection: "The earlier the influence, the more important it is. It was formerly thought that the personality was completed only when one became an adult. Then the limit was shortened to the age of adolescence. Later it was said that the personality was virtually set by five years of age, and now one hears that the most important influences have got in their work by two years of age [age set by Watson]." He continues, "The studies of disorders of personality, as they appear in neuroses and psychoses, rank the affectional elements as most significant," adding with a Watsonian flourish, "perhaps because of their possibly greater variability and the

readiness with which conditioning occurs in connection with love." Ogburn, "Social Heritage," pp. 26–27. According to Ruth Reed, "It is important . . . that foundations for later good health be laid by proper feeding and suitable hours and surroundings for sufficient rest. These conditions can be provided only in an adequately equipped and *well-regulated* household conducted by a person of sufficient initiative to establish and *maintain the necessary routine.* . . . Physical *habits of self-control* and proper eating and resting are easily formed in early years, and upon the establishment of such *fundamental mental habits depends* the probability of *future efficiency.*" Reed, *Modern Family,* p. 95 (my italics). For a study very much influenced by Watson, yet retaining the belief in the efficacy of emotional intimacy, see Leonard, *Problems of Freshman College Girls.* Leonard was particularly concerned that emotionalism in the home not sap independence, which would prevent proper adjustment to college life and the outside world.

79. James S. Plant, "The Child as a Member of the Family," *Annals, AAPSS.* 160 (1932), 71–72.

80. Ernest Burgess, "The Family as a Unity of Interacting Personalities," *Family,* 7 (1926), 6; Mowrer, *Family,* p. 23. For culture-lag theory, see, for example, F. Stuart Chapin, "The Lag of Family Mores in Social Culture," *Journal of Applied Sociology,* 9 (1925), 241–249. For a summary of this view, see Folsom, *Family,* p. 235. Among the more notable urban disorganization studies, see Thomas and Znaniecki, *The Polish Peasant;* William I. Thomas, *The Unadjusted Girl* (Boston, 1923); Ernest Mowrer, *Family Disorganization* (Chicago, 1927), and Mowrer, *Family,* pp. 186–206, and for disorganization generally, pp. 145–249; E. Franklin Frazier, *The Negro Family in the United States* (Chicago, 1939).

81. Mowrer, *Family,* p. 19. Even when the urban family was seen as a refuge, however, the very emotions sought for also led to frustrations and threatened unity and stability; see Mowrer, *Family,* pp. 52–53, 277–278.

82. Ernest Burgess, "The Family and the Person," *Publications of the American Sociological Society,* 22 (1928), 133, which elaborates the views Burgess presented earlier in "The Family as a Unity of Interacting Personalities." According to Mowrer, "The introduction of the idea of interaction into the study of the family is, perhaps, one of the most revolutionary accomplishments of the present century in this field." *Family,* p. 84. And in their textbook collection of all the relevant authorities on the subject, Reuter and Runner noted that "the paper by Mr. Burgess we are disposed to regard as perhaps the most significant single contribution that has been made to a fundamental analysis of the family." *The Family,* p. 47.

83. Burgess, "Interacting Personalities," 5; "The family as a going concern," Burgess noted, "depends more on the natural unity that arises and de-

velops through the personal interaction of its members than upon any attempt to enforce the family obligations which the law imposes"; Burgess, in Reuter and Runner, *The Family,* pp. 55–56.

84. Miriam Van Waters, *Youth in Conflict* (New York, 1925), p. 80; *Parents on Probation* (New York, 1927), p. 314. For different emotional needs of adolescents, see *Youth,* p. 83; *Parents,* p. 84.

85. Van Waters, *Youth,* pp. 73–74.

86. WHC, *The Adolescent in the Family,* ed. Ernest Burgess (New York, 1934), and *The Young Child in the Home,* John B. Anderson, Chairman (New York, 1936).

87. WHC, *Adolescent,* pp. 7, 29.

88. De Schweinitz, "In Familia," 115, 116.

89. Mowrer, *Family,* pp. 52–53.

CHAPTER 3

1. Caroline M. Tryon, "The Adolescent Peer Culture," in *Adolescence, 43rd Yearbook of the National Society for the Study of Education,* ed. Nelson B. Henry (Chicago, 1944), p. 236.

2. For a discussion of the psychological problems confronting the adolescent during this transition from what I call the personal to the social sphere, see Erik H. Erikson, "Youth: Fidelity and Diversity," in *The Challenge of Youth* (Garden City, N.Y., 1965), pp. 1–28. Erikson is, of course, primarily concerned with the problem of ego integration, but his identification of the two areas of acute concern, sexuality and "calling," are specifically problems of social role.

3. See S. N. Eisenstadt, "Archetypal Patterns of Youth," in *The Challenge of Youth,* ed. Erik H. Erikson, pp. 29–50, for a short discussion of what Eisenstadt has more completely dealt with in *From Generation to Generation: Age Groups and Social Structure* (New York, 1956).

4. In 1900 there were 284,683 students in American institutions of higher education. By 1930, there were 1,178,318, an increase of 300%. See Charles Judd, "Education," in *Recent Social Trends in the United States, Report of the President's Research Committee on Social Trends,* one-volume ed. (New York, 1933), p. 329; also, Frank M. Phillips, "Statistics of Universities, Colleges and Professional Schools, 1927–1928," *U.S. Bureau of Education Bulletin, 1929,* no. 38, pp. 2–3, and "Statistical Survey of Education, 1927–1928," *U.S. Bureau of Education Bulletin, 1930,* no. 3, p. 8. According to Phillips, in 1890, of all those aged 19, 20, 21, and 22, 2.43% were in school. By 1928, nearly 12% were in colleges and universities on a full-time basis, excluding those in professional

work enrolled at these institutions. Eighteen per cent were enrolled in some kind of program full-time. This does not include junior colleges and normal schools.

Even more striking are the figures for high-school attendance. In 1900 there were 630,048 youths in secondary schools. By 1920 there were 4,740,580, an increase of more than 650%. In 1911, there were still fewer than one million (984,677), so that the increase in that decade had been only 50%. The major increase took place in the teens and twenties. In 1930, about 60% of all high-school-age youths were in school. See Judd, "Education," p. 329; Emery M. Foster, "School Survival Rates," *School Life,* 22 (1936), 12–13, 21; "Biennial Survey of Education, 1928–1930, Vol. 2," *U.S. Bureau of Education Bulletin, 1931, no. 20.*

In addition to traditional high schools and colleges, the twenties saw the first full flowering of the junior colleges. In 1920, only 15,000 students were enrolled in junior colleges. This increased to 70,000 by 1930. See Goodwin Watson, *Youth After Conflict* (New York, 1947), p. 100.

5. *Daily Illini,* January 6, 1922; *Ohio State Lantern,* February 5, 1923. All items from college newspapers will be identified by the name and date of the school paper. Editorials are implied unless otherwise specified.

6. Between 1918 and 1930 there was a ten-fold increase in enrollments in junior high schools, and, in cities of 10,000 or more, there were five times as many junior high schools by the latter date. See Judd, "Education," p. 338, Table 10. For junior colleges, see Leonard V. Koos, *The Junior College Movement* (Boston, 1925).

7. Reporting on the situation among high-school youths in the late twenties, Warren W. Coxe and Wayne W. Soper claimed that these students had no clear idea of why they were attending school. They seemed to attend because "going to school has become an individual and group habit, the customary thing to do." See "Why Do Pupils Attend High School?" *New York State Education,* 18 (1930), 372. See also E. Davenport, "What a Man Loses in Going to College," *Saturday Evening Post,* 193 (November 13, 1920), 29–30, 98.

8. Henry Seidel Canby, *College Sons and College Fathers* (New York, 1915), p. 97. Paul Nystrom, *Economics of Fashion* (New York, 1928), p. 74.

The following ad appeared in the UCLA paper: " 'College style' has a definite meaning. To the layman it spells—debonair smartness—an individual trimness that is particularly the insignia of the young man of today. Fall '23 can almost be called the young man's season with the style pace set by the collegian"; *Cub Californian,* October 18, 1923. Because the UCLA newspaper went through a number of name changes during the twenties, all future references to the UCLA student newspaper will be called *UCLA Daily,* in order to facilitate identification.

9. *Daily Illini,* November 18, 1922; also, February 6, 1924. *Ohio State Lantern,* October 19, 1926; also, November 2, 1926. *UCLA Daily,* September 15, 1925; also, April 10, 1929. For "glamor" associated with college, see Davenport, "What a Man Loses," 45.

10. For a sense of the variety of schools available to the undergraduate in the twenties, see the handbook by Rita S. Halle, *Which College?* (New York, 1929), which lists and briefly describes 325 different schools—men's, women's, coeducational, and Negro colleges. The very fact that such a guide to colleges was published at this time suggests that the choice of college had become a problem for many students.

11. See Walter J. Greenleaf, "Self-Help for College Students," *U.S. Bureau of Education Bulletin, 1929,* no. 2, p. 59, Table 1. Sixty-eight per cent of all men and 59% of all women were enrolled in such schools. Of a total of 1068 institutions of higher education in the United States in 1929 (including professional schools, junior colleges, and Negro colleges), 365 were coeducational universities and colleges.

For insularity of residential colleges, see R. H. Edwards, J. M. Artman, and Galen M. Fisher, *Undergraduates: A Study of Morale in Twenty-three American Colleges and Universities* (Garden City, N.Y., 1928), Chapters 2 and 3; Christian Gauss, *Life in College* (New York, 1930), Introduction; Niles Carpenter, "Courtship Practices and Contemporary Social Change in America," *Annals, AAPSS,* 160 (1932), 38–44. For one example among many in the college papers, *Cornell Sun,* October 14, 1922.

12. At a meeting of the American Association of Colleges and Universities in 1925, administrators noted that enrollments had reached "crisis" proportions. See *New Student,* (National Student Forum of the Paris Pact, New York, vols. 1–8, April 19, 1922–June 1929), November 11, 1925, p. 1. See also, "Biennial Survey of Education, 1920–22, vol. 1," *U.S. Bureau of Education Bulletin, 1924,* no. 13, p. 82. For a discussion of the growing trend toward admissions restrictions even at state schools, see Ralph Philip Boaz, "Who Shall Go to College?" *Atlantic Monthly,* 130 (1922), 441–448. See also the editorial comments in the *Daily Princetonian,* April 3, 1924; *Cornell Sun,* February 12, 1921, February 21, 1921, December 7, 1923; *New Student,* April 18, 1925, p. 1.

13. Greenleaf, "Self-Help for College Students," p. 59, Table 1. A small proportion of the students at these schools lived at home—about 7% of the men and 11% of the women. See O. Edgar Reynolds, *The Social and Economic Status of College Students,* Contributions to Education, Teachers College, Columbia University (New York, 1927), p. 52.

14. For residential distribution at UCLA, see *UCLA Daily,* December 11, 1925. In 1925, of 4000 women at UCLA, 70% lived at home, 18% lived with relatives, 3% were in lodgings, and 5% kept house.

According to Greenleaf, "Self-Help for College Students," (p. 2), 29% of all four-year liberal arts colleges were under church control. For the residence characteristics of church schools, see F. W. Reeves, *The Liberal Arts Colleges* (Chicago, 1932), p. 392. At some denominational schools, largely those in cities, as many as three-fourths of the students lived at home. For high schools, see Chapter 4 herein. For Negro colleges in the twenties, Raymond Walters, *The New Negro on Campus: Black College Rebellions of the 1920's* (Princeton, N.J., 1975).

15. A variety of services were being introduced in the twenties to help personalize this formal structure. These included various kinds of guidance programs and counseling systems, such as freshman orientation, networks of deans and advisers, mental health experts, and vocational guidance bureaus. For mental health interest, see Milton A. Harrington, "The Mental Health Problem in the College," *Journal of Abnormal and Social Psychology*, 23 (1928), 293–314.

16. Defenders of extra-curricular activities asserted that they stimulated leadership, developed initiative and "social intelligence," helped in the task of "social adjustment," and provided good training for adult occupations. They were also defended as providing training in democracy, simulating the life situation, being civilizing, and developing social manners and training in etiquette, as well as providing an arena for self-expression not provided in the curriculum. See F. Stuart Chapin, *Extra-Curricular Activities at the University of Minnesota* (Minneapolis, 1929), p. 118; Beulah Van Wagenen, *Extra-Curricular Activities in the Colleges of the United Lutheran Church in America*, Contributions to Education, Teachers College, Columbia University (New York, 1929), pp. 3–7; Robert C. Angell, *A Study in Undergraduate Adjustment* (Chicago, 1930), p. 122; Elbert K. Fretwell, *Extracurricular Activities in Secondary Schools* (Boston, 1931), Introduction; International Committee on the YMCA, Student Department, *A Study of the Present Position of the Young Men's Christian Association in Relation to Higher Education* (New York, 1925), pp. 3, 18; Gerald W. Johnson, "Should Our Colleges Educate?" *Harper's*, 155 (1927), 723–727; *Report of the Faculty-Student Committee on the Distribution of Students' Time at the University of Chicago* (Chicago, 1925), p. 3.

The most telling rationale, and the one most frequently invoked by the students themselves, was that these activities stimulated the competitive instinct and fostered social interaction and contacts that would be valuable in later business life. See especially Max McConn, "Tired Business Men of the Campus," *North American Review*, 226 (1928), 545–550; R. E. Thornhill and Carney Landis, "Extra-Curricular Activity and Success," *School and Society*, 28 (1928), 117–120; Henry F. Pringle, "Young Men on the Make," *Harper's*, 158 (1929), 149–157; Wilbur Abbott, "The Guild of Students," *Atlantic*

Monthly, 128 (1921), 618–625. For the students' views, see Chapter 5 herein.

17. For a sample of the variety of rules that affected women at the Big Ten, see *Ohio State Lantern,* November 13, 1925, p. 1; for women's rules at Louisiana State University, *The Reveille,* October 12, 1919, October 7, 1921, p. 2. At the University of Texas, the administration outlawed the wearing of "Oxford bags," the very wide slacks popular among men; see *Daily Illini,* November 12, 1925. Regulation about women's dress was more frequent. See, for example, *Cornell Sun,* February 14, 1925, on dress regulations at Union College, Nebraska. For student reaction to administrative regulations, see, for example, *Cornell Sun,* November 15, 1926; LSU *Reveille,* October 19, 1928.

18. In *Exile's Return* (New York, 1934; revised, 1963) Malcolm Cowley rightfully insists on the importance of leisure at the colleges in the development of the specific college styles and understanding, although he deplores the unreal life that this creates. "College students inhabit an easy world of their own, except for very rich people and certain types of childless wives they have been the only American class that could take leisure for granted" (p. 36).

19. Gauss, *Life in College,* p. 30; Davenport, "What a Man Loses," 29. Davenport asserted that the contacts of youth had become so age-restricted that they even affected their perception of older people: "In their conception all people older than themselves are old, and . . . the student makes practically no discrimination between thirty-five and up, except in decrepitude which he recognizes as awful old" (30).

20. There was considerable ambiguity in the attitude of the young toward the working student. On the one hand, students argued that the society was democratic and that working students were heroes of a sort; see *Ohio State Lantern,* February 28, 1922; *Daily Illini,* November 4, 1920, letter to the editor; LSU *Reveille,* February 2, 1923. On the other hand, students believed that there was no glamor in working and that by doing so the working student missed out in the peer society both in activities and social life. Youths were often urged not to work unless absolutely necessary. See *Daily Illini,* September 16, 1924, September 14, 1925; *UCLA Daily,* April 15, 1925; LSU *Reveille,* March 21, 1930.

21. Greenleaf, "Self-Help for College Students," pp. 59–60; Reynolds, pp. 27–29; Christian Gauss, "Other Side of Paradise," *Saturday Evening Post,* 105 (July 9, 1932), 6; "Self-Supporting Students at Yale University," *School and Society,* 32 (1930), 834–835. These were all pre-Depression figures.

At the University of Chicago, a coeducational private institution, 65.1% of the men and 34.2% of the women were working; *Faculty-Student Committee, Chicago,* p. 20. At the University of Minnesota, more than 50% of the sophomores, juniors, and seniors reported working; freshmen, understandably, were less frequently employed; Chapin, *Extra-Curricular Activities,* p. 22. At Syracuse, about one-half of all students reported working; Daniel Katz and Floyd H. Allport, *Students' Attitudes* (Syracuse, N.Y., 1931), p. 45. At Illinois, 56.5% of the students earned at least part of their expenses; *Daily Illini,* February 16, 1921. At LSU about 30% of the students worked; *The Reveille,* April 26, 1929, p. 1. At the University of Michigan, 59% of the students were employed—64% of the men and 28% of the women; Angell, *Adjustment,* p. 101. At Wisconsin, 59% of all students worked; "Self-Supporting Students at the University of Wisconsin," *School and Society,* 34 (1931), 829. In a study of 23 junior colleges in California, 54% of the men and 19.7% of the women reported employment; Walter C. Eels and Romayne R. Brand, "Student Opinion in Junior Colleges in California," *School Review,* 38 (1930), 183. At Stanford, only 38% of the students worked; Reynolds, *Social and Economic Status,* p. 29. At Barnard College, an Eastern women's school, 30% of the students reported employment; *Barnard Bulletin,* October 17, 1924, p. 1. See also various editorials asking for non-needy students to refrain from applying for the limited jobs available until those who really needed them were served; *Daily Illini,* September 24, 1923; *Cornell Sun,* September 24, 1921. See also *UCLA Daily,* March 16, 1928, p. 1.

22. According to Greenleaf, one-sixth or 16.6% of all students were self-supporting. More men were self-supporting than women, a ratio similar to that of working men to working women—two to one. Twenty-two per cent of the men and 14% of the women were largely self-supporting; Greenleaf, "Self-Help for College Students," p. 61. See also Reynolds, *Social and Economic Status,* pp. 26–28. Figures for individual schools substantiate these general percentages. At Wisconsin, 23% of the men worked, "Self-Supporting Students, Wisconsin," 829; Syracuse, 16% reported meeting three-quarters or more of their expenses, and 27% one-half or more; Katz and Allport, *Students' Attitudes,* Table 11, p. 45. At Illinois, 9.3% of the men earned all their expenses; *Daily Illini,* February 16, 1921. At Ohio State, 20% of the men were wholly self-supporting; *Ohio State Lantern,* September 29, 1927. At Trinity-Duke, about one-quarter of the seniors were self-supporting; Duke *Chronicle,* December 3, 1924, p. 1. Trinity College in Durham, North Carolina became Duke University in 1925. All references to Trinity College in the notes will be given as Trinity-Duke. In the text the name Trinity College will be retained for the period before 1925. All citations to the Trinity *Chronicle* will be given as Duke *Chronicle* to facilitate identification.

23. Katz and Allport, *Students' Attitudes,* p. 231; Chapin, *Extra-Curricular Activities,* p. 22; *Faculty-Student Committee, Chicago,* p. 26. For commuting students at different kinds of institutions, see Reynolds, *Social and Economic Status,* Tables 33, 34, p. 52. At uni-sex schools, the proportion of commuting students was lower, about 8% at men's colleges and 11% at women's colleges; Reynolds, *Social and Economic Status,* p. 52.

24. Katz and Allport, *Students' Attitudes*, pp. 45–46; *Faculty-Student Committee, Chicago*, pp. 14, 26; Chapin, *Extra-Curricular Activities*, p. 69; Angell, *Adjustment*, p. 101; *Ohio State Lantern*, October 21, 1924.

25. Russell A. Beam, *The Religious Attitudes and Habits of College Freshmen* (Chicago, 1934), pp. 28, 27. See also, Katz and Allport, *Students' Attitudes*, pp. 297–317.

26. Duke *Chronicle*, February 27, 1924, March 7, 1928, November 18, 1925. For decline in religious enthusiasm, see also Duke *Chronicle*, February 27, 1924, April 23, 1924; for loss of YMCA prestige, October 21, 1925, October 24, 1924, November 14, 1928; for demands that chapel be reformed and opposition to other regulations, December 7, 1927, September 30, 1925, p. 1, January 23, 1929, April 21, 1926, December 1, 1926, p. 1, April 20, 1927.

27. Duke *Chronicle*, May 5, 1926, May 12, 1926, January 5, 1927, April 1, 1925, December 2, 1925, February 3, 1926, February 16, 1927.

28. Ernest H. Wilkens, President of Oberlin College, "The Questions Raised by Thinking Students," in Galen M. Fisher, ed., *Religion in the Colleges* (New York, 1928), pp. 6–8. See also the other comments in this volume. Edwards *et al.*, *Undergraduates*, p. 247; Ruth Strang, *Behavior and Background of Students in College and Secondary School* (New York, 1937), p. 243; Lincoln B. Hale, *From School to College: A Study of the Transition Experience* (New Haven, 1939), p. 253; Angell, *Adjustment*, p. 140; Katz and Allport, *Students' Attitudes*, p. 317. Even at a deep-South school like LSU, students condemned evangelist religion; see LSU *Reveille*, October 11, 1929.

29. Vincent Sheean, *Personal History* (Garden City, N.Y., 1934). p. 9.

30. There were no sororities at the elite Eastern women's schools during the period. See *Baird's Manual of American College Fraternities*, 13th ed., Francis W. Shepardson, ed. (Menasha, Wis., 1935).

31. For the general devaluation of literary-aesthetic interests and Bohemian styles among the mass of students, see, for example, *Ohio State Lantern*, December 7, 1925; *Daily Illini*, February 11, 1923. For the ostracism of those with radical views on politics or with intense political interests generally, *Ohio State Lantern*, April 3, 1924. An indication of the disdain for these fringe groups is the following advice: "For those of the intelligentsia, self-styled, who gather around their tea tables to lament the lack of American literature, we would prescribe a liberal dose of the best sports columns of the newspapers"; *Ohio State Lantern*, December 17, 1925. On the self-conscious literary circles, see also *Daily Illini*, review of *Town and Gown*, February 1, 1923.

32. Quoted in Edwards *et al.*, *Undergraduates*, p. 283. For derisive comment about the funny habits and inhabitants of the YMCA, see *Daily Illini*, January 11, 1923, letter to editor. For the difference between students with strong religious orientations and others at Syracuse University, see Katz and Allport,

Students' Attitudes, pp. 24–49. As one student president of the YMCA at a small university explained, "The YM reaches the ungrouped men better than the grouped. It provides rooms, jobs and some social life. . . . Few fraternity men come to the YM. I believe their lack of interest is due to fraternity men having homes of their own and being content with the fellowship of their own groups." Quoted in Edwards *et al.*, p. 279. See also, Angell, *Adjustment*, p. 115.

33. See, for example, the article in the Duke *Chronicle*, March 7, 1928, which notes that religious idealism among students had been turned into active political channels, which was far better than a passive Christianity. For a discussion of this phenomenon, see Chapter 8 herein.

34. For early fraternities, see John Addison Porter, "College Fraternities," *The Century*, 36 (1888), 749–760. For the transition from the tight academies to the greater freedom of the colleges, see Frederick P. Keppel, *The Undergraduate and His College* (Boston and New York, 1917), pp. 12–18; William Clyde DeVane, *Higher Education in Twentieth-Century America* (Cambridge, Mass., 1965), pp. 14–33.

35. P. F. Piper, "College Fraternities," *Cosmopolitan Magazine*, 22 (1897), 646. Using one student newspaper, the *Rutgers Targum*, as a test case, the growing number of activities sponsored by fraternities toward the end of the century is clearly documented in its pages. In the 1870's there was practically no mention of meetings of fraternities, except as they met to issue a statement of condolence on the death of a member. By the late eighties and into the nineties, there were frequent teas, dances, dinners, etc.

36. See DeVane, *Higher Education*, pp. 19–21; C. H. Freeark, *A College Career and the American Fraternity System* (Lincoln, Neb., 1935), p. 9; R. J. Watts, "Development of University Residence Halls and the Effect Thereof on Fraternities and Sororities," *Central Association of College and University Business Officers, Twenty-fourth Annual Meeting, 1934*, p. 79. Watts' estimate of property values was based on only those organizations which reported them.

37. Freeark, *American Fraternity System*, pp. 9–10; *Daily Illini*, December 7, 1921, January 14, 1922, and October 26, 1921. In another Midwestern school, Ohio State, ten new fraternity chapters were established in one year; *Ohio State Lantern*, April 20, 1923. Kenneth L. Roberts, "Smoldering Illini," *Saturday Evening Post*, 201 (January 12, 1929), 13; Chapin, *Extra-Curricular Activities*, pp. 8–9; Angell, *Adjustment*, p. 112.

38. See Chapin, *Extra-Curricular Activities*, Table 6, p. 28, for a breakdown by schools at Minnesota; Katz and Allport, *Students' Attitudes*, p. 129, for Syracuse. *Which College?*, a handbook of colleges by Rita Halle, indicated those schools where fraternities were strong. Almost all state universities were so categorized. Of the more than 300 schools listed (including Catholic insti-

tutions where fraternities were weak), more than half were said to have strong fraternities.

39. Quoted in Edwards *et al.*, *Undergraduates*, p. 65; quoted in Piper, "College Fraternities," 647. See also James Anderson Hawes, *Twenty Years Among the Twenty Year Olds* (New York, 1929), pp. 72–73; DeVane, *Higher Education*, pp. 19–21. Among the many editorials advocating fraternity expansion and the reasons for such expansion, see the Duke *Chronicle*, November 1, 1922.

40. See the elaborate description of guests entertained at fraternity dances in the 1890's in the *Rutgers Targum;* for example, January 15, 1890, September 30, 1896, December 7, 1892. In the late 1880's and 1890's the paper for the first time listed new fraternity members. See, for example, October 15, 1889, October 7, 1896. By the late nineties there was a regular news column for fraternity functions and activities. In 1890, the editor of the *Targum* noted the change that had taken place in the college: "In many ways our college is undergoing a change which will materially alter the conditions of life among the students. The fraternity men, who are in many respects the leading men in college, realize that the acquiring of chapter houses is bringing them nearer together than ever before. When a man joins a fraternity he decides, once and for all, who shall be his nearest friends for the entire course"; January 15, 1890. At Cornell in 1923, non-fraternity men for the first time joined fraternity men in an all-college dance. Before then almost all dances were restricted, centering around fraternity occasions; *Cornell Sun*, February 9, 1923.

41. See *Rutgers Targum*, April 21, 1897, for a story about school, fraternity, and class monograms. At this time there was still more demand for class insignia than for fraternity insignia. For further discussion, see Chapter 4 herein.

42. For the decline in "class spirit" because of the increase in class size, see *Daily Illini*, December 7, 1921; also, *Cornell Sun*, March 16, 1920. Attempts to re-establish senior garb, for example, never caught fire; see *Cornell Sun*, March 23, 1921. UCLA tried the most intricate set of class apparel, including "sombreros" for seniors and "cords'" for juniors, but rather than distinguish classes, the articles became status symbols worn as a general fad; *UCLA Daily*, October 12, 1923. At Princeton, a committee was appointed to reinstate "Certain Extinct Patterns," but the editor of the *Daily Princetonian* noted that "A custom to be salutory must be a custom and not a rule," and that while development of class spirit was a worthy end, it was a lost cause (February 21, 1924). See also the Duke *Chronicle*, December 10, 1925, March 3, 1926.

UCLA provides an important demonstration of how fraternity life replaced the academic class structure. The transformation that had taken place over a period of 50 years elsewhere was here compressed into a short time because of the transformation of UCLA from a minor teachers institution to a major university and youth center. Before the war, the institution was a normal school with an almost exclusively female population. (In 1916, of 1675 students, only 86 were men; *UCLA Daily,* January 28, 1916.) By a series of legislative enactments, the school began first to offer a two-year liberal arts program in 1919, then a three-year, and finally in 1924 a full four-year program (December 12, 1923, p. 1). During this time, the college was still considered a minor division of the University at Berkeley, a feeder school, called the Southern Branch of the University of California. It had few clubs and very little sorority life, none of the sororities having a national affiliation. Almost from the first, when it began to offer liberal arts courses, the editors of the paper, invigorated by a new sense of the importance of the institution, began to campaign to make the college a youth center with a full contingent of traditions and rituals for creating student loyalty and a sense of group affiliation. "Traditions are to college spirit what the foundation is to a building," noted the editor on January 26, 1923. The first traditions that came to mind were those associated with the academic class system, and the first attempts to establish traditions concerned freshman rules and regulations, distinctive apparel, and the granting of upper-class privileges. It was soon apparent that a social system based on class affiliation had failed. The last freshman class to be hazed officially was in 1925 (February 11, 1926).

In the meantime, a real social system based on fraternity affiliation and extra-curricular participation was growing on the campus. In 1922 the eight fraternities on campus formed an inter-fraternity council for the first time (*UCLA Daily,* September 15, 1922); the first nationally affiliated fraternity was established in 1923 and the first national sorority in the same year (February 27, 1923, April 17, 1923). The first all-fraternity-sorority dance was held in 1924 (January 19, 1924). In 1925, the newspaper began a series of articles on "prominent campus personalities" (November 13, 1925). By 1927, fraternity rushing had become a problem because of increased enrollment and the increase in fraternity chapters (February 7, 1927). By 1927, a UCLA editor was already talking about a very different kind of tradition, the tradition "that a man or woman who doesn't rate in the select group that hangs out in Millspaugh Hall between classes, has no chance of being one of the popular set on the campus. This tradition is being formed unconsciously but it is about the strongest we have" (November 2, 1927). The campus had evolved a social structure based on association and prominence.

43. See, for example, Angell, *Adjustment,* p. 115 and *passim;* Edwards *et al., Undergraduates,* pp. 76, 90; Ruth Vesta Pope, *Factors Affecting the Elimination of Women Students from Selected Coeducational Colleges of Liberal Arts,* Con-

tributions to Education, Teachers College, Columbia University (New York, 1931), pp. 87–90.

44. The fraternities' sacrosanct position began to give way toward the end of the decade as more and more criticism was heard from within the student body about the fraternities' grip on the campus. Criticism of the fraternities, which was almost non-existent at the beginning of the decade, became a regular feature of college newspapers by the end of the decade. This criticism went hand-in-hand with a growing lament over excessive concentration on extra-curricular activities and the denigration of academic pursuits. The twenties saw the zenith of the social side of college life, encouraged by the fraternities and fed by increased student enrollments, and it witnessed the beginning of a reaction against the extremes to which this development led. The over-aggressiveness of fraternities was in part responsible. For example, in 1924, students at the University of Miami lodged a strong protest against fraternity control over athletics which permitted a fraternity sophomore to be elected basketball manager over a non-fraternity junior (*New Student,* April 26, 1924). By the latter part of the decade, criticism was often heated; see, for example, *Cornell Sun,* October 28, 1926; LSU *Reveille,* January 19, 1927.

After 1930, there was a marked decline in fraternity membership. Certainly a response to financial conditions and the inability of many to carry the expensive obligations of membership, it also reflected the return to interest in academic and intellectual matters on the campus as a whole.

45. Quoted in Edwards *et al., Undergraduates,* p. 14; *Daily Illini,* January 23, 1923.

46. *Cornell Sun,* December 7, 1925. Canby, *College Fathers,* and Keppel, *The Undergraduates,* describe college life in the prewar period.

47. Edwards *et al., Undergraduates,* p. 49. At Cornell in 1925, the fraternities, or "men on the hill," as they were called, published a "blue book" of BMOC's, or Big Men on the Campus; see *Cornell Sun,* March 26, 1925; also October 28, 1926.

48. In explaining why the distinction between the "ins" and the "outs" on the campus—those who were in fraternities and those who were not—was "so keenly felt," the LSU *Reveille* described it as "but natural that the pledge should look upon himself as one of the chosen few. Has he not been singled out from the multitude?" (October 7, 1927).

49. Rita S. Halle, "Greek or Barb?" *Good Housekeeping,* 91 (November, 1930), 43. At Duke University, the editor of *The Chronicle* was forced to assure freshmen who had not received fraternity bids that this did not automatically exclude them from campus prominence and leadership (October 26, 1927, February 18, 1925). Freshmen had associated the two so closely that it was necessary to make public statements to the contrary. See also Katz and

Allport, *Students' Attitudes*, pp. 134–135; Angell, *Adjustment*, p. 115; Robert Cooley Angell, *The Campus* (New York, 1928), pp. 28–31, for "types" and conformity on the campus.

50. *Daily Princetonian*, December 8, 1926. Despite the common knowledge of social exclusivity practiced by the clubs, a referendum supported the continuation of the status quo; *Daily Princetonian*, April 23, 1926, p. 1. See also the interesting letter to the editor which notes that election to the clubs subsumes all other considerations, even taking precedence over previous friendships; March 10, 1926. The short story, "The Strangest Serenade," in Lois Montross and Lynn Montross, *Town and Gown* (New York, 1923), describes the effect of continuing fraternity aspirations. According to the *Ohio State Lantern*, April 26, 1921, many fraternities did in fact honor personal achievements by later election.

51. The following "joke" appeared in the Duke *Chronicle*, February 13, 1924:

Stranger: "What do you think about fraternities?"
Freshman: "I'm not booting one; I don't much believe in them."
Stranger: "How about joining ours?"
Freshman: "Er-well-all right. Which one do you belong to?"

The joke makes very plain that even most self-conscious opposition to fraternities was often a case of sour grapes. Note also that the freshman agrees even before he knows which organization he is accepting.

52. Jorgen Holck, "Fraternities," *The Survey*, 50 (1923), 391.

53. See *Baird's Manual*, which lists Jewish fraternities with the others, but lists the Negro fraternities separately (1935 edition). See *Ohio State Lantern*, May 2, 1924, for exclusion of Negro chapters.

54. Sheean, *Personal History*, pp. 11–19.

55. At Syracuse, for example, the bid of a black fraternity for membership in the Interfraternity Council was turned down (*New Student*, March 10, 1923, p. 3). Also, *Daily Illini*, May 3, 1924, May 7, 1924, letter to editor, and May 9, 1924 for the situation at Illinois. According to Katz and Allport, Negroes were the lowest on the list of those with whom fraternities and other student living associations would willingly room. This study makes clear that students were very exclusive in their choice of acceptable roommates. Katz and Allport found that fraternity members were the most exclusionary in their views (*Students' Attitudes*, pp. 143–157).

56. *Cornell Sun*, December 4, 1920; Katz and Allport, *Students' Attitudes*, pp. 183–184, 146; McConn, "Tired Business Men," 546.

57. At Princeton, the eating clubs were in fact very socially exclusive. Very few high school students, as opposed to those from the elite preparatory

schools, were members of the organizations; see *Daily Princetonian*, February 28, 1924, p. 1. See *Cornell Sun*, December 13, 1921, for prep-school "type." But see also the story of Carl Peters, Hugh Carver's roommate in *The Plastic Age*, by Percy Marks (New York, 1924). Peters appears to have all the earmarks of class but had merely learned to affect the mannerisms.

58. McConn, "Tired Business Men," 546; quoted in Edwards *et al.*, *Undergraduates*, p. 53. See David Riesman with Nathan Glazer and Reuel Denney, *The Lonely Crowd*, abridged ed. (New Haven, 1964), for the characteristics of personality and sociability in the other-directed personality.

59. Edwards *et al.*, *Undergraduates*, p. 18. See *Daily Illini*, March 27, 1925, on costly clothes as a means to popularity. Also, *Daily Illini*, February 1, 1924, p. 1, which notes that chapter house building amounting to one-half million dollars was under way among ten fraternities, and February 2, 1924, letter to editor.

60. *Daily Northwestern*, reprinted in *Daily Illini*, October 19, 1921. See also the *Ohio State Lantern*, April 25, 1923, p. 1, for the qualities that coeds desired in an ideal man. These included appearance, clothes, manner, ability to socialize, dancing skills, and ownership of a car.

61. Many administrators feared that early rushing prevented freshmen from first being introduced to the academic side of college before they were thrown into the social. Many schools moved to delay rushing. This was the case at Ohio State, where 24 credits of acceptable academic work were required before a youth could belong to a fraternity; see *Ohio State Lantern*, October 6, 1921, p. 1.

62. LSU *Reveille*, October 7, 1924.

63. Angell, *Campus*, p. 7. For social culture, see Gerald Johnson, "Should Our Colleges Educate?" 723–727; also, Thomas Arkle Clark, *The Fraternity and the College*, (Menasha, Wis., 1915); Freeark, *American Fraternity System*, *passim*. See *New Student*, November 15, 1924, p. 3, discussing the iconoclastic magazine *The Circle* published at the University of Chicago, and October 10, 1925 (editorial) reprinted from *The Dartmouth*, which gives a good summary of their criticisms.

64. *Present Position of the Student YMCA*, p. 37. Students with strong religious orientations and those who were active in the student Y's showed different patterns in their attitudes toward work, social life, extra-curricular activities, and athletics than did fraternity members. See Katz and Allport, *Students' Attitudes*, pp. 24–49.

65. Quoted in Edwards *et al.*, *Undergraduates*, p. 12.

66. Quoted in Edwards *et al.*, *Undergraduates*, p. 57. See also LSU *Reveille*, February 3, 1928.

67. Originally the signs and rituals were in fact secret, partly because

college officials tried to weed out the members of the secret brotherhoods; see Piper, "College Fraternities," 641–643. The pins, too, were secret and not to be seen by outsiders. But by the nineties, the fraternities no longer feared officials, and the pins were worn proudly. By the nineties, the pin had become something to be granted as a sign of devotion to a girl friend. See the story in *Rutgers Targum*, May 17, 1895, p. 365. For "pinning" in the twenties, see *Ohio State Lantern*, October 15, 1924, p. 1.

68. Edwards *et al.*, *Undergraduates*, p. 58; quoted in Edwards *et al.*, pp. 59–60.

69. Edwards *et al.*, *Undergraduates*, p. 71; quoted in Edwards *et al.*, p. 59; *Faculty-Student Committee, Chicago*, p. 39.

70. Holck, "Fraternities," 391. According to Katz and Allport, fraternity members gave as reason for excluding certain kinds of individuals the preservation of the reputation of the group much more frequently than other residence units (*Students' Attitudes*, pp. 149–157). See also Edward Y. Hartshorne, "Undergraduate Society and the College Culture," *American Sociological Review*, 8 (1943), 321–332. Hartshorne contends that the criticism which the individual permits members of his own group, "if pressed by an outsider, would elicit violent indignation." He permits such group criticism because it helps to maintain group solidarity which is basic to his sense of confidence.

71. Edwards *et al.*, *Undergraduates*, p. 62.

72. Quoted in Edwards *et al.*, p. 60.

73. Quoted in Edwards *et al.*, p. 60.

74. Quoted in Edwards *et al.*, p. 60.

75. *Cornell Sun*, October 14, 1924, December 7, 1925.

76. *Faculty-Student Committee, Chicago*, p. 39.

77. Katz and Allport, *Students' Attitudes*, p. 136; quoted in Edwards *et al.*, *Undergraduates*, pp. 63–64; Clarence C. Little, *The Awakening College* (New York, 1930), p. 69; *Faculty-Student Committee, Chicago*, p. 40. See also *UCLA Daily*, November 21, 1927, "The Stray Cat."

78. *Faculty-Student Committee, Chicago*, p. 40.

79. Reprinted in *Daily Illini*, January 26, 1922. Princeton actually took the unprecedented step of cutting in half the length of competition for editorial posts on the newspaper in order to cut down on wear and tear among competitors. See *Daily Princetonian*, April 15, 1926. Some students spent as many as nine hours a day working on the newspaper; see *Daily Princetonian*, December 17, 1925. For abuses in competition, see, for example, *Cornell Sun*, September 30, 1920. Also, *New Student*, special issue on the Yale Conference on Activities, March 29, 1924. For fraternity assistance, *Cornell Sun*, October 25, 1923, letter to editor.

80. Angell, *Campus*, p. 9; LSU *Reveille*, January 19, 1927. At Ohio State,

non-fraternity students caucused to attempt united support for a non-fraternity man for president of student government in order to break fraternity control; see *Ohio State Lantern,* March 21, 1923. Also, *UCLA Daily,* March 25, 1927; Duke *Chronicle,* May 17, 1923, March 31, 1926, April 14, 1926, March 7, 1928; LSU *Reveille,* December 2, 1921, May 19, 1919, for politicking on campus. For the assignment of political appointments to fraternities, see, for example, *Daily Illini,* October 24, 1923.

81. See *Daily Illini,* October 24, 25, 26, 1921; also, October 24, 1923. In 1924, *Daily Illini* dropped its usual non-partisan stance to applaud the election of a non-organization candidate to the presidency of the senior class, a break in the stranglehold that fraternities had over campus politics and their "steamroller" tactics; see February 23, 1924.

CHAPTER 4

1. Caroline M. Tryon, "The Adolescent Peer Culture," in *Adolescence, 43rd Yearbook of the National Society for the Study of Education,* ed. Nelson B. Henry (Chicago, 1944), p. 226.

2. See the following for the transformation of higher education from the nineteenth-century colleges and academies to their modern descendants; Frederick Rudolph, *The American College and University: A History* (New York, 1965); Laurence R. Vesey, *The Emergence of the American University* (Chicago, 1965); Robert A. McCaughey, "The Transformation of American Academic Life: Harvard University, 1821–1892," *Perspectives in American History,* 8 (1974), 239–332; William Clyde DeVane, *Higher Education in Twentieth-Century America* (Cambridge, Mass., 1965); also Richard Hofstadter and Walter P. Metzger, *The Development of Academic Freedom in the United States,* Part 2 (New York, 1955). Walter C. John, "Requirements for the Bachelor's Degree," *U.S. Bureau of Education Bulletin, 1920,* no. 7, pp. 1–322 describes changing college requirements.

3. Rudolph, *College and University,* pp. 287–306. For nineteenth-century students, Rudolph, pp. 136–155, and Vesey, *Emergence,* pp. 268–302.

4. Vesey, *Emergence,* p. 301.

5. R. H. Edwards, J. M. Artman, and Galen M. Fisher, *Undergraduates* (Garden City, N.Y., 1928), p. 91.

6. According to Lincoln B. Hale, *From School to College: A Study of the Transition Experience* (New Haven, 1939), "The most frequent ideal was the student making an average grade and participating successfully in several college activities" (p. 141). See also Robert Cooley Angell, *The Campus* (New York, 1928), pp. 2, 10; *Cornell Sun,* December 18, 1920; Duke *Chronicle,* May 2,

1923. For published grade averages at various schools see, for example, *Daily Illini,* April 11, 1920, May 2, 1920; *Ohio State Lantern,* May 23, 1921. At Louisiana State, only one-third of all students passed all their courses; see *The Reveille,* January 26, 1923, p. 1. More women than men were normally elected to Phi Beta Kappa; see, for example, *Ohio State Lantern,* May 1, 1923; *UCLA Daily,* November 7, 1924; *Daily Illini,* January 22, 1921; Duke *Chronicle,* April 4, 1928, p. 3.

For students' expectation of degree benefits, see, for example, *Cornell Sun,* December 7, 1920; LSU *Reveille,* October 16, 1925; also the survey by H. F. Weeks, "Factors Influencing the Choice of Courses by Students in Certain Liberal Arts Colleges," *Teachers College Record,* 33 (1932), 443–444. Weeks surveyed 500 seniors at ten colleges and found that 40% of all courses were taken because of requirements; 19% because of occupation; 15% because of subject matter; and 8% because of culture. Only 3% were taken out of curiosity and 4% because of the professor (444).

7. *Report of the Faculty-Student Committee on the Distribution of Students' Time at the University of Chicago* (Chicago, 1925), pp. 11, 14, 45, 41. One-sixth of the men and one-tenth of the women spent more time on activities than studies, and one-twelfth of the men and one-tenth of the women an equal amount of time. A similar situation existed at other schools. According to the *UCLA Daily,* April 23, 1923, the average number of hours spent in study was six to eight per work day. At the University of Idaho, an average of five hours and 50 minutes was spent in class and associated study per day; men spent slightly more and women slightly less. See Alfred G. Goldsmith and C. C. Crawford, "How College Students Spend Their Time," *School and Society,* 27 (1928), 399–402. A study of Vassar College revealed the same situation, with an average of 38 hours and 20 minutes of academic work per week. At Mt. Holyoke, students gave 39 hours and 40 minutes to academic work, while Bryn Mawr College women averaged 42 hours and 30 minutes on studies, probably the highest average for any school. See Ruth Gillette Hutchinson and Mary H. Connard, "What's a College Week?" *School and Society,* 24 (1926), 771.

8. For example, *Daily Illini,* October 22, 1920, April 4, 1922; *Ohio State Lantern,* February 20, 1928.

9. *Cornell Sun,* May 15, 1920; *Daily Illini,* October 8, 1921; Duke *Chronicle,* October 10, 1923.

10. *Rutgers Targum,* October 7, 1924. Compare *Rutgers Targum,* March 4, 1887 with *Columbia Spectator,* May 23, 1919 for change between nineteenth- and twentieth-century evaluations.

11. *Cornell Sun,* February 20, 1922, April 14, 1925; Duke *Chronicle,* March 10, 1923, April 7, 1926, March 2, 1927; *Barnard Bulletin,* March 25, 1921;

for Syracuse see Daniel Katz and Floyd H. Allport, *Students' Attitudes* (Syracuse, N.Y., 1931), pp. 37, 81–82; *Ohio State Lantern,* December 7, 1922, also December 2, 1926; *Daily Princetonian,* March 22, 1926; LSU *Reveille,* October 27, 1923, also February 24, 1928. See *Ohio State Lantern,* May 18, 1922 for Yale case. The preference was registered again in 1926; see the account in the *UCLA Daily,* April 5, 1928, "Lantern Column." According to the *Daily Princetonian,* January 24, 1925, acquiring a Phi Beta Kappa key was not worth the sacrifice of keeping one's "nose to the educational grindstone."

Phi Beta Kappa's were frequently criticized for contributing nothing to college life; see, for example, *Daily Illini,* November 2, 1921. For the vogue of criticizing Phi Beta Kappa, see LSU *Reveille,* January 15, 1926. See also R. E. Thornhill and Carney Landis, "Extra-Curricular Activity and Success," *School and Society,* 28 (1928), 117; Angell, *Campus,* p. 8.

12. Katz and Allport, *Students' Attitudes,* pp. 74, 75; quoted in Edwards *et. al., Undergraduates,* p. 13. See also Hale, *School to College,* p. 141; and the random poll of Louisiana State University students, *The Reveille,* May 11, 1923, p. 1. In her study of Lutheran denominational schools, Beulah Van Wagenen noted a similar divergence: "Presidents and older members of the faculty think that the undergraduates are attempting to change the college into an institution entirely different from the one intended in the original purpose"; *Extra-Curricular Activities in the Colleges of the United Lutheran Church in America,* Contributions to Education, Teachers College, Columbia University (New York, 1929), p. 57.

13. Katz and Allport, *Students' Attitudes,* p. 209; Ruth Strang, *Behavior and Background of Students in College and Secondary School* (New York, 1937), p. 76. *Cornell Sun,* February 20, 1920, and February 23, 1920, discusses the cheating problem. For a discussion of how honor codes were failing all over the country, *Cornell Sun,* October 4 and 5, 1920.

14. Vesey, *Emergence,* p. 299. For objections to honor codes, see *Ohio State Lantern,* March 30, 1926; *Cornell Sun,* February 28, 1921; LSU *Reveille,* February 24, 1926; *New Student,* November 8, 1924, March 24, 1926; also Katz and Allport, *Students' Attitudes,* pp. 212–214. Katz and Allport, pp. 231–233, 163–165, 57–58, discuss differences in student cheating. At Illinois, as at most schools, the dean often called the presidents of organizations together to urge that they help to spread "honor" among their members; see *Daily Illini,* January 17, 1924, p. 1.

15. *Cornell Sun,* January 12, 1927; January 14, 1927, letter to the editor. See also Katz and Allport, *Students' Attitudes,* pp. 222–223.

16. For one such reminder, see *Cornell Sun,* May 10, 1920. Usually fraternities were required to maintain a high "D"; see Clarence C. Little, *The Awakening College* (New York, 1930), pp. 76–77. At the University of Illi-

nois, the administration stiffened the requirements for fraternities. Even so, the average needed to initiate new students was only a low "C"; *Daily Illini,* January 22, 1921. A similar action was taken at Louisiana State University, see *The Reveille,* June 5, 1925, p. 1. Fraternity men had lower averages than non-fraternity men at most schools; see, for example, *Ohio State Lantern,* February 23, 1927; *Cornell Sun,* November 17, 1926, "Innocents Abroad"; *Daily Illini,* April 7, 1920, September 23, 1920, p. 1.

17. For time spent in studies, see *Faculty-Student Committee, Chicago,* p. 11; *UCLA Daily,* April 23, 1923; Hutchinson and Connard, "A College Week," 768–772; Strang, *Behavior and Background,* p. 312; Little, *Awakening College,* p. 209. For social adjustment, Robert C. Angell, *A Study in Undergraduate Adjustment* (Chicago, 1930), p. 32; Ruth Vesta Pope, *Factors Affecting the Elimination of Women Students from Selected Coeducational Colleges of Liberal Arts,* Contributions to Education, Teachers College, Columbia University (New York, 1931), pp. 42–51. According to Francis M. Vreeland and Stephan M. Corey, "A Study of College Friendships," *Journal of Abnormal and Social Psychology,* 30 (1935), 229–236, college friendships were rarely based on intellectual compatibility.

18. In 1924, Princeton was testing out a new scheme which gave students more freedom to pursue intellectual interests; see *Daily Princetonian,* February 2, 1924, September 26, 1924, April 8, 1925, June 16, 1925, April 16, 1926. In 1924 and 1925, the editorial staffs of the *Cornell Sun* were bitterly critical of the prevailing attitudes toward intellectual interests; see, for example, April 14, 1925, February 13, 1925. In an editorial of January 4, 1924, the *Sun* observed, "Too often are the epithets 'bookworm' and 'grind' attached to the individuals, often a mere handful, who find in the selected thoughts of a master mind greater stimulus than in the patter of the actor or in the glowing excitement of the double three-no-trump." See also the editorial platform of the 1924 board (April 12, 1923), whose first plank reads, "The stimulation of greater interest, among the students, in learning for its own sake." The editorials, the coverage, and the tone of the paper changed during these years with far less attention paid to rah-rah activities and athletics. For similar expressions at Illinois, *Daily Illini,* April 13, 1924, March 30, 1924, and most issues in 1925. At this same time, too, the editorial board at the *Ohio State Lantern* was seized by a paroxysm of iconoclasm. Their observations about freshman rules, activities, and even sports seem like heresy when placed side by side with editorials in previous and succeeding years. In conjunction with this new mood there was a new appreciation of intellect. At mid-decade (1925–1926) the Duke *Chronicle* was similarly filled with criticism of philistinism, repression of speech, and the boorishness of students, and the newspaper newly emphasized the need for students to think for themselves;

see, for example, October 7, 1925, October 21, 1925. The paper also ceaselessly warned students against the many "jackass" professors who wanted students merely to mouth their own words. The articles throughout the year also paid specific homage to the *American Mercury,* Mencken, and destructive criticism; see, for example, October 28, 1925. See also January 13, 1925, where the editor notes that *The Chronicle* was accused of being too "high brow" even for the faculty.

For a discussion of the *New Student,* see Chapter 8 herein. Many editors acknowledged their acquaintance with the *New Student,* and many were clearly in its debt. See *Ohio State Lantern,* February 18, 1926; *UCLA Daily,* December 10, 1925, March 24, 1926; *Cornell Sun,* April 28, 1925; LSU *Reveille,* February 13, 1925. The *Daily Northwestern* published a remarkable editorial in 1925 which reflected the new iconoclasm. It was prominently reprinted in various journals; see *UCLA Daily,* December 15, 1925, *Cornell Sun,* November 4, 1925. It was, of course, cited in the *New Student* (March 21, 1925, p. 3). *The Northwestern* was clearly conscious of its aggressive reversal of trend when it concluded the editorial with, "If this be treason, make the most of it."

19. Robert C. Angell, "The Trend Toward Greater Maturity Among Undergraduates due to the Depression," *School and Society,* 38 (1933), 392; also, "The Influence of the Economic Depression on Student Life at the University of Michigan," *School and Society,* 34 (1931), 649–657. Dorothy D. Bromley and Florence H. Britten, *Youth and Sex: A Study of 1300 College Students* (New York, 1938), p. 17. See also "Youth in College," *Fortune,* 13 (June 1936), 99–102. For decline in fraternity membership, C. H. Freeark, *A College Career and the American Fraternity System* (Lincoln, Neb., 1935), p. 10; for decline in importance at two formerly strong club schools, see Evelyn Seeley, "Student Trends at Swarthmore and Princeton," *Literary Digest,* 119 (April 20, 1935), 22–23.

20. Although time expended is not the only or even the most suitable gauge of seriousness in studies, it gives some measure of academic interest. At Chicago, about 15% of the students could be defined as serious scholastically, spending more than 50 hours per week in study; 18% spent six or more hours per week in serious outside reading (*Faculty-Student Committee, Chicago,* p. 10). Angell estimated that about one-third of all students at Michigan were doing well in studies (*Adjustment,* p. 112). At Syracuse, a small minority, less than 10%, believed their studies gave them good scope for self-expression (Katz and Allport, *Students' Attitudes,* pp. 40–41). In all the studies, fraternity students showed up least well on these measures.

21. Like a refrain the newspapers urged that students see their instructors as human and drop the curtain of hostility that separated students from faculty. For example, *UCLA Daily,* March 6, 1923; *Ohio State Lantern,* May 21, 1919;

Daily Illini, March 11, 1922; *Daily Northwestern,* reprinted in *Daily Illini,* April 7, 1922. For student hostility toward professors, see *UCLA Daily,* May 20, 1921; Duke *Chronicle,* December 15, 1926. In his fiction re-creation of college life, *The Plastic Age* (New York, 1924), Percy Marks described the attitude toward the faculty at the college: "He had supposed that all professors were wise men, that their knowledge was almost limitless, and he was finding that many of the undergraduates were frankly contemptuous of the majority of their teachers" (p. 167). See also the complaints of students about formal academic methods and various reform proposals in *The Students Speak Out, New Republic* ed., (New York, 1929).

22. *Daily Illini,* January 18, 1922. Also *Daily Illini,* March 18, 1924; *UCLA Daily,* December 4, 1930; Duke *Chronicle,* April 4, 1928; Katz and Allport, *Students' Attitudes,* Table 4, p. 26. Only 5.1% of the students at Syracuse considered contact with the faculty the most important part of their college experience. There was a marked correlation between those who valued contacts with instructors and those who admired the brilliant or industrious student (Katz and Allport, Table 6, p. 33). Fraternity and sorority students tended to be most suspicious of students who cultivated faculty contacts. For invidious characterizations of professors, see *Cornell Sun,* December 1, 1920 and February 5, 1926; also, *Daily Illini,* September 24, 1921; *Ohio State Lantern,* February 8, 1926; Duke *Chronicle,* September 23, 1925; LSU *Reveille,* February 24, 1928.

23. E. Davenport, "What a Man Loses in Going to College," *Saturday Evening Post,* 193 (November 13, 1920), 30.

24. Vincent Sheean, *Personal History* (Garden City, N.Y., 1934), p. 9.

25. *Daily Illini,* September 22, 1921.

"When we all decide to put a shoulder to these activities and push forward together," the Duke *Chronicle* declared, "we, as students, have done our share for our college" (November 12, 1919). The following appeared in the *Purdue Exponent,* reprinted in *Daily Illini,* December 2, 1922: "The student who starts early through participating in activities to build, and builds every day, will realize a more beautiful and endearing name than the student who sticks his nose in his books and ignores everything else." See also LSU *Reveille,* November 7, 1924. Barnard appears to have been exceptional in this regard. See, for example, *Barnard Bulletin,* November 4, 1922, November 28, 1924, and March 24, 1922, where the editor observes, "If extracurricular activities do not seem worthwhile to individual students, there is no reason why they should enter them. After all there is no abstract Barnard to be heartened by a mob of shouting adherents."

26. *UCLA Daily,* September 9, 1920; *Ohio State Lantern,* October 5, 1925.

27. *Daily Illini,* October 4, 1921; also *UCLA Daily,* September 28, 1928;

LSU *Reveille*, October 9, 1919, November 17, 1925. For elimination of hazing, see *Daily Illini*, September 25, 1920, p. 1; LSU *Reveille*, November 17, 1925. Stanford and the University of Southern California eliminated hazing in 1923 (*UCLA Daily*, February 16, 1923), and UCLA in 1925 (*UCLA Daily*, February 11, 1926). Hazing was prohibited at Lutheran colleges, Van Wagenen, *Extra-Curricular Activities*, p. 69. These are just a few among the many schools which eliminated hazing during the twenties.

One example of the abuses which drew national attention was the disappearance of a Northwestern student because of hazing; see *Daily Illini*, September 24, 1920. For hazing disorders, see *Ohio State Lantern*, March 30, 1920; LSU *Reveille*, October 9, 1919; *Cornell Sun*, December 12, 1922. The issue of hazing became so potent that even President Coolidge took an official position against hazing; see *UCLA Daily*, May 8, 1925.

28. *Ohio State Lantern*, October 7, 1919; *Daily Illini*, October 5, 1921; *Kansas State Collegian*, reprinted in *Daily Illini*, February 27, 1923.

29. *Cornell Sun*, September 26, 1921; also Duke *Chronicle*, May 13, 1925, where caps were first used in 1925 as a substitute for badges. In the spring, freshmen were to burn their caps in a celebration ritual. Only then did freshmen become "responsible members of the community," according to the *Cornell Sun*, May 21, 1921. But freshmen appear to have taken these things less and less seriously; see *Daily Illini*, March 15, 1922.

30. See, for example, *Cornell Sun*, September 23, 1922; *UCLA Daily*, March 5, 1920; *Daily Iowan*, reprinted in *Daily Illini*, October 29, 1921; *Purdue Exponent*, reprinted in *Daily Illini*, September 21, 1922; LSU *Reveille*, February 2, 1923, p. 1.

Among the "Tips to Freshmen" in the handbook at Roanoke College was the following: "Don't wear any preparatory or high school athletic insignia. Maybe you were a big man in a little school, but now you are a little man in a big school." Reprinted in Van Wagenen, *Extra-Curricular Activities*, p. 69.

31. *Daily Illini*, November 4, 1921. For declining interest in the rush, see *Ohio State Lantern*, October 5, 1925. The Cornell Student Council decided to abolish the rush in 1923 because the custom had outlived its usefulness and interest was slight. See *Cornell Sun*, October 17, 1923, p. 1; also, November 2, 1923 on the insincerity of the rite. For pep rallies, see, for example, *UCLA Daily*, October 15, 1929.

32. At Cornell, freshmen were warned to stop wearing knickers, "the stamp inviolate of the upper classes," and golf stockings, "the dearest prerogative of upper-class underpinnings;" *Cornell Sun*, October 7, 1920. For rules against sitting on the senior bench, *Daily Illini*, September 21, 1922. At Michigan no freshman was permitted to date; see *Daily Illini*, October 4, 1921. Rules at UCLA prohibited "queening," that is, dating, or making

passes at women; see *UCLA Daily*, September 17, 1920; also LSU *Reveille*, November 17, 1925. For some freshman rules at denominational schools, Van Wagenen, *Extra-Curricular Activities*, pp. 70, 72.

Even the freshman cap rule was being called into question at some schools and it was retained at Northwestern and the University of Wisconsin only after long consideration (*Daily Illini*, October 1, 1921).

In general, freshman rules at coed schools applied only to men, but UCLA, for example, tried to enforce certain restrictions against women; see *UCLA Daily*, September 24, 1920, September 19, 1922. Women at Louisiana State were required to wear freshmen caps; see LSU *Reveille*, November 25, 1921, p. 6, September 29, 1922. It was likely that the coeds' more recent advent on the campus at a time when the rites were falling away precluded their involvement in these traditions. So too, a certain deference to women as the weaker sex may have excluded them from the rough-house which was the normal treatment of freshmen and from the humiliation with which it was associated. The older women's schools did have traditional rites and rules which were almost wholly organized along academic class lines. At Barnard College, for example, the annual Greek Games event was a contest of grace and agility between the freshman and sophomore classes. But despite the symbolic rivalry, it had become more a fête and an all-college event than a real rite of passage. Barnard also had an event which served as a kind of initiation, the Night of Mysteries, when freshmen as a group were led into the cafeteria and sophomores dressed in black robes informed them of the mysteries and responsibilities of college life (*Barnard Bulletin*, October 27, 1922).

33. See *Cornell Sun*, April 21, 1921, also letters to the editor, April 19, 1921 and April 30, 1921; *UCLA Daily*, October 3, 1927. For the Michigan incident, see *Daily Illini*, April 27, 1922. For the UCLA lobby to bring back hazing, *UCLA Daily*, November 21, 1927.

34. *Daily Illini*, September 27, 1923; *UCLA Daily*, October 3, 1922; also LSU *Reveille*, September 29, 1922, which calls for publication of freshman rules.

35. *UCLA Daily*, October 18, 1923; *New Student*, December 7, 1922.

36. *Ohio State Lantern*, April 28, 1922, p. 1. According to Angell, "One of the most powerful incentives to participation in campus activities is conformity," *Campus*, p. 127. See the condemnation of the "professional joiner" in the *Wisconsin Daily Cardinal*, reprinted in *Daily Illini*, October 4, 1921, and the *Illini* condemnation of those who were "dead wood" in the organizations, March 9, 1922; also Duke *Chronicle*, October 31, 1923.

37. *Cornell Sun*, October 11, 1924; *Ohio State Lantern*, March 10, 1925; *UCLA Daily*, November 4, 1927, October 16, 1928, "Lantern Column"; *Daily Princetonian*, February 14, 1925; LSU *Reveille*, October 16, 1925.

38. *Daily Illini,* December 7, 1921, February 8, 1922. For complaints about over-organization, *Ohio State Lantern,* October 6, 1925; *Cornell Sun,* April 2, 1926, October 30, 1926; *The Johns Hopkins News Letter,* reprinted in *New Student,* October 28, 1925, p. 3; *Daily Princetonian,* December 18, 1925; Duke *Chronicle,* February 23, 1927; the LSU *Reveille,* March 23, 1928, April 11, 1930.

39. *Cornell Sun,* especially September 30, October 4, October 5, 1920; also *Ohio State Lantern,* March 14, 1921; *Daily Princetonian,* March 31, 1924. At Trinity-Duke, *The Chronicle* urged that special consideration be accorded active students and that academic discipline take activities into consideration. So too, the editor suggested that extra-curricular activities become a part of a student's formal record so that future employers might consider them as a counterweight to poor grades: "The most important advantage of this innovation is the expectation that it will give added value to extra-curricular activities which, it is argued, occasionally gives [*sic*] a more correct index to a student's after-college career than does his scholarship standing"; May 6, 1925. For students' evaluation of the role of activities in their education, see Chapter 5 herein.

40. Frederick J. Kelly, *The American Arts College; A Limited Survey* (New York, 1925), p. 143. For opposition to the point system, see, for example, *Daily Illini,* April 21, 1922, October 15, 1922; Duke *Chronicle,* May 3, 1922. For the system at Ohio State, see *Ohio State Lantern,* March 12, 1919, and for women at Illinois, *Daily Illini,* September 28, 1920, p. 1; for women at Duke, see *The Chronicle,* March 2, 1927, p. 1 and March 9, 1927; for women at Louisiana State, see *The Reveille,* October 7, 1927, p. 1 and editorial. For a description of how the system operated at a number of Lutheran colleges, Van Wagenen, *Extra-Curricular Activities,* pp. 25–26. On the whole, small colleges appear to have adopted the system more readily than large universities.

41. F. Stuart Chapin, *Extra-Curricular Activities at the University of Minnesota* (Minneapolis, 1929), pp. 4, 41, 45, 82, 84, 89; Angell, *Adjustment,* p. 118; *Faculty-Student Committee, Chicago,* pp. 41, 45; F. W. Reeves, *The Liberal Arts Colleges* (Chicago, 1932), p. 382; O. Edgar Reynolds, *The Social and Economic Status of College Students,* Contributions to Education, Teachers College, Columbia University (New York, 1927), p. 45; Hutchinson and Connard, "A College Week," 772.

At Minnesota, the freshman class was the only one to have less than a majority participating, 51.1% taking no part. The proportion decreased steadily with each class; sophomores had only one-third not taking part in activities and one-quarter of the juniors and seniors did not participate; Chapin, *Extra-Curricular Activities,* p. 41. Of the "prominent" men and women at Minnesota (those who were either leaders in extra-curricular activities or were well known because of their widespread participation) 75% belonged to fraternities and sororities compared with 38.9% of all students in fraternities (Chapin, p. 54).

At the University of Chicago, the majority of all students, men and women, averaged between 15 and 20 hours a week on activities, but almost 40% spent considerably more. Among fraternity men and women, 56% spent more than 20 hours each week. Of all students at Chicago, almost one-quarter spent as much or more time on activities as they did on classroom attendance and studies. Again, fraternity members were disproportionately represented in this group. See *Faculty-Student Committee, Chicago*, pp. 45, 41. But at the University of Idaho, the average amount of time given to activities was reported to be only ten minutes per day, with men spending 25 minutes and women only five. Even the most active group, seniors, spent only 30 minutes a day, which equalled a mere three-and-a-half hours per week; Goldsmith and Crawford, "Students Spend Their Time," 399–402.

42. For denominational schools, Reeves, *Liberal Arts Colleges*, p. 382. For women's schools, Hutchinson and Connard, "A College Week," 771; Reynolds, *Social and Economic Status*, p. 50; Chapin, *Extra-Curricular Activities*, p. 62. Newspapers in Southern schools generally appeared less often; see LSU *Reveille*, September 29, 1925.

43. See Chapin, *Extra-Curricular Activities*, pp. 21, 37–46; Angell, *Adjustment*, pp. 119–121; Reynolds, *Social and Economic Status*, p. 50, who found that once women did join they tended to belong to more organizations than men.

44. Chapin, *Extra-Curricular Activities*, p. 62. At Minnesota, only a small portion of the prominent students engaged in fewer than three activities. Also, Angell, *Adjustment*, p. 118.

45. For disproportionate fraternity membership among prominent students, Chapin, *Extra-Curricular Activities*, p. 54; *Faculty-Student Committee, Chicago*, pp. 41, 45. For newspaper assurances, see, for example, Duke *Chronicle*, October 26, 1927. See also LSU *Reveille*, October 7, 1927, which warns fraternity pledges not to be smug in their new sense of importance and reassures non-pledges that they can still become important in college.

See Katz and Allport, *Students' Attitudes*, pp. 134–135 for different perceptions by fraternity and non-fraternity members about whether those not in organizations could succeed. At Syracuse non-fraternity students believed that they could participate in the extra-curricular field but that achieving leadership positions was more difficult for them than for those in fraternities. Also, Angell, *Adjustment*, p. 115.

46. Chapin, *Extra-Curricular Activities*, p. 45; Angell, *Adjustment*, p. 118; also LSU *Reveille*, October 16, 1925.

47. For sports, Chapin, *Extra-Curricular Activities,* pp. 51–52, 55, 14–15. For YMCA status, Edwards *et al., Undergraduates,* p. 283. At Minnesota, for example, prominents tended to participate less than others; Chapin, p. 52. Ohio State appears to have been an exception. Here fraternity men were actively involved in the Y; see *Ohio State Lantern,* December 9, 1920. This may help to explain why the YMCA activities and functions were prominently featured in the newspaper. For YMCA activities, see *Daily Illini,* May 10, 1922, January 21, 1922; LSU *Reveille,* October 21, 1927. For a history of the YMCA and its activities on the campus, see Owen Pence, *The YMCA and Social Need* (New York, 1939), pp. 123–144; York Lucci, *The YMCA on the Campus* (New York, 1960), pp. 11–14; Edwards *et al., Undergraduates,* pp. 252–309. On differences between Y students and fraternity members, see Angell, *Adjustment,* p. 115; also, Katz and Allport, *Students' Attitudes,* pp. 30–44.

48. Angell, *Campus,* p. 6; *The New York Times,* reprinted in the *Daily Illini,* December 5, 1922. See also James Hawes, *Twenty Years Among the Twenty Year Olds* (New York, 1929), p. 49.

49. *Colgate Maroon,* reprinted in *Daily Illini,* January 4, 1922; *Daily Illini,* January 23, 1923; also *Ohio State Lantern,* October 25, 1922.

50. For example, *Daily Illini,* October 9, 1921; *UCLA Daily,* May 3, 1922; *Daily Illini,* November 25, 1922; Duke *Chronicle,* October 8, 1924; LSU *Reveille,* October 9, 1919, p. 3.

51. *Cornell Sun,* October 14, 1924; Duke *Chronicle,* September 23, 1925. One fraternity apologist noted with approval, "One of the real thrills enjoyed by the faculty and teachers who are in a position to observe students at college is to watch the development of the new students. Many of them appear on the campus in out-of-date clothes, unkempt hair, careless and slovenly appearance. Their manners are crude, their talk is loud and boisterous, they are awkward and bashful. . . . Within a few weeks some of them catch on and begin to discard the funny clothes and gradually round off the rough edges. It takes others a year and sometimes two years to take a tumble to their new environment but eventually *all come out of the fabricating process a more finished product."* Freeark, *American Fraternity Sytem,* p. 6 (my italics).

52. Quoted in *Cornell Sun,* February 20, 1922; *Daily Illini,* March 6, 1923; *Ohio State Lantern,* October 21, 1927.

53. *Cornell Sun,* January 7, 1921; Wisconsin protest reported in *Cornell Sun,* May 21, 1923; *Cornell Sun,* May 1, 1925; LSU *Reveille,* October 28, 1927; Michigan protest reported in *Cornell Sun,* December 18, 1925; *Ohio State Lantern,* December 18, 1925; also *Daily Illini,* October 20, 1925. See also *Daily Illini* editorial which gives strong approval to Princeton's move to turn over complete control of student morals to student committees, March 24, 1921; and LSU *Reveille,* September 30, 1925 (p. 1 and editorial), October

10, 1925, for students' outraged reaction to the administration prohibitions against off-campus dances.

54. *Cornell Sun*, November 14, 1921; also, November 23, 1921. Chicago incident reported in the *Cornell Sun*, November 9, 1926, p. 6. At Ohio State, two Greek-letter organizations were suspended for failing to observe administrative rules regarding proper behavior at dances (where they were drinking), but the organizations appear to have continued to operate anyway; see *Ohio State Lantern*, May 14, 1920.

55. *Daily Illini*, September 22, 1925. Three girls were sent home from Smith College for smoking; see *New Student*, June 21, 1924, p. 6. This is only one example among many. For smoking and drinking habits, see Chapter 7 herein.

56. See *Daily Princetonian*, May 1, 1925; *Ohio State Lantern*, January 20, 1919, May 2, 1919; October 26, 1920, April 5, 1922; letters to the editor *Daily Illini*, February 24, 1923, April 29, 1921, May 10, 1921; *Cornell Sun*, May 21, 1923; *Daily Kansan* in *Ohio State Lantern*, January 21, 1920; LSU *Reveille*, May 22, 1919, February 13, 1920, p. 1; Thomas Arkle Clark, "The Passing of the Chaperone," *Atlantic Monthly*, 129 (1922), 516–519. See also the short stories, "The Faculty and the Creaking Shirt," and "Bass Drums," in Lynn Montross and Lois Montross, *Town and Gown* (New York, 1923), a fictionalized account that rings true-to-life.

57. *Daily Illini*, December 5, 1923; also, LSU *Reveille*, September 28, 1928. For curfew violations, *Ohio State Lantern*, February 5, 1924; Mabel Barbee Lee, "Censuring the Conduct of College Women," *Atlantic Monthly*, 145 (1930), 444–450; also, Duke *Chronicle*, October 3, 1923, "Campus Chatter."

58. For smoking petitions, *New Student*, October 28, 1925; February 26, 1925. The Vassar administration finally relented; see *Daily Princetonian*, March 2, 1926. For Wellesley, *Daily Illini*, January 26, 1925. For compulsory chapel, *New Student*, November 18, 1925, p. 1; *Daily Princetonian*, November 10, 1925; *Cornell Sun*, March 31, 1925, February 16, 1926. More and more schools were banning automobiles on campus in the twenties. By 1927, 17 of 35 leading institutions had such a ban (*UCLA Daily*, March 24, 1927). For student resentment of the interference, *Daily Illini*, February 24, 1922, November 1, 1922; *UCLA Daily*, October 16, 1925; *Cornell Sun*, February 15, 1922; LSU *Reveille*, October 30, 1925.

59. Little, *Awakening College*, pp. 75, 85–86. Little believed that "in the past ten or fifteen years the fraternity has frequently been the most powerful organized source of moral misbehavior on the campus" (p. 78).

60. Reported in *Cornell Sun*, November 29, 1926; reported in *UCLA Daily*, February 11, 1926, p. 3. See also the Duke *Chronicle*, March 26, 1924, "Campus Chatter," which commends the women's self-government association

for its efficient handling of student conduct by setting codes rather than regulations. The association had apparently been able to deprive six coeds of social privileges for six weeks; on the other hand, the Trinity-Duke Men's Association had earlier been blamed for failure to solve the drinking problem; see April 11, 1923.

61. *Cornell Sun,* October 28, 1920.

62. Duke *Chronicle,* January 13, 1925. Dean Thomas Arkle Clark of Illinois sent letters to fraternities urging that their members obey and enforce anti-drinking rules (*Daily Illini,* November 5, 1921). At Brown, the president was urging fraternities to obey Prohibition (*Daily Illini,* December 3, 1922, p. 1). See also *Ohio State Lantern,* October 15, 1924; Duke *Chronicle,* December 16, 1925; LSU *Reveille,* November 2, 1928.

63. Such a system for non-fraternity members was established at Illinois. For continuous coverage, see the *Daily Illini,* fall, 1923 and spring, 1924. A series of editorials were published on the system, beginning September 27, 1923. A similar system was initiated at Ohio State and at Cornell. There was also a move at Princeton for non-clubs; *Daily Princetonian,* October 29, 1926.

64. *Cornell Sun,* March 17, 1921.

65. See, for example, *Cornell Sun,* February 12, 1921 and February 11, 1922 on new "independent associations."

66. The social life of the university was also the staple of college humor. The foibles and behaviors of the "social types," like the flapper, the lounge lizard, the naïve coed, the sharpie with the smooth line, the vamp, and the activities man were all matter for jest and humor. Often, too, there were "in jokes" concerning specific fraternities, campus groups, or campus personalities, whose prominence was accentuated by the humorous thrusts. This was a kind of "razzing" humor—[at Cornell the newspaper column was called the "Berry (razz-berry) Patch"]—also used in numerous campus "rag" sheets whose function was to deride the self-conscious styles of the famous. The individuals who were the butt of this kind of humor, with names and identities barely veiled, were well known and their goings-on of sufficient interest to warrant the publication of such scandal sheets. The effect of this razzing was to give recognition to prominence. It was a sure sign of belonging if one made a scandal sheet, and humor, not shame, was the result of their security and belonging. Occasionally a joke or an exposé went too far and some individual or group was offended, but usually razzing of this kind was accepted in a spirit of fun and a demonstration of welcome notoriety. For a discussion of exposé sheets to reveal the sex lives of campus figures, see Ernest Burgess, "The Sociological Aspects of the Sex Life of the Unmarried Adult," in Ira Wile, ed., *The Sex Life of the Unmarried Adult* (New York, 1934), p. 129.

67. *New Student,* January 31, 1925; Angell, *Adjustment,* p. 46; Chapin,

Extra-Curricular Activities, Table 6, p. 28; *Faculty-Student Committee, Chicago*, p. 42; *Ohio State Lantern*, February 10, 1926, p. 1. Northwestern incident reported in *UCLA Daily*, November 13, 1925.

Even at denominational colleges like Trinity-Duke, where church auspices tended to keep a tight rein over social affairs and students balanced academic achievements with extra-curricular activities, editors frequently complained that the number of social events crowded out time for serious study; see, for example, *The Chronicle*, March 29, 1922, February 21, 1923, February 27, 1924. The number of activities had skyrocketed at Trinity-Duke from a mere handful in the prewar years to a full daily, weekly, and semester round by mid-decade.

At most large universities, women's engagements were carefully supervised in line with the stricter view of the parental obligation of universities in regard to female conduct. For some of the rules that circumscribed female conduct at the Big Ten, see *Ohio State Lantern*, November 13, 1925, p. 1; February 12, 1923, p. 1. For some of the rules at women's colleges, *Barnard Bulletin*, November 25, 1921. At church-controlled Trinity-Duke the rules for women were very strict indeed. All lights had to be put out in the dorms by 11 p.m.; a chaperone had to accompany a coed on any automobile rides with men; women could have dates only until 10:45 on Friday and Sunday nights; women could not attend any theater or movie not approved by the Dean. See *The Chronicle*, September 28, 1921. The rules were later relaxed somewhat to permit women more engagements and later hours.

68. Katz and Allport, *Students' Attitudes*, Table 5, p. 29. At the School of Liberal Arts, 40.7% chose social contacts as opposed to 36.0% who opted for college studies. See also Chapin, *Extra-Curricular Activities*, p. 23; *Faculty-Student Committee, Chicago*, p. 45. At Chicago about one-fifth of all women but only one-tenth of all men spent ten or more hours on social events each week. Also, Angell, *Adjustment*, p. 46.

69. See Chapin, *Extra-Curricular Activities*, p. 33, Table 6, p. 28. More students in these divisions were also members of fraternities and sororities. At Syracuse, students at these divisions selected daily social contacts much more often than students at divisions like Applied Science or the Graduate School; Katz and Allport, *Students' Attitudes*, Table 4, p. 26.

70. *Daily Illini*, December 20, 1922; February 2, 1924 letter to the editor. See also *Daily Princetonian*, May 7, 1925, and the *Ohio State Lantern*, March 30, 1922, which notes that the colleges had become matrimonial bureaus. William Waller is usually credited with developing this concept. ("The Rating-and-Dating Complex," *American Sociological Review*, 2 (1938), 727–734), but the term and its meaning were used during the twenties; see Rita S. Halle, "Greek or Barb?" *Good Housekeeping*, 91 (November, 1930), 43; Ed-

wards *et al., Undergraduates,* p. 76. For the role of clothes, see *Daily Iowan,* reprinted in *Daily Illini,* March 27, 1925 and Chapter 6 herein.

71. See, for example, *Ohio State Lantern,* May 23, 1923; *Daily Illini,* October 27, 1923, letter to the editor.

72. Halle, "Greek or Barb?" 201. According to the *Faculty-Student Committee, Chicago* (p. 41), one of the foremost rights fraternities reserved to themselves was that of overseeing the associations of their members with the right women.

73. Quoted in Halle, "Greek or Barb?" 202; *Daily Illini,* May 5, 1922.

74. See the Duke *Chroncile,* October 13, 1926, for the universal desire for popularity.

75. *Daily Illini,* February 9, 1921. For prom publicity, see, for example, *Ohio State Lantern,* January 28, 1924, p. 1. On the popularity of coke and other soda-fountain concoctions, see *Daily Illini,* November 30, 1920; *UCLA Daily,* October 24, 1929, p. 1.

76. *Daily Illini,* November 21, 1924, November 26, 1924.

77. *Faculty-Student Committee, Chicago,* p. 67. Howard J. Savage, *American College Athletics,* The Carnegie Foundation for the Advancement of Teaching, *Bulletin,* no. 23 (New York, 1929), describes the obsession of youths with athletics and the enormous investment of money in stadia and the management of teams. Also, John R. Tunis, "The Great God Football," *Harper's,* 157 (1928), pp. 742–752. Athletics inspired an almost religious reverence among the young, and the fervor expressed was not unlike that of religious revivals. See the comments of Willard L. Sperry, Dean of the Harvard Divinity School, in *Religion in the Colleges,* Galen M. Fisher, ed., (New York, 1928), p. 46. Also, Edwards *et al., Undergraduates,* pp. 128–148; Hawes, *Twenty Years,* pp. 83–90. For fuller discussion, see Chapter 5 herein.

78. *Daily Illini,* October 27, 1923. A group of Illinois students achieved national notoriety when, on one such occasion, they rigged up a baggage car and used it as a dance hall; *Daily Illini,* January 18, 1922. See also, *Daily Illini,* November 4, 1920, p. 1, and *Ohio State Lantern,* November 2, 1920. The University of Chicago was forced to issue a proclamation against attendance at out-of-town games because drinking was a regular occurrence on the trains; see *Ohio State Lantern,* September 30, 1926, p. 1. The habit of following the team was also becoming common in the South. In 1928, 400 students out of a total of 1600 were recorded as having gone with the Duke team to Annapolis; see Duke *Chronicle,* October 24, 1928.

79. See Edwards *et. al., Undergraduates,* pp. 203–204; also Max McConn, "Tired Business Men of the Campus," *North American Review,* 226 (1926), 545–550; Henry F. Pringle, "Young Men on the Make," *Harper's,* 158 (1929), 149–157; Kenneth L. Roberts, "Harvard: Fair and Cooler," *Saturday*

Evening Post, 201 (February 9, 1929), 16–17; *Daily Princetonian,* January 28, 1927; Hutchinson and Connard, "A College Week," 769.

80. *Daily Princetonian,* April 4, 1924. For example, "Girls from Smith, Vassar, Wellesley, etc., Welcomed to House Parties," *Daily Princetonian,* May 9, 1924.

81. Edwards *et al., Undergraduates,* p. 204. She noted that this averaged seven-and-one-half passes per student, which meant that some girls were gone every weekend to make up for those who never went.

82. For a newspaper conference among the Big Ten, *Daily Illini,* May 24, 1922; student activities conference, *Cornell Sun,* April 18, 1921; West Coast Conference, *UCLA Daily,* November 13, 1922; International Student Convention of the YMCA at Des Moines, *UCLA Daily,* November 21, 1919; YMCA conference at Indianapolis, Duke *Chronicle,* January 9, 1924, p. 1; Princeton Disarmament Conference, *Cornell Sun,* October 15, 1921, November 21, 1921; Women's Conference on Disarmament, *Barnard Bulletin,* November 17, 1922. Many more of this sort were sponsored, much too many to enumerate here.

83. See *New Student,* April 19, 1922. For the increase in intercollegiate news exchange, see *Cornell Sun,* September 21, 1921. For National Student Federation meeting, see *Daily Illini,* February 23, 1924; *UCLA Daily,* January 6, 1926. For student organizations, see Chapter 8 herein.

84. Chapin, *Extra-Curricular Activities,* Table 3, p. 19, p. 33; *Faculty-Student Committee, Chicago,* p. 68.

85. See letter to the editor, *Daily Illini,* February 18, 1921; October 8, 1920. The same situation appears to have prevailed at Michigan; see *Ohio State Lantern,* January 25, 1923. Chapin found that at Minnesota there was an inverse relation between attendance at theaters and movies and involvement in extra-curricular affairs; *Extra-Curricular Activities,* p. 69. Some students argued that those who spent much time at the movies were insufficiently engaged in peer concerns; for example, *Daily Illini,* February 28, 1922.

86. See *Daily Illini,* March 11, 1922, September 27, 1923; *Ohio State Lantern,* June 1, 1922; *Daily Princetonian,* April 7, 1924; *Daily Illini,* February 2, 1921, letter to the editor.

87. Eunice Fuller Barnard, "The New Freedom of the College Girl," *New York Times Magazine* (March 12, 1932), p. 8. For attempts to keep students on campus, see *Daily Illini,* "Women's Building Opens for Dances, Union Increases Capacity to Attract Students from City Resorts," October 8, 1920, p. 1; Duke *Chronicle* January 5, 1927, also December 1, 1926, p. 1, December 16, 1926, p. 1. One of the arguments against automobiles was that they provided a too-ready means of escape from the campus; see *Daily Princetonian,* March 24, 1926.

Town-and-gown incidents remained common throughout the period. There was a bloody confrontation at Illinois, for example, at which one student was killed by the town police and a number of others were injured; see *Daily Illini,* March 18, 1924. A similar incident occurred in 1926; see *Daily Illini,* March 19, 1926, p. 1.

88. *Faculty-Student Committee, Chicago,* p. 56; also Chapin, *Extra-Curricular Activities,* p. 23. *Ohio State Lantern,* February 16, 1923, p. 1. A survey of Syracuse University students found that men spent an average of three hours each day and women one hour each day in bull sessions; see Duke *Chronicle,* April 4, 1927. For bull sessions, see *Columbia Spectator,* April 11, 1919, reprinted in *Ohio State Lantern,* February 10, 1922 and *Cornell Sun,* November 27, 1922; LSU *Reveille,* April 20, 1928, p. 3.

An editorial in the *Daily Illini* claimed that "shows" were a chief amusement among non-fraternity men because of the dearth of informal residential interaction available to them (February 28, 1922). In response, one student, a non-fraternity man, asserted that this was not the case and that non-organization men had a host of informal diversions and many occasions for group interaction; *Daily Illini,* March 2, 1922, letter to the editor. See also Duke *Chronicle,* November 30, 1924, "College Collections," for the story of Emory University non-fraternity men who rented a house to serve as a hang-out or social center, so that they might enjoy the informal socializing available to fraternity men.

89. Angell, *Adjustment,* p. 118. Colleges and universities were in the process of developing informal facilities to meet the needs of increasing student enrollment and the demand by students for congenial meeting places. Illinois women, for example, complained that there were no facilities where they could prepare and eat lunch and asked for kitchens and lounges in which they could relax. They noted that such places were provided at the University of Chicago and elsewhere; *Daily Illini,* November 23, 1923, letter to the editor. See also a similar plea on behalf of "town girls" at Duke in *The Chronicle,* May 8, 1929. There was frequent complaint made in the newspapers of the fact that the libraries were too often used as social centers. See, for example, *Ohio State Lantern,* March 14, 1922.

90. Pope, *Elimination of Women Students,* p. 19. At the denominational colleges studied by F. W. Reeves, the range of student retention was from a high of 42% at Allegheny College to a mere 12% at Oklahoma College. Reeves found that one-half of all students who would eventually drop out did so at the end of the freshman year. The percentages of these returning students were as follows: 60.3% after freshman year; 37.6% of the original students returned for junior year; 28.5% returned for senior year. The high drop-out after sophomore year was related to the high incidence of student transfers to

professional schools at this point (*Liberal Arts Colleges,* pp. 52–55). In a sample study of 629 students, Pope found that the largest drop-out occurred at the end of the second semester (after freshman year)—49% of all students who would leave before graduating left at this time, a figure highly comparable to Reeves. By the end of the sophomore year, 88% of those who would leave had done so (pp. 16–18).

91. See Pope, *Elimination of Women Students,* pp. 42–45, 25, 85–90. At the University of Minnesota, 31.7% of the women who withdrew claimed they did so for financial reasons. At Chicago, the reasons most often cited were finances, health, and home conditions (Pope, pp. 44, 45, 46).

92. Charles Judd, "Education," in *Recent Social Trends in the United States, Report of the President's Research Committee on Social Trends,* one-volume ed. (New York, 1933), p. 338; Emery M. Foster, "School Survival Rates," *School Life,* 22 (1926), 13–14. In 1915, before the war, there were 1,328,984 students in grades 9–12; in 1920, 2,200,389. By 1924, there was a 50% increase to 3,389,878 and by 1930 there were 4,399,422, an increase of 100% in the ten years of the decade and 350% over the prewar figure. See U.S. Bureau of the Census, *Historical Statistics of the United States, Colonial Times to 1957* (Washington, D.C., 1960), p. 207, Table H223–233. To use Middletown as a convenient example, where the city population increased three-and-one-half times from 1890 to 1924, the high-school population increased nearly eleven times, and the number of graduates 19 times. In 1889–90, there were only 170 pupils in the high school, 8% of the school population. By 1923–24, there were 1849 pupils, 25% of the total school enrollment; Robert S. and Helen Merrill Lynd, *Middletown* (New York, 1929), pp. 182–183.

93. In terms of social environment, the local junior colleges were similar to the high schools. One investigation called them "glorified high schools." In a questionnaire study of 3000 California junior-college students (Walter Crosby Eells and R. Romayne Brand, "Student Opinion in Junior Colleges in California," *School Review,* 38 (1930), 176–190), almost one-half of all students questioned believed that the social life at their school was insufficient and did not live up to their expectations of college life. Most students (73.9%) believed that there was not enough "college atmosphere, traditions, and spirit." The major deficiency of the junior colleges, according to the investigators, was the absence of the qualities which the young valued above all: "Undoubtedly, the students want and expect something more than a glorified high school. They want real college life when they enroll in the junior college" (184).

94. Elbert K. Fretwell, *Extracurricular Activities in Secondary Schools* (Boston, 1931), vi, vii. See also the discussion of extra-curricular activities in *The Proceedings of the National Educational Association,* 1922 (hereafter cited as *NEA Proceedings*); *National Society for the Study of Education, Twenty-fifth Yearbook,*

"Extra-Curricular Activities," (Bloomington, Ill., 1928), Part 2, pp. 1–235; Thomas M. Deam and Olive M. Bear, *Socializing the Pupil Through Extra-Curricular Activities* (Chicago, 1928).

According to Deam and Bear, "A democratic society is in a way dangerous, as it brings together all kinds of pupils regardless of training. Many lack the advantage of proper home life. They are often crude and timid, or sophisticated and blasé. Some sort of refining influence, such as exists in a real home or a properly conducted lab . . . is as helpful to the school group as the work of Jane Addams in Hull House is to that community" (p. 206).

95. Some studies which contain such data are Inez M. Cook and T. V. Goodrich, "How High School Pupils Spend Their Time," *School Review,* 36 (1928), 771–778; Alice L. Dement, "Values in Extra-Curricular Organizations in the High School," *School Review,* 32 (1924), 40–48; George B. Smith, "Combinations of Extra-Curricular Activities Engaged in by Students in High School and the University," *School and Society,* 44 (1936), 716–720; Sarah M. Sturtevant and Ruth Strang, "Activities of High School Girls," *Teachers College Record,* 30 (1929), 562–571; Strang, *Behavior and Background,* p. 306; J. G. Masters, "Place of Social Affairs in the High School," *Seventh Yearbook, National Association of Secondary School Principals* (1923), pp. 71–75, (hereafter cited as *Seventh Yearbook, NASSP*).

96. Quoted in G. B. Morrison, "Report of Committee on Secret Fraternities," *NEA Proceedings,* 1905, p. 448. For laws against fraternities, William R. Hood and Bertha Y. Hebb, "State Laws, School Board Regulations, and Judicial Decisions Relating to High School Fraternities," *City School Leaflet No. 7,* Bureau of Education (Washington, D.C., May, 1923). Also, William E. Jones, "Legal Status of High School Fraternities," *American School Board Journal,* 75 (1927), 53, 156. The Mississippi law banned all secret societies at all state educational institutions, effectively destroying college fraternities as well (Jones, "High School Fraternities," 53). For opposition to fraternities, see Gilbert B. Morrison, "Social Ethics in High School Life," *School Review,* 13 (1905), 361–370; and G. B. Morrison, "Secret Fraternities," pp. 445–451; Deam and Bear, *Socializing the Pupil,* pp. 198–203. "Fraternities, Democracy and the High School," *Educational Review,* 67 (1924), 158.

97. See, for example, Deam and Bear, *Socializing the Pupil,* p. 201; "Fraternities, Democracy," 157–158.

98. See Olivia Pound, "Social Life of High School Girls: Its Problems and Opportunities," *School Review,* 28 (1920), 55; Frederick T. Shipp, "Social Activities of High School Boys," *School Review,* 28 (1931), 774; Harriet Hayes, "The Social Life of the High School and Some of its Problems," *NEA Proceedings,* 1923, pp. 874, 877; see also, Sarah M. Sturtevant, "The Relations of the Work of a Real Dean of Girls to High School Girls," *Seventh Yearbook,*

NASSP, pp. 121–126; Deam and Bear, *Socializing the Pupil*, especially pp. 213 ff.; Cecil K. Reiff, "Social Life of Pupils," *Seventh Yearbook, NASSP*, pp. 48–53; Margaret Kiely, "The Significance of the Dean to the High School Girl," *Seventh Yearbook, NASSP*, pp. 115–121.

99. Masters, "Social Affairs," 75. As one investigator noted, of the various kinds of social activities, "it would be putting the case mildly indeed to say that dancing is the most interesting of all" (Masters, p. 73). But not everyone could or would dance and there were proposals for alternative social events like teas. See Harold Johnson, "Psychology of the High School," *School Review*, 30 (1922), 127–130.

100. "Letter Used in Lakewood High School, Ohio, in Campaign for Conservative Dress Regulation," *Seventh Yearbook, NASSP*, p. 126.

101. Shipp, "Social Activities," 768, 770; H. S. Dimrock, "A Research in Adolescence: Part II, The Social World of the Adolescent," *Child Development*, 6 (1935), 285–302; Strang, *Behavior and Background*, p. 306. In the Shipp sample, only one-fifth of all sophomore high-school youths were never permitted by their parents to go out on school nights. By the time they were seniors, less than 6% were so completely confined. Of all the high-school youths in this sample, 26.5% went out with girls once a week or more often, and only 32% admitted to never going out with girls. The proportion of boys dating increased markedly with academic class. Where 14.7% of the sophomores went out with girls at least once a week, 36.3% of the seniors dated regularly. Of these, two-thirds did so more often than once a week.

102. Quoted in Lynd and Lynd, *Middletown*, p. 257. For movie attendance, Shipp, "Social Activities," 771; William Clark Trow, "The Leisure Activities of Students and Their Instructors," *Pedagogical Seminary and Journal of Genetic Psychology*, 34 (1927), 406–414; Frank W. Shuttleworth and M. A. May, *The Social Conduct and Attitudes of Movie Fans* (New York, 1933), p. 8. Although attendance with parents was common, attendance with friends was more common. In Middletown, 60% of the girls and 70% of the boys attended at least once a week; Lynd and Lynd, *Middletown*, pp. 264–265. For motoring, see Reiff, "Social Life," p. 50; Shipp, "Social Activities," 772; Lynd and Lynd, *Middletown*, p. 137. The effect of cars on family relations is not clear. On the one hand, motoring was a family occasion and provided an important form of family recreation; see White House Conference on Child Health and Protection, *The Adolescent in the Family*, ed. Ernest Burgess (New York, 1934), pp. 163–164. On the other hand, the automobile provided a means for the young to escape from family and community supervisions; see Reiff, "Social Life," p. 50.

103. Lynd and Lynd, *Middletown*, pp. 163, 164. For consumerism, see Chapter 5 herein.

104. Lynd and Lynd, *Middletown*, p. 135. See also Phyllis Blanchard and Carlyn Manasses, *New Girls for Old* (New York, 1930), Chapter 9 for parent-adolescent conflicts and the importance of peer example.

CHAPTER 5

1. Frederick Van de Water, quoted in *Daily Princetonian*, March 11, 1924; *Daily Illini*, March 27, 1925; *Ohio State Lantern*, February 16, 1926. See also *Ohio State Lantern*, December 27, 1922; *UCLA Daily*, February 27, 1923, September 18, 1923, January 7, 1924; *Daily Illini*, November 25, 1922, June 13, 1924.

2. *UCLA Daily*, March 29, 1926; LSU *Reveille*, October 10, 1928, p. 6; *Daily Princetonian*, December 1, 1924; Duke *Chronicle*, October 5, 1927.

3. *The Green Onion*, humor magazine at Michigan State College, sarcastically twitted students: "Neck, drink, occasionally study, and all will be well. Whatever you do, freshmen, don't be original. Be collegiate. Wear the right clothes at the right time. Think as few original thoughts as possible. It's collegiate to bull the prof into a "B" when you rated a "D". It's collegiate to sleep in lectures, crib in exams, copy themes, and get by. It's collegiate to prefer an Afro-American fox trot to a Beethovian sonata. Ah, by all means let's be collegiate. None of the herd will raise shocked hands and say begone miserable, radical, pink socialists." Reprinted in *New Student*, November 4, 1925, p. 3.

4. The editor of the *Daily Princetonian* noted that Princeton men do "not bother about the latest dictates of fashion which emanate from the semitic sartorial salons of New York and New Haven" (March 11, 1924). For contrast, see the report on the latest fashions in *UCLA Daily*, November 18, 1925, p. 2, which advised women to discard all of last season's clothes because all the styles had changed; also, *Ohio State Lantern*, December 11, 1922.

5. *UCLA Daily*, November 29, 1927; Duke *Chronicle*, March 19, 1924; *Daily Illini*, December 30, 1922, "Millicent Meows." See also the ad in the *Daily Illini*, November 12, 1924, describing fashions at other institutions; *Ohio State Lantern*, November 5, 1924, January 13, 1920; *Daily Princetonian*, January 21, 1924. One correspondent at UCLA complained that too many students were collegiate in a caricatured way because they were imitating the Harold Lloyd imitation of the college student as presented on the movie screen; see *UCLA Daily*, October 21, 1925, letter to the editor.

6. Galoshes were advertised at every school which had women students, and they seem to have been sold out as soon as they came in. Shoe stores frequently apprised coeds that they were back in stock. This fad called forth

considerable editorial comment. The girls, editors noted, were just waiting for the first rain or snow to show off their new galoshes. For some examples among many see *Daily Illini*, January 14, 1921, and the poem "Flappers," January 18, 1921; *Cornell Sun*, January 10, 1920; *Ohio State Lantern*, December 1, 1920, p. 1, and February 15, 1922. See also Duke *Chronicle*, October 10, 1928, p. 1. For yellow slickers, see *UCLA Daily*, January 9, 1925; *Ohio State Lantern*, October 29, 1923. For raccoon coats, see *Daily Princetonian*, January 31, 1924, and the almost daily ads for Gunther Furs in the *Cornell Sun* beginning in 1922 (for example, November 23, 1922). For knickers and oxford bags, see Duke *Chronicle*, March 19, 1924; LSU *Reveille*, September 25, 1925.

7. See *UCLA Daily*, September 18, 1923; also, *Ohio State Lantern*, March 20, 1923; Duke *Chronicle*, May 11, 1927.

8. For crossword puzzles, see *Cornell Sun*, November 10, 1924, p. 1 "Cross Word Puzzle Craze Gripping American Campuses;" *Ohio State Lantern*, February 16, 1925, p. 1; *UCLA Daily*, December 16, 1924; *Daily Princetonian*, December 5, 1924, December 19, 1924; *Barnard Bulletin*, December 13, 1924; *New Student*, December 6, 1924, p. 4, and January 17, 1925, p. 3; Duke *Chronicle*, December 10, 1924; LSU *Reveille*, January 3, 1925.

For Coué, see *Ohio State Lantern*, February 5, 1923, p. 1; *Daily Illini*, February 22, 1923; *Cornell Sun*, January 8, 1925, cartoon, and the article and photo of Coué, January 10, 1923; Duke *Chronicle*, February 14, 1923, "Paragraphics." The following jingle appeared in the *UCLA Daily* (March 6, 1923): "There was a man in our town/Who was so wondrous wise/He made and drank synthetic gin/and put out both his eyes./ And when he found his eyes were out/Did he curse with might and main?/ Oh, not at all! he tried Coué/ and put them back again." See also *Daily Illini*, June 15, 1924. For bridge and Mah Jongg parties in sorority houses, *UCLA Daily*, May 2, 1924; for Mah Jongg teacher, *Cornell Sun*, October 13, 1923. See also the *Daily Illini*, February 24, 1924 ad for a "Mah Jongg Coat," and February 6, 1924, editorial; *Daily Princetonian*, April 7, 1924. For *The Plastic Age*, *Ohio State Lantern*, March 3, 1924; *Daily Princetonian*, December 5, 1924 ("Booksellers inform us that next to *The Plastic Age* and the Bible the Crossword Puzzle books enjoy the largest sales."), also review, February 18, 1924, p. 4; *Daily Illini*, January 17, 1924; *Cornell Sun*, September 23, 1925; *New Student*, February 16, 1924, p. 8; LSU *Reveille*, January 23, 1925, March 13, 1925. For *Town and Gown*, see *Daily Illini*, February 1, 1923, which declares that *Town and Gown* was sold out immediately on arrival. For the review, *Daily Illini*, February 1, 1923, and the controversy over how real the stories are, February 2, 1923, February 6, 1923, and February 2, 1923, letter to the editor. For *Main Street*, *Daily Illini*, February 19, 1921, April 3, 1921, and *Harvard Crimson*, reprinted in *Daily Illini*, May 19, 1921. For dancing see Chapter 7 herein.

9. *Ohio State Lantern,* February 26, 1923; *UCLA Daily,* September 19, 1925; *UCLA Daily,* November 29, 1927. See also Duke *Chronicle,* April 20, 1927, "Wayside Wares." For some slang expressions current on campus, see *Ohio State Lantern,* March 27, 1922; *UCLA Daily,* September 29, 1925, p. 4, March 29, 1926, November 29, 1927.

10. See the LSU *Reveille,* January 30, 1925, "Ye Griddle." "To bull is to tell wild, true or near true tales about your experiences to an interested group, each member of which is, at the same time, trying to recall a similar story that will outdo yours."

11. *UCLA Daily,* April 10, 1929; January 12, 1928. At Cornell, the editor lamented the "Disappearing College Man," who was copied and imitated by everyone (reprinted in *UCLA Daily,* April 22, 1929). See also *Daily Illini,* March 6, 1923.

12. *Cornell Sun,* April 29, 1922.

13. For example, *Daily Princetonian,* November 27, 1924; Duke *Chronicle,* May 11, 1921; *Cornell Sun,* January 23, 1920.

14. Daniel Katz and Floyd H. Allport, *Students' Attitudes* (Syracuse, N.Y., 1931), pp. 196, 197, 203, 189, 196–197.

15. *Columbia Spectator,* September 23, 1919; *Cornell Sun,* September 27, 1921, December 17, 1921.

16. *Daily Illini,* April 5, 1921; Duke *Chronicle,* May 18, 1921 (italics mine).

17. *Ohio State Lantern,* October 25, 1921; Duke *Chronicle,* May 17, 1923, May 18, 1921; *Ohio State Lantern,* December 1, 1921, letter to the editor. See also *Cornell Sun,* November 9, 1926, "Innocents Abroad."

18. Willard L. Sperry, in *Religion in the Colleges,* ed. Galen M. Fisher (New York, 1928), p. 46. See also John R. Tunis, "The Great God Football," *Harper's,* 157 (1928), 743; Robert Cooley Angell, *The Campus* (New York, 1928), pp. 210–211; Duke *Chronicle,* October 20, 1923.

19. The editor of the Duke *Chronicle,* May 11, 1921, denounced students for sitting in the grandstands where they could better see and enjoy the game, rather than in the cheering section of the bleachers where they belonged as part of the "team." "It is nothing more than an act of disloyalty" to do otherwise. See also LSU *Reveille,* November 14, 1919.

20. Duke *Chronicle,* September 22, 1920. For loss of football to public interest, see *Cornell Sun,* January 4, 1926; Duke *Chronicle,* February 6, 1924. For reactions against football, *New Student,* December 9, 1925, p. 1, March 21, 1925; *Cornell Sun,* October 13, 1926; Duke *Chronicle,* January 13, 1926, p. 1 and editorial. See also the special football edition of the *New Student,* November 29, 1924. The *New Student* generally kept close watch on what it considered the absurdities of the football mania and its commercialism; see, for example, April 11, 1925, p. 1. For schools planning stadia, see *Daily Illini,*

January 27, 1921; Duke *Chronicle,* March 6, 1919, p. 1, and November 26, 1924, p. 1.

21. The Duke *Chronicle* made clear the relationship between all members of the college community and an athletic victory when it described the effect of a decline in cheering enthusiasm: "This tendency to slacken display of pep on the part of students often proves fatal. . . . The situation is just this, the *student body* weakens in its yelling; there is a quiet spell; some player relaxes; his opponent puts one over on him; the crowd becomes pessimistic; the team loses heart; and the game is lost" (January 30, 1919). For complaints that varsity men were not wearing letters, see, for example, *Cornell Sun,* December 2, 1919; *Daily Illini,* October 29, 1921, March 19, 1922.

See also the complaint in the Duke *Chronicle,* March 26, 1923, that many were wearing letters who didn't deserve them, because they borrowed a friend's. "Such careless or indifferent action if continued will result in a general lowering of the value of a 'T' in the eyes of the men who earn one and in the eyes of the student body at large. Acts of this nature are certainly violations of 'the eternal fitness of things,' and are deplored by all thinking students."

22. *Columbia Spectator,* October 21, 1919; Duke *Chronicle,* March 14, 1923, September 19, 1923.

23. *Ohio State Lantern,* June 4, 1923. "When we go home for our vacations, let us not be just self-sufficient college men and women; let us be boosters for Illinois"; *Daily Illini,* December 20, 1921; also December 21, 1922. A correspondent at Duke expressed the same sentiment when he advised all students to imitate the spirit of the Duke gift to the college: "From now on let every man in the college community be a 'Booster for a Greater Duke' "; *The Chronicle,* May 6, 1926, letter to the editor; also, November 12, 1919, April 28, 1920. See also *Ohio State Lantern,* April 19, 1922, for a special "boost" committee; *Cornell Sun,* December 20, 1919, before the day when spiralling applications for admissions diminished Cornell's fervor to enlist high-school students. At Louisiana State, there was an annual high-school rally to attract potential students; see, for example, *The Reveille,* January 23, 1920, April 25, 1924.

24. *Cornell Sun,* April 1, 1920; also, *Daily Illini,* April 15, 1920.

25. *Daily Illini,* November 13, 1924; see also *Cornell Sun,* November 18, 1920. For condemnations of unkempt appearance, see, for example, *Daily Illini,* "Freaks," March 11, 1922, and February 11, 1923. See also the ad for "Oleaqua" hair cream in the *Daily Princetonian,* which noted, "Don't go around looking like a Bolsheviki, Use Oleaqua"; January 18, 1924.

The one protest against fashion and business neatness came early in the decade when the post-war inflation sent clothes prices zooming. This was the abortive overalls campaign started at schools across the country. See, for example, *UCLA Daily*, May 7, 1920; *Columbia Spectator*, April 21, 1920, April 24, 1920; *Cornell Sun*, April 17, 1920, April 21, 1920; Duke *Chronicle*, April 14, 1920, April 21, 1920; LSU *Reveille*, April 15, 1920, p. 1, April 23, 1920.

26. *Columbia Spectator*, September 27, 1919. The editor of the *Spectator* compared a university to a business firm: "A college or University resembles a business firm in one way. Each man is expected to give a part of himself for the value received"; October 21, 1919. See also *UCLA Daily*, October 18, 1923.

27. *Ohio State Lantern*, May 4, 1923, also March 27, 1925; *Oregon Sunday Emerald*, reprinted in *Daily Illini*, March 6, 1923.

28. *Daily Illini*, April 12, 1924, letter to the editor; Duke *Chronicle*, December 19, 1923; also, *The Chronicle*, April 13, 1927, "Wayside Wares."

29. *Cornell Sun*, February 4, 1927; University of Denver coed, quoted in D. E. Phillips, "Jazz Age: Some Expressions of Opinion from the Young People Themselves," *Sunset*, 56 (1926), 35; Alice Anderson and Beatrice Dvorak, "Differences Between College Students and Their Elders in Standards of Conduct," *Journal of Abnormal and Social Psychology*, 23 (1928), 287–288. See also the impressionistic evaluation by Avis Carlson, "Wanted: A Substitute for Righteousness," *Harper's*, 154 (1927), 148–157.

30. David Riesman, with Nathan Glazer and Reuel Denney, *The Lonely Crowd*, abridged ed. (New Haven, 1964), pp. 66–82.

31. *Daily Illini*, December 18, 1923; also, November 26, 1921; *Cornell Sun*, March 14, 1921. An excellent example of the subtle emphasis on competition within conformity is the view of one young woman that she wore cosmetics like everyone else in order to be able to compete with the women who did; see *Daily Illini*, January 15, 1921.

32. See *Daily Illini*, September 20, 1924; Duke *Chronicle*, October 13, 1923. One Duke editor compared rushing to the haggling at a bargain counter; see *The Chronicle*, October 20, 1923, p. 1.

33. *Daily Illini*, June 14, 1924; *Ohio State Lantern*, April 6, 1922.

34. *Cornell Sun*, October 20, 1920; *Ohio State Lantern*, March 29, 1922. See also the letter to the editor, *Daily Princetonian*, March 10, 1926, which notes that the desire for prestigious association in the exclusive club system took precedence over even loyal friendships at Princeton. The Western schools tended to give much lip service to the idea of democratic free play. See, for example, *Ohio State Lantern*, April 26, 1921 and June 4, 1923; also, *Daily Illini*, March 17, 1925, which condemned the Yale decision to give admission preference to the sons of alumni.

35. Duke *Chronicle*, March 10, 1926.

36. For example, *Ohio State Lantern,* January 11, 1922.

37. Edward Y. Hartshorne, "Undergraduate Society and the College Culture," *American Sociological Review,* 8 (1943), 326. See Riesman *et al., The Lonely Crowd,* Chapters 3–6. For example, in noting the difference between the ambitions of inner- versus other-directed individuals, Riesman says, "Ambition I define as the striving for clear goals characteristic of the period of inner-direction. . . . Competition in the era depending on inner-direction is frequently ruthless, but at the same time people are in no doubt as to their place in the race—and that there is a race. If they feel guilt it is when they fail, not when they succeed. By contrast, antagonistic cooperation may be defined as an inculcated striving characteristic of the groups affected by other-direction. Here the goal is less important than the relationship to the 'others.' In this new-style competition people are often in doubt whether there is a race at all, and if so, what its goals are. Since they are supposed to be cooperative rather than rivalrous, they may feel guilt about success and even a certain responsibility for others' failure" (p. 101). While Riesman is no doubt correct that the goal may be less important than the "relationship to the others," he gives personal ambition too subordinate a place than was true for the youth of the twenties, at least. Riesman implies that effort and ambition will be limited or tempered by fear of success which would alienate the individual from the affections and approvals of the group. Since the youth in the 1920's believed unreservedly in success, it is highly unlikely that they would underplay the impulse to succeed.

38. *Daily Princetonian,* March 25, 1924; *Daily Illini,* October 15, 1922; LSU *Reveille,* November 16, 1925. See, also, *Ohio State Lantern,* April 6, 1922; *Daily Illini,* March 8, 1924, April 7, 1926.

39. *Ohio State Lantern,* February 8, 1926; *Cornell Sun,* March 14, 1921, October 3, 1919; *Daily Illini,* November 26, 1921. See also the letter to the editor of the *Daily Illini,* January 5, 1922, appropriately entitled, "Theory and Practice"; and Duke *Chronicle,* September 28, 1927; University of Kansas *Dove,* reprinted in LSU *Reveille,* February 17, 1928. According to the *Purdue Exponent,* "There is more in college education than merely making grades. . . . College life should train you to adjust yourself to environment. . . . There is no better way of spending one's leisure time than in doing something useful; and this 'something useful' should be the development of the mind for the responsibilities of life." Reprinted in *Daily Illini,* December 2, 1922.

40. *Ohio State Lantern,* October 21, 1927; *UCLA Daily,* February 23, 1927. See also LSU *Reveille,* October 7, 1924; *Ohio State Lantern,* April 25, 1922.

41. *Ohio State Lantern,* March 10, 1922; *Oregon Sunday Emerald,* reprinted in *Daily Illini,* March 6, 1923; *UCLA Daily,* March 8, 1927; *Ohio State Lantern,* March 21, 1923; Duke *Chronicle,* September 28, 1927.

42. See the mixed results obtained from an alumni questionnaire in Frederick J. Kelly, *The American Arts College* (New York, 1925), pp. 194–197; F. Stuart Chapin, *Extra-Curricular Activities at the University of Minnesota* (Minneapolis, 1929), pp. 90–110. Also, R. E. Thornhill and Carney Landis, "Extra-Curricular Activity and Success," *School and Society,* 28 (1928), 117–120.

43. *Daily Princetonian,* June 3, 1924; *UCLA Daily,* November 4, 1926; Duke *Chronicle,* February 7, 1923, p. 3; *Cornell Sun,* March 30, 1923; *Ohio State Lantern,* December 9, 1926. See also *Cornell Sun,* September 30, 1924, February 11, 1921; *Daily Illini,* December 24, 1925. Even when students were urged to study, the advice was usually given in terms of the benefits that would come to them later in business life; see, for example, Duke *Chronicle,* November 13, 1924.

For estimations of the money value of a college education, see, for example, *Ohio State Lantern,* November 3, 1924, p. 4, November 4, 1924; *Cornell Sun,* October 18, 1924, p. 1; *Daily Illini,* December 24, 1925, May 28, 1924; Duke *Chronicle,* December 3, 1924, p. 1, January 18, 1928; LSU *Reveille,* May 9, 1924, April 17, 1925. For businessmen's evaluation of college students, see, for example, *Cornell Sun,* April 4, 1923; *Ohio State Lantern,* March 3, 1925, p. 1; *Daily Illini,* February 27, 1922.

44. *Daily Princetonian,* January 7, 1925; *Cornell Sun,* March 11, 1924. See also *UCLA Daily,* May 20, 1927, "We Honor Our Executives"; *Daily Illini,* October 19, 1924; *Cornell Sun,* March 11, 1924 and December 14, 1922, editorial on John Wanamaker. The eulogy by the Duke *Chronicle,* October 14, 1925, on the death of the school's benefactor might well have been expected, but the memorial issue went well beyond Duke to praise the role of American businessmen in general.

45. *Cornell Sun,* December 13, 1924. See also the Duke *Chronicle,* September 17, 1919, which notes that the new economic offerings in the curriculum "will be valuable training for a business career." According to a survey of course selection among male seniors in liberal-arts colleges, after requirements, courses were most frequently chosen because they provided training for occupations. See H. F. Weeks, "Factors Influencing the Choice of Courses by Students in Certain Liberal Arts Colleges," *Teachers College Record,* 33 (1932), 443–444. According to Weeks, of all subjects, economics and sociology were least often selected simply because they were required.

CHAPTER 6

1. Erik H. Erikson, "Youth: Fidelity and Diversity," in *The Challenge of Youth,* ed. Erik H. Erikson (Garden City, N.Y., 1965), p. 10.

2. For the sexual revolution argument in surveys of sexual behavior, see, for example, Alfred G. Kinsey *et al.*, *Sexual Behavior in the Human Female* (New York, 1965, paperback ed.), pp. 300–302; Lewis M. Terman, *Psychological Factors in Marital Happiness* (New York, 1938), pp. 321–322; Winston Ehrmann, *Premarital Dating Behavior* (New York, 1959), p. 56, and "Changing Sexual Mores," in *Youth and Values*, ed. Eli Ginsberg (New York, 1961), pp. 56–67. For historians who argue along these lines, see Carl Degler, "Revolution Without Ideology: The Changing Place of Women in America," in *The Woman in America*, ed. Robert Jay Lifton (Boston, 1965); William E. Leuchtenburg, *The Perils of Prosperity, 1914–1932* (Chicago, 1958), pp. 158–177; Lois W. Banner, *Women in Modern America: A Brief History* (New York, 1974), pp. 131–154. Among the contemporary documents, Freda Kirchwey, ed., *Our Changing Morality: A Symposium* (New York, 1924); Judge Ben Lindsey and Wainwright Evans, *The Revolt of Modern Youth* (New York, 1925); V. F. Calverton, *The Bankruptcy of Marriage* (New York, 1928); and, of course, that omnipresent historical source, Frederick Lewis Allen, *Only Yesterday* (New York, 1931). See also the judicious examination by the philosopher James Hayden Tufts, who places the sexual mores in the context of broad social changes, in *America's Social Morality* (New York, 1933), Chapter 6.

Sex researchers were convinced that if they could only find a statistically significant increase in premarital intercourse among women, they could chart a turning point. Terman found just such a phenomenon: more than 50% of the women in his sample (born 1900–1909 and less than 25 years old at marriage) were not virgin at marriage (*Psychological Factors*, p. 331). Moreover, he found that the likelihood of marrying young or at all was related to a woman's willingness to have sexual relations before marriage. He thus implies that premarital coitus had become a new norm. Terman's sample, small and select, is open to grave questions of reliability, and his conclusions are therefore highly suspect. For an examination of Terman's reliability, see Ernest W. Burgess and Paul Wallin, *Engagement and Marriage* (New York, 1953), pp. 331–332. Alfred Kinsey's data and conclusions are more modest than Terman's, but on the basis of the fact that twice as many women who came to maturity in the twenties as those who matured in the period before the war were non-virgin at marriage, Kinsey concludes that the twenties witnessed a revolution in sexual mores. After the twenties, the proportion of women who had premarital coitus remained nearly constant (Kinsey *et al.*, *Sexual Behavior*, pp. 298–300). For a fuller consideration of the implications of Kinsey's data, see note 28 herein.

Recently historians have tried to locate the revolution in sexual behavior in the prewar period. See especially James R. McGovern, "American Women's Pre-World War I Freedom in Manners and Morals," *Journal of American His-*

tory, 55 (1968), 315–333. McGovern's discussion is largely unconvincing, because he remains victim to the trap of trying to locate the start of a sudden revolution. For a more important attempt to trace long-term trends, see Daniel Scott Smith's perceptive re-examination of the revolution issue, "The Dating of the American Sexual Revolution: Evidence and Interpretation," in *The American Family in Social-Historical Perspective,* ed. Michael Gordon (New York, 1973), pp. 321–335. David M. Kennedy, *Birth Control in America: The Career of Margaret Sanger* (New Haven, 1973), pp. 36–71, provides important insights into the gradual changes in attitude toward the family, women, and sex that came in the late nineteenth and early twentieth centuries.

3. For example, *Indiana State Student,* reprinted in *Ohio State Lantern,* March 30, 1922.

4. For dating, see Burgess and Wallin, *Engagement and Marriage,* pp. 63–67. Much was made of the distinctions between petting and necking in the 1920's and after. To some, necking described milder forms of embrace and was largely restricted to kissing; petting described more intimate forms of physical fondling short of intercourse. To others, the terms were reversed. The very fact that there now seemed to be a need to differentiate stages of sexual behavior preliminary to coitus is indicative of the new patterns being elaborated. To avoid confusion, the term "petting" is used here to mean all forms of erotic behavior short of intercourse. It was this broad range of activities which campus youths implied in using the term "petting."

Floyd Dell in his discussions of sexual mores, was a more perceptive analyst of sexual behavior among the young than were sexologists like Terman and Kinsey who succeeded him. See the discussion of *Love in the Machine Age* in the author's doctoral dissertation, "The Fruits of Transition: American Youth in the 1920's" (Columbia, 1974), Chapter 2.

There is little question that family proscriptions about sexual behavior continued along traditional lines in the twenties. According to Ernest Burgess, "The influence of the family . . . is relatively constant and consistent in the inculcation of the traditional ideals of family life. It is outside the family that social groups show the greatest complexities and variations." "Sociological Aspects of the Sex Life of the Unmarried Adult," in *The Sex Life of the Unmarried Adult,* ed. Ira Wile (New York, 1934), p. 128.

5. See Burgess and Wallin on "keeping company," *Engagement and Marriage,* p. 64. Joseph K. Folsom, *The Family* (New York, 1934), p. 230, on pairing; also *Daily Illini,* April 24, 1924, letter to the editor, whose correspondent complains about the lack of group activities between the sexes on campus—all contacts were restricted to paired dates.

6. Phyllis Blanchard and Carlyn Manasses, *New Girls for Old* (New York, 1930), p. 70. These authors noted that petting had become "an end in itself

. . . a substitute for more advanced sexual activity," and the fear that it would lead to intercourse for the young was unfounded (p. 69).

7. Such a bill was introduced in the North Carolina legislature as late as 1927; see Duke *Chronicle*, February 16, 1927.

8. Duke *Chronicle*, April 25, 1923, December 5, 1923; Blanchard and Manasses, *New Girls*, p. 75; Ira Wile, "Introduction," *The Sex Life of the Unmarried Adult*, pp. 38, 32. See also Dorothy Bromley and Florence Britten, *Youth and Sex* (New York, 1938), who observe that the girl who "waits for marriage" had the same standard of absolute virtue as the prewar girl, but "many of them permit themselves a degree of petting which would have been considered decidedly improper, even with a fiancé, by pre-war college girls" (pp. 56–57).

9. *Daily Illini*, April 8, 1923. For the various words used as synonymous with "spooning," see *Ohio State Lantern*, December 15, 1924, p. 1. For petting generally, see, for example, *Cornell Sun*, October 3, 1926; Duke *Chronicle*, April 29, 1925, April 1, 1925. See also the "pro-necking" article from *The Vagabond* (University of Indiana), reprinted in the *New Student*, April 7, 1926, p. 7; LSU *Reveille*, April 23, 1927; *UCLA Daily*, September 19, 1928, "Lantern" column.

10. Geraldine Frances Smith, "Certain Aspects of the Sex Life of the Adolescent Girl," *Journal of Applied Psychology*, 8 (1924), 347–349; Wile, "Introduction," p. 33; Burgess, "Sociological Aspects," p. 138. Blanchard and Manasses, *New Girls*, p. 3; also, pp. 62–66. At the University of Michigan, Robert Angell found that the attitude of women toward petting was fairly permissive; the strictest standard was maintained by those who were least well adjusted socially—not well oriented toward peers. He concluded that the "stricter morally one is in college today the more difficult it is to get along well socially." Robert C. Angell, *A Study in Undergraduate Adjustment* (New York, 1928), p. 94. R. H. Edwards, J. M. Artman, and Galen M. Fisher, *Undergraduates* (Garden City, N.Y., 1928), p. 189.

11. See Edwards *et al.*, *Undergraduates*, p. 189; Burgess, "Sociological Aspects," pp. 129, 136. According to Burgess, most campus scandals involved "town women" (pp. 135-136). At the University of Illinois, a coed disappeared from the campus and was found living with her boy-friend in Chicago. The editors noted that they believed it was best to give students a full account of the affair rather than have them learn of it from the national press as an exposé. See *Daily Illini*, April 13, 1921, p. 1, and April 15, 1921. The newspaper account suggests both how uncommon this was and that students still considered it scandalous. It also hints that similar events were often censored from the campus press by the college administration.

"Sexual irregularities" was not listed among the most prevalent "worst practices" by students at the University of Texas in 1922, according to a study of student ethics by A. P. Brogan, "A Study of Statistical Ethics," *International Journal of Ethics,* 33 (1922–23), 119–134. But it was listed as one of the worst practices in the "home community." This clear differentiation may indicate that while sexual offenses were not common on the campus, they were common with town girls. It is always possible that while sexual intercourse was infrequent for college women, it was common for those in high school. Indeed, many Jeremiahs in the twenties feared that the high-school girl was the real problem. One must, however, guard against too readily accepting this conclusion, for it was often appended to fears about "democracy" in the schools and the evil example of the lower classes. See, for example, Thomas M. Deam and Olive M. Bear, *Socializing the Pupil through Extracurricular Activities* (Chicago, 1928), pp. 224–231; Margaret Kiely, "The Significance of the Dean to the High School Girl," *Seventh Yearbook, NASSP* (1923), pp. 117–120. For an assault on the effect of lower moral standards among the newly rich and how they were debasing the standards of the "better" college women, see Eleanor Rowland Wembridge, "Petting and the Campus," *The Survey,* 54 (1925), 393–395.

12. *Daily Illini,* February 8, 1923, letter to the editor; Edwards *et al., Undergraduates,* p. 190. See also *Daily Illini,* January 6, 1926, where the editor notes that the "first-nighter" always observes the amenities. "It used to be," observed the Duke *Chronicle,* April 23, 1924, "that the mention of a woman's neck was taboo in good society. Now it is the favorite topic of conversation among the younger set." Note also the following half wistful ode:

> *She had the looks,*
> *She had the class,*
> *And yet they say she was too fas';*
> *It may be so.*
> *We feared it from the first.*
> *But now we've heard the worst;*
> *And may the rest be cursed;*
> *She had to go.*

The Chronicle, December 6, 1922.

13. A. P. Brogan, "Group Estimates of the Frequency of Misconduct," *International Journal of Ethics,* 34 (1923–24), 254–271; Daniel Katz and Floyd H. Allport, *Students' Attitudes* (Syracuse, N.Y., 1931), pp. 252–253 for the double standard at Syracuse University.

14. In Brogan's studies, sexual indiscretion was ranked as the worst practice among women in all four universities studied—Texas, Kansas, Chicago, and Wisconsin. Moreover, he found that women generally believed that there

was a lack of indulgence in sexual intercourse among coeds, thus accepting no intercourse as a norm of behavior as well as a value. They acquiesced in that norm much more frequently than did men. In general, Brogan found that women's personal standards and their estimates of the conduct of other women was more strongly correlated than men's standards and conduct. The differences were all statistically significant. See Brogan, "Group Estimates," *passim,* and Brogan, "Moral Valuations About Men and Women," *International Journal of Ethics,* 35 (1925), 105–124.

In Bromley and Britten's sample, of the 375 girls who indicated that they would wait for marriage before having intercourse, 187 gave fear of pregnancy as at least one of their reasons; 168 mentioned moral or religious scruples; *Youth and Sex,* (p. 59). According to Blanchard and Manasses, 92% of the girls classed extramarital sexual relations as immoral or unwise. Of these, 45% were unconcerned with the moral implications but based their view on expediency: "However emancipated intellectually the modern girl may be, she apparently realizes that social customs are still too powerful for the individual to defy them without risking personal happiness" (*New Girls,* p. 70). Too often practical considerations are narrowed to the problem of pregnancy, but maintaining one's status is also a practical consideration.

15. The data on the male attitude toward a future wife's virginity and the women's views of their husbands' expectations are ambiguous. In general, virginity may be said to have been prized, but no longer considered an absolute prerequisite. Blanchard and Manasses concluded that the views of the men they interviewed suggested that "there seems to be a consensus of opinion among young men that while virginity is desirable in a bride, it is less necessary than other qualifications, such as congenial tastes, ability to take an interest in the husband's work, tact, understanding and sympathy" (*New Girls,* p. 238). See also Clifford Kirkpatrick, "Student Attitudes Toward Marriage and Sex," *Journal of Educational Sociology,* 9 (1936), 545–555; Bromley and Britten, *Youth and Sex,* p. 5; Katz and Allport, *Students' Attitudes,* pp. 252–253; Brogan, "Moral Valuations," 108–111. Katz and Allport and Brogan found that men still condemned sexual irregularity much more severely in women than in men. The decline in importance of virginity in a bride was, I believe, related to the growing acceptance of sexual intercourse among engaged couples rather than to an acceptance of premarital promiscuity. Thus men may not have expected their brides to be chaste but may still have expected that their experience had been limited to relations with themselves.

According to Blanchard and Manasses, only 22% of the girls questioned believed that lack of virginity would impede their chances for marriage; only one-half of these girls were certain that it would make no difference and a good many doubted that they would be honest about their past experiences (*New Girls,* pp. 73-75). For some of the fears of women about lost virginity, see Ruth White Beebe, "The Sex Questions of Undergraduate College Students" (M.A. thesis, Columbia University, 1936), pp. 7, 11, 18–19. Also, Horace Kallen, "Sex Morals and the Unmarried Adult," in Wile, *Sex Life,* p. 248.

16. Bromley and Britten, *Youth and Sex,* pp. 16, 64–65; Burgess, "Sociological Aspects," p. 124. It is interesting that the concept of "technical virginity," or what the French call *demi-vierge,* should have become useful during this time; see Folsom, *Family,* p. 71; Kinsey *et al., Sex Life,* p. 231.

The following exchange took place among undergraduate men at an all-night bull session in Percy Marks' *The Plastic Age* (New York, 1924), a realistic re-creation of college mores and customs: " 'Some fellows say it's all right to have a woman, and some fellows say it's all wrong, but *I notice none of them have any use for a woman who isn't straight.'* . . . 'The old single-standard fight. . . . I don't see any sense in scrapping about that any more. We've got a single standard now. The girls go just as fast as the fellows.' . . . Ferguson smiled pleasantly at Hugh and drawled: 'Shut up, innocent; you don't know anything about it. I tell you the old double standard has gone all to hell.' 'You're exaggerating, Don, just to get Hugh excited,' Ross said in his quiet way. *'There are plenty of decent girls. Just because a lot of them pet on all occasions isn't any reason to say that they aren't straight'* " (pp. 156–157, my italics). Note the stress on a woman's "straightness" and the differentiation between petting and remaining straight. See also *UCLA Daily,* February 11, 1928.

17. See Mary Ware Dennett, "Sex Enlightenment for Civilized Youth," in *Sex in Civilization,* ed. V. F. Calverton and S. D. Schmalhausen (New York, 1929), pp. 99–103; *Daily Illini,* January 11, 1923, "Millicent Meows."

18. Warner Fabian, *Flaming Youth* (New York, 1923).

19. Theodore Newcomb, "Recent Changes in Attitudes Toward Sex and Marriage," *American Sociological Review,* 2 (1937), 662; Bromley and Britten, *Youth and Sex,* pp. 15–16. According to Bromley and Britten, by the mid-thirties petting was a widespread and generally accepted phenomenon which embodied "a social revolution in manners and morals" among the young (p. 3). See also "Youth in College," *Fortune,* 13 (1936), 99–102.

20. Quoted in Bromley and Britten, *Youth and Sex,* pp. 19–20, and p. 52; Bromley and Britten, p. 26. For liberalization in attitudes, see Walter Buck, "A Measurement of Changes in Attitudes and Interests of University Students over a Ten-Year Period," *Journal of Abnormal and Social Psychology,* 31 (1936), 12–19.

21. This game has dominated the sexual relations of unmarried youths throughout the twentieth century and is only recently losing its hold. See Ehr-

man, *Pre-Marital Dating,* Ira L. Reiss, *Premarital Sexual Standards in America* (Glencoe, Ill., 1960).

22. Blanchard and Manasses, *New Girls,* p. 71. Quoted in Blanchard and Manasses, pp. 65, 71; Duke *Chronicle,* March 31, 1926, "Wayside Wares"; Bromley and Britten, p. 5.

23. *Ohio State Lantern,* April 18, 1922; also *Daily Illini,* March 29, 1923. Henry Seidel Canby observed, "Romance suffused the American nineties and romance was incompatible with our quite realistic knowledge of sex." "We learned to associate amorous ardors with the vulgar or, worse, with the commonplace, and to dissociate them sharply from romance. Our sensual emotions escaped from the control of our imaginations so that in love and marriage later we found it difficult to bring the two together again;" "Sex and Marriage in the Nineties," *Harper's* 169 (1934), 428, 430.

24. *Daily Illini,* March 29, 1923. One Duluth high-school student, noting the endless discussions about the immorality of youth, observed, "The majority of fellows here at school, and the majority of the girls, too, don't go in for that stuff [petting] as much as a lot of these later-day Jeremiahs would like to have people believe. We may be a bit freer than they were in their youth, but we *still* hold close to old ideals and standards." Quoted in Duke *Chronicle,* April 27, 1927, "Wayside Wares."

25. Katherine Bement Davis' study, *Factors in the Sex Life of Twenty-Two Hundred Women* (New York, 1929) was concerned with older women, mostly in their thirties, whom she ingeniously surveyed by mail. For difficulties in surveying women, see Harry Elmer Barnes, "Sex in Education," in Calverton and Schmalhausen, *Sex in Civilization;* Blanchard and Manasses, *New Girls,* pp. 250–251.

Some investigations of male sexual behavior are M. W. Peck and F. L. Wells, "On the Psycho-Sexuality of College Graduate Men," *Mental Hygiene,* 7 (1923), 697–714; Peck and Wells, "Further Studies on the Psycho-Sexuality of College Graduate Men," *Mental Hygiene,* 9 (1925), 501–520; Walter L. Hughes, "Sex Experiences of Boyhood," *Journal of Social Hygiene,* 12 (1926), 262–273; P. S. Achilles, *The Effectiveness of Certain Social Hygiene Literature* (New York, 1923), who differentiated in the questions asked of men and women. Also, Angell, *Adjustment,* who asked only men whether they had had sexual intercourse (p. 93). For deviant sexual behavior among women, see, for example, the highly moralistic early study, Edith L. Smith, "A Study of Sexual Morality," *Social Hygiene,* 2 (1916), 541; and the equally offensive study by Mabel Seagrave, "Causes Underlying Sex Delinquency in Young Girls," *Journal of Social Hygiene,* 12 (1926), 523–529.

26. Bromley and Britten interviewed 1344 college students at 46 colleges in the late thirties. The age cohort would therefore have been born

1910–1920. Burgess and Wallin conducted their interviews between 1937 and 1939 and used a sample of 1000 engaged couples from metropolitan Chicago. The group was born between 1910 and 1920 and was therefore highly comparable to that used by Bromley and Britten (*Youth and Sex,* pp. 44–55).

27. Bromley and Britten, *Youth and Sex,* pp. 4–5; Burgess and Wallin, *Engagement and Marriage,* p. 331. The age difference of first experience is consistent with the findings of most studies which show that men become more liberal and tolerant while in high school while women do so in college. See Buck, "Measurement of Changes," 12–19, who ascribes the difference to the fact that high-school women were "kept closer to the conventions and more influenced by the home," but when they got to college, they experienced a "marked freeing of thought and attitude" (14).

28. A careful examination of the Kinsey data collected at a later date (1953) leads to the same conclusion. Kinsey found that the incidence of premarital coitus among women born between 1900 and 1910, who came to maturity in the 1920's, increased markedly over the previous generation. He therefore concluded that the twenties witnessed the critical shift to modern permissive sexuality. But in Kinsey's sample, the prevalence of premarital intercourse among the younger age groups remained low. Only 18% of the women reported sexual experience by the age of 20 (after the median age of first experience for the Bromley-Britten group). Even among women 21–25 years of age, the proportion admitting sexual experience was only 36% (Tables 83 and 84, *Sexual Behavior,* p. 339). It was not until women had reached the age of 30 and were still unmarried that more than 50% reported premarital sexual experience. Not only were these women no longer young, but the period of their experience would have taken place not in the twenties, but in the depression thirties, at which time, if not already married, their chances of marriage would be fast declining. In this case, the mores of the peer culture would no longer direct behavior and the advantage of preserving chastity in terms of marriage goals would have been strongly undercut. Moreover, of all women born 1900 to 1910 and reporting premarital coitus, 48% had coitus with a fiancé only. Since the proportion reporting coitus with a fiancé only was considerably higher among those who married young than among those who married at an older age (this is true of all birth cohorts), at least one-half of the young women in the twenties who had intercourse before marriage did so only with a future spouse (Table 78, p. 336).

29. Buck, "Measurement of Changes," 14; Blanchard and Manasses, *New Girls,* p. 72; Bromley and Britten, *Youth and Sex,* p. 5. Kirkpatrick found about half of the men asked willing to marry a non-virgin; "Students' Attitudes," 547.

In a study of 758 Miami University (Oxford, Ohio) students, Read Bain found that between 1928 and 1934, there was a decline in the idea that sex was dirty and concluded that this reflected "a real and enduring change in sex mores which has been going on rapidly during the lifetime of these students"; see Read Bain, "Changed Beliefs of College Students," *Journal of Abnormal and Social Psychology*, 31 (1936), 1–11. Also, Niles Carpenter, "Courtship Practices and Contemporary Social Change in America," *Annals, AAPSS*, 160 (1932), 38–44; Newcomb, "Recent Changes," *passim;* Buck, *"Measurement of Changes,"* *passim:* Blanchard and Manasses, *New Girls,* pp. 71–76; Brogan, "Group Estimates," 259–260, 266–270.

30. Burgess, "Sociological Aspects," 125. See also Ernest Groves, "Sex Adjustment of College Men and Women," in Wile, *Sex Life,* p. 357; Newcomb, "Recent Changes," *passim;* Blanchard and Manasses, *New Girls,* p. 70; Talcott Parsons, "Youth in the Context of American Society," in Erikson, *The Challenge of Youth,* p. 127.

31. For example, *Daily Illini,* February 8, 1923; also, April 8, 1922. For similar expressions, *Cornell Sun,* December 1, 1920, May 1, 1920 and January 21, 1921. For fuller discussion, see Chapters 7–8 herein.

32. *Wisconsin Daily Cardinal,* reprinted in *Daily Illini,* October 15, 1921. See also *Ohio State Lantern,* June 2, 1920, letter to the editor, which differentiates women into four types: "goody-goody"; "baby doll"; "vamp"; and "real woman," who "understands a fellow" and is his "pal."

33. For the importance of "sex appeal," *UCLA Daily,* March 15, 1929; *Daily Illini,* December 18, 1924, letter to the editor.

34. Very few things were untouched by the new sexual sophistication and interests of youth. According to one humorist in the Duke *Chronicle,* February 13, 1924, not even the sacred was immune: "Some girls go to church not so much for the sermons and music as for the 'hims.' " See also the complaint of the editor of the *Daily Iowan* that all the interest in fashion on campus had one object in view, cultivating popularity with the opposite sex; reprinted in *Daily Illini,* March 27, 1925. According to Angell, *Adjustment,* "this mass of evidence points unerringly to the large part played by sex interest in undergraduate life" (p. 101). See also S. M. Stoke and E. D. West, "The Conversational Interests of College Students," *School and Society,* 32 (1930), 567–570. As might be expected, sex and subjects related to sex were the most common subjects in the conversations of both men and women. Also, Stoke and West, "Sex Differences in Conversational Interests," *Journal of Social Psychology,* 2 (1931), 120–126. See also *UCLA Daily,* May 2, 1927 and Newcomb, "Recent Changes," 663–665, for the new sophistication in sexual knowledge. For women as pals and companions, see, for example, *UCLA Daily,* November 17, 1922, September 28, 1923; *Daily Illini,* November 25, 1922.

35. I have tried to survey the ads and photographs in various papers, and

from these it appears that in 1918–1919, long hair was still the prevailing fashion, but there was already a sprinkling of bobbed heads. By 1922–23, the bobs were clearly in the ascendent; most women, in the photos at least, sported the new style. The ads now showed the new hair styles uniformly. In 1922, there was some talk that the bob was doomed (for example, *Daily Illini*, February 10, 1922), but there is no evidence for this. What declined was the amount of talk about bobbed hair. Most of the criticism as well as the humor came at the beginning of the decade. See the witty and amusing take-off on the Hamlet monologue, "Clipped Locks," in *UCLA Daily*, September 26, 1922, humor column, which begins "To bob or not to bob, that is the question." In 1925, the *Ohio State Lantern* reported that no more than three out of ten girls still had long hair and belonged to the "old brigade"; February 24, 1925, p. 4. At Mt. Holyoke College in 1925, 53% of the women reported having short hair, an increase from the 42.5% the preceding year (*New Student*, May 30, 1925, p. 4). See also *UCLA Daily*, October 21, 1926; *Cornell Sun*, January 13, 1927, "Innocents Abroad"; Duke *Chronicle*, October 17, 1923, p. 1; LSU *Reveille*, January 27, 1928, p. 5. For the practicality of bobbed hair, see *Daily Illini*, February 16, 1921, letters to the editor; Duke *Chronicle*, December 2, 1925, letter to the editor. In a survey taken by the *Barnard Bulletin*, March 2, 1923, p. 3, women declared that short hair needed only little attention and was especially convenient in the morning rush to class. This was also the reason often given by coeds at Duke, according to *The Chronicle*, November 10, 1923, p. 3. But the editor notes that all the explanations were window dressing, that women bob their hair and wear short skirts quite simply because they like them.

36. Women emphatically believed that bobbed hair made them more attractive but that it was not a symbol of promiscuity as so many of the elders thought; see the letter to the editor, *Daily Illini*, April 22, 1922. In defending the bob as not promiscuous, women demonstrated their very keen awareness that the bob was in fact a sexually-loaded issue. Many school officials considered bobbed hair an irksome problem. According to the *UCLA Daily* (April 22, 1924), a Pennsylvania school board voted a $100 salary increase to all school teachers who did not bob their hair. The editor noted, "the board is about one hundred fifty years behind the majority of the American nation. . . . We tremble to think what a panic would ensue should a similar measure be adopted in Southern California." Bobbed hair was usually one of the prohibited items in those schools which adopted sumptuary regulations.

37. See *Daily Illini*, April 21, 1923, movie ad; May 22, 1924, ad for *Photoplay Magazine*. Note also the *UCLA Daily* announcement (October 21, 1926), "Bobbed Heads Still Reign in Hollywood." See also *Daily Illini*, September 23, 1922, and March 31, 1920, humor column.

38. Duke *Chronicle*, November 25, 1925, letter to the editor.

39. Silk stockings, explained one Trinity-Duke editor, were the sign of modernity on the part of men as well as women. "An old-fashioned young man, the mother's boy type," he mused, "will give his best girl a volume of Tennyson for a Christmas present instead of a pair of silk stockings"; Duke *Chronicle,* December 9, 1923. Ungartered rolled stockings were a fad that remained even after skirts had become so short that the top of the stockings were exposed. An ad in the *Daily Illini,* March 18, 1922, "Women are rolling their own," contained the intentional *double entendre* of cigarettes and stockings, both indications of female liberation and both having a certain sexual connotation. By the end of the decade, some women wore no stockings at all; see *UCLA Daily,* October 2, 1928. See also Eleanor Rowland Wembridge, "Silk Stockings," *The Survey,* 52 (1924), 28–30, for the importance of silk hose for the working girl and her image of glamor. For silk stockings and the high-school girl, see Robert S. Lynd and Helen Merrill Lynd, *Middletown* (New York, 1929), p. 163.

40. For example, *UCLA Daily,* July 3, 1924; *Daily Illini,* January 3, 1926. Also, *Daily Illini,* March 27, 1925, April 11, 1925, June 13, 1924; *UCLA Daily,* May 10, 1928, p. 1.

41. See *Daily Illini,* March 3, 1923, which talks about the new woman's "morbid horror of fleshiness"; and *UCLA Daily,* April 14, 1926, addressed to "members of the dieting table." The *UCLA Daily,* February 21, 1928, notes that there was now a nutrition clinic at the University of Minnesota because of the "diet fad." Also, *UCLA Daily,* "Best Way to Reduce," November 4, 1926; *Ohio State Lantern,* November 24, 1925, p. 1; LSU *Reveille,* May 15, 1926, p. 3 and February 10, 1928, p. 4.

42. For defense in terms of practicality, *Daily Illini,* October 8, 1920, letter to the editor, and *Daily Illini,* February 16, 1921. Also, Mary Alden Hopkins, "Woman's Rebellion Against Fashion," *New Republic,* 31 (August 16, 1922), 331–332.

43. See the letter to the editor, *Daily Illini,* April 20, 1922, by a "strictly Old-Fashioned Girl," which points out the association between modern fashions and the trend toward female participation in traditionally male pursuits. Objecting to modern dress, hair styles, and manners for women, the correspondent asserts, "After all, women's place is really in the home." By opposing the symbols of liberation, she voiced her opposition to the essence of that liberation and supported the old domestic ideal. For the new access between men and women in clerical professions and the effect on women's self-image, see Mary E. Adams, "Women in the Office: Business, Society, and Women's Role 1880–1930" (private manuscript, by permission of the author).

44. See the defense of sleeveless evening gowns in LSU *Reveille,* May 22, 1919.

45. For male reactions on aesthetic grounds, see *Daily Illini,* December 14, 1920, letter to the editor; Duke *Chronicle,* December 2, 1925, letter to the editor. At the University of California, men fought back against the public powdering by women by shaving in class; see *UCLA Daily,* March 17, 1926, p. 2.

At Duke, women were rouging and powdering so much in the school corridors that *The Chronicle* believed they were beginning to cause massive traffic jams; see February 11, 1925. One dean complained that the carpet in front of the hall mirror was being worn out by the constant trek of girls going to powder and rouge their faces; see *UCLA Daily,* January 16, 1920, p. 1. See also the comments of Dean Thomas Arkle Clark, "Painting the Lily," *Daily Illini,* December 12, 1920, "8 O'Clock" column.

46. See *UCLA Daily,* November 30, 1926, p. 3, a column on makeup which notes that sharp contrasts were going out of style.

47. John F. Cuber, "Changing Courtship and Marriage Customs," *Annals, AAPSS,* 229 (1943), 31.

48. Burgess, "Sociological Aspects," p. 124. See the formal approval of cosmetics used "in moderation" by the Woman's Affairs Committee of UCLA; *UCLA Daily,* November 21, 1924. The *Ohio State Lantern,* April 19, 1923, p. 1, contrasts the views of women about the effect of cosmetics on their appearance and that of professors. See also *Daily Illini,* April 26, 1922, letter to the editor, where a male correspondent denies that cosmetics have anything to do with morals. Too much makeup, he notes, has nothing to do with evil intent, but reflects deficient knowledge in the art of application. In general, this male correspondent concluded, makeup increases a woman's popularity. "The men seem to like it, for they respond to the women who use the cosmetics." In the *Daily Illini,* January 15, 1921, the editor points out that one reason women used cosmetics was that they would be at a competitive disadvantage with their sisters if they did not.

49. Quoted in Blanchard and Manasses, *New Girls,* p. 132; Blanchard and Manasses, p. 139. For cosmetics, clothes, and mother-daughter relationships, Eugenie Andruss Leonard, *Problems of Freshmen College Girls: A Study of Mother-Daughter Relationships and Social Adjustments of Girls Entering College,* Child Development Monographs, Teachers College, Columbia University (New York, 1932), p. 43.

At Union College, Nebraska, college officials passed rigid dress regulations and completely prohibited the use of cosmetics, having completely misread the girls' intentions; see *New Student,* April 4, 1925, p. 4. Union College was not a unique case of this kind of fear; an Arkansas coed was dismissed for using cosmetics; see *Daily Illini,* April 8, 1922. It is also not surprising that Catholic colleges should have had very strict rules which prohibited the wearing of various kinds of apparel and outlawed the use of cosmetics. This was true at the College of St. Elizabeth in New Jersey; see LSU *Reveille*, January 15, 1927, p. 4.

At the beginning of the decade, even coeds sometimes took offense at cosmetics. At Newcomb College (Tulane University), one coed shocked the woment's student council by proposing to limit the amount of cosmetics a woman could buy each semester. The response of the students is appropriate: "It strikes at a fundamental right. . . . It is unconstitutional, unnecessary, and impossible. . . . It could not possibly be enforced. Why, if we really wanted rouge, we would smuggle it in just as bootleggers do." See LSU *Reveille*, March 11, 1921, p. 3.

50. Duke *Chronicle*, November 25, 1925; *Ohio State Lantern*, February 5, 1925. See also the defense of women's clothes in the *Arkansas Weekly*, reprinted in LSU *Reveille*, January 16, 1920; *Chicago Daily Maroon*, reprinted in *Daily Illini*, January 31, 1922.

51. This duality of roles sometimes led to conflicting expectations. This appears especially to have been true in the South, where Southern "femininity" often found it difficult to adjust to the new "buddy" relationship. In an interesting editorial, the Duke editor took women to task for failing to take an adequate part in campus activities and for being unable to forget their sexual prerogatives and become equal with men. He asked that they give over older deferences and "for the time being . . . forget that they are women, especially Southern women—who expect Southern gentlemen to treat them accordingly." He asked women to live by the same standard as the men; see *The Chronicle*, September 23, 1925.

At Louisiana State, students and faculty voted against the Women's Suffrage Amendment in a college poll; see *The Reveille*, May 13, 1920. See also the editorial immediately after the time when women were granted the vote which warns women against going to extremes in behavior by becoming either "baby-doll" parasites or moral "reformers" (May 21, 1920). One correspondent also urged women to stick to teaching and shun business careers (May 21, 1920). But as the decade progressed, women even in this deep South school began actively to participate with men in school activities and functions, and editors here as at Duke demanded that they not use the old excuse of their femininity to shirk their equal responsibilities; see May 11, 1923.

52. *Barnard Bulletin*, November 26, 1920, p. 6; Eunice Fuller Barnard, "Our Colleges for Women: Co-ed or Not?" *New York Times Magazine* (March 26, 1933), p. 4.

53. *Daily Illini*, November 25, 1923; LSU *Reveille*, October 30, 1925, p. 4; Duke *Chronicle*, March 19, 1924; March 17, 1927. See also *Daily Illini*, "Male Flappers," November 11, 1922, and November 30, 1922; *Ohio State Lantern*, October 28, 1921, p. 1; *UCLA Daily*, September 28, 1923. At the

University of Chicago, men formed a "Five-Minute Egg Club" to enroll those males who refused to wear the perfume and to cultivate the effeminate manners they believed dominated male fashions; *Ohio State Lantern*, February 28, 1922.

54. Lounge-lizard was the most common of many phrases used to describe this species of smooth, almost rakish man; see *Daily Illini*, February 10, 1923, "Millicent Meows" column. Princeton men especially suffered from the association of their school with a country club and bore the opprobrium of the "tea-hound" appellation; *Daily Princetonian*, September 25, 1924. See also *Daily Illini*, January 6, 1923, "Jaundiced Eye"; *Ohio State Lantern*, January 14, 1926. The *Daily Illini* complained that the excessive attention that was given to cultivating female company threatened to deprive the campus of its air of male virility (May 14, 1922). At Princeton, the editor of the *Princetonian* scolded men for elevating a new campus goddess, woman, in place of the old god, athletics (April 7, 1924). For the "cooky pusher" and his manners, *Daily Illini*, February 10, 1923, "Millicent Meows."

For male fashions, see, for example, *Cornell Sun*, November 5, 1921, p. 8. In the middle of the decade there was a definite trend toward outdoorsman clothes, what was called the "lumberjack" style, complete with boots, corduroy trousers, wool or flannel shirts, sports coats, and sheepskin jackets; see *Ohio State Lantern*, December 12, 1923. The informality of day-time wear, as it was for women, was offset by the smooth elegance of evening wear—dinner jacket, black tie, and highly polished shoes—the costume of the debonair socializer.

55. Duke *Chronicle*, October 22, 1924. At Ohio State, a line was listed as one of the essential qualities coeds sought in a man; *Ohio State Lantern*, April 23, 1923, p. 1. See also *UCLA Daily*, April 14, 1926, which notes that women were, in turn, trying to impress their dates with their "naughtiness." But see the attack on the affectation of cynicism which lay behind male lines in *Daily Illini*, January 19, 1923 and December 15, 1922, "Millicent Meows."

56. See *UCLA Daily*, October 23, 1929.

CHAPTER 7

1. Quoted in D. E. Phillips, "The Jazz Age: Some Expressions of Opinion from the Young People Themselves," *Sunset*, 56 (March, 1926), 35.

2. For the heated debate about smoking in the early twenties, see, for example, the ongoing discussion in the letters-to-the-editor column of the *Daily Illini*, Spring, 1920, especially April 14, 15, 16, 1920, and the editorials of

April 15 and 17. Also, *Ohio State Lantern,* November 22, 1926; *Cornell Sun,* November 30, 1926, "Innocents Abroad."

3. *Ohio State Lantern,* November 30, 1925, p. 1; Dean of Rhode Island College, quoted in Duke *Chronicle,* December 17, 1924, "College Collections"; seminary incident cited in *Daily Illini,* April 14, 1920, letter to the editor. Dismissals or suspensions for smoking violations were frequent; see *New Student,* June 21, 1924, p. 6, for dismissal of three women at Smith College.

4. *UCLA Daily,* November 30, 1927, letter to the editor. See also *Daily Illini,* April 17, 1920, letter to the editor, which denounces the tendency of putting women on pedestals and links this idealization to smoking bans, and April 15, 1920, letter to the editor, which asserts that smoking undermines an ideal of "pure womanhood"; also remarks by the Dean of Women at Rhode Island State College, quoted in Duke *Chronicle,* December 17, 1924, "College Collections."

At UCLA the dean asserted, "The question is not is it right or is it wrong for women to smoke, but rather, does smoking on the campus cast reflections upon the good name of the University? While smoking among women is becoming more and more common, as yet it is not accepted by the mass of people as the correct thing to do. . . . It is the duty of the students to uphold the ideals of the mass of the people"; *UCLA Daily,* October 14, 1927.

5. Barnard College, for example, had more liberal rules than those at Bryn Mawr, but they had not been similarly publicized; see *Barnard Bulletin,* April 24, 1924. At M.I.T. women had been given permission to smoke just prior to the action at Bryn Mawr; see *New Student,* October 28, 1925. For rejection of petitions at Vassar and Wellesley, see *New Student,* January 19, 1924, December 9, 1925; *Daily Illini,* January 26, 1926.

6. *New Student,* January 31, 1925, p. 1, January 19, 1924, January 10, 1925, p. 3, January 21, 1925, p. 1; *Cornell Sun,* November 29, 1926, "Innocents Abroad." Vassar lifted the ban on smoking the next year on petition by students; see *Daily Princetonian,* March 2, 1926.

7. Quoted in *New Student,* December 9, 1925, p. 3; *New Student,* October 28, 1925; quoted in *New Student,* December 9, 1925, p. 3; quoted in Duke *Chronicle,* December 17, 1924, "College Collections"; quoted in *Ohio State Lantern,* November 30, 1925, p. 1; quoted in *New Student,* December 9, 1925, p. 3. For Eastern college meeting, see *New Student,* October 28, 1925. As early as 1921, smoking was one of the topics discussed at a conference of deans of Western colleges at Berkeley. The deans agreed that they should do something before the problem became "serious"; see, *LSU Reveille,* November 25, 1921, p. 7. By 1925, the problem had become serious; see *Ohio State Lantern,* November 30, 1925, p. 1.

8. *New Student,* November 18, 1925, p. 1.

9. *UCLA Daily,* February 18, 1927; Duke *Chronicle,* October 10, 1927, for Old Golds ad. For prevalence of smoking, see C. M. Whitlow, "Attitudes and Behavior of High School Students," *American Journal of Sociology,* 40 (1935), 492; R. H. Edwards, J. M. Artman and Galen Fisher, *Undergraduates* (Garden City, N.Y., 1928), p. 181; *Daily Illini,* November 10, 1925. Brogan found that the frequency of women's smoking and the permissive attitude toward smoking increased significantly at the University of Texas, but that permissiveness still lagged behind Northern institutions. At the University of Chicago, the habit was more common and approved earlier than at the Southern school. Smoking at Texas increased in frequency from fifteenth to tenth among bad practices among women between 1922 and 1924. See A. P. Brogan, "Group Estimates of the Frequency of Misconduct," *International Journal of Ethics,* 34 (1923–24), 259–260, 266–270. By 1927, *The Reveille* of Louisiana State University, a Deep-South school, was remarking that coeds were learning the habit of "bumming" cigarettes just like their brothers; see February 26, 1927.

10. For Ohio State, see *New Student,* December 19, 1925, p. 1. For similar results at Mt. Holyoke and Wellesley, *New Student,* November 18, 1925. For Bowdoin survey, *Cornell Sun,* February 22, 1927, "Innocents Abroad." Rhode Island State leader quoted in Duke *Chronicle,* December 17, 1924, "College Collections."

11. *Daily Illini,* November 10, 1925.

12. *Daily Illini,* April 12, 1924, letter to the editor; New York University incident reported in *UCLA Daily,* October 12, 1925; Phyllis Blanchard and Carlyn Manasses, *New Girls for Old* (New York, 1930), pp. 66, 68. In a referendum on smoking at Wellesley College, 80% of the women were in favor of allowing women to smoke; see *Daily Illini,* January 24, 1926.

13. *Daily Illini,* September 22, 1925; LSU *Reveille,* March 9, 1928. For lost male prerogative, see, for example, *UCLA Daily,* November 17, 1922; *Cornell Sun,* January 17, 1925, January 9, 1926; LSU *Reveille,* November 13, 1925. See also the interview of LSU cadets on the question of women's smoking in *The Reveille,* December 1, 1925, p. 5. On the whole, the attitudes were of humorous condescension and objections were largely limited to the fear that coeds would soon be bumming cigarettes. No one was morally outraged.

For general approval by male editors, see *Daily Princetonian,* March 2, 1926; *Daily Illini,* September 22, 1925, March 11, 1921. Also LSU *Reveille,* March 9, 1928, which links banning smoking with banning drinking. In fact, all smoking, for men as well as women, was prohibited at Syracuse early in the decade; see *Cornell Sun,* March 14, 1921. Most editors believed that women had a right to smoke but some still asserted that "most of them smoke simply because it has come to be considered smart and the thing to do. With them it is incense burned in worship of the god of fashion"; *Ohio State Lantern*, November 22, 1926.

14. *Daily Illini*, April 14, 1920, letter to the editor; *Ohio State Lantern*, August 19, 1925; *Barnard Bulletin*, February 24, 1922. At Rhode Island State College, students circulated a petition of remonstrance against school authorities who had dismissed coeds for smoking. The action, students believed, was patently unjust because it punished women for what male students could do with impunity; see Duke *Chronicle*, December 17, 1924, "College Collections."

15. Blanchard and Manasses, *New Girls*, p. 2; Eunice Fuller Barnard, "The New Freedom of the College Girl," *New York Times Magazine* (March 19, 1933), p. 8. See also "Youth in College," *Fortune*, 13 (1936) 99–102. According to Walter Buck, the decrease in the disapproval of smoking for women between 1923 and 1933 was significant, a change of 20%. Moreover, this was true of under-classmen, freshmen and sophomores, as well as seniors and juniors, indicating that the new approbation was already incorporated into the mores of high-school students; see "A Measurement of Changes in Attitudes and Interests of University Students Over a Ten-Year Period," *Journal of Abnormal and Social Psychology*, 31 (1936), 16. Brogan found that although there was a decided decline in the tendency to differentiate between what was bad for women and men, the double standard still lingered. Smoking, for example, was at all times still considered worse for women than for men, but the differences were narrowing; see A. P. Brogan, "Moral Valuations About Men and Women," *International Journal of Ethics*, 35 (1925), 120–121.

16. See the *Daily Illini*, April 14, 1925, letter to the editor: "Every girl likes to appear just a bit daring and just a bit worse than she really is. To pretend a thing is not immoral yet unconventional is to invite her to do one of the things she likes best; breaking the conventions."

A history could be written about the changes in cigarette advertisements. Where at the beginning of the decade photos showed women in the same room while men smoked, by the end of the decade women were not only smoking themselves, but many ads concentrated on the act of men offering or lighting women's cigarettes. There were constant overtones of sexual intimacy. The association between cigarettes and sexuality was not overlooked by the advertisers. One ad for Camels (in the *American Mercury*) featured two young couples, in the chic Fitzgerald-Zelda manner, in close proximity, with the provocative title, "Pleasure Ahead," and continued, "Those who love life for its own sake instinctively choose the cigarette which gives them the greatest pleasure." By the late twenties, women, often starlets, were used as spokesmen for the cigarette brands and their sexual and languorous manners usually implied much more than that they merely indulged a taste for tobacco.

17. See petition by denominational University of Richmond students, in the Duke *Chronicle,* April 14, 1926, "Wayside Wares"; also, F. W. Reeves, *The Liberal Art Colleges* (Chicago, 1932), p. 403. At Duke, students voted overwhelmingly, 704 to 6, for university-sponsored dances; *The Chronicle,* December 1, 1926. Despite this, however, the Methodist board of governors refused to lift the official ban against the school sponsoring such events; see March 30, 1927. For popularity of dancing, see Blanchard and Manasses, *New Girls,* p. 16; Robert Cooley Angell, *The Campus* (New York, 1928), p. 165; Edwards *et al., Undergraduates,* pp. 185–189. The investigators called dancing "the chief social diversion of college men and women" (p. 185). Newspaper after newspaper documents the fact that dancing was an invariable part of college life. At the University of Wisconsin, there were approximately 30 all-college dances and 80 fraternity dances sponsored each month; see *New Student,* January 31, 1925. The *Daily Illini* editor scolded students at the University of Michigan for permitting their dance fervor to interfere with attendance at a football game, both the dance and the game being scheduled for the same day; see February 14, 1923. See also the statement by the Dean of the University of Kansas in the Duke *Chronicle,* November 13, 1924, "College Collections."

The popularity of dancing was by no means restricted to the colleges. High-school students were avid disciples of the dance craze. In general, more girls than boys danced. According to Whitlow, of 623 students at a high school in Cheyenne Wells, Colorado, 53% of the girls and 27% of the boys danced frequently, and 32% of the girls and 29% of the boys danced occasionally; "Attitudes and Behavior of High School Students," 493.

Even by the 1930's, although the frequency of dancing had subsided, the popularity remained strong. Dancing was still the most desirable kind of social recreation. See Robert C. Angell, "The Trend Toward Greater Maturity Among Undergraduates Due to the Depression," *School and Society,* 38 (1932), 394.

Of all morally "bad" practices, dancing was consistently ranked least bad by men and women in Brogan's studies; see A. P. Brogan, "A Study of Statistical Ethics," *International Journal of Ethics,* 33 (1922–1923), 122–126. It was also the most frequently indulged by women, second only to gossip; see Brogan, "Group Estimates," 259. Among men, its frequency was slightly lower (262). See also Joseph K. Johnson and Kingsley Davis, "An Attempt to Discvoer Change in Moral Attitudes of High School Students," *International Journal of Ethics,* 44 (1934), 244–251. According to the investigators, dancing was ranked least bad of all practices among high-school students throughout the period 1926–1932.

18. The city of Syracuse prohibited jazz bands and jazz dancing; see *Cornell Sun,* February 22, 1921, p. 1. So did East St. Louis; see *Daily Illini,* February 8, 1921, p. 1. At Columbus, Ohio, the city appointed a dance censor in the

early twenties; see *Ohio State Lantern*, February 9, 1920. He was reported to be aghast at the fact that the "majority of boys and girls were dancing cheek-to-cheek." See also the rumpus caused by cheek-to-cheek dancing at Louisiana State, *The Reveille*, May 5, 1919.

19. See the cartoon, *Cornell Sun*, May 21, 1921; *Ohio State Lantern*, January 12, 1920. The jazz lingo was catchy and used in youth parlance for a variety of descriptions other than music. To call someone jazzy or snappy was a mark of approval. At UCLA, things highly favored were called "jazzy," at Ohio State, "snappy" or "peppy." On the enormous popularity of jazz, see *Ohio State Lantern*, January 12, 1920, November 30, 1920.

20. Edwards *et al.*, *Undergraduates*, p. 185; quoted in *UCLA Daily*, October 23, 1929. For dancing and the high-school girl, see Margaret V. Kiely, "The Significance of the Dean to the High School Girl," *Seventh Yearbook, NASSP*, 1923, p. 115. Among the requirements listed by coeds at Ohio State as basic to their ideal man was the ability to dance well; see *Ohio State Lantern*, April 25, 1923, p. 1. University of Washington women noted that in order to be popular one had to know how to dance; see *UCLA Daily*, March 15, 1929. See also *Daily Nebraskan*, reprinted in *Daily Illini*, October 19, 1921. The dean at Ohio State said that she often feared that girls would marry men simply because they were such wonderful dancers without considering their other qualifications; see *Ohio State Lantern*, April 26, 1921.

In instructing potential freshmen about the situation they could expect to find when they arrived at college, Kate W. Jameson and F. C. Lockwood, *The Freshman Girl* (New York, 1925), noted that "of fundamental importance to the girl in her relations with the men of the community are problems in dancing" (p. 93). At the University of Minnesota, "practically all evening parties are dancing parties," according to Jessie S. Ladd, "Recreation and the University Mixer," NEA *Proceedings*, 1922, p. 733.

21. The editor of the *Ohio State Lantern*, September 19, 1919, noted that city officials were issuing orders against certain kinds of dancing: "No more of this snuggling up and dreaming around the room; no more shimmying and shivering to nervous music; no more of this head-to-head business. Actually, it is demanded that there be some air space between the people who are doing the dancing. Isn't it cruel? What's to become of the evenings of those accustomed to cheek-to-cheek to a soothing sea of jazz?" At Smith College, girls were forbidden to practice the charleston in their dorm rooms because it was disturbing so many girls. At the State College for Women in Atlanta, Georgia, a floor caved in when 500 girls tried furiously to learn the latest dance steps, but at Oberlin College the dance was already taught in gym classes; see *New Student*, January 27, 1926, pp. 1, 3; also *Daily Princetonian*, January 25, 1926. At the University of Kansas, a move was under way to have

the latest steps taught in class; see Duke *Chronicle,* November 13, 1924, "College Collections." For the fast-paced changes in dancing, see LSU *Reveille,* June 18, 1927.

22. *Daily Illini,* December 19, 1920, January 22, 1921. The Women's League at Illinois, for example, reacted to the warnings of school officials by requesting the presidents of fraternities and sororities and the captains of other residence units (for unorganized students) to carry the message to their groups in order to insure that the extreme steps would be avoided; see *Daily Illini,* October 13, 1920. Later in the same year, the Women's Panhellenic at Illinois (an inter-sorority council) put a ban on "improper dancing" and called for the raising of standards and an end to the lights-out policy; see April 14, 1920, p. 1.

23. *Daily Illini,* December 21, 1920, letter to the editor; May 10, 1921, p. 1. See also the response to "Dad Elliott," who called dancing in college "one of the greatest menaces to the moral standards of our young people"; October 3, 1922.

24. Jingle in *Daily Illini,* April 20, 1920; *Daily Illini,* February 18, 1921, letter to the editor; January 22, 1921; *Ohio State Lantern,* November 30, 1920. See also *Ohio State Lantern,* January 24, 1922, January 12, 1920; Duke *Chronicle,* October 13, 1926.

25. *Ohio State Lantern,* February 10, 1920; *UCLA Daily,* December 14, 1923; LSU *Reveille,* February 13, 1920, p. 1, and editorial; Duke *Chronicle,* March 30, 1927.

26. Quoted in Ladd, "University Mixer," p. 735; *Ohio State Lantern,* February 11, 1920. See also *UCLA Daily,* December 21, 1921. Many feared that other immoral behavior, including petting and drinking, went along with the dancing; see, for example, *Cornell Sun,* March 24, 1926; LSU *Reveille,* November 2, 1928.

27. *Daily Illini,* October 15, 1920; LSU *Reveille,* June 2, 1926.

28. *Ohio State Lantern,* January 9, 1922, p. 1 (my italics).

29. *Ohio State Lantern,* January 11, 1922, p. 1 (my italics).

30. *Daily Illini,* February 15, 1921, letter to the editor. See also Duke *Chronicle,* February 23, 1926, letter to the editor; *Daily Princetonian,* January 22, 1927.

31. For the Michigan incident, see *Cornell Sun,* December 18, 1926. Officials at Michigan also called on federal authorities to inspect fraternity houses; see *UCLA Daily,* November 2, 1928. According to Brogan, "Group Estimates," 256, drinking had increased among male students between 1919 and 1922. Dean Clark of Illinois believed, "There is no question but that there is drinking among college students, both men and women. . . . I don't believe that there is any more than before Prohibition"; quoted in *Cornell Sun,*

November 9, 1926, "Innocents Abroad." For the opinions of other adminis-
trators, see "College Student Drinking Since Prohibition," *Literary Digest,* 90
(July 10, 1926), 30–31; also Alfred E. Stearns, "Liquor and the Schools,"
Harper's, 153 (1926), 773–778. But see also the comments by the *UCLA
Daily,* July 20, 1926, LSU *Reveille,* February 3, 1926, and the *Daily Prince-
tonian,* November 5, 1926 criticizing officials for trying to hide the truth
from the public. For some student dismissals for drinking, see *Cornell Sun,*
March 25, 1920, p. 1; Duke *Chronicle,* February 17, 1926; LSU *Reveille,*
March 3, 1926.

32. *U.S. Congress, House Committee on the Judiciary,* "Hearings on the Prohibition Amendment," 71st Congress, 2nd Session, 1930, Part 3, pp. 1456,
1453, 1451; Table 4, p. 1299. See also J. H. Barnett, "College Seniors and
the Liquor Problem," *Annals, AAPSS,* 163 (1932), 130–146, for similar
results of another poll.

33. *Cornell Sun,* November 14, 1921; reported in *Daily Illini,* December 1,
1923. For the decline in drinking see, for example, *Daily Illini,* October 6,
1923, October 10, 1924; *Cornell Sun,* January 18, 1923, December 16, 1922;
Daily Princetonian, May 13, 1924; *Ohio State Lantern,* December 5, 1922; *New
Student,* December 30, 1922, p. 3. By 1923, however, the *Cornell Sun* already
predicted that Spring Day activities would be wet; see May 11, 1923.

In 1924, the fraternities at Louisiana State unanimously pledged to "ban
drinking at all dances" and "to report violations of the pledge"; see *The Reveille,* April 11, 1924, p. 1. The editor noted, "That this movement comes
from the students is to be highly commended. It is the only way in which
drinking may be stopped at L.S.U."; April 11, 1924. Another campaign was
manned by the fraternities at LSU in 1926; see February 6, 1926, p. 1.

At Trinity-Duke, the administration blamed the student self-government
association for failing to halt drinking on the campus, but the editor of *The
Chronicle* noted that this was grossly unfair since the association was not only
diligently doing its best to gain the cooperation of students, but because
drinking had, in fact, decreased since the students took control; see February
17, 1926.

34. *Cornell Sun,* January 14, 1921; *Daily Princetonian,* January 15, 1926.
Also *Cornell Sun,* January 29, 1926; December 12, 1922. On January 25,
1924, the *Daily Princetonian* declared, "Prohibition, like a new car, takes time
to be broken in." But the *Daily Princetonian,* like most papers, was soon to
despair of the experiment.

35. See *Daily Illini,* March 31, 1922; Duke *Chronicle,* December 16, 1925,
"Wayside Wares," for statement by North Carolina *Tar Heel* editor.

36. *Daily Princetonian,* February 16, 1927; *Cornell Sun,* October 23, 1923.

37. For the attempt to suppress Prohibition jokes, see *Cornell Sun,* November 3, 1925.

38. *Daily Illini*, November 3, 1920; November 2, 1920, letter to the editor.

39. *Cornell Sun*, January 31, 1921; *Ohio State Lantern*, January 18, 1921; Duke *Chronicle*, April 2, 1924; *Ohio State Lantern*, October 27, 1921; Duke *Chronicle*, November 28, 1923; *Cornell Sun*, January 13, 1921. See also *Daily Illini*, January 25, 1921.

40. See *Ohio State Lantern*, October 15, 1926; *Daily Illini*, December 15, 1922 and January 11, 1923, "Millicent Meows."

41. *Cornell Sun*, October 29, 1921; December 3, 1921; Wisconsin protest reported in *Daily Illini*, November 18, 1923. For "proper" drinking form, see *Daily Illini*, November 10, 1921.

Drinking by women in the early twenties was rarely considered a problem; see, for example, Edwards *et al.*, *Undergraduates*, pp. 183–185. In Brogan's study of the University of Texas, men and women agreed that drinking was very uncommon among women, and women disapproved of drinking much more strongly than did men; "Group Estimates," 257. In addition, both men and women believed that it was worse for women to drink than for men to do so; "Moral Valuations," 105, 108, 111. Drinking was believed to be an almost exclusively male problem; "Group Estimates," 262. At the University of Chicago, the double standard with regard to drinking was still effective, although it was waning more rapidly than at Texas; Brogan, "Moral Valuations," 121. Students at Syracuse University considered drinking for women far worse than for men; in fact, of all female offenses, this received the greatest condemnation. Seventy-four per cent of the students believed that it was worse for women than for men; Daniel Katz and Floyd H. Allport, *Students' Attitudes* (Syracuse, N.Y., 1931), p. 253. See also the responses from editors at women's schools, in "College-Student Editors on College Drinking," *Literary Digest*, 90 (July 17, 1926), 24–25, and the views about the situation at women's schools by administrators in "College Student Drinking," *passim*.

42. *Daily Illini*, November 10, 1921.

43. *Cornell Sun*, October 25, 1920; *The Dartmouth*, reprinted in LSU *Reveille*, March 22, 1929. See also Duke *Chronicle*, April 13, 1927, where the editor asks students to think of their school before engaging in the drunken displays common at vacation time: "Every vacation is . . . marked by a great amount of drinking among college boys. Now if the boys must drink, we suggest that he [*sic*] do so privately, and not get out and advertise his university by getting gloriously drunk in public." See also the comments by Dean Ames of Johns Hopkins on the smartness of drinking, in "College Student Drinking," 69. For the new drinking ethic, see *Cornell Sun*, February 22, 1927, "Innocents Abroad"; *Daily Illini*, March 26, 1928.

44. *Cornell Sun*, January 10, 1927, "Innocents Abroad"; Duke *Chronicle*, March 26, 1924; *Daily Texan*, reprinted in *Daily Illini*, March 26, 1926.

45. Quoted in Edwards *et al.*, *Undergraduates*, p. 182; cited in *Daily Princetonian*, December 3, 1926; *Daily Illini*, May 13, 1926; Duke *Chronicle*, January 13, 1926, p. 1; quoted in *UCLA Daily*, November 2, 1928. See also *Cornell Sun*, November 23, 1921; Clarence C. Little, *The Awakening College* (New York, 1930), pp. 96–97. In 1925, the President of Duke cancelled all dancing until after Easter because of the amount of drinking which had taken place at fraternities during the Thanksgiving week dances; see *The Chronicle*, January 13, 1925, p. 1. At Louisiana State, after repeated attempts to deal with the problem of liquor at dances the authorities cancelled all off-campus dances (usually fraternity dances at LSU) and once again called on fraternities to deal with the situation; see *The Reveille*, November 2, 1928. The appeal to fraternities took place several times during the decade at LSU.

46. *New Student*, April 28, 1926, p. 1.

47. *Harvard Crimson*, reprinted in *Daily Illini*, April 14, 1920; *Cornell Sun*, March 24, 1926; *Daily Princetonian*, January 25, 1925, for Yale; *Daily Princetonian*, May 7, 1926, p. 1, and May 24, 1926, for Princeton; *Daily Illini*, April 14, 1926, p. 1; "College-Student Editors," 50, for Ohio Wesleyan; LSU *Reveille*, February 24, 1926, p. 1, for Midwest and South Convention statement.

48. "Hearings," pp. 1456, 1299, 1453; "Poll in 10 Colleges is 95% Wet," *New York Times*, June 1, 1932. Conducted by Princeton Publications, the poll was of the following schools: Amherst, Bryn Mawr, Dartmouth, Harvard, University of Pennsylvania, Princeton, Sarah Lawrence, Smith, Wellesley, and Vassar.

49. *Daily Princetonian*, April 28, 1926, p. 1; *Wisconsin Daily Cardinal*, reprinted in Ohio State Lantern, October 15, 1926.

50. *Daily Illini*, March 31, 1922; *Wisconsin Daily Cardinal*, reprinted in *Ohio State Lantern*, October 15, 1926. See also the remarks of Dean Clark of Illinois, in *Daily Illini*, February 20, 1921, "8 O'Clock" column. But see especially the letter to the editor by a Trinity-Duke student informing the editor that he was going to get drunk and would like everyone to know about it: "My ma, you know, always wanted me to be in the fashion; . . . its the fashion to or rather its not the fashion to drink water at Trinity. . . . I have preserved that all the I Ate A Pie [a pun on fraternity letters] men and also the Pie Betty Cap A men get drunk, and if they do I guess its the fashion." *The Chronicle*, February 24, 1924, letter to the editor.

51. For example, *Daily Illini*, September 8, 1925; *UCLA Daily*, December 2, 1929; Duke *Chronicle*, December 16, 1925, "Wayside Wares." The editor of the North Carolina *Tar Heel* noted that "students have no precedent against drinking because public opinion in North Carolina sets no precedent against drinking"; quoted in Duke *Chronicle*, December 16, 1925, "Wayside Wares."

52. Duke *Chronicle,* March 26, 1924.
53. Duke *Chronicle,* October 3, 1923.

CHAPTER 8

1. See Joseph Gusfield, *Symbolic Crusade* (Urbana, Ill., 1963); Andrew Sinclair, *Prohibition: The Era of Excess* (Boston, 1962).

2. See Stuart M. Stoke and Elmer D. West, "The Conversational Interests of College Students," *School and Society,* 32 (1930), 567–570.

3. *Daily Illini,* March 9, 1921; *Cornell Sun,* April 23, 1923. See also *Daily Illini,* February 9, 1924, which called Wilson the greatest president since Lincoln; *Cornell Sun,* February 6, 1924; Duke *Chronicle,* February 6, 1924; *Daily Princetonian,* February 4, 1924, and the discussion of Wilson in an editorial on Davis' foreign policy, October 4, 1924.

4. At Cornell, for example, a large number of students voted in one such poll (2314). Of these, 924 voted for straight ratification, 464 for the Lodge reservations, 700 for compromises, and 227 against the League (*Cornell Sun,* January 14, 1920, p. 1). At Trinity-Duke, students favored the League two to one in a poll which had a large turnout of students (*The Chronicle,* January 14, 1920). Harvard, Princeton, and Brown voted for the League with amendments, each school showing a large voter turnout (*Cornell Sun,* January 14, 1920, p. 1). But at Illinois the turnout was light, and the Wilson League was turned down, five to one, and barely approved with reservations (*Daily Illini,* October 29, 1920, p. 1). At Ohio State, there was a very small voter turnout, and the League carried two to one, 256 to 121. Many who voted on other issues at the same poll did not register an opinion on this matter, and the editor noted that students appeared not "enough interested in the matter to care whether the United States entered the League" (*Ohio State Lantern,* November 3, 1919). A later poll at the same school turned out a much larger vote, with the largest single response calling for a declaration of peace without the League (January 14, 1920). At Louisiana State, only 200 students out of 1000 turned out to vote; the League carried without amendments or reservations (*The Reveille,* January 23, 1920, p. 1). See also the complaint by the editor of *The Reveille,* February 16, 1920, that students lacked interest in national and international affairs.

Princeton initiated a call for a student disarmament conference, which was held in 1921; see *Cornell Sun,* October 7, 1921. There was also a disarmament conference held by delegates from 22 women's colleges; see *Barnard Bulletin,* October 28, 1921, p. 1. See *New Student,* April 19, 1922, p. 1, for a discussion of the organization; also, John Rothschild's account, "Retrospect, Fore-

School	Straight League	Lodge Reserves	No League	Compromises
Barnard	194	57	45	164 *
Amherst	132	26	69	94 *
Massachusetts	131	9	69	109 *
Western Reserve	203	119	201	820 *
Boston	3	113	578	16 **
Mt. Holyoke	70	6	30	670 *
Smith	305	14	159	1149 *
Colby	40	12	42	111 *
Bowdoin	. 48	5	72	254 *
Beloit	—	6	—	56 **
Dickinson	85	1	195	41 **
Pittsburgh	211	95	242	123 ꞊
Wisconsin	563	312	609	0 **
Buffalo	0	3	398	72 **
Northwestern	113	11	38	91 *
Michigan	924	227	464	700 *
Pennsylvania	341	223	323	235 *
Swarthmore	85	11	85	11 ꞊
Georgia	472	35	154	56 *
South Carolina	159	3	10	60 *
Lafayette	69	22	43	223 *

* indicates that the League was carried; i.e., the total of votes for the straight League or with compromises was in the majority.
** indicates that the League was defeated; i.e., No League and Lodge Reservations are in the majority.
꞊ indicates an approximately equal division.

cast, and a Personal Confession," *New Student,* February 2, 1923, pp. 1–2.

The *Barnard Bulletin* published a list of the League vote at 46 schools (January 16, 1920, p. 3). The above table is selected from that source.

5. *Ohio State Lantern,* November 3, 1919. At the University of Illinois, more students turned out to vote on a proposed new athletic stadium than on the League issue; see *Daily Illini,* December 10, 1920. According to the *Cornell Sun,* December 13, 1919, students were ignorant of the relative merits of the different proposals and the "peace treaty has occupied only a slight place in Cornell conversations." See also *Daily Illini,* October 21, 1920.

6. *Daily Illini,* April 14, 1921. Syracuse and Wisconsin incidents reported in *Cornell Sun,* October 22, 1919, May 21, 1923. When Louisiana State was forced to cancel a planned conference on the World Court because of the lack of student interest, the editor was forced to ask, "Do our small minds prefer the Charleston to the World Court?" (*The Reveille,* December 4, 1925). At LSU, as elsewhere, the answer was yes.

7. *Cornell Sun,* October 7, 1921. See also the editorial in the *Daily Illini,* January 3, 1926, which praises the noble ideals expressed at the Evanston Interdenominational Student Conference but doubts that all the talk about student opposition to war could ever effect any kind of change. This is not to imply that the original impulse to express student opposition to war did not gather some momentum. Pennsylvania State University, for example, urged that undergraduate opinion on the matter be ascertained and the results submitted to the conferees in Washington. The *Cornell Sun* considered this a feasible proposal, much more so than that of the Princeton conference which, the editor believed, would only express the views of the delegates (October 11, 1921).

8. *Daily Illini,* October 18, 1921, October 22, 1921. See also *Cornell Sun,* October 26, 1921.

9. Quoted in Duke *Chronicle,* March 1, 1922. For Bok Peace Prize, see *New Student,* February 16, 1924; *Ohio State Lantern,* January 18, 1924; Duke *Chronicle,* December 13, 1924, p. 1. The *Ohio State Lantern,* December 11, 1925, p. 1, reported an astonishing turnout on the World Court poll, 4113 ballots. Of these, 3568 favored and only 545 opposed United States cooperation in the international organization. See also *Cornell Sun,* December 5, 1925; *UCLA Daily,* December 4 and 5, 1925, which gave the Court substantial coverage. The poll on the World Court appears to have been one of the most successful in UCLA history (*UCLA Daily,* January 7, 1926). But see also the editorial by the *Yale Daily News* opposing the proposal for U.S. participation in the World Court, reprinted in Duke *Chronicle,* December 2, 1925, and a similar sentiment by the Duke editor on December 16, 1925.

10. See Heber Reece Harper, *What European and American Students Think on International Problems: A Contemporary Study of the World-Mindedness of University Students,* Contributions to Education, Teachers College, Columbia University (New York, 1931). Also, George Vetter, "The Measurement of Social and Political Attitudes and the Related Personality Factors," *Journal of Abnormal and Social Psychology,* 25 (1930), 162, question 34; G. A. Lundberg, "Sex Differences on Social Questions," *School and Society,* 23 (1926), 595–600, question 20; W. J. Boldt and J. B. Stroud, "Changes in the Attitudes of College Students," *Journal of Educational Psychology,* 25 (1934), Table 4, 616; K. C. Garrison and Margaret Mann, "A Study of the Opinions of College Students,"

Journal of Social Psychology, 2 (1931), 172; Hilding B. Carlson, "Attitudes of Undergraduate Students," *Journal of Social Psychology,* 5 (1934), 202–213; Genevieve Sowards, "A Study of the War Attitudes of College Students," *Journal of Abnormal and Social Psychology,* 29 (1934), 329, who found that attending college increased the tendency toward pacifism; and Gwyn Moore and Karl C. Garrison, "A Comparative Study of Social and Political Attitudes of College Students," *Journal of Abnormal and Social Psychology,* 27 (1932), 195–208.

For the contrary view about young adults and children, see R. C. Peterson and Louis Leon Thurstone, *Motion Pictures and the Social Attitudes of Children* (New York, 1933), pp. 10–11. For high-school youths, Robert Frederick, "An Investigation into Some Social Attitudes of High-School Pupils," *School and Society,* 25 (1927), 411–412, who claimed that high-school youths demonstrated a rigid patriotism lacking in intelligence. For a good discussion of the strong nationalist sentiments of high-school youths and their general internationalist views, see George B. Neumann, *A Study of International Attitudes of High School Students,* Contributions to Education, Teachers College, Columbia University (New York, 1926). Neumann believed that high-school students showed a general satisfaction with American foreign policy as it was (p. 50) and that although they were internationally oriented, their nationalism got in the way of a full expression of humanistic impulses and international viewpoints (p. 56).

11. Oliver La Farge, "Colleges and War," *Scribner's,* 78 (1925), 13, 17.

12. For the Indianapolis Convention, see *New Student,* January 19, 1924, pp. 1–2, March 15, 1924, p. 2. For a report on the conference, Milton T. Stouffer, ed., *Christian Students and World Problems,* Report of the 9th International Convention of the Student Volunteer Movement for Foreign Missions, Indianapolis, Indiana, December 28, 1923 to January 1, 1924 (New York, 1924), pp. 238–255; for the discussion groups, see pp. 229–233. For the vote on the war issue at the succeeding convention at Milwaukee in 1926–1927, Frances P. Miller, ed., *Religion on the Campus,* The Report of the National Student Conference, Milwaukee, December 28, 1926 to January 1, 1927 (New York, 1927), p. 194.

For action of Methodist students, see *New Student,* May 10, 1924, p. 2; also, article by Stanley High in same issue, p. 3. For Evanston Conference, *Daily Illini,* January 3, 1926. See also the report of the conference, *Youth Looks at the Church,* National Interdenominational Student Conference, Evanston, Illinois, December 29, 1925–January 1, 1926 (New York, 1926). For the strong anti-war position, see p. 177. For the Garrett pledge, see *Daily Illini,* April 4, 1924; *New Student,* May 10, 1924, p. 5. For some of the reactions to the pledge, *New Student,* June 21, 1924, p. 10, and April 12, 1924, p. 3. When the 38 Garrett students voted to refuse service in the military in case of war, the officials of Northwestern University reacted in anxious anger with a vehement denial that the group represented the view of the majority of students; see *Daily Illini*, March 26, 1924, p. 1. Also, in response a large number of Northwestern students turned out in a massive patriotic rally; see *Daily Illini*, April 9, 1924 and April 14, 1924. For Missouri students, *Cornell Sun*, November 18, 1924. For the organization of a pacifist group at Syracuse University, *New Student*, June 21, 1924, p. 1. For Chicago-Northwestern meeting, *New Student*, June 2, 1923, p. 4. See also the pledge by Vassar College students to do everything possible to oppose war; *New Student*, April 3, 1923.

13. For link between pacifism and Christian idealism, see, for example, "Compulsory Military Training in Colleges," by A Sophomore, *New Student*, January 13, 1923, p. 1; also the views of the Methodist students, *New Student*, May 10, 1924, p. 2, for the link to Christian idealism. For the resignation of a pre-ministerial student at Syracuse because of his refusal to cooperate with the ROTC, see *New Student*, March 15, 1924, p. 2. For the dismissal of a student at the University of California for failure to comply with military training regulations, *New Student*, December 2, 1925, p. 3.

The Des Moines and Indianapolis conventions and reorganization of Student Volunteers is discussed by W. H. Morgan, *Student Religion During Fifty Years* (New York, 1935), pp. 133–141, 154, and The Student Department of the National Council of YMCAs, Report, 1924–25, *American Students and the Christian Way of Life*, pp. iii, 1–2, in which Walter Judd, the chairman, declares, "This *is* a student convention." The title of the Indianapolis conference volume reflected the new activist emphasis—*Christian Students and World Problems*. See the introduction and especially the description of the informal discussion groups which all dealt with social issues, pp. 229–270. By the time of the Milwaukee convention (1926–27), the conference was no longer sponsored by the Student Volunteers; see the report of the conference, *Religion on the Campus, passim*. For topics discussed in Milwaukee, see Morgan, *Student Religion*, p. 156n. Although 327 students at Milwaukee took the pacifist position, the overall vote was much smaller than at the conference in Indianapolis; *Religion on the Campus*, p. 194. For declining student interest in the convention, see Morgan, *Student Religion*, p. 176.

14. York Lucci, *The YMCA on the Campus*, Bureau of Applied Social Research (New York, 1960), p. 11; Stanley High, in *Youth Looks at the Church*, introduction. High was interested in world youth movements; see his description of the European scene in *The Revolt of Youth* (New York, 1923).

15. See, for example, *Religion on the Campus*, pp. 185–186; and the statement by Kirby Page in the same volume, p. 108.

16. *New Student*, April 19, 1922, pp. 2, 3, 7, February 24, 1923, p. 4, October 6, 1923, p. 4. Also, *Cornell Sun*, April 4, 1921, p. 1.

17. See, for example, *New Student*, March 10, 1923. The emphasis and di-

rection of student cooperation was especially strong during the early years of publication when it had a traveling editor in Europe, first John Rothschild and then George Platt, who reported on conditions and developments among European students. See, for example, October 7, 1922, p. 1; and November 4, 1922. The *New Student* also carried a running account of the ideals and postwar hardships of students in Europe; for example, Henry Israel, November 18, 1922, p. 5, and the special issues like March 3, 1923 and December 20, 1924. The YMCA also sought to promote international student fellowship on Christian grounds and often sponsored student relief and fellowship funds. See, for example, *New Student,* January 19, 1924, p. 7.

18. *New Student,* October 6, 1923, p. 4.

19. *Daily Illini,* May 7, 1925; *Cornell Sun,* November 18, 1924; *Daily Illini,* April 4, 1924; Duke *Chronicle,* January 9, 1924, p. 1. In one editorial, the *Illini,* March 29, 1924, asserted that there were many tasks students could perform at "quietly and thoroughly without interference with the government under whose protection he is privileged to live and study. Liberal education will play an important factor in world brotherhood when such a state does arrive. Until such a time *it does not seem sensible to trust blindly to the good will of other nations toward the United States* when many of them have standards of education far below the level of our own" (my italics).

For an example of letters condemning pacifism, see *Daily Illini,* January 12, 1924. The controversy raged in the letters-to-the-editor column for more than a week; see, for example, January 5, 1924. The editor finally proclaimed an end to the issue on January 13, 1924, but it reappeared; see April 8, 1924. See also the astonishing letter of April 25, 1924 which asserts that Christ himself was a militarist.

20. *Daily Illini,* April 4, 1924; see also April 22, 1924. *Ohio State Lantern,* April 3, 1924. See also *UCLA Daily,* November 11, 1924, which asserts that the world is not yet rational so there continues a need for national preparedness "to resist aggression on the part of other nations."

21. See the editorial in the *Ohio State Lantern,* December 11, 1925, which condemns America for its selfish aloofness: "Our state of mind is shown in the case of the League of Nations and the World Court. America doesn't consider what is best for the world. America considers what is best for herself. The United States tells all other peoples to go hang." For the general spirit of internationalism, *Daily Illini,* March 28, 1922. See also Lundberg, "Sex Differences," 597, question 20; Vetter, "Social and Political Attitudes," 162, question 34. Vetter found that the majority of students at the three universities took a liberal-centrist position—advocating cooperation with the international organizations but not so as to endanger American safety. For related studies, see note 10 above.

22. The vote at City College was 2049 opposed to compulsory drill to 349 supporting. See Joseph P. Lash, *The Campus Strikes Against War,* Student League for Industrial Democracy (New York, 1935). Also *Ohio State Lantern,* December 11, 1925; *Cornell Sun,* November 27, 1925; *Daily Illini,* December 31, 1925. Many newspapers began to sponsor polls after the CCNY incident. One such poll at Ohio State resulted in a vote of 1099 opposed to 701 in favor of drill, with one-third of the student body voting; *Ohio State Lantern,* January 22, 1926. Anti-ROTC clubs and organizations began to form at various schools to urge the abolition of the requirement. See, for example, *UCLA Daily,* January 5, 1926. At Louisiana State, *The Reveille* recorded that students had begun to debate the issue and attended the various lectures which presented the issues pro and con. By 1927, *The Reveille* noted, the "overwhelming majority would be in favor of abolishing the compulsory feature of the University's military training" (March 12, 1927); this at a school which had long been a military training academy and was affectionately known to its students as "The Old War Skule."

23. For early reactions to ROTC, see, for example, *Cornell Sun,* January 10, 1921, March 9, 1922, December 13, 1922. In an editorial of October 18, 1923, the *Sun* noted that drill existed for two reasons: it was required by the Morrill Act, and it was a good means of insuring military preparedness. As late as 1925, the editor at UCLA claimed that drill was a national necessity; see *UCLA Daily,* November 30, 1925, December 3, 1925, December 8, 1925, December 9, 1925. For the Morrill Act, see *Ohio State Lantern,* May 10, 1924; *Cornell Sun,* October 18, 1925. It is not surprising, of course, that when campus patriotism during the war was fervid, ROTC, rather than an enemy, was seen as something highly desirable. At Trinity-Duke, for example, students clamored to have a branch introduced on the campus; see *The Chronicle,* March 28, 1917.

24. See, for example, letters to the editor in the following: *Daily Illini,* October 20, 1921, February 16, 1922, October 19, 1922; *UCLA Daily,* December 3, 1925, December 14, 1925. For student withdrawals, see *New Student,* March 15, 1924, p. 2. Also *UCLA Daily,* November 19, 1925, letter to the editor.

25. LSU *Reveille,* December 11, 1925; *Daily Illini,* April 22, 1924. The *Reveille* editor went on to add that students were probably shocked, but that "such a shock might be survived if for the sake of right and truth and freedom." *The Reveille* subsequently turned the carefully phrased description of the issue into a resounding clamor to have compulsory training done away with; see April 6, 1926, March 5, 1927, April 26, 1929; and especially the strongly phrased responses to the letters to the editor on March 12, 1927 and March 3, 1928.

26. See *Ohio State Lantern*, November 25, 1925: "The *Lantern* believes that compulsory military drill has no educational value, but is rather opposed to education. . . . It is not in accord with American tradition. . . . Just what American tradition does a conscript army in peace time represent? . . . Compulsory drill teaches men to allow other men to think for them. That is the basis of the system. That is not the basis of education. Education teaches men that war is unnecessary." A week later, the *Lantern* clarified its position by announcing that it did not oppose all drill on campus, only compulsory drill; see November 30, 1925.

See also the heavy criticism of Prussianism and the demands for servility made in the ROTC in the LSU *Reveille* throughout 1927; especially March 12, 1927, March 26, 1927, and the letters to the editor on the same dates. See also the letter to the editor which defended the rights of the pacifists, January 27, 1926.

27. *Daily Illini*, December 15, 1924. See also *Cornell Sun*, October 18, 1923, for another anti-compulsion argument based on the efficiency of voluntarism; also, *Utah Chronicle*, reprinted in *UCLA Daily*, April 18, 1927; Duke *Chronicle*, April 29, 1928, January 19, 1927.

28. *UCLA Daily*, December 8, 1925, letter to the editor; *Ohio State Lantern*, January 22, 1926, p. 1. See also *Ohio State Lantern*, January 14, 1927; *Cornell Sun*, January 12, 1925.

29. *Daily Illini*, October 24, 1925; also, January 12, 1926; *Cornell Sun*, March 3, 1925. The editor of the *Daily Princetonian* congratulated Princeton for having non-compulsory drill, November 30, 1925. The conjoining of concrete practicality with abstract idealism is demonstrated in a letter to the editor of the *UCLA Daily* which berated ROTC for being militaristic but also noted that it was inconvenient for students who had to work because the hours that were usually reserved for training interfered with jobs (November 19, 1925).

30. *Cornell Sun*, October 14, 1926.

31. The *New Student* gave the election a special issue which discussed in detail all the parties and platforms, from the American Party to the Socialist Labor and Workers Parties, and reviewed the issues and the records of candidates; see *New Student*, October 18, 1924, Section 3. The results of the student poll were recorded in *New Student*, November 1, 1924, p. 1. Unless otherwise specified, all election returns in this chapter are from this issue of the *New Student*.

32. *New Student*, November 1, 1924, p. 2.

33. Except for the Negro colleges, where the vote was almost unanimous for Coolidge. At Knoxville College, Tennessee, Coolidge got 100% of the vote and Atlanta University in Georgia, 97%.

34. At UCLA, Coolidge won, but LaFollette led Davis two to one. The vote was 619 Coolidge, 250 LaFollette, 140 Davis; *UCLA Daily,* November 4, 1924, p. 1.

35. Calvin Coolidge, "Enemies of the Republic," *Delineator,* 98 (June, 1921), 4–5; (July, 1921), 10–11; (August, 1921), 10–11.

36. *Daily Princetonian,* October 29, 1924. The faculty vote was Davis 95, Coolidge 76, LaFollette 7. See *New Student,* October 18, 1924, p. 3, for faculty support for Davis. As a newspaper, the *Daily Princetonian* carefully refrained from taking a strong partisan stand, but the editor was very strongly pro-Davis (September 30, 1924) and used the paper for continuous coverage of the Davis campaign and constant praise for the candidate; for example, October 3, 1924. Davis made a personal appearance at Princeton; see October 3, 1924. For Hibben's support for Davis, see *New Student,* October 11, 1924; *Daily Princetonian,* September 30, 1924, p. 1.

Because of Davis' position on the League, he often won faculty support at other schools as well. Former President Eliot of Harvard was among those who looked to Davis to reinvigorate the League; see *Ohio State Lantern,* November 3, 1924; also *New Student,* October 18, 1924, p. 3; *Daily Princetonian,* October 4, 1924. The *Princetonian* noted, "To those who have blushed at the timorous attitude of our government toward Europe during the past forty years the message [Davis' foreign policy statement] came as an assurance that the lofty idealism which led us through the greatest war in history to victory still burns in the breast of a new leader of American Democracy. Nothing vague in Mr. Davis' pledge of participation in world problems; no equivocation."

37. For example, *Cornell Sun,* January 19, 1924, March 15, 1923; *Ohio State Lantern,* April 30, 1924; *Daily Illini,* January 19, 1924; *UCLA Daily,* October 21, 1924; *New Student,* October 18, 1924.

38. Gordon W. Allport, "The Composition of Political Attitudes," *American Journal of Sociology,* 35 (1929), 228, 238, 232n.

39. The *Daily Illini,* December 5, 1925, reprinted the following: "The American undergraduate almost invariably accepts popular judgments. He doesn't think much about politics one way or another, and he goes Republican because that is the direction which the crowd takes." This was a reprint of an article by Heywood Broun. See also "The College Radical Myth," *Daily Illini,* November 9, 1924. At the beginning of the decade, a student poll at the University of Illinois produced a very conservative response by students on three issues: the League was voted down five to one, 1144 to 275 (without reservations); open shop and compulsory arbitration of labor disputes carried, 1062 to 371; Harding received 1150 votes to 361 for Cox and 50 for Debs (*Daily Illini,* October 29, 1920).

40. Allport, "Political Attitudes," 220; Vetter, "Social and Political Attitudes," 153–156, questions 1, 2, 4, 17, 18, 11; Lundberg, "Sex Differences," 596, questions 14 and 15. Vetter found some differences between students at the three schools, but the differences were minor compared with the overall similarities. As might well be expected, students at New York University were consistently more liberal and radical than those at the other schools. The overall correlations between schools were very high, however—.914 (Vetter, 173). See Arthur W. Kornhauser, "Results from a Quantitative Questionnaire on Likes and Dislikes Used with a Group of College Freshmen," *Journal of Applied Psychology*, 11 (1927), 85–94, who discovered that most students either did not know whether they liked socialists or indicated that they disliked them. They were much stronger in disliking the IWW's. See also Moore and Garrison, "A Comparative Study," which compared a group of North Carolina College students with the Vetter sample; and Edward S. Jones, "Opinions of College Students," *Journal of Applied Psychology*, 10 (1926), 427–436, which showed a strong pro-capitalist sentiment.

41. *Ohio State Lantern*, May 1, 1924; *Cornell Sun*, December 17, 1920.

42. *Cornell Sun*, November 15, 1919, November 19, 1919; Duke *Chronicle*, April 27, 1927; *Barnard Bulletin*, April 23, 1919. Barnard had initiated a move to have all state schools protest the bill. At Vassar, the protest failed to receive the support of only 12 students out of 1100. At Wells the vote was unanimous, and at Barnard it carried 350 to 13. For other actions on the law, see *New Student*, June 7, 1922, p. 5. The *Cornell Sun* also protested the ousting of five socialists from the New York State Assembly (January 14, 1920) and an avowed socialist from the school system (January 20, 1921).

43. Duke *Chronicle*, May 5, 1926, May 12, 1926; North Carolina *Tar Heel*, reprinted in Duke *Chronicle*, December 2, 1925; LSU *Reveille*, March 13, 1926, March 27, 1926; see also *The Reveille*, May 19, 1926 concerning the pending legislation in Louisiana.

44. *Cornell Sun*, October 30, 1925; Duke *Chronicle*, March 10, 1926; *Daily Illini*, February 20, 1925, January 3, 1926. See also *Cornell Sun*, December 15, 1925 and February 4, 1926. For protest of the Karolyi affair, see also *Daily Illini*, April 23, 1925.

45. See *Religion on the Campus* (Milwaukee), pp. 194–195; *Christian Students and World Problems* (Indianapolis), pp. 93–96, 234–238, 247–249; *Youth Looks at the Church* (Evanston), pp. 183–184. The race issue exploded at the Detroit Student-Faculty Conference on Religion and Education, which was concerned with the development of "enlightened Christian character," when black delegates were refused admission to the convention dining halls. See *Education Adequate for Modern Times*, Discussions and Proposals of the National Student-Faculty Conference on Religion and Education, Detroit, (New York, 1931).

As a result of the experience, the conference proposed that racism was the most important social problem in America. For Duke, Swarthmore, and other meetings, see Duke *Chronicle*, February 22, 1928; March 16, 1921 for an address by the President of Tuskegee; *New Student*, April 12, 1924, April 26, 1924; *Barnard Bulletin*, May 9, 1924.

46. LSU *Reveille*, December 5, 1925, p. 1. At a later conference of students from the Midwestern region (including the South), delegates agreed not to seat any Negroes as representatives of the South and to reserve a separate seat to the Negro colleges; see *The Reveille*, February 24, 1926, p. 1.

47. LSU *Reveille*, December 5, 1925. See the Duke *Chronicle*, May 19, 1923, where an outraged observer berates the college community for its unthinking treatment of blacks. At issue was an incident where students baited a black man with a dog: "Verily we are victims of our prejudices. The little incident . . . is only one of many which illustrate this truth. . . . Something similar to this happens on the campus every day. . . . One day an old Negro drove on the campus with a barrel of apples. For some reason, or no reason at all, a number of students . . . deemed it great fun to take possession of the barrel and distribute the apples. . . . It seems to me that part of a college man's education should consist in learning how to behave with other groups of people."

For the refusal of the University of Virginia track team to meet with the Harvard team because the latter had a Negro runner, see *Cornell Sun*, January 18, 1921; for the same kind of problem between Washington and Lee and Washington and Jefferson Universities, *UCLA Daily*, October 12, 1923. The unwillingness of the inter-fraternity council of Ohio State to welcome the membership of a Negro fraternity caused a furor at that university; see *Ohio State Lantern*, April 2, 1924. See also the editorial on racism, *Ohio State Lantern*, May 2, 1924. A similar situation occurred at Illinois; see *Daily Illini*, May 3, 1924, May 6, 1924. See also the exchange in the letters to the editor column which raises the issue of social equality as opposed to racial inferiority; *Daily Illini*, May 6, 7, 10, 17, and 20, 1924.

48. LSU *Reveille*, October 11, 1929, p. 1; March 7, 1930. But see the response by students to the Ku Klux Klan in a random poll taken on the campus. On the whole, students supported the aims of the organization but opposed its violent methods; *The Reveille*, January 19, 1923, p. 1.

For anti-Semitism, see *Cornell Sun*, December 16, 1924, April 12, 1923. At Illinois, one correspondent was careful to differentiate the Jewish problem from the Negro issue, claiming that Jews had proven themselves ready for social equality, but blacks had not (*Daily Illini*, May 7, 1924). See also the editorial of the same day, which observes that both groups were discriminated against, and the letter of May 9, 1924: "The Jew has a far better time of it than any Negro, we grant, but he is far from being accorded an equal chance with the rest."

49. See the debate in the *Daily Illini,* cited in note 46 above; also, Daniel Katz and Floyd H. Allport, *Students' Attitudes* (Syracuse, N.Y., 1931), pp. 146–147. The discussion about racial differences did not, however, lack racist overtones. See, for example, the stereotypes of Jews in the *Cornell Sun*'s discussion of President Eliot's claims that Jews were unassimilable (December 16, 1924): "'The candid statements by Harvard's President concerning the unassimilable nature of the Jewish people have occasioned controversy, possibly because their truth is admitted. Save in rare instances, the *innate racial characteristics of Jews* so conflict with Christian customs and prejudices that happy unions are impossible" (my italics). The *Sun* went on to object to Zionism on the grounds that Jews could never cultivate the soil or provide themselves with other necessary social and economic services. See also the angry letter in response to the accusation, which in its own way is full of stereotyped racism (December 19, 1924). Also the editorial on Jewish violators of the Honor Code, January 12, 1927. For a "Jew joke," see LSU *Reveille,* May 6, 1920, p. 10.

Moreover, sometimes conscious beliefs are less telling than unconscious patterns. At Trinity-Duke, for example (which prided itself on being the most enlightened Southern school on racial matters), an article praising the tolerance and open discussion on racial issues at a recent student conference was followed on the same page by a miserable "nigger joke"; see *The Chronicle,* January 9, 1924. Even at liberal Columbia University, students attempted to oust a black student from the dormitory; see *New Student,* April 12, 1924, p. 1.

50. Vetter, "Social and Political Attitudes," 161–162, questions 31, 33, 35, 36. For racial and ethnic dislikes, see Kornhauser, "Likes and Dislikes," *passim.* The English, German, and Protestant groups were generally well-liked, while considerable distaste was indicated for Jews, blacks, and Orientals. Interestingly, Jews were more intensely disliked than blacks, who evoked many more neutral responses. See also J. P. Guilford, "Racial Preferences of a Thousand American University Students," *Journal of Social Psychology,* 2 (1931), 179–204. See also the amazing array of groups that most Syracuse University students indicated they would not be willing to room with or have enter their fraternities: Jews, grinds, Orientals, "queer-looking students," Bolsheviks, loafers, anarchists, Negroes—to mention just a few; Katz and Allport, *Students' Attitudes,* pp. 146–147.

For opposition to Oriental immigration, *Daily Princetonian,* March 4, 1924, letter to the editor, which takes a venomous anti-Oriental attitude; *Cornell Sun,* December 10, 1920, p. 1, cartoon. For assimilation problems, *Daily*

Princetonian, March 4, 1924; *Cornell Sun,* June 2, 1921, cartoon, December 10, 1920, cartoon; LSU *Reveille,* December 9, 1921, in support of an Americanization policy in education.

51. The first large student organization, the National Student Federation, was founded in 1925 in Princeton at a meeting of 245 colleges and universities called together to discuss the World Court. See *UCLA Daily,* January 6, 1926; Thomas Neblett, "Youth Movements in the United States," *Annals, AAPSS,* 194 (1937), 141–151.

52. *Daily Illini,* April 25, 1924. See also *Daily Illini,* December 17, 1925, which comments on the possibilities of an American "Youth Movement"; *Cornel Sun,* May 9, 1923, April 16, 1923. In general, the Cornell paper, the most liberal and politically alert of all those sampled here, was a year or two ahead of other schools in presenting political and social issues.

53. Duke *Chronicle,* May 5, 1926, December 7, 1927; February 2, 1927, March 23, 1927, February 23, 1927.

54. *Cornell Sun,* January 9, 1926; see also *Daily Princetonian,* January 19, 1925. For an explanation of why most college students are conservative, see the Literary Supplement to the *Daily Illini,* November 1, 1925, "The College and the Conservative," by Paul Robert Beatle.

55. Duke *Chronicle,* February 23, 1927; *Daily Illini,* November 8, 1925.

56. *UCLA Daily,* April 27, 1926.

57. *Cornell Sun,* May 1, 1920; Duke *Chronicle,* February 3, 1926; *Cornell Sun,* March 15, 1927. See also *Cornell Sun,* December 1, 1920; LSU *Reveille,* April 15, 1920.

58. The *UCLA Daily* (September 22, 1926) defended Mencken and the young against the *Nation's* accusation that "the young college generation speaks a degenerate Menckenese." "Speaking for college youth, we do believe Mencken is becoming popular. Who isn't tired of high pressure drives, join-this-or-that, Big Brotherism, wear-the-banner Rotarianism, and anti-everything; why not tear off the mask from our civilization and let us look at things as they are?" See also *Daily Illini,* December 23, 1925; *Cornell Sun,* November 28, 1925, November 6, 1926; Duke *Chronicle,* October 21, 1925, "Fig Leaves"; LSU *Reveille,* June 5, 1926; *Daily Kansan,* reprinted in LSU *Reveille,* May 22, 1925.

Every paper at mid-decade turned to a more self-critical stance and began to question those staples of college life, activities and football; see, for example, *Ohio State Lantern,* February 18, 1926, March 1, 1926, November 12, 1924. See also the widely reprinted "We Are Tired" editorial from the *Daily Northwestern,* in *Cornell Sun,* November 4, 1925. Almost every paper reprinted the article, since it was prominently displayed in the *New Student.* The change in tone at this time was especially notable at Ohio State and Louisiana State.

Before 1925, editors at Louisiana mouthed administratively underwritten pieties. But after 1925, the editors became critical and gave a sharp slap to administrative censorship of the paper; see *The Reveille,* June 5, 1926, February 6, 1926, p. 1. After this there was a change in the coverage and attitude expressed by *The Reveille.* For a completely out-of-character veneration of elitism in the *Ohio State Lantern,* see March 6, 1925, January 5, 1925, and February 26, 1925 on art, and November 13, 1925. The whole year was archly Menckenesque.

59. *Ohio State Lantern,* February 11, 1925.

60. *Ohio State Lantern,* February 11, 1925; Tulane *Hullaballoo,* reprinted in LSU *Reveille,* May 17, 1929; *Cornell Sun,* December 18, 1928. See also Duke *Chronicle,* April 27, 1927, "Wayside Wares"; LSU *Reveille,* February 19, 1927. At a conference on the religious attitudes of students, Princeton's President Hibben observed that the young extolled the virtues of self-expression and personality. The young, he noted, found religion a real obstacle to "freedom of expression": "They say this not only of religion, but they go so far as to say that old-fashioned standards of morality cannot be accepted, because they hamper the great adventure of self-expression." In Galen Fisher, ed., *Religion in the Colleges* (New York, 1928), p. 4.

61. For the Clark uproar, see, for example, *Cornell Sun,* April 3, 1922; *Barnard Bulletin,* March 31, 1922, p. 1; *Daily Illini,* April 12, 1922. The *New Student,* of course, took this *cause célèbre* of freedom to its heart; see April 9, 1922, p. 5; May 17, 1922, p. 3; and the continuing coverage on reactions and development thereafter throughout 1922 and 1923. At Clark, the elected student officers of the undergraduate associations condemned the action on behalf of the student body and issued a statement which called for complete freedom of speakers. At the same time it made a pointed denunciation of "Socialism, Bolshevism, Communism, or Anarchism." See *New Student,* April 19, 1922, p. 6. A number of schools, including Miami University, Columbia, Barnard, George Washington University, Bryn Mawr, and Harvard, sent petitions to Atwood denouncing his action; see *New Student,* May 17, 1922, p. 3. See also the condemnation of the suppression of a speech by former Attorney-General Wickersham by the University of Michigan Board of Regents in *Cornell Sun,* October 12, 1923.

For marriage and birth control discussions at California, *Cornell Sun,* February 13, 1926, December 11, 1925. The Debate Council of California issued a statement strongly opposing the action of the administration; see, *New Student,* December 2, 1925, p. 3. For anti-fundamentalism, see, for example, *Ohio State Lantern,* December 4, 1923; *Daily Princetonian,* January 18, 1927, February 19, 1927; *Cornell Sun,* March 25, 1925; Duke *Chronicle,* May 5, 1926, May 12, 1926, January 5, 1927; LSU *Reveille,* March 13, 1926, March 19,

1926. See also the heated attack on the administration for forcing all students to attend a session by a noted evangelist making his rounds of the colleges; LSU *Reveille,* October 11, 1929; and the attack on fundamentalist intolerance at Methodist Duke; *The Chronicle,* December 12, 1923, December 2, 1925, November 18, 1925. The attack on fundamentalism was nationwide, but the examples of two Southern schools, in the heart of Bryan country, are most illustrative. For Denison University action, see *Daily Illini,* May 26, 1922; *New Student,* June 7, 1922, p. 7. For private school bans, see *Ohio State Lantern,* November 10, 1924. Among countless examples that could be cited on censorship issues are, *Ohio State Lantern,* August 24, 1927, April 26, 1923; *Cornell Sun,* March 15, 1927, September 25, 1924; Duke *Chronicle,* February 8, 1928, January 23, 1929. For the general attack on Prohibition, see Chapter 7 herein. The *Wisconsin Daily Cardinal* asserted, "As students, we do not believe we deserve the censure that has been heaped upon our heads by militant reformers on the outside. *We lay the blame* for whatever law violation there happens to be in our midst *on the professional protectors of our morals* who have foisted this unjust, radical, and unreasonable law upon us." Reprinted in *Ohio State Lantern,* October 15, 1926 (my italics).

See *Daily Princetonian,* March 24, 1926, for the relationship between morality and motors in the minds of officials. All the papers cried out against the infringement of personal liberty represented by the bans on automobiles passed by growing numbers of schools during the decade; see, for example, *UCLA Daily,* October 16, 1924. While the prohibitions were in part warranted by the terrible traffic and parking situation, they were largely enacted because officials feared that autos threatened morality. The *Daily Illini* urged students to police themselves to forestall regulations: "We believe in freedom and personal liberty, not paternalism and restriction" (November 13, 1924).

Compulsory chapel was one of the big campus issues of the twenties, and school after school found students agitating for repeal of the requirement. See *Cornell Sun* on the Yale vote to eliminate compulsory chapel, February 12, 1926; *Daily Princetonian,* November 10, 1925; *Daily Illini,* December 15, 1925; Duke *Chronicle,* December 7, 1927. The *New Student* provided continuing coverage of the anti-chapel successes and failures at various schools.

62. A variety of measures of this modernist inclination is available from surveys of the attitudes of youths in the twenties. In the Vetter sample (students from New York University, Syracuse University, and the University of Washington), for example, there were a number of broadly cultural issues. One such question concerned *Birth Control.* In all three schools, the response was heavily liberal, urging that the government supply information and even materials to married couples and even to the unmarried; "Social and Political Attitudes," 155, question 7. On *Divorce,* the responses were conservative to

liberal, most students urging that there be provisions for divorce when satisfaction was lacking, and a considerable number asserting that divorces be granted on demand (155, question 9). On *Prohibition*, the majority of responses favored modification (156, question 12). There was an overwhelmingly liberal turnout on the question of *Academic Freedom*, urging the strongest possible right to freedom of expression by instructors (156–157, question 13). The question on *Freedom of Speech* brought large student response for maximum freedom except in times of war or national emergency (the investigators provided no really liberal alternative on this question (157, question 14). On *Respect for Traditions*, the responses were broadly liberal, arguing that customs could become outworn and that behavior should conform to new conditions. Traditions should be respected only when in conformity to need, not for themselves (159, question 24).

The Moore-Garrison results from the same questionnaire with students at North Carolina College produced more reactionary views on questions of race, sex, and family, but a large liberal response on *Individual Freedom;* "A Comparative Study," 197–198. The investigators also found a slight tendency toward increased liberalism with academic class, seniors being more liberal than freshmen. A critical break seemed to come between freshman and sophomore years (Table 3, 201–202). See also Lundberg, "Sex Differences," especially on equality of pay for men and women (question 25), divorce on demand (question 32), petting by non-engaged couples (question 33), birth control (question 35), the single standard (question 30), and on enforcing blue laws (question 43). On all questions, the responses were generally liberal. See Jones, "Opinions of College Students," on divorce for the unhappily mated (question 9) and dancing (question 20); Robert C. Angell, *A Study in Undergraduate Adjustment* (Chicago, 1930), p. 141, for modernism.

63. The suppressions were legion. The following are a few illustrations. The suspension of a Berkeley magazine for "radicalism" when it attacked the Immaculate Conception, see *UCLA Daily,* November 16, 1924; the suspension of the *Syracuse Orange Peel* for a drinking pun and risqué humor, see *Daily Illini,* March 11, 1923; the gagging of the CCNY editor, see *Cornell Sun,* November 27, 1925; dismissal of a Baylor University editor for an anti-ROTC position, see *Cornell Sun,* February 12, 1926; suppression of the Columbia College humor magazine for ridiculing the church, see *Cornell Sun,* April 14, 1926; suspension of a Trinity-Duke editor for asserting that he preferred radicals to conformist goosesteppers, see *Cornell Sun,* November 5, 1925, *Duke Chronicle,* February 23, 1926, April 14, 1926. Again, countless examples might be cited. For a general attack on suppression, see *Daily Illini,* November 29, 1925, April 15, 1925, April 23, 1925; *Daily Princetonian,* April 20, 1925.

64. In "Dreams of Plenitude, Nightmares of Scarcity," Edward Shils argues that the highly competitive academic system of the 1960's in American colleges and universities had a great deal to do with the political rebellions of the sixties. Thus, while the ideals taught students were of an ever-expanding prosperity, the reality that confronted them was of diminished opportunities for which they had to compete vigorously. This is a suggestive hypothesis and might well be used to explain the lack of political radicalism in the 1920's, for then the dreams were predominant and the nightmares at bay. Academic competition was at a minimum, and even a little college education was still a large insurance toward business placement. Thus the lack of interest in academic competition was a realistic appraisal of its insignificance in terms of long-term goals. Students' complacency in politics was a result of their perception that the political system as it was, offered them ample opportunity and great hope for prosperity. See Shils article in *Students in Revolt,* ed. Seymour Martin Lipset and Philip G. Altbach (Boston, 1969). See also Lipset's introduction to the same volume, where he notes, "Opinions as to the place of politics in the university are inherently related to feelings about the larger society" (xxii). Again, the argument can be applied to conditions in the 1920's where politics on campus were at a very low ebb precisely because students felt no desire to change political priorities in the larger society. Note also that where student consciousness was keenest—on issues of personal liberty—they were consciously upholding American traditions about freedom. Shils has rightfully argued that an assault on traditional liberties is usually very important in provoking student protest.

CONCLUSION

1. Duke *Chronicle,* January 9, 1924; *Ohio State Lantern,* November 3, 1925. For a charming story which draws out the resemblances between lodges and fraternities, see "The Apostate," by George Milburn, in *Short Stories from the New Yorker* (New York, 1940).

2. *Ohio State Lantern,* October 20, 1924. For reading interests, see, for example, *Daily Illini,* November 8, 1922; *Daily Princetonian,* October 14, 1926, p. 1 and May 27, 1924; Duke *Chronicle,* April 14, 1924. Also, Robert Cooley Angell, *The Campus* (New York, 1928), p. 154; Arthur W. Kornhauser, "Results from a Quantitative Questionnaire on Likes and Dislikes Used with A Group of College Freshmen," *Journal of Applied Psychology,* 11 (1927), 85–97. For favored actors, see, for example, *UCLA Daily,* October 27, 1925; *Daily Princetonian,* May 25, 1924; *Ohio State Lantern,* April 19, 1926.

3. *Daily Californian,* reprinted in *Daily Illini,* October 3, 1922. For the in-

tellectual antecedents for twenties values and attitudes, see Henry F. May, *The End of American Innocence: A Study of the First Years of Our Own Time, 1912–1917* (New York, 1959).

4. S. N. Eisenstadt, *From Generation to Generation: Age Groups and Social Structure* (New York, 1956), especially Chapters 1, 2, 6; also, "Archetypical Patterns of Youth," in Erik H. Erikson, ed., *The Challenge of Youth,* (Garden City, N.Y., 1965), pp. 29–59.

5. In "Age-Groups and Youth Culture," in *Essays on Comparative Institutions* (New York, 1965), pp. 107–174, Eisenstadt admits the insufficiency of his earlier model and amplifies it with an examination and explanation of "deviant or non-normative behavior," which he now recognizes to be far more common than he once assumed.

6. See, for example, Kenneth Keniston, "Social Change and Youth in America," in Erikson, ed., *The Challenge of Youth,* pp. 191–222; Erik H. Erikson, "Identity and the Life Cycle," *Psychological Issues,* 1 (New York, 1959); "Youth: Fidelity and Diversity," in *The Challenge of Youth,* pp. 1–28.

7. David Matza, "The Subterranean Traditions of Youth," *Annals, AAPSS,* 338 (1961), 102–118.

8. Kingsley Davis, "The Sociology of Parent-Youth Conflict," *American Sociological Review,* 5 (1940), 523–535, and "Adolescence and the Social Structure," *Annals, AAPSS,* 236 (1944), 8–16; Lewis Feuer, *The Conflict of Generations* (New York, 1969).

INDEX